PAUL

THE APOSTLE

PAUL

THE APOSTLE

Jimmy Swaggart

Jimmy Swaggart Ministries
P.O. Box 262550 • Baton Rouge, Louisiana 70826-2550
Website: www.jsm.org • Email: info@jsm.org
(225) 768-7000

ISBN 978-1-934655-64-1
09-108 • COPYRIGHT © 2011 World Evangelism Press®
13 14 15 16 17 18 19 20 21 22 23 24 / RRD / 13 12 11 10 9 8 7 6 5 4 3 2

TABLE OF CONTENTS

INTRODUCTION

Several years back, one of the billionaire philanthropists from Texas gave Yale University some three million dollars in order that a *"chair"* be established, with the intent of teaching a course on the origin of Western Civilization. A considerable period of time passed when there seemed to be no action in this regard, which prompted the benefactor to call the President of Yale.

"What is the holdup as it regards the teaching of this subject?" the philanthropist inquired.

The president of Yale answered and said to the benefactor, *"Mr. Bass, we are very grateful for your gift of three million dollars to Yale University, with the intent that the subject of the origin of Western Civilization would be taught as a college level course; however,"* the President of Yale went on to say, *"we simply don't know how to teach the subject."* He continued, *"We do not know how Western Civilization began."*

PAUL, THE APOSTLE

If the President of Yale had known the Bible, he would have had some understanding as it regards this subject. The truth is, the Source of Western Civilization is the Lord Jesus Christ, with all that He has given to us, made possible by the Cross of Christ. But the human instrumentation used by our Lord was Paul, the Apostle. Of course, the Lord used many; however, the Book of Acts, written by Luke, characterizes the formation of the Early Church and, above all, the Ministry of the Apostle Paul, gives us the origin of the greatest way of life known to mankind—Western Civilization.

DEMOCRACY AND THE GOSPEL

It must be understood, however, that there can be no true Democracy, which is the greatest form of government in this present world, without such being based on the Judeo-Christian concept. This means that our government spending hundreds of billions of dollars trying to establish democracy in places like Iraq and Afghanistan, which are governed by the Muslim religion, i.e., the *"Koran,"* will prove to be a fruitless task. Democracy and the Koran are not on the same page. In fact, they are really not on the same Planet. So, for Democracy to be what it ought to be, the Gospel of Jesus Christ must be paramount; otherwise, it becomes no more than another vapid philosophy.

THE BEGINNING OF WESTERN CIVILIZATION

The beginning of this way of life, of course, had its start with the Holy Spirit; however, the physical demonstration of the origin of the Western way of life under Christ began with the Macedonian Call. The Scripture says, and I quote from THE EXPOSITOR'S STUDY BIBLE, as will be all the Biblical quotes in this Volume:

> "And a Vision appeared to Paul in the night *(proclaims the Holy Spirit now telling the Apostle exactly where He wanted him to go)*; there stood a man of Macedonia *(the northern part of modern Greece, from the Adriatic to the Hebrus River)*, and prayed him, saying, Come over into Macedonia, and help us *(thus was ushered in the most momentous event in the history of the world, the going forth of Paul to take the Gospel to the nations of the West)*.
> "And after he had seen the Vision, immediately we endeavored to go into Macedonia *(by the use of the pronoun 'we,' we know that Luke, the writer of this Book of Acts, now joins Paul here at Troas)*, assuredly gathering that the Lord had called us for to preach the Gospel unto them *(they knew they now had the Mind of the Lord)*" (Acts 16:9-10).

PHILIPPI

> "Therefore loosing from Troas, we came with a straight

course to Samothracia, and the next *day* **to Neapolis** *(this would be the very first presentation of the Gospel on European soil, which would have such a bearing on what is presently referred to as 'Western Civilization')*;

"**And from thence to Philippi, which is the chief city of that part of Macedonia** *(Paul's destination)*, *and* **a colony** *(was a colony of Rome)*: **and we were in that city abiding certain days** *(represents tremendous hardships, but a Church was established here)*.

THE FIRST CONVERT

"**And on the Sabbath we went out of the city by a riverside, where prayer was wont to be made** *(evidently meant there was no Synagogue in the city; what few Jews were there met by the riverside)*; **and we sat down, and spoke unto the women which resorted** *thither (seems to tell us that no men were present other than Paul and his party)*.

"**And a certain woman named Lydia, a seller of purple, of the city of Thyatira** *(she was a businesswoman)*, **which worshipped God** *(proclaims her as a Gentile who had probably begun visiting a Jewish Synagogue in Thyatira)*, **heard** *us (Paul evidently was asked to speak to these women, thus proclaiming the Story of Jesus Christ and His Redemption afforded by the Cross of Calvary)*: **whose heart the Lord opened** *(presents her hungry for God)*, **that she attended unto the things which were spoken of Paul** *(she gave her heart to Christ, and was, thereby, the first convert on European soil)*.

"**And when she was baptized** *(evidently took place some days later)*, **and her household** *(refers to the fact that all of those with her accepted the Lord as well, and were baptized)*, **she besought** *us*, **saying, If you have judged me to be faithful to the Lord, come into my house, and abide** *there (as well, her house was probably the first Church on European soil)*. **And she constrained us** *(means*

*they did not acquiesce at first, feeling perhaps that it may
be an imposition on her; but she would not take no for an
answer)*" **(Acts 16:11-15).**

THE SPREAD OF THE GOSPEL

From the first convert in Europe, who was Lydia, to the
first Church established on European soil, which was in Lydia's
house, the Gospel spread westward.

We do know that after Paul had been to Rome, he wanted
to go to Spain (Rom. 15:24, 28); however, there is no historical
or Scriptural proof that this desire was realized. But we do
know that ultimately the Gospel went to France and England,
along with all the other European countries, and eventually to
North, Central and South America. That is the origin of Western Civilization. But again we emphasize that the true source
of the prosperity and freedom of this way of life has its origin
totally and completely in the Lord Jesus Christ and the price
that He paid at Calvary's Cross. To misunderstand that is to
misunderstand what Western Civilization is all about.

PAUL, THE GREATEST EXAMPLE FOR CHRISTIANITY EVER PRODUCED BY CHRIST

I know that Paul would never have made such a statement
as that given in our heading of himself. Actually, he said:

"**For I am the least of the Apostles** *(not mock mod-
esty, but rather the most deep humility)*, **that am not meet**
(worthy) **to be called an Apostle, because I persecuted
the Church of God** *(before his conversion)*.

"**But by the Grace of God I am what I am** *(concerns
the Favor or Mercy of God)*: **and His Grace which *was*
bestowed upon me was not in vain** *(it was not without
effect, telling us that it is without effect with many)*; **but I
laboured more abundantly than they all** *(proclaims that*

which Grace enabled Paul to do because he had a greater grasp of Grace than anyone else, which speaks of the Cross, the means of Grace): **yet not I, but the Grace of God which was with me** *(is with all Believers who look toward the Cross [I Cor. 1:17])*" **(I Cor. 15:9-10).**

But at the same time, when we realize certain things about Paul, I think one would be hard put to find any human being who has ever lived, other than Christ, who can match this man.

• First of all, it was to Paul that our Lord gave the meaning of the New Covenant. Considering that the New Covenant is the greatest Word, the greatest Plan, and the greatest Covenant that has ever been given to man, and ever will be given to man, then we have to realize that the Lord, considering the vast significance of this all-important Word, would not have given it to just anyone. This is the Covenant to which everything else pointed. In fact, as great as the First Covenant was, and we speak of the Law of Moses given to that great Patriarch, it pointed in every capacity to the New Covenant that was to come. In fact, Paul said of the New Covenant:

MEDIATOR

"**But now** *(since the Cross)* **has He** *(the Lord Jesus)* **obtained a more excellent Ministry** *(the New Covenant in Jesus' Blood is superior, and takes the place of the Old Covenant in animal blood)*, **by how much also He is the Mediator of a Better Covenant** *(proclaims the fact that Christ officiates between God and man according to the arrangements of the New Covenant)*, **which was established upon better Promises.** *(This presents the New Covenant, explicitly based on the cleansing and forgiveness of all sin, which the Old Covenant could not do.)*

"**For if that first** *Covenant* **had been faultless** *(proclaims the fact that the First Covenant was definitely not faultless; as stated, it was based on animal blood, which* *was vastly inferior to the Precious Blood of Christ)*, **then should no place have been sought for the Second** *(proclaims the necessity of the New Covenant)*" **(Heb. 8:6-7).**

• **As well, the Lord gave the responsibility to Paul of founding the Church. In fact, the Apostle, under the guidance of the Holy Spirit, referred to himself as the** *"Masterbuilder of the Church."* **He said:**

> **"According to the Grace of God which is given unto me, as a wise masterbuilder** *(in essence, Paul, under Christ, founded the Church)*, **I have laid the foundation** *(Jesus Christ and Him Crucified)*, **and another builds thereon** *(speaks of all Preachers who followed thereafter, even unto this very moment, and have built upon this Foundation)*. **But let every man take heed how he builds thereupon.** *(All must preach the same Doctrine Paul preached, in essence, 'Jesus Christ and Him Crucified.')*
>
> **"For other foundation can no man lay than that is laid** *(anything other than the Cross is another foundation and, therefore, unacceptable to the Lord)*, **which is Jesus Christ** *(Who He is, God manifest in the flesh, and what He did, Redemption through the Cross)*" **(I Cor. 3:10-11).**

• **The mystical Body of Christ: of course, we speak of the Church, the true, Blood-bought Believers, all of whom make up the Body of Christ. While Jesus Christ is the Builder of the Church, He did so, even as the Book of Acts grandly proclaims, through the Holy Spirit, but with the Holy Spirit using Paul. So, if we have to select a man, all under Christ, Paul stands out as no other, even as he referred to himself, and the Holy Spirit wanted him to do so, as the** *"Masterbuilder of the Church."* **And this refers to the Church all over the world. It does not refer to denominations, but rather to every called-out Believer, called out from the darkness of this world, and we speak of those who are truly Born-Again. And, to be sure, this Church is** *"a glorious*

Church, not having spot, or wrinkle, or any such thing; but that it should be Holy and without blemish" (Eph. 5:27).

THE MAN AND HIS MESSAGE

Unequivocally and grandly so, Paul preached the Cross. In fact, he used the *"Cross"* as a synonym for the Gospel, which means that's how prominent his teaching was as it regarded this all-important subject (I Cor. 1:17-18; Phil. 3:18; Gal. 6:14).

The meaning of the Cross is actually the meaning of the New Covenant. In fact, one could turn it around and say the meaning of the New Covenant is the meaning of the Cross. When Paul spoke of the Cross, he wasn't speaking of a wooden beam, but rather what Jesus there did, the price that was there paid, and the tremendous all-inclusive Victory that He there purchased with His Own Precious Blood (Eph. 2:13-18). If we fail to grasp the Message of this man, which is the Cross of Christ, then we totally misunderstand Paul, who he was, and what he did. Unfortunately, in today's spiritual climate, the Cross of Christ has been so little preached that the modern church hardly knows what it is and what was there done. As a result, there is much preaching done about the Gospel, but very little True Gospel that's actually being preached. The truth is and the facts are, if the preacher is not preaching the Cross of Christ, then whatever it is he is preaching will be of precious little good to those who hear him.

THE REVELATION

In 1997, after six years of prayer meetings morning and evening, the Lord began to open up to me that which I refer to as the *"Revelation of the Cross."* It definitely was not new, having been given to the Apostle Paul nearly 2,000 years ago, which the great Apostle gave to us in his 14 Epistles. I'm sure that quite possibly the Lord has given this Revelation, or at least a part of it, to others down through the centuries. At any rate, it totally revolutionized my life and my Ministry. As it regarded the Cross of Christ and Salvation, I had always preached this strongly all over the world, with the Lord helping me to see, and I exaggerate not, hundreds of thousands of souls brought to a Saving knowledge of Jesus Christ. But as it regarded the Cross of Christ and Sanctification, of that I had no knowledge. And when I speak of *"Sanctification,"* I am speaking of the manner in which we live for God, the way we order our behavior, and how we overcome the world, the flesh, and the Devil, even as this latter phrase was coined by the Early Church Fathers. In fact, while one can certainly be Saved and not understand this great Truth, the simple fact is, one cannot successfully live for the Lord, as it regards daily life and living, without a working knowledge of this great Truth. This means that the sin nature will rule such a person to some degree, which, you can be sure, will make life miserable. Every single Believer in the world has *"more abundant life"* (Jn. 10:10), but the truth is, only a tiny portion of the modern church is enjoying this more Abundant Life.

THE SIN NATURE

The very first thing the Lord showed me in that Revelation was the meaning of the sin nature. To do that, He took me to the great Sixth Chapter of Romans. In fact, the Holy Spirit through Paul has given over this entire Chapter to explaining this all-important subject. This, not understanding the sin nature, is the cause of most, if not all, failure in the hearts and lives of the Children of God.

THE CROSS OF CHRIST

Then some days later, the Lord showed me the solution to this problem, which is the Cross of Christ, and related forcibly to me that the Cross of Christ is the only solution. There is no other! Not understanding this, which means the Cross of Christ relative to Sanctification is not understood, means that most modern Christians simply do not know how to live for God. The Cross alone is the answer. For this great Truth, the Lord once again took me to the Sixth Chapter of Romans.

THE HOLY SPIRIT

And then last of all, and of extreme significance, the Lord showed me how the Holy Spirit works in all of this. Regrettably, not understanding the Cross of Christ relative to Sanctification, most of the modern church doesn't understand, as well, how the Holy Spirit works within our lives. It is the Cross of Christ, the Lord showed me from Romans 8:2, through which the Holy Spirit works. In other words, it is the Cross which gives the Holy Spirit the legal means to do all that He does. As a result, while the Lord doesn't require very much of us, He most definitely does require that our Faith be exclusively in Christ and the Cross, without which, the Holy Spirit is greatly limited.

I learned all of this, which we will elaborate on much more fully in the body of this Volume, from the Apostle Paul.

If this Book opens up to you to a greater degree that which was taught by Paul, which the Holy Spirit gave to him, then your time in perusing its contents will not be wasted.

"But God forbid that I should glory *(boast)*, save in the Cross of our Lord Jesus Christ *(what the opponents of Paul sought to escape at the price of insincerity is the Apostle's only basis of exultation)*, by Whom the world is crucified unto me, and I unto the world. *(The only way we can overcome the world, and I mean the only way, is by placing our Faith exclusively in the Cross of Christ and keeping it there.)*

"For in Christ Jesus neither Circumcision avails any thing, nor uncircumcision *(blows all of man's religious ceremonies to pieces)*, but a new creature *(new in every respect, which can only be brought about by trusting Christ and what He did for us at the Cross).*

"**And as many as walk** *(to direct one's life, to order one's conduct)* **according to this rule** *(the principle of the Cross)*, **peace** *be* **on them, and mercy** *(which comes only by means of the Cross)*, **and upon the Israel of God.** *(This refers to all who look to the Cross for their Redemption. They alone are the true Israel)*" **(Gal. 6:14-16).**

PAUL

THE APOSTLE

CHAPTER ONE

Paul, The Apostle
Before Conversion, Paul's Early Life

PAUL, THE APOSTLE

BEFORE CONVERSION, PAUL'S EARLY LIFE

We are given very little information as it regards Paul's life before conversion. We know next to nothing about his family or his upbringing, except that which led to his conversion. So, we must deduce that what Luke gave us concerning Paul, and what Paul gave us concerning himself, is all that the Holy Spirit wanted us to know. Yet, we do know some few things, which are of immense interest.

TARSUS

There is no doubt about the place in which Paul was born. He says, when addressing the Jews in Acts, Chapter 22, Verse 3, *"I am verily a man which am a Jew, born in Tarsus, a city in Cilicia, yet brought up in this city at the feet of Gamaliel, and taught according to the perfect manner of the Law of the Fathers, and was zealous toward God, as you all are this day."*

Tarsus was the capital of the region of Cilicia, which was situated in the southeastern part of Asia Minor, and which is today modern Turkey. In fact, Tarsus was located in the extreme southern part of this country, about halfway of its modern borders. The city then was about eight miles from the Mediterranean Sea but had an excellent harbor by the means of the River Cydnus, which flowed to the Sea. It is believed by many presently that Tarsus must have had a population of no less than half a million in Roman times. So, it was a city of considerable importance. In fact, it was one of the university centers of the period, ranking with Athens and Alexandria. As well, it was an exceedingly corrupt city, being the chief seat of *"a special Baal worship of an imposing but unspeakably degrading character."* Because of information gathered from some of the things Paul said, there are some modern scholars who believe that Paul attended the university at Tarsus after his training in the Law of Moses by the great Law scholar of that day, Gamaliel; however, that is only speculation with no concrete proof.

PAUL, THE ROMAN CITIZEN

We know, as stated, that Paul was born a Roman citizen, but no clue is given as to how all of this was brought about.

Some have speculated that something happened in the city of Tarsus of which the Emperor took notice and granted Roman citizenship to the entirety of the city, and for all time. Others speculate that possibly Paul's parents, or maybe his grandparents, did something noteworthy as it regarded the Romans, and they granted his family perpetual citizenship. But all of that is speculation with no proof either way. The one thing we do know is that Paul was born a Roman citizen, which carried with it any number of privileges. For instance, a Roman citizen was not to be bound by a rope, etc., or put to torture in any capacity.

As well, few would ever venture the claim of being a Roman citizen when such was not the case. The penalty for such was death.

PHILIPPI

For instance when Paul and Silas were beaten (Acts, Chpt. 16), it was a grossly unlawful act, which could have gotten the Magistrates into serious trouble. As to exactly why Paul and Silas didn't relate to them that they were Romans at the beginning, we aren't told. But maybe they did and were not believed. At any rate, the Scripture says concerning this situation:

"And when it was day, the Magistrates sent the serjeants *(probably refers to the same men who had administered the beating to Paul and Silas)*, saying, Let those men go *(the Codex Bezae says that the Magistrates came into*

Court that morning feeling that their treatment of Paul and Silas had brought on the earthquake; they were right!).

"And the keeper of the prison told this saying to Paul, The Magistrates have sent to let you go: now therefore depart, and go in peace.

"But Paul said unto them, They have beaten us openly uncondemned, being Romans *(presents a scenario which puts an entirely different complexion on the matter; it was against Roman Law for Romans to be beaten; so, in beating them, the Magistrates had broken the law, evidently not realizing they were Romans)*, and have cast us into prison; and now do they thrust us out privily? *(They were treated as common criminals.)* No verily; but let them come themselves and fetch us out *(in this way, the city of Philippi would know that the charges were false).*

"And the serjeants told these words unto the Magistrates: and they feared, when they heard that they were Romans *(if Paul and Silas so desired, they could have brought charges against these individuals, which could have resulted in severe consequences).*

"And they came and besought them, and brought *them* out *(refers to the fact that the 'Magistrates' now came to Paul and Silas)*, and desired *them* to depart out of the city *(has reference to the fact that they were pleading with the Apostles not to bring charges against them, but rather depart in peace).*

"And they went out of the prison, and entered into *the house* of Lydia *(they were somewhat the worse for wear in the physical sense, but greatly encouraged in the spiritual sense)*: and when they had seen the Brethren, they comforted them, and departed *(these were new converts in the Philippian Church)*" (Acts 16:35-40).

JERUSALEM

We have another account of Paul referring to his Roman

citizenship. It occurred in Jerusalem.

After a great tumult in the Temple, instigated by certain Jews, they would have killed him but for a Chief Captain of the Roman army.

Concerning this event, Luke wrote:

"The Chief Captain commanded him *(Paul)* to be brought into the castle, and bade that he should be examined by scourging *(a most terrible form of torture)*; that he might know wherefore they cried so against him *(considering that Paul was speaking in Hebrew, the Roman Captain little knew what was taking place)*.

"And as they bound him with thongs *(getting him ready for the beating that would now be inflicted)*, Paul said unto the centurion who stood by, Is it lawful for you to scourge a man who is a Roman, and uncondemned? *(Paul did not shrink from torture when it was directly connected with the Name of Jesus, but he quietly and with much dignity avoided it when ordered by official ignorance.)*

"When the centurion heard *that*, he went and told the Chief Captain, saying, Take heed what you do: for this man is a Roman *(the rights of Roman citizens were guarded as something sacred by Rome)*.

"Then the Chief Captain came, and said unto him, Tell me, are you a Roman? He said, Yes *(in fact, the Chief Captain had broken the law even by binding Paul)*.

"And the Chief Captain answered, With a great sum obtained I this freedom *(proclaims one of the ways Roman citizenship could be gained)*. And Paul said, But I was *free* born *(Paul was born a Roman citizen, either through some service performed for Rome by his family, or else because of living in the city of Tarsus)*.

"Then straightway *(immediately)* they departed from him which should have examined him *(refers to those who were going to scourge Paul quickly retiring)*:

and the Chief Captain also was afraid, after he knew that he was a Roman, and because he had bound him" (Acts 22:24-29).

CAESAREA

As a result of the uproar in Jerusalem, Paul was transferred by the Romans to Caesarea, where he was there imprisoned for some two years. He was kept in the capital building in a place called *"Herod's Judgment Hall"* (Acts 23:35). It was a part of the lavish palace built by Herod the Great. It served as the capital building as well as the official residence of the Roman Governors, and evidently had some prison cells within its confines.

After appearing before any number of notables and noting that Festus, the Roman Governor:

"**Willing to do the Jews a pleasure, answered Paul, and said** *(Festus feared these Jewish leaders, knowing that if they were willing to bring these types of false charges against Paul, they would not hesitate to do the same against him to Rome)*, **Will you go up to Jerusalem, and there be judged of these things before me?** *(This presents the compromise of the Governor.)*

"**Then said Paul, I stand at Caesar's judgment seat, where I ought to be judged** *(proclaims the Apostle seeing through this ploy, knowing that if he went to Jerusalem, the Jews would find some way to kill him)*: **to the Jews have I done no wrong, as you very well know** *(proclaims that which is true, and which Paul hammers home, and rightly so!)*.

"**For if I be an offender, or have committed any thing worthy of death, I refuse not to die** *(in effect, Paul is attempting not so much to save his life, but rather to declare his innocence)*: **but if there be none of these things whereof these accuse me, no man may deliver me unto** them. I appeal unto Caesar *(means it is the Will of God for him to stand before Caesar, not the Jews)*.

"Then Festus, when he had conferred with the Council, answered *(refers to the legal advisory Council of the Governor, which evidently advised Festus that he acquiesce to Paul because of Roman Law)*, Have you appealed unto Caesar? unto Caesar shall you go" (Acts 25:9-12).

This was another privilege or right held by Roman citizens who appealed to Caesar, if they felt they were not being duly treated in other courts. This didn't mean that Caesar personally would attend these trials, but that he or someone appointed by him would officiate.

During the time of Paul, Roman citizenship, as stated, was highly prized. While some, who were not born a Roman citizen, paid large sums of money for this privilege, Paul rather was born a Roman citizen.

HIS TRAINING AS A BOY

Paul said:

"I am a Pharisee, the son of a Pharisee" (Acts 23:6). He also said, "I was circumcised the eight day, of the stock of Israel *(he was a pure-blooded Jew)*, *of* the Tribe of Benjamin *(Benjamin was the only Tribe that stayed with Judah at the time of the division of the nation)*, an Hebrew of the Hebrews *(goes all the way back to Abraham)*; as touching the Law, a Pharisee. *(In fact, Paul had been the hope of the Pharisees, touted to take the place of Gamaliel)*" (Phil. 3:5).

From the way that Paul said, *"I am a Pharisee, the son of a Pharisee,"* we would assume that his father and mother were Jews of the stricter sort.

When Paul used the term *"an Hebrew of the Hebrews,"*

he was referring to the fact that he had clung to the Hebrew tongue and followed Hebrew customs. Other types of Jews of that day were called *"Hellenists,"* who spoke Greek by preference and adopted, more or less, Greek views and civilization.

And yet, Paul could probably be said to be a *"Hebraist,"* which means that even though he was unabashedly Hebrew, still, at the same time, he was a master of the Hellenistic Greek language.

Farrar said, *"Although Paul was a Hebrew by virtue of his ancestry, and by virtue of the language which he had learned as his mother-tongue, and although he would probably have rejected the appellation of 'Hellenist,' which is indeed never applied to him, yet his very Hebraism had, in one most important respect, and one which has very little attracted the attention of scholars, an Hellenic bias and tinge."*[1]

The world that Paul was born into was a world of acute skepticism. Sell said, *"While the gods and goddesses in the great heathen temple still had their rites and ceremonies observed yet the people to a large degree, had ceased to believe in them."* Sell went on to say, *"The Roman writers of the period are agreed in the slackening of religious ties and of moral restraints. Yet it was the policy of the state to maintain the worship of the gods and goddesses. Any attack on them or their worship was regarded as an offense against the state."*[2] So, Paul faced several powerful obstacles. They were:

• As we have previously alluded, to attack the religion of the state in any capacity constituted an offense punishable by beatings and even imprisonment. So, there was precious little freedom of religion.

• To take a stand against the sins of man and the evils of the times stirred up bitter opposition.

• On top of all of that, to proclaim a crucified and risen Christ as the Messiah to the Jews, when they were expecting rather a conquering hero, most of the time put them into a rage.

• And, even among Christian Jews, the idea that the Law of Moses was totally finished in Christ did not sit well either.

In the midst of all of this, especially considering the opposition he encountered, the fact that Paul could preach *"Christ Crucified"* and establish Churches, seeing great numbers Saved, portrays to us the truth that he did not allow these obstacles to stop the propagation of the Gospel.

Along with his education regarding the Mosaic Law under Gamaliel, to which we will address ourselves more particularly momentarily, he seems also to have been quite well acquainted with Greek philosophy and literature. In fact, he quotes from the Greek poets, Aratus, Epimenides, and Menander. It is this that pushes some scholars to believe that Paul also attended the university at Tarsus. But, of course, that is only speculation.

PAUL AS A BOY

At the age of five every Jewish boy would begin to study the Bible with his parents at home. At the age of six he would enter into the synagogue to begin formal education. At the age of ten he would begin to study those earlier and simpler developments of the oral law, which were afterwards collected in the Mishna. Some even say that all Jewish boys had to memorize the entirety of the Book of Leviticus.

At any rate, by the age of thirteen he would, by a sort of *"confirmation,"* become a *"Son of the Commandment."*

As well, at the age of thirteen, if he were destined for the position of a Rabbi, he then entered the school of one of the great masters. Farrar said, *"The master among whose pupils the young Saul was enrolled was the famous Rabban Gamaliel, son of Rabban Simeon, and a grandson of Hillel, 'a doctor of the law had in reputation among all the people.' There were only seven of the Rabbis to whom the Jews gave the title of Rabban, and three of these were Gamaliels of this family, who each in turn rose to the high distinction of President of the School."*[3]

At the feet of Gamaliel sat Saul of Tarsus, in all probability, for several years. It is said that the Jewish Rabbis sat on lofty chairs, and their pupils sat at their feet, either on the ground or on benches.

It is also said that Paul as a young scholar was so learned in the Scriptures, absorbing all that Gamaliel taught him, that he was being groomed by the Pharisees to take the place of the great Gamaliel. In other words, he was the darling of the Pharisees, and in today's modern terminology, their *"fair haired boy."*

THE PHARISEES

The Jewish world into which Jesus came, and Paul, as well, was a world that had lost all of the real meaning of the Law of Moses. In fact, the Law of Moses had been turned into some 248 commands and 365 prohibitions, totaling some 613 oral laws, all formulated by men, oftentimes referred to as *"fence laws."*

For instance, a woman could not comb her hair on the Sabbath, nor could anyone drag a chair across the floor, because dust might be parted in the hair or on the floor, which could be construed as plowing, with the latter being forbidden by the Law. They had so taken it to extreme that it was now a burden that was literally impossible to be borne. The Pharisees demanded that a rigidly scrupulous obedience was due. This was what God absolutely required, they said! This, and this only, came up to the true conception of the blameless Righteousness of the Law.

In their minds, so very much depended upon this scrupulous obedience to the Law, which took it far beyond what the Lord originally intended. In fact, this was the cause, or at least part of the cause, of the great hatred of the Pharisees for Christ. He portrayed the true meaning of the Law, which infuriated them. And it must be understood that the Pharisees in that particular time claimed to believe all of the Bible, which consisted of the Books beginning with Genesis and concluding with Malachi. They were the fundamentalists of that day. Actually, it is said that there were seven kinds of Pharisees:

1. The bleeding Pharisees;

2. The mortar Pharisees;

3. The Shechemite Pharisees;

4. The timid Pharisees;

5. The tumbling Pharisees;

6. The painted Pharisees; and,

7. And the Tell-me-anything-more-to-do-and-I-will-do-it Pharisee!   Paul probably belonged to this group.

EZRA

The Pharisee party probably began under Ezra, the ambition of which was to master the Text and teachings of the Mosaic Law in every detail. Actually, the first Pharisees would have borne no resemblance to those of Paul's day. The Scribes, who for the most part hated Christ, were their spiritual descendants.

The Pharisees were always a minority group. Under Herod they numbered something over 6,000, but they held great sway as it regarded the religious life of Israel.

The Pharisees held the belief that the Babylonian Exile was caused by Israel's failure to keep the Law, and that its keeping was an individual as well as a national duty. In their minds' eyes, at least by the time of Christ, they thought that if they could keep the Law minutely, this would usher in the Messiah, which would enable them to throw off the Roman yoke, and once again Israel would be the leading Nation in the world, as it had been under David and Solomon. But, as stated, they had so twisted and perverted the Law that they didn't even recognize their Messiah when He came. In fact, they crucified Him.

They reasoned that God would not have demanded obedience to the Law if that obedience were not possible! So, in their efforts to obey, they completely disobeyed, and in their legalism, they pushed themselves further and further away from God. Understanding this, we can see how their hatred for Paul was so rabid after he gave his heart to Christ on the road to Damascus.

But something was about to enter into the life and living of

Paul (then called Saul) that would serve to push him in a different direction altogether. That something was Stephen.

STEPHEN

Now begins the spread of the Gospel around the world, the propagation of the Message that was to confront humanity as no other Message in the annals of human history. It is the Gospel of Jesus Christ, and more particularly, *"Christ and Him Crucified."* Strangely enough, even as the Ways of God often are, it begins with death, the death of Stephen, but whose death plants a seed in the heart of a young man nearby by the name of Saul, which seed would ultimately spring to life. Much preparation over several centuries, actually from the time of Abraham, one might say, was all for this moment. Going back for half a millennia, we see three vast and worldwide events, all designed for the purpose of the spread of the Gospel. They are:

1. *"The Jews of the Dispersion:"* Josephus tells us that they crowded every corner of the habitable globe of that day and built their synagogues, which served as a staging point for the presentation of the Gospel by a young man who viewed the death of Stephen and even, in a sense, played a part in that death—Paul.

2. The second great effort by the Holy Spirit involved a pagan by the name of Alexander the Great. He gave to the civilized world of that day a unity of language, the Greek language, without which it would have been, humanly speaking, impossible for the earliest Preachers to have made known the good tidings in every land which they traversed. It was the language of the world of that day, which made it much easier for the Gospel to be preached, as should be obvious.

3. The rise of the Roman Empire on the ashes of the Greek Empire created a political unity which reflected in every direction the doctrines of the New Faith. In fact, the high morality of Christianity eventually replaced the paganism of Rome. Ultimately, that Gospel spread to all of Europe, and finally, to

the shores of North America, and Central and South America, which launched it to the entirety of the world. Our Ministry (Jimmy Swaggart Ministries) played a part in this, airing television over a large part of the world, with the Gospel translated into the languages of the people and, as well, with massive Crusades in capital cities all over the world.

Getting back to the Greek language, in every considerable city of the Roman Empire the service of the synagogue was held in Greek, and these services were opened to anyone who desired to be present at them. Greek, too, became emphatically the language of Christianity, with the entirety of the New Testament originally written in Greek.

THE CHURCH IN JERUSALEM

Jesus remained on Earth some forty days after His Resurrection (Acts 1:3). As well, from the time of His Ascension to the Day of Pentecost was another ten days. The Day of Pentecost, for all practical purposes, was the visible beginning of the Church. Peter preached the inaugural Message, one might say. At the conclusion of his message, the Scripture says that *"about three thousand souls"* were added to the Kingdom of God (Acts 2:41). And then, the Scripture says, without giving any numbers, *"And the Lord added to the Church daily such as should be Saved"* (Acts 2:47).

Some days later, with the healing of the lame man at the gate called Beautiful, Peter once again preached to the multitudes which gathered, and the Scripture says, *"Howbeit many of them which heard the Word believed; and the number of the men was about five thousand"* (Acts 4:4).

While we are not told in the Scripture as to exactly how large was the Jerusalem Church, it is believed it could have been regarding numbers anywhere between 30,000 and 50,000 people. When one considers the following, it is easy to see how this number could have easily been won to the Lord. The Word says:

MIGHTY HEALINGS AND MIRACLES

"**And by the hands of the Apostles were many signs and wonders wrought among the people** *(the Church was founded on the Power of God, and is meant to continue by the Power of God)*; **(and they were all with one accord in Solomon's porch** *(portrays a roofed colonnade bearing Solomon's name, which ran along the eastern wall in the Court of the Gentiles of Herod's Temple)*.

"**And of the rest does no man join himself to them** *(to the Apostles)*: **but the people magnified them** *(they knew the Apostles were of the Lord and that the Lord was greatly using them, so they found no fault with them)*.

"**And Believers were the more added to the Lord, multitudes both of men and women.)** *(It could have been as many as forty or fifty thousand, or even more.)*

"**Insomuch that they brought forth the sick into the streets, and laid *them* on beds and couches** *(evidently refers to two or three different streets on which Peter and the Apostles came to the Temple each day; the crowds were so large they could not all get into the Temple Court)*, **that at the least the shadow of Peter passing by might overshadow some of them** *(implying that when this happened, healing resulted)*.

"**There came also a multitude *out* of the cities round about unto Jerusalem, bringing sick folks** *(proclaims the extent to which this Move of God had reached)*, **and them which were vexed with unclean spirits** *(probably implying that much of the sickness was caused by demon spirits)*: **and they were healed every one** *(delivered and healed)*" (Acts 5:12-16).

FIRST DEACONS?

Due to the growth of the Church in Jerusalem, and due to the persecution, severe problems developed.

When anyone in Jerusalem accepted the Lord Jesus Christ as their Saviour, immediately they were excommunicated from the synagogue. In fact, they were not allowed to attend the services there anymore. As well, if they had children, due to the fact that the schooling for little boys was carried on in the synagogues, such children were not allowed to continue in school (girls did not attend school).

If they were renting an apartment or a house, they were immediately evicted. As well, if they were working for an employer, as most were, they were automatically terminated from their jobs. Consequently, the Church in Jerusalem was faced with tremendous hardships of trying to take care of the thousands of people who found themselves in this situation. In fact, the following Scriptures are addressing themselves to this situation. The Bible says:

> "Neither was there any among them who lacked *(those who lost their employment, etc., had their needs met)*: for as many as were possessors of lands or houses sold them, and brought the prices of the things that were sold *(refers to extra possessions, etc.)*,
>
> "And laid *them* down at the Apostles' feet *(they were entrusted with this largesse)*: and distribution was made unto every man according as he had need *(no hint of communism here, as some have suggested)*" (Acts 4:34-35).

In fact, the great dissertation that the Apostle Paul gave in II Corinthians, Chapters 8 and 9, pertains to this need. He was receiving an offering from all of the Churches in order to take such to Jerusalem, which he did (II Cor. 9:12-15; Acts 20:4).

Regarding these difficulties, a problem arose in the Church in Jerusalem concerning certain *"widows which were neglected in the daily ministration"* (Acts 6:1). At this juncture the Twelve Apostles told some of the Elders in the Church to:

> ". . . look you out among you seven men of honest

report, full of the Holy Spirit and wisdom *(is thought by some to represent the first Deacons, even though they are not called that in this Chapter)*, **whom we may appoint over this business** *(the Holy Spirit told the 'Twelve' what to do, the number to choose, and how they were to be chosen)*" **(Acts 6:3).**

The Scripture says that they chose *"Stephen, a man full of Faith and of the Holy Spirit, and Philip, and Prochorus, and Nicanor, and Timon, and Parmenas, and Nicolas a proselyte of Antioch"* (Acts 6:5).

Little did they realize that when they chose Stephen, how much this would play into the great Plan of God as it regarded the one we now know as the Apostle Paul. As it regards Stephen, we have but one account of a Message he preached, which cost him his life. Yet, the Message he brought that day, which was before the Jewish Sanhedrin, without a doubt influenced the greatest of the Apostles, and we continue to speak of Paul. As someone has well said:

"God works in mysterious ways,
"His Wonders to perform,
"He plants His Feet upon the seas,
"And rides upon the storm."

Stephen's death was the earliest martyrdom.

Up to this period, the name of Stephen has not occurred in Christian history, and as the tradition that he had been one of the seventy Disciples is valueless, we know nothing of the circumstances of his conversion to Christianity.

And yet, there is a good possibility that Stephen actually saw and heard the living Jesus, which turned his life completely around. So, we know him only for a moment, only as this first Martyr steps into the full light of history. Farrar said, *"Our insight into his greatness is derived almost solely from the record of a single Message and a single day – the last Message he ever uttered – the last day of his mortal life.* "[4]

The Holy Spirit plainly tells us that Stephen was *"full of Faith, and of the Holy Spirit."* Nothing could be said about a man greater than that! Like Philip, he was an Evangelist as well as a Deacon, with the following given to us as to what the Holy Spirit wanted us to know. It is considerable! The Scripture says:

FULL OF FAITH AND POWER

"And Stephen, full of faith and power *(speaks of a great knowledge of the Word of God, and of the Holy Spirit controlling this man, and, thereby, using him)*, did great wonders and miracles among the people *(these things were Divinely done)*.

"Then there arose certain of the Synagogue, which is called *the Synagogue* of the Libertines *(speaks of Jews who had been taken as slaves to Rome or elsewhere in the Roman Empire, but now had been set free, consequently coming back to Jerusalem; they had a Synagogue in Jerusalem, and perhaps several. In fact, at that time, the Rabbis stated there were 480 Synagogues in Jerusalem)*, and Cyrenians, and Alexandrians, and of them of Cilicia and of Asia *(pertains to each one of these groups of Jews who had a Synagogue in Jerusalem)*, disputing with Stephen *(it is thought by some that Paul, then known as Saul, was the leading disputer against Stephen; he could have been associated with the Synagogue that pertained to Cilicia, as Tarsus, the hometown of Paul, was in that region)*."

PAUL AND STEPHEN?

"And they were not able to resist the wisdom and the spirit by which he spoke *(if it was Paul who led the dispute against Stephen, it would have been most interesting, considering that Paul was the hope of the Pharisees at that time and, therefore, reputed to have great knowledge of the Law;*

the difference is that the Holy Spirit anointed Stephen!).

"**Then they suborned men** *(they planned and formed a scheme together, which held no validity or truth)*, **which said, We have heard him speak blasphemous words against Moses, and** *against* **God** *(concerns their concocted scheme).*

"**And they stirred up the people, and the Elders, and the Scribes** *(refers to the lies they told and kept telling respecting Stephen)*, **and came upon** *him*, **and caught him, and brought** *him* **to the Council** *(refers to them getting permission from the Sanhedrin to arrest Stephen, which they did),*

"**And set up false witnesses, which said** *(proclaims the similarity of Stephen's trial with that of our Lord)*, **This man ceases not to speak blasphemous words against this holy place, and the Law** *(this was their charge, which was false)*:

"**For we have heard him say** *(represents a distortion of what Stephen had probably said; they probably based their accusation upon some semblance of Truth, but totally distorted its meaning)*, **that this Jesus of Nazareth** *(said in such a way as to be most contemptuous)* **shall destroy this place** *(probably referred to the Words said by Jesus in the Olivet discourse [Mat. 24:2])*, **and shall change the customs which Moses delivered us** *(it is true that the customs were to be changed as a result of the New Covenant and, in fact, were meant to be changed).*

"**And all who sat in the Council** *(Sanhedrin)*, **looking stedfastly on him** *(gazed intently, and for purpose and reason)*, **saw his face as it had been the face of an Angel** *(pertains to the Glory of the Lord shining on the face of Stephen)*" **(Acts 6:8-15).**

THE MESSAGE

Looking at Stephen and the Message he delivered to the

Sanhedrin, which was, no doubt, similar to the ones he was delivering in the synagogues, we learn from this how different was his preaching from that of the Twelve, and how much earlier he had arrived at the true appreciation of the Words of Jesus respecting the extent and nature of His Kingdom. Concerning that, Farrar said, *"That which, in the mind of Peter, was still but a grain of mustard seed, sown in the soil of Judaism, had already grown, in the soul of Stephen, into a mighty tree."*[5] The truth is, the Twelve were still lingering in the portals of the synagogue. For them the new wine of the Kingdom of Heaven had not yet burst the old wine-skins. There is no trace up to this time that they ever dreamed of the abrogation of the Law of Moses or the free admission of uncircumcised Gentiles into a full equality of Spiritual privileges. At this time, anyone who held back from the seal of the Covenant made to Abraham, which speaks of circumcision, would not be regarded as a full Believer any more than he would be regarded as a full Jew.

If indeed the early Believers had never advanced beyond this position, Christianity might have been regarded to the last as nothing more than a phase of Phariseeism, heretical for its acceptance of a crucified Messiah, but worthy of honor for its devotion to Spiritual Life. But had Christianity never been more than this, then it would have died aborning. The Church, under the Ministry of Paul, would come to know that it was necessary that all Christians, whether Jews or Gentiles, should see how impossible it was to put a new patch on an old garment.

In fact, this Truth had been preached by Jesus to His Apostles, but like many other of His Words, this great Truth lay long dormant in their minds. After some of His deepest Statements were made, in full consciousness that He could not at once be understood, He would say, *"He who has ears to hear, let him hear."* And as they themselves frankly confess, the Apostles had not always been among those *"who had ears to hear."* As plainly and clearly as it was, as it regarded the Prophecies, which He had addressed to them respecting

His Own Crucifixion and Resurrection, the Prophecy regarding the Crucifixion plunged them into despair and horror. In fact, so much so, despite the fact that He repeated this several times, still, not a single Apostle believed that He would rise from the dead. He who commanded the light to shine out of darkness had, indeed, shone in their hearts *"to give the light of the knowledge of the Glory of God in the Face of Jesus Christ;"* but, still, they were well aware that they had this treasure *"in earthen vessels."*

JAMES AND PAUL

Jumping ahead, why was James, the Lord's brother, so highly respected by the people, as tradition tells us that he was? Why was Paul regarded by them with such deadly hatred?

Farrar said, *"It was because Paul recognized more fully than did James the future universal destiny of a Christianity separated from Judaic institutions."* He went on to say, *"The Crucifixion had, in fact, been the protest of the Jews against this Faith; however, from that moment the fate of the nation was decided. Her religion was to kill her. But when the Temple burst into flames, Christianity had already spread its wings and gone out to conquer an entire world."⁶* The truth is, even as Paul faced on a daily basis, it required many years for Jewish converts to understand the meaning of the saying that, *"He came not to destroy the Law but to fulfill."*

THE MINISTRY OF STEPHEN

As short as it was, I think we should by now understand that Stephen seemed to have a grasp of Who Jesus was and what Jesus did possibly, at this time, more so than anyone else in the world of that day.

As we have asked, was it possible when Stephen was ministering in the synagogues in Jerusalem that at some point his opponent could have been Paul?

If, in fact, this happened, though the Saul of this period must have differed greatly from that Paul, the Apostle of Jesus Christ, Whom we know so well, the main features of his personality must have been the same. He had to have seen something in Stephen that was totally different than anything he had ever known. Surely he felt the contrast between a dead theology and a living Faith. He would have heard preaching that stirred the inmost depths of his troubled heart. For the first time in his life, if, in fact, he heard Stephen, and possibly even debated him, he would have sensed the Presence of the Lord. He would have felt the result of the Anointing of the Holy Spirit. He would have seen, even though he would have smothered it at the time, the secret of a light and joy, and of love and peace, compared with his own condition, which was that of one who was chained to a corpse. The truth is, during all of this time, Paul, despite his great religiosity, despite having studied the Law of Moses under the greatest teacher of that day, and despite devoting his entire life to that of the Mosaic institution, still, this man was not Saved. He was religious but lost, as were so very, very many in the Israel of that day, and including his religious leadership, and especially including its religious leadership.

If Paul debated Stephen, Paul being at that time possibly the greatest authority on the Law of Moses in Israel other than Gamaliel himself, to have lost this debate, considering who Paul was and considering who Stephen was, who was nothing in their eyes, the immediate effect would have been anger on the part of these religionists.

These Rabbis would have been nonplussed to find that the one they were dealing with was no illiterate, but one who rather could meet them with their own weapons, and who could speak Greek as fluently as themselves.

Farrar said, *"Steeped in centuries of prejudice, ingrained with perditions of which the Truth had never been questioned, they must have imagined that they would win an easy victory, and convince a man of intelligence how degrading it was for him to accept a faith on which, from the full height of their own ignorance, they complacently looked down."* **Farrar went on to say,** *"How great must have been their discomfiture to find that what they had now to face was not a mere personal testimony which they could contemptuously set aside, but arguments based on premises which they themselves admitted, enforced by methods which they recognized, and illustrated by a learning which they could not surpass!*

"How bitter must have been their rage when they heard this man open the Scriptures, which surpassed even their most learned Scholars. But when Stephen said that Jesus of Nazareth was the promised Messiah, to prove from the Scriptures that all the splendid Prophecies of the Patriarchs, and Seers, and Kings, from the Divine Voice which spoke to Adam in Paradise, to the last utterance of the great Prophet Malachi – all pointed to, all centered in, One Who had been the carpenter of Nazareth, and Whom they had seen crucified between two brigands – to say that their very Messiah had been 'hung' by Gentile tyrants at the insistence of their own Priests; – this, to most of the hearers in the Synagogue, would have seemed wicked if it had not seemed so absurd. Was there not one sufficient and decisive answer to it all in the one Verse of the Law – 'Cursed by God is he who hangs on a tree?'

"Yet this was the thesis which such a man as Stephen, no ignorant Galilean, but a learned Hellenist, who undertook to prove, and in fact did prove with such power as to produce silence if not assent, and hatred if not conviction.

"These men who listened to Stephen that day, with Paul possibly among them, would have at that time come face-to-face with the realization of Jesus of Nazareth, as they had not previously seen, heard, or known. They came face-to-face with their blasphemy, face-to-face with their rejection, face-to-face with what they had done in crucifying the Lord Jesus Christ."

Farrar also said, *"How could they possibly miss the conception of a 'suffering' as well as of a 'triumphant' Messiah, which might very well amaze us, if there had not been proof in* *all ages that men may entirely overlook the statements and perfect the meaning of their own sacred Books, because, when they read those books, the veil of obstinate prejudice is lying upon their hearts."* Farrar continues, *"But when the view of ancient prophecy, which proved that it behooved Christ thus to suffer and to enter into His Glory, was forcibly presented to them by the insight and eloquence of one who was their equal in learning and their superior in illumination, we can understand the difficulties to which they were reduced. How, for instance, could they allude the force of the 53rd Chapter of Isaiah, to which their Rabbis freely accorded in Messianic interpretation?"*[7]

So now, the Pharisees will forcibly take Stephen before the Sanhedrin, the highest tribunal in the land of Israel.

THE SANHEDRIN

The history of the Jewish Sanhedrin is not clear at all points. Traditionally it originated with the seventy Elders who assisted Moses (Num. 11:16-24). Ezra is supposed to have reorganized this body after the exile.

Under the Romans, except for a short period of time, the Sanhedrin had wide powers. It was Julius Caesar who extended the power of the Sanhedrin over all Judea, although during the reign of Herod (37-4 B.C.), its powers were severely curtailed. During the years of A.D. 6-66, the powers of the Sanhedrin were extensive, actually, the internal government of the country being in its hands. But under Herod the Great, its direct powers were, however, limited to Judaea, meaning it had no power over Jesus while He was in Galilee.

After A.D. 70, when Jerusalem and the Temple were destroyed by the Romans, the Sanhedrin was abolished, with the group taking its place whose decisions had only moral and religious authority.

According to Josephus, and it seems which the New Testament bears out, the High Priest was president (Mat. 26:57; Acts 5:17; 7:1; 22:5; 24:1). Thus, Caiaphas was president at the trial of Jesus and Ananias at the trial of Paul (Acts 23:2). It seems that the High Priest had supreme authority, but this was curbed somewhat later. The appointment was no longer hereditary, thereby, in the lineage of Aaron, but had become political, with Rome making the decision as to who was appointed, which by and large was to the one who could pay Rome the most money.

THE EXTENT OF JURISDICTION

As far as the area of Jewish jurisdiction regarding the Sanhedrin, it varied from Caesar to Caesar. As we have stated, during the time of Christ as far as the area was concerned, the Jewish Sanhedrin had no authority in Galilee but did have authority in Judaea. And yet, at the time of Christ, its jurisdiction in the area that it did control was fairly wide. It exercised not only Civil jurisdiction according to Jewish Law but also criminal jurisdiction in some degree. It had administrative authority and could order arrest by its own officers of justice, so-called (Mat. 26:47; Mk. 14:43; Acts 4:1; 5:17; 9:2). It was empowered to judge cases that did not involve capital punishment. Capital cases required the confirmation of the Roman procurator (Jn. 18:31), though the procurator's judgment was normally in accordance with the demands of the Sanhedrin, which in Jewish Law had the power of life and death (Mat. 26:66).

For instance, in the special case where a Gentile passed the barrier that divided the inner court of the Temple from that of the Gentiles, the Sanhedrin was granted the power of death by Roman administrators (Acts 21:28).

The only case of capital sentence in connection with the Sanhedrin in the New Testament is that of our Lord, but the execution was carried out by the judgment of the Roman Governor. The case of Stephen had some features of an illegal mob act.

TYPES OF CASES

A study of the New Testament will give a cross-section of

the kinds of matters that came before the Sanhedrin. Thus, Jesus was charged with blasphemy (Mat. 26:57; Jn. 19:7); Peter and John were charged with teaching the people false doctrine (Acts, Chpt. 4); and, Paul was charged with transgressing the Mosaic Law (Acts, Chpts. 22-24). And yet, the Romans reserved the right to interfere in any area whatsoever, if necessary, independently of the Jewish court. Paul's arrest in Acts, Chapter 23 is a case in point.

FACE OF AN ANGEL

As Stephen ministered in the synagogues, the Holy Spirit so anointed him that the Scripture says, *"And they were not able to resist the wisdom and the Spirit by which he spoke"* (Acts 6:10). So they appointed certain men to go before the high council (Sanhedrin), and there to accuse Stephen of *"speaking blasphemous words against Moses, and against God."* They set up witnesses, as well, to further accuse him, and there is a great possibility that Paul was in this group.

And as Stephen was brought before the high court of Israel, the Scripture says:

> "And all that sat in the Council *(Sanhedrin)*, looking stedfastly on him *(gazed intently, and for purpose and reason)*, saw his face as it had been the face of an Angel *(pertains to the Glory of the Lord shining on the face of Stephen)*" (Acts 6:15).

Even though they saw this, still, it had no bearing upon their evil intent. It is amazing how that man can come face-to-face with the Lord, so to speak, see God's Power manifested in a great way, and still fight against it. That shows the acute evil of the human heart. No wonder that Paul later wrote, *"Their throat is an open sepulcher; with their tongues they have used deceit; the poison of asps is under their lips: whose mouth is full of cursing and bitterness: their feet are swift to shed blood:*

destruction and misery are in their ways" (Rom. 3:13-16).

RELIGIOUS EVIL

Religious evil is the worst evil on the face of the Earth. Most of the blood that has been shed in wars from the beginning until now has been religious in intent. All of this stems back to Cain and Abel. The sacrifice of Cain was rejected by the Lord, while the sacrifice of Abel, who followed the commands of the Lord, was accepted. Cain's reaction was to murder his brother. That spirit has not changed from then until now.

While presently the law of the land does not allow such in the U.S.A., those who function accordingly do the next best thing, and that is to make every effort to murder a person's reputation with their tongues. Religious evil is always spawned by self-righteousness. In fact, it was self-righteousness which nailed Christ to the Cross. It was not the drunks and the gamblers and the harlots who did such a thing, as evil as those sins are, but rather the religious leaders of Israel. And so now with Stephen, they will continue in their murderous ways.

STEPHEN'S MESSAGE

It is positive that Stephen full well knew and understood the danger which he now faced. These murderous rakes were the ones who had crucified Christ, so he expected no mercy from that source. And yet, even though he was very conscious of the danger that now presented itself, it never occurred to him to try to defend himself in any way. He saw it was the time to speak out even as the Holy Spirit urged him to do so. He was to bear witness to the Kingdom of his Lord. And there is every evidence that his countenance maintained the Glory of the Lord, *"as it had been the face of an Angel,"* throughout the entirety of his Message.

In truth, the Message that he would bring that day would lead to consequences that changed the Church from a Jewish sect at Jerusalem into the Church of the Gentiles and of the world. It is noteworthy to understand that the Message preached by Stephen and recorded in the Seventh Chapter of Acts is the longest Message recorded by the Holy Spirit in the New Testament, with the exception of the two Messages preached by Christ, referred to as the *"Sermon on the Mount"* (Mat., Chpts. 5-7) and the *"Olivet Discourse"* (Mat., Chpts. 24-25). It is ironical that Jesus began His Ministry with a Sermon on the Mount and closed it with a Sermon on the Mount.

Stephen's Message was, in a sense, a compendium of God's Dealings with Israel from the very beginning, the Call of Abraham. As it regarded what he said, there was really nothing with which they could disagree because his history of the Nation was perfect as God anointed him.

And then he begins to remind the Sanhedrin as to how the fathers would not obey the Word given by God to Moses. But when he came down to the close of his Message, the Holy Spirit began to move upon him in even a greater way, and to be sure, he pulled no punches.

THE CONCLUDING REMARKS

"You stiffnecked and uncircumcised in heart and ears *(presents Stephen using the same language as Moses when he conveyed God's rebuke to Israel [Deut. 10:16])*, you do always resist the Holy Spirit: as your fathers *did*, so *do* you *(everything carried out by God on Earth is through the Person and Office of the Holy Spirit; to resist Him is to resist God, for He is God; they resisted Him by resisting the Plan of God, Who and what was Jesus Christ)*."

BETRAYERS AND MURDERERS

"Which of the Prophets have not your fathers persecuted? *(This is very similar to that stated by Christ [Mat. 5:21; 23:30-31, 34-37; Lk. 13:33-34].)* and they

have slain them which showed before of the coming
of the Just One *(they killed the Prophets who pointed to
the One Who was to come, namely Jesus)*; of Whom you
have been now the betrayers and murderers *(is about
as strong as anything that could be said; how different this
is from most of the modern preaching!)*:

"Who *(Israel)* have received the Law *(Law of Moses)*
by the disposition of Angels *(speaks of the myriads of
Angels who were present and were used to help give the
Law of Moses to Israel [Ps. 68:17])*, and have not kept *it*
(contradicted their claims!)" (Acts 7:51-53).

THE ANSWER OF THE SANHEDRIN

As he closed his Message, he could hardly have addressed
them in words more calculated to kindle their fury than what
he said. Farrar said, *"To call them uncircumcised in heart
and ears was to reject with scorn the idle fancies that circumcision alone was enough to save them from God's wrath, and that
uncircumcision was worse than crime."*

Rabbi Juda had previously stated, *"Circumcision is equiva-
lent to all the Commandments which are in the Law."*

Farrar continued, *"To convict them of being the true sons of
their fathers, and to brand consciences, already ulcerated by a
sense of guilt, with a murder worse than the worst murder of the
Prophets, was not only to sweep away the prestige of an authority which the people so blindly accepted, but it was to arraign his
very judges and turn upon them the tables of accusation."*[8]

PAUL

Now we must understand, Paul was witnessing all of this and
heard every word uttered by Stephen, but as to what impression all of this made upon his heart, Luke does not mention,
nor does the Apostle himself; but the traces of that impression
present a series of coincidences which confirm, I personally

believe, the impact that Stephen had on him, of which we will say more momentarily.

ANGER AT A WHITE HOT PITCH

"**When they heard these things, they were cut to the heart** *(refers to the depth to which the Holy Spirit took Stephen's words, which, in effect, were the 'Words of the Lord')*, **and they gnashed on him with** *their* **teeth** *(proclaims their answer to Stephen and the Holy Spirit)*.

"**But he, being full of the Holy Spirit** *(the second time this is said of him [Acts 6:5])*, **looked up stedfastly into Heaven** *(means that Stephen saw something in Heaven which immediately seized his attention)*, **and saw the Glory of God** *(he saw the Throne of God)*, **and Jesus standing on the Right Hand of God** *(Christ is usually presented as sitting at the Right Hand of God [Heb. 1:3], but here He is seen standing, as rising to welcome His Faithful martyr and to place on his head the Crown of Life)*,"

HEAVEN IS OPENED

"**And said, Behold, I see the Heavens opened** *(proclaims Jesus in His Glory as God, just as the Heavens had opened to see Jesus in His humiliation on Earth as Man [Jn. 1:51])*, **and the Son of Man standing on the Right Hand of God** *(proclaims His rightful place by virtue of His Achievements and Exaltation to original Glory [Jn. 17:5; Eph. 1:20-23; Phil. 2:9-11; Heb. 1:3-4])*" **(Acts 7:54-56).**

THE FIRST MENTION OF PAUL

"**Then they** *(members of the Sanhedrin)* **cried out with a loud voice** *(had they cried out in Repentance, the future of Israel could have been drastically changed for the better)*, **and stopped their ears** *(means that they no* *longer desired to hear anything he desired to say)*, **and ran upon him with one accord** *(all of the religious leadership of Israel were guilty)*,

"**And cast** *him* **out of the city, and stoned** *him (this was their answer to the plea of God for their souls)*: **and the witnesses laid down their clothes at a young man's feet** *(they took off their outer garments so as to be free to hurl the stones at their victim with greater force)*, **whose name was Saul** *(presents the first mention of this man who would have a greater positive impact on Christianity than any other human being who has ever lived; the death of Stephen, no doubt, played a part in the later conversion of Paul)*" **(Acts 7:57-58).**

THE DATE OF THIS HAPPENING

Actually, there is no date given in the Bible as to exactly when the martyrdom of Stephen took place. Some scholars state that it was A.D. 33, with others claiming it was as late as A.D. 37. There is no way to truly know.

We know the High Priest, whomever he may have been, was president of the Sanhedrin. But the Scripture simply says, *"Then said the High Priest, Are these things so?"* (Acts 7:1). But no identification is given in the Scriptures as to who he was.

If this took place in A.D. 37, Jonathan, son of Hanan, could have been High Priest at the time. His son-in-law, Caiaphas, stained his hands in the Blood of the Lord Jesus Christ. Theophilus, another son of Hanan, was the High Priest who, during the utmost heat of the first persecution, gave Saul his commission to go to Damascus and imprison followers of Christ. Matthias, another son of Hanan, was probably one of those leading Jews whom Herod Agrippa tried to conciliate by the murder of James, the brother of John, and the son of Zebedee. And then, the youngest son of this man called *"Hanan"* murdered James, the brother of our Lord. Thus, all of these judicial murders were aimed at the followers of the Lord Jesus, and all of them directed or sanctioned by the cunning, avaricious, and unscrupulous members of a single family of Sadducean Priests.

Let us say it again, there is no evil in the world like religious evil. And I remind the reader again that it was not the thieves and the harlots who crucified Christ, as vile as those sins might be, but rather the religious leaders of Israel.

THE LAST WORDS OF STEPHEN

The Scripture says:

"And they stoned Stephen, calling upon *God* *(presents a monstrous offense on the part of his murderers; we must remember, he was murdered by the religious leaders of Israel)*, and saying, Lord Jesus, receive my spirit *(presents Stephen rendering Divine Worship to Jesus Christ in the most sublime form, and in the most solemn moment of his life)*.

"And he kneeled down, and cried with a loud voice, Lord, lay not this sin to their charge *(presents him dying on his knees, without malice toward his murderers)*. And when he had said this, he fell asleep *(portrays the body falling asleep, while his soul and spirit instantly went to be with Jesus; due to what Jesus did at the Cross; death is now looked at as merely going to sleep)*" (Acts 7:59-60).

A YOUNG MAN WHOSE NAME WAS SAUL

To carry out this terrible task of murdering Stephen, those who were guilty of this perfidious act had taken off their garments, and they laid them *"at the feet of a young man whose name was Saul."*

Farrar says, *"It is the first allusion in history to a name, destined from that day forward to be memorable forever in the annals of the world.*

"Saul stands, not indeed actively engaged in the work of death; but keeping the clothes, consenting to the violence, of those who, in this brutal manner, snuffed out the life of a man whose face looked like that of an Angel.

"Stephen sank in his own blood, but miracle of miracles, his place was ultimately taken by the young man who stood there to incite his murderers. Some months, or even possibly several years after Jesus had died upon the Cross of infamy, Stephen was stoned for being His Disciple and His worshipper; some thirty years after the death of Stephen, his deadliest opponent died also for the same holy faith."[9]

"I hear the words of love,
"I gaze upon the Blood,
"I see the mighty Sacrifice,
"And I have peace with God."

"'Tis everlasting peace!
"Sure as Jehovah's Name;
"'Tis stable as His steadfast Throne,
"Forevermore the same."

"The clouds may come and go,
"And storms may sweep my sky,
"This Blood-sealed friendship changes not:
"The Cross is ever nigh."

"My love is oft-times low,
"My joy still ebbs and flows;
"But peace with Him remains the same,
"No change Jehovah knows."

"I change, He changes not,
"The Christ can never die;
"His Love, not mine, the resting place,
"His Truth, not mine, the tie."

PAUL
THE APOSTLE

CHAPTER TWO

Paul's Conversion

PAUL'S CONVERSION

The time from Stephen's death, which Paul witnessed, unto the time he was stricken down on the Road to Damascus by the Power of God, with him actually seeing the Lord Jesus Christ and even speaking with Him, was filled with, one might say, inhuman persecution of the Church, and it was all headed up by the one then known as Saul.

Some even think that Paul, during this time, was a member of the vaunted Jewish Sanhedrin. This supposition is derived from the statement that Paul made when he ministered before king Agrippa. He said:

"I verily thought with myself, that I ought to do many things contrary to the Name of Jesus of Nazareth *(presents Paul taking himself back to his dreadful time of unbelief).*

"Which thing I also did in Jerusalem: and many of the Saints did I shut up in prison, having received authority from the Chief Priests; and when they were put to death, I gave my voice against *them (we know of Stephen; however, there may have been more).*

"And I punished them oft in every Synagogue, and compelled *them* to blaspheme *(should have been trans-lated, 'and attempted to compel them to blaspheme,' because the Greek Text implies that he was not successful in this effort)*; and being exceedingly mad against them, I persecuted *them* even unto strange cities *(indicates that Damascus was not the only city, other than Jerusalem, where Paul was practicing his deadly wares).*

"Whereupon as I went to Damascus with author-ity and commission from the Chief Priests *(intending to continue his persecution in that city)*" (Acts 26:9-12).

WAS PAUL A MEMBER OF THE SANHEDRIN?

Some think Paul was a member of the Sanhedrin from the

statement he made, *"I gave my voice against them."* They state that from the Greek Text, the word *"voice"* could have been translated *"vote."*

This seems to me to be too little information to give a clear-cut answer. As well, if Paul had been a member of the Sanhedrin, he would have to have been at least 30 years of age, and also a married man. That among other things was the rule followed as it regarded being a member of the Sanhedrin. While such is possible, I seriously doubt that it was the case. While Paul definitely was the shining light of the Pharisees at that time, and as previously stated, groomed to take the place of the vaunted Gamaliel, still, members of the Sanhedrin were normally older men.

BREATHING OUT THREATENINGS
AND SLAUGHTER

As stated, the time between Stephen's death and the conversion of Paul on the Road to Damascus presents a time frame anywhere from several months to as much as three or four years. During that time, he was the heart and soul of the effort to stamp out the followers of Christ. Paul, then called Saul, felt duty bound to stamp out anything that proved to be a challenge to the Law of Moses. Had the early followers of Christ been content to have proclaimed him to be but a great Teacher and Prophet, they would in all probability have become a Jewish sect and then speedily lost to sight. But claims were boldly made that Jesus Christ was the promised Messiah (Acts 2:25-40), that He was also the Son of God (Acts 3:26), and, as such, a forgiver of sins (Acts 2:38; 5:31). In the midst of all this, the claim was being boldly made, with many even claiming to have seen Him, that He had risen from the dead (Acts 4:33). As well, and unequivocally, thousands were claiming obedience to Him over and above their Jewish rulers (Acts 4:18-20). Furthermore, they were bold in proclaiming how that the religious leaders of Israel had wickedly slain

Christ (Acts 3:14-15), and on top of that, they were claiming that Salvation was only through Him (Acts 4:12). And then, on top of all of that, the Apostles began to perform Miracles, all in the Name of Jesus (Acts 3:2-8, 16; 2:43; 5:12).

It became very clear, and very soon, that the followers of Christ would enter into no truce, and propose to keep no truce, which called in question or denied the Supremacy of Christ.

To a man of Paul's temperament and zeal, and inasmuch as he was a stickler for the Law of Moses, there could be no halfway measures in a case like this. He could not be content to merely bide his time. Either the claims of Christ were true or they were false. If false, then they were doing harm and His Doctrine and Teaching must be eradicated at any cost. All who hated Christ, which included most all the religious leaders of Israel, found a champion in this Saul of Tarsus. As Paul led this fight, the cruelty and thoroughness of this man in his work are shown in his instituting a house-to-house canvass, seeking for the Christians and sparing neither age nor gender (Acts 8:1-3).

At the beginning, the religious leaders of Israel had been content to arrest and imprison those who publicly preached Christ, but now, the policy was changed, and that policy now is that these followers of Christ, sometimes called *"the Way,"* had to be exterminated root and branch. All believers in Christ were to be hunted out.

The character of Saul, the lead persecutor in all of this, is shown in the characterization of him by Luke, when he represented him as breathing out *"threatenings and slaughter against the Disciples of the Lord"* (Acts 9:1).

The truth is, the Law of Moses at this time had been so diluted, so perverted, and so twisted by the Israel of that day, that it little more represented anything that was the original Law of Moses. Furthermore, over 600 oral laws had been enjoined to the original Law of Moses, with many at that time even claiming that the oral laws were more binding and more important than the original Law. Jesus said concerning all of this:

"... Well has Isaiah prophesied of you hypocrites *(said this to their faces. 'You hypocrites' actually says in the Greek, 'You, the hypocrites,' which means the outstanding ones of all time)*, as it is written, This people honor Me with *their* lips, but their heart is far from Me *(hits at the very heart of what true Salvation is and isn't [Isa. 29:13])*.

"Howbeit in vain *(means empty nothings, no profit)* do they worship Me, teaching *for* doctrines the commandments of men *(the state [Herod] put to death the Preacher of Righteousness [Mat. 14:10], and the Church [the Scribes], corrupted the Word of Righteousness)*.

"For laying aside the Commandment of God, you hold the tradition of men, *as* the washing of pots and cups: and many other such like things you do *(said with sarcasm; they washed cups and pots but not their hearts; the ceremonial washing of their hands could not remove the guilt that stained them)*.

"And He said unto them, Full well you reject the Commandment of God, that you may keep your own tradition *(it was a studied and deliberate rejection)*" (Mk. 7:6-9).

Furthermore, Jesus called the religious leaders of that day, *"hypocrites, blind guides, fools, serpents, vipers"* (Mat., Chpt. 24). That was the Israel of Jesus' day and the Israel of Paul's day. So, Paul was a product of a perverted, ungodly, and one might even say, insane religion that had lost all sense as to Who God was and who they were. Their idea was that they would keep the Law perfectly, then the Messiah would come, throw off the Roman yoke, and once again make them the Nation that they had been under David and Solomon. But, they were so perverted spiritually that when the Messiah did come, and not because they were perfectly keeping the law, but because it was God's Time, the truth is, they didn't even recognize Him, despite every sign they needed to see. In fact,

Jesus fulfilled every Prophecy, met every standard, and did so many times over.

JESUS, THE MESSIAH

As far as His genealogy was concerned, it was perfect. All they had to do was to go to the Temple and look through the records, and they would see that Joseph, Jesus' foster father, went all the way back to David through Solomon. They would see that His mother Mary went all the way back to David through another son of David, who was Nathan. As well, they would have seen, had they bothered to look, that He was born in Bethlehem, exactly as the Prophet Micah had said, even some 700 years before Christ (Mic. 5:2). Also, they would have seen how that it had been prophesied by Zechariah that the Messiah would be sold for 30 pieces of silver, which word was given some 500 years before Christ (Zech. 11:12). Jesus was sold by Judas for 30 pieces of silver (Mat. 26:14-16). Thirty pieces of silver, incidentally, was the price of a slave. It was predicted by the Prophet Isaiah that the Messiah would be buried in a rich man's tomb. This was prophesied nearly 800 years before Christ (Isa. 53:9). Isaiah also prophesied that the Messiah would be virgin born (Isa. 7:14). Thus it was with our Lord, but Israel would not believe it. In fact, they concocted a most blasphemous story, claiming that Jesus was born as the result of Mary being with a drunken Roman soldier.

This was the Israel of Jesus' time and of Paul's time as well.

There is evidence that Paul had hit the followers of Christ hard in Jerusalem, with many put in prison, and with many even put to death. When he was speaking to the Jews as recorded in Acts 22:4, he portrayed the fact that the blood of Stephen was not the only blood that had been shed, and not the only blood of which the stains had pricked his conscience, and did so deeply. He tells the mob that day not only of the binding and imprisonment of women as well as men, but also that he *"persecuted this way unto the death."* In fact, he was so successful in Jerusalem, with his terrible hatred demanding that every follower of Christ be apprehended, that there were no more Apostles preaching in Solomon's Porch in the Temple; no more throngs that gathered in the streets to wait the passing shadow of Peter, when they would be healed; and, no more multitudes in the house of Mary, the mother of Mark. No doubt, when the Believers did meet, they did so in secrecy and in diminished numbers. So now he turns his attention to Damascus.

DAMASCUS

Saul now heard that there was a nest of these Believers of this hateful delusion in the city of Damascus. To the High Priest, therefore, he went, asking permission in his breathings of threatenings and slaughter to do the same in Damascus as he had done in Jerusalem.

The High Priest, it is said, in all probability was Theophilus, who was promoted by Vitellius to this position in A.D. 37. He was a Sadducee and a son of the hated house of Hanan. And yet, it was with Saul, not with Theophilus, that the demand originated to carry out this hateful design in Damascus. Farrar said, *"Theophilus gave the letters which authorized Saul to set up his court at Damascus, and to bring from thence in chains all whom he could find, both men and women, to await such mercy as Stephen's murder might lead them to hope for at the hands of the supreme tribunal."*[1] The upshot is, they could expect no mercy at all!

And so, with the credentials given to him by the High Priest in Jerusalem, he started on his journey to Damascus of approximately 150 miles. Even though the Scripture doesn't say, considering who he was, the naked arm of the High Priest, so to speak, he and those with him, no doubt, were given horses to ride.

Because of the manner in which they had to travel then, the journey would have taken several days.

WHAT WAS PAUL THINKING AT THAT TIME?

From something that Jesus said to him when the appearance was made, which we will address to a greater degree momentarily, it is positive that Paul was under great conviction. No doubt, he could not get Stephen's face out of his mind. He could not forget the words that Stephen spoke. Was it possible that Stephen was right, these followers of Christ were right, that Christ was actually the Messiah, and that Israel had murdered her Messiah? Could they be right and the vaunted Sanhedrin be all wrong?

At this time, Paul was eaten up with pride—the pride of system, the pride of nature, the rank pride of the self-style theologian, and the exclusive national Pharisaic pride in which he had been trained; all of this weighed heavily upon him. There was no humility there, as should be obvious. And without humility, there can be no sincerity; without sincerity, no attainment of the Truth. Farrar said, *"He could not and would not admit that much of the learning of his thirty years of life was a mass of worthless cobwebs, and that all the righteousness with which he had striven to hasten the coming of the Messiah was as filthy rags. He could not and would not admit the possibility that people like Peter and Stephen could be right, while people like himself and the Sanhedrin could be mistaken; or that the Messiah could be a Nazarene who had been crucified as a malefactor; or that after looking for Him so many generations, and making their whole religious life turn on His expected Advent, Israel should have been found sleeping, and have murdered Him when at last He came."*[2] These ignorant people, in his mind, did not know the Lord and were, therefore, *"accursed."*

It is my thought that Paul, then called Saul, slept very little the nights he was on the road. Again, I feel he could not get away from Stephen's face! He kept hearing the last words of this man before he died. They wouldn't leave his mind, seemingly transfixed on his brain. But despite how much he tried to force it from his thinking, deep down inside he had to admit that there was a serenity about these people, a peace that he did not have. Could he have died as did Stephen? And then again, making the matter even worse for him, he saw Stephen's face shine like an Angel, and especially so when he was dying. And then he had stated in his dying breath, and with a loud voice, *"Lord, lay not this sin to their charge"* (Acts 7:60). How could anyone, even with his dying breath, forgive people who were killing him? If this man were wrong in his direction, if his hope of Jesus as the Messiah were only a pipe dream, how could a confused mind be so serene, so peaceful, even when the stones were thudding upon his body? Could a deceived and deluded mind bring about such peace?

For a moment, Saul might have tried to put himself in the place of Stephen, asking himself if he could have forgiven those who had murdered him. The answer he would have received would not have given peace to his troubled soul.

While the mob was howling their thirst for blood, and then it was obvious that Stephen was dead, Saul nodded his head in approval, *"consenting unto his death"* (Acts 8:1). It was at that moment that he made the decision to stamp out these followers of the Nazarene. And the Scripture would say, *"As for Saul, he made havock of the Church, entering into every house, and haling men and women committed them to prison"* (Acts 8:3).

HIGH NOON

They are now close to Damascus and Paul presses on. It is *"high noon,"* even as he related the time to the Jews in the Temple compound, on his last trip to Jerusalem (Acts 22:6). At this time, most travelers sought for shade to shield them from the blazing sun, but Paul presses on. Damascus is just ahead; the trip is almost over. Even though the Syrian sun was shining down that noon day with all of its brilliance and brightness, still, something now happened, which shone with a light that was far brighter than anything this future Apostle had ever seen. All with Saul saw the light and even heard a sound, but they could not tell what was said. Only Paul would understand what Jesus said to him. In fact, ever how many were with Paul, this Vision was not for them. They saw something, the light, and they heard something, the sound, and they, no doubt, felt something as well; however, there is no record that those with Paul ever knew Christ as their Saviour. Perhaps they did, and we certainly hope they did, but there is no record of it.

To be a participant, even if in a small way, of one of the greatest incidents and experiences in history, and not be moved the right way, is unthinkable. This was an opportunity of unparalleled proportions with all of it lost, if, in fact, that's what happened. At this moment, if they died lost, they are in Hell, and they have relived this scene 10,000 times, and will relive it forever and forever. Such an opportunity but no favorable response.

PAUL'S CONVERSION

The Scriptural account of what might be called the greatest conversion in human history is as follows:

"And as he journeyed, he came near Damascus *(approximately 175 miles from Jerusalem)*: and suddenly there shined round about him a Light from Heaven *(proclaims the appearance of Christ in His Glory)*:

"And he fell to the earth *(implies that the Power of God knocked him down, and if on a horse, he fell to the ground)*, and heard a voice saying unto him, Saul, Saul, why do you persecute Me? *(To touch one who belongs to the Lord in a negative way is to touch the Lord!)*

"And he said, Who are You, Lord? *(Paul uses this in the realm of Deity, not merely as respect as some have claimed.)* And the Lord said, I am Jesus Whom you persecute *(presents the Lord using the Name that Paul hated)*: *it is* hard for you to kick against the pricks *(has reference to sharp goads, which were placed immediately behind the oxen and were attached to the plow; to kick against it, would cause sharp pain).*

"**And he trembling and astonished said** *(he was stupefied and astounded),* **Lord, what will You have me to do?** *(This constitutes the moment that Paul was Saved.)* **And the Lord** *said* **unto him, Arise, and go into the city, and it shall be told you what you must do** *(pertains to the Plan of God for Paul, which, in effect, would change the world).*

"**And the men which journeyed with him stood speechless** *(they were very much aware that something had happened, but they did not know exactly what),* **hearing a voice, but seeing no man** *(but Paul saw the Man, and that Man was Christ).*

"**And Saul arose from the earth; and when his eyes were opened, he saw no man** *(it seems that his eyes had been blinded by the Glory of the Lord):* **but they led him by the hand, and brought** *him* **into Damascus** *(Paul, the champion of the persecutors, is now led like the blind man he temporarily is).*

"**And he was three days without sight** *(speaks only of the physical sense; in fact, for the very first time he was now able to see),* **and neither did eat nor drink** *(presents him fasting three days and nights)*" **(Acts 9:3-9).**

THE LIGHT FROM HEAVEN

Jesus, a lowly carpenter's son, or so they thought, not at all of the aristocracy of Israel, just a humble peasant, so how could anyone think that He could be the Messiah? He was from a family of abject poverty, for it must be remembered, in those days there were only the obscenely rich and the extremely poor. There was no middle class.

But when Jesus now appears to Paul, it will not be as the lowly Galilean, but He will rather appear in a Light that is so bright and so glorious that when the Vision ends, Paul will be left blinded.

The Scripture is quick to say that this *"Light was from Heaven."*

When John the Beloved some years later would give an account of his Vision of Christ, as well, he would state of Him, *"And His Countenance was as the sun shines in His Strength"* (Rev. 1:16). This was the *"Light"* that penetrated the darkness that enveloped Paul. He would never be the same again!

One thing is certain about that which he saw and heard, he would never waver from the account exactly as it happened. It was the conviction of his soul, the crisis of his life. He would never doubt what he saw, what he heard, and what happened to him. As stated, without a doubt, this could be referred to as the greatest conversion in human history.

WHY WOULD THE LORD CHOOSE SOMEONE LIKE PAUL?

That's a good question!

Here was a man who hated the very Name of Jesus Christ. Here was a man who had vowed with all that was within him to stamp out this ridiculous idea that Jesus was the Messiah. He had rid Jerusalem of this parasitic evil and now he would rid Damascus of the same. He burned with hate, with bitterness, and with bile, all directed at the One Who had been crucified! And yet, out of all the human beings on Earth, even passing over the Twelve which our Lord chose, even passing over the seventy, and the myriads of those whom He had healed and even raised from the dead, instead, He would choose Paul.

Why?

Perhaps the great Prophet Samuel had answered this question nearly 1,100 years before Christ. When David was chosen by the Lord to be the future king of Israel, *"The LORD said unto Samuel . . . the Lord sees not as man sees; for man looks on the outward appearance, but the LORD looks on the heart"* (I Sam. 16:7).

The Lord doesn't choose a person because of what he is but because of what He can make of him. It is obvious that the Lord, despite the anger, the hate, and the terrible evil practiced by Paul, saw something in him, which He Alone could see. It would be something that would brave every hardship, and that would be unfailing in his dedication and consecration to the Lord. Paul would never forsake the great Message, which the Lord would give him, and to be sure, to this man, *"Saul of Tarsus,"* would be given the greatest Revelation that any human being has ever known—*"the meaning of the New Covenant."*

So, this great Vision, that is, if one would refer to such as that, this appearance that would change Paul and change him forever and, in fact, would do so instantly, would begin with *"Light."*

As it regarded the First Advent of Christ, that which had been denied by Paul, the Scripture says:

"That it might be fulfilled which was spoken by Isaiah the Prophet, saying *(Isaiah prophesied of Christ more than any other Prophet)*,

"The land of Zabulon, and the land of Nephthalim, *by* the way of the sea *(Sea of Galilee)*, beyond Jordan, Galilee of the Gentiles *(the great Roman Road ran near the Sea of Galilee from Damascus; almost all Gentiles traveling in this direction did so on this road; the Headquarters of Christ was within the confines of the Tribe of Naphtali)*;

"The people which sat in darkness *(implies a settled acceptance of this darkness; the moral darkness was even greater than the national misery)* saw great Light *(Christ is the Light of the world, and the only True Light)*; and to them which sat in the region and shadow of death *(spiritual death is the result of this spiritual darkness)* light *(spiritual illumination in Christ)* is sprung up" (Mat. 4:14-16).

For the first time, despite all of his religiosity, despite all his study of the Law, all of which had been darkness, he now sees the Light.

PAUL FELL TO THE EARTH

As we have stated, he was probably riding a horse, as were the others with him, but actually the Scripture does not say. At any rate, the advent of this Light, which did *"shine round about him from Heaven,"* which incorporated the Power of God, is why Paul fell. In other words, the Power of God knocked him to the ground. To be sure, this proud Pharisee, this hater of Jesus Christ, this hater of those who followed Christ, and this hater of those who claimed that our Lord had risen from the dead, now, in front of all who were with him, was greatly humbled. But as it regards the Lord, the way up is always down. In other words, we have to decrease before He can increase. And when He increases in our lives, then we increase as well!

The first thing that Paul experienced was the *"Light,"* which was the Glory of God. The next thing he experienced was the *"Power"* of God. The truth is, the modern church, for all practical purposes, has denied the Power of God. Listen to what Paul would later write. He said to us:

APOSTASY

"This know also, that in the last days *(the days in which we now live)* **perilous times shall come.** *(This speaks of difficult dangerous times, which Christians living just before the Rapture will encounter.)*

"For men *(those who call themselves Christians)* **shall be lovers of their own selves, covetous, boasters, proud, blasphemers, disobedient to parents, unthankful, unholy,**

"Without natural affection, trucebreakers, false accusers, incontinent, fierce, despisers of those who are good,

"Traitors, heady, highminded, lovers of pleasures

more than lovers of God *(and remember, this is describ-*
ing the Endtime Church, which has been totally corrupted
[Mat. 13:33; Rev. 3:14-22]);

"**Having a form of Godliness** *(refers to all the trap-*
pings of Christianity, but without the power), **but denying**
the power thereof *(the modern church, for all practical*
purposes, has denied the Cross; in doing this, they have
denied that through which the Holy Spirit works, and in
Whom the power resides [Rom. 8:1-2, 11; I Cor. 1:18]):
from such turn away. *(No half measures are to be adopted*
here. The command is clear! It means to turn away from
churches that deny or ignore the Cross)" **(II Tim. 3:1-5).**

The modern church has by and large denied the Cross and
denied the Holy Spirit, and in doing so, has denied Christ. The
Power of God is invested in the Holy Spirit, Who works exclusively within the Finished Work of Christ, i.e., *"the Cross,"*
which demands ever that the Cross of Christ be the Object of
our Faith. Paul taught us this, which we will address later on
in this Volume.

JESUS SPEAKS TO SAUL

The Passage says, *"And heard a voice saying unto him, Saul,*
Saul, why do you persecute Me?"
Nothing is said in this account given to us by Luke that
Paul actually saw Christ; however, in the account given by
Paul in I Corinthians, he plainly stated, *"And last of all He was*
seen of me also, as of one born out of due time" (I Cor. 15:8).
The question, *"Why do you persecute Me?"* was the first
thing the Lord said to this headstrong Pharisee.
The idea is, when one persecutes God's Children, at the
same time, one is persecuting the Lord. And to be sure, that's
a position in which one doesn't want to find oneself.
Every single Believer in this world belongs to the Lord Jesus
Christ. We were bought with a great price, in fact, the Life of

our Lord and Saviour, Jesus Christ. He has much invested in us. This means that every single Believer is precious in the Sight of God. Please note the following:

EVERYTHING THAT HAPPENS TO A BELIEVER IS EITHER CAUSED OR ALLOWED BY THE LORD

Of course, as should be obvious, the Lord does not cause Believers to sin. But, He will allow us to do this if we are so minded. He will speak to us, deal with us, and move upon us, in order that we not sin, but if we insist on doing so, He will allow it to go forward, but at the same time, helping us time and time again, that Satan not take advantage of us to steal, kill, and destroy. To be sure, for any Believer who fails the Lord, there is always a penalty attached to that failure. However, in all of this, it should be quickly stated, the Lord does not leave us. In fact, if He did, there wouldn't be any Christians left. The reason is simple; all of us are a work in progress.

So, if we seem to find ourself in a hard place, whether by our own laxity or through no fault of our own, we should understand that the Lord is teaching us a lesson, and then we should try to learn that lesson, whatever it might be.

The Lord could have led Israel, after their deliverance from Egypt, into the Promised Land in several different ways. But He chose to take them through a howling wilderness where there was no sustenance, no water, etc. Why did He do that?

He did that to show them the incurable evil of their own hearts and, as well, His Ability to provide even in impossible circumstances. The Lord always has a purpose and always has a reason!

Getting back to the original Text, when Saul *(Paul)* was dragging followers of Christ into prison and to torture, with some of them dying, the Lord looked at this situation as if it were being done directly to Him.

That's the reason it's a very serious thing for people to lay their hands in a hurtful way on the Lord's Anointed. And regrettably, most of the time, it's religion that does this. Please note carefully the following statement:

When a person is down and can do nothing to defend himself, and anyone can do any negative thing to him that they so desire and not fear any reprisal whatsoever, but rather approval, one then finds out very quickly just how many good Christians there are. Regrettably, there aren't many!

Saul was to learn to his utter dismay that all that he had been doing was in opposition to the Lord of Glory, a battle he could not hope to win. What a shock that must have been to him! Considering that this was the first word given by the Lord to Saul, no doubt, he had no idea as to what next to expect.

WHO ARE YOU, LORD?

Paul uses the appellative *"Lord"* because it is unmistakably clear that he is dealing with Deity. This he knows, and beyond the shadow of a doubt.

In this question that Paul asked of the Lord as to His Identity, we find a man who has had everything pulled out from under him. The great foundation of the Law on which he had stood all of his life now crumbled beneath him. His own so-called righteousness was instantly shown up for what it really was, self-righteousness. All of this happened in a moment's time.

Even though the Sacred Text does not give us a clue, I personally feel that Paul, when he asked this question as to the Lord's Identity, greatly suspected in the depths of his soul as to what the answer would be. As he sees this Form and hears this Voice, his mind must have gone to Stephen, who professed in his dying moment to seeing *"the Son of Man standing on the Right Hand of God."*

If men are to be Saved, this is what they must see. Men must have a Vision of Jesus, at least an acknowledgement in their souls as to Who Christ is and what Christ has done. In fact, it's not possible to bring men to Christ any other way. If we try to intellectualize people into Christ, it simply won't work.

If we try to entice them in with the dangling carrot of riches, that won't work either. All of that is man's way and definitely not God's Way. The sinner must see Jesus! While he may not see Christ as Paul saw him, nevertheless, the Born-Again experience demands a Revelation of Christ to the soul, which can only be carried out by the Power of the Holy Spirit, with everything based exclusively on the Word of God (Jn. 3:3, 16).

"And he said, Who are You, Lord?" It was the greatest question that he had ever asked in all of his life!

Pharaoh of long, long ago asked the question, *"Who is the Lord?"* Pharaoh rejected Him, and he was to find out the hard way just exactly Who the Lord was. Thankfully, Paul humbly accepted what He heard and saw, and was changed forever, and changed for the good!

I AM JESUS WHOM YOU PERSECUTE

Why did Jesus answer him as He did? He could have said to Paul, *"I am the Son of Man,"* or *"I am the Messiah,"* or *"I am the Son of God!"* But instead, He used the Name which Paul hated more than any other name on the face of the Earth, *"Jesus."*

Jesus answered this way, no doubt, for many reasons. However, He wanted Paul to know, and to know instantly, that the Jesus Who had lived in Israel for some thirty three and one half years, Who had walked among its people, Who had healed the sick and cast out demons, Who had proclaimed the Gospel as no man had ever proclaimed the Gospel, Who had been accused by the Jewish Sanhedrin, the same body that had empowered Paul to come to Damascus, and Who had been crucified, was indeed Israel's Messiah, the Saviour of mankind, the Son of the Living God, in fact, God manifest in the flesh. The Name of *"Jesus"* summed it all up. It told the story as nothing else or no other name could have told it. This, then, was the Messiah Whom he had hated! What must he have thought when Jesus identified Himself? What ran through his mind at that time when Jesus identified Himself? But one thing is certain, every evidence is that he believed immediately. Then Jesus said to him:

"IT IS HARD FOR YOU TO KICK AGAINST THE PRICKS"

As we previously stated, the pricks had reference to sharp goads, which were placed immediately behind the oxen and were attached to the plow; to kick against it would cause sharp pain, as would be obvious.

It is this statement uttered by Christ to Paul that makes me believe that Paul had been under great conviction as a result of Stephen's death. Of course, with all the scores of men and women he had arrested, without a doubt, he had seen the same attitude and spirit in them as he had seen in Stephen.

THE CONVICTING POWER OF THE HOLY SPIRIT

Unbelievers respond in varied ways to the administration of the Holy Spirit. In the first place, they don't understand it all, but it is definitely true that something is happening to them. They feel it! In some ways, they see it! But they cannot really identify it. This, no doubt, happened to Paul as he witnessed the death of Stephen.

Some respond by accepting the Lord immediately, and some grow harder and meaner, even as did Paul. The *"breathing out threatenings and slaughter against the Disciples of the Lord,"* was his response to the Spirit of God. He would show these followers of Christ! He would take every one of them down! Whatever damage he could do to them, that they deserved. The very idea of anyone following this despised Nazarene! So, he was *"kicking against the goads,"* and he was feeling the pain!

There is one thing about the Moving and Operation of the Holy Spirit on the heart of an individual, it never leaves one neutral. One either gets meaner, as did Paul, or one softens and accepts the Lord.

I personally think, and from many years of experience, that the reaction that Paul had regarding his threatenings and slaughter is the reaction of most as it regards the Holy Spirit. During this time, ever how long it lasts, everything becomes confused to the individual in question. The sins he once loved and enjoyed seemingly do not now bring the satisfaction they once did. The people he once enjoyed being with, the enjoyment is now gone! Everything seems to be upside down, and he does not know or understand why, even as Paul, no doubt, did not understand what was happening to him. Yes, it was hard to kick against the goads then, and it's hard to kick against the goads now.

TREMBLING AND ASTONISHED

This was Paul's reaction to the events at hand. In other words, he was scared to death, and rightly so! In the word *"trembling,"* we find Paul's guilt. He knew what he had done to countless Believers simply because they were followers of Christ. They had broken no laws, had hurt no one, in fact, had been a blessing everywhere they were, but still, because of his hatred for Christ, he had decimated their lives, with many of them even losing their lives. He now knows this is Jesus Who has appeared to him. He also knows there is Power here beyond the scope of imagination. What will the Lord do to him?

Let me hurriedly say that the Lord has nothing but good for anyone and everyone. Irrespective as to what a person has done, and no matter how bad it may have been, if that individual will humble himself or herself before the Lord, and I mean truly humble oneself, realizing how wrong we are and how right He is, the Lord will always, and without fail, give good things to that person. He will forgive all sin. He will cleanse of every iniquity. He will start that person out on a road of success and in every capacity. No one need fear the Lord in the sense of wrath, unless that person is rebelling against God and refusing to humble himself before the Lord. That being the case, there can be dire consequences.

The word *"astonished"* in the Greek is *"thambeo,"* and means, *"to be dumbfounded, stupefied, amazed."* In modern vernacular, his whole world has just turned upside down, or possibly one should say, *"right side up."* In a moment's time, everything has changed! Everything he has believed has been proven false! His course of life has suddenly done an about-face. But the question he now asks the Lord is exactly what he should have done and signals that he is now *"born from above."* He said:

LORD, WHAT WILL YOU HAVE ME TO DO?

At that moment, Paul was *"Born-Again,"* and as stated, *"born from above."* At that moment, his entire world changed, never to go back to the old way again. Whatever the Lord wanted, whatever path that was to be taken, and whatever direction he was to go, all the Lord had to do was to show him, which is exactly what happened. When he uttered this question, that was the moment that he came from darkness to light, from death to life, from sin to Salvation, from spiritual sickness to Spiritual health, from Law to Grace. One might say that this was the greatest Revival that's ever been preached, and yet, only one soul was Saved. But that soul, under the guidance of the Lord Jesus Christ, would change the world.

IT SHALL BE TOLD YOU
WHAT YOU MUST DO

The Lord answered the Apostle immediately, for at that moment his apostleship was likewise born, and he would be told in unmistakable terms *"what he must do."*

Concerning these instructions given to Paul, the first word used at that time by our Lord to Paul was, *"arise."* The Lord doesn't push men down but rather picks them up. But to be sure, the Paul who had fallen to the ground a short time before was not the same Paul who would now arise.

PAUL WAS BLIND

Paul was blind physically but very much sightful spiritually. Three days later, Ananias will lay hands on him, with the Lord at that time giving him back his sight, as well as baptizing him with the Holy Spirit.

The statement as written here by Luke is somewhat strange, *"and when his eyes were opened, he saw no man."* The idea is as follows:

His eyes were opened Spiritually in that he could now see what was right and what was wrong. In other words, he now knew that the Lord Jesus Christ was Israel's Messiah and, as well, the Son of the Living God. His eyes were opened to these Truths plus countless others we don't have the space to innumerate.

And yet, *"he saw no man,"* meaning that physically he could not see, which, as stated, would be rectified shortly.

THEY LED HIM BY THE HAND

He had meant to enter the city of Damascus with all of the importance and pomp of an emissary from the Sanhedrin. He would be received with distinction. This is the man who is going to stamp out this *"Jesus"* religion. In his mind's eye, he would leave Damascus when his work was finished, to the applause of his fellow countrymen and, as well, with a captive train of dejected Nazarenes in tow. But it was not to be that way. How different were his actual entrance and his actual exit!

He is led by the hand into the city, probably meaning that someone is leading the horse on which he is riding, if, in fact, he was on a horse, coming in a stricken, dejected, and trembling state, no longer breathing threats and slaughter, but rather the very opposite.

When he would leave sometime later, it would be in the dead of night, let down through a window in the wall, in a basket, so as to escape those who would have killed him had they found him.

ANANIAS

Without a doubt, Luke, who wrote the Book of Acts, questioned Ananias about the following events and then gave it to us as it was given to him. The Lord, no doubt, superintended this account in that it be given to us exactly as it happened. The Scripture says:

THE LORD SPEAKS TO ANANIAS

"And there was a certain Disciple at Damascus, named Ananias *(the word 'Disciple,' as used without exception in the Book of Acts, refers to followers of Christ)*; and to him said the Lord in a vision, Ananias *(he actually saw the Lord, but in Vision form)*. And he said, Behold, I *am here*, Lord *(proclaims an extensive familiarity with the Lord, far beyond the normal)*.

"And the Lord *said* unto him, Arise, and go into the street which is called Straight *(proclaims the street, which still exists even after nearly 2,000 years)*, and enquire in the house of Judas for *one* called Saul of Tarsus *(expresses the name of the man who was the most notorious scourge of the followers of Christ in the world of that time)*: for, behold, he prays *(Paul had much to pray about)*,

"And has seen in a vision a man named Ananias coming in *(proclaims the second Vision that Paul had in a very short period of time)*, and putting *his* hand on him, that he might receive his sight" (Acts 9:10-12).

WHO WAS ANANIAS?

• Paul said that Ananias was *"a devout man according to the Law"* (Acts 22:12). With the meaning of the New Covenant not yet having been given, Ananias was walking in all the light he had. Little did he realize at the time that the man on whom he laid his hand would be given the meaning of the New Covenant, which would be the greatest Word the Lord ever gave to a human being. How privileged he was to have a part in this, which the Lord was doing.

• Paul also said that Ananias, *"had a good report of all the Jews which dwelt in Damascus."* While he definitely was a follower of Christ, still, he was loved and respected by the Jews who were not friendly to Christ.

• Ananias was close enough to the Lord that he was given a Vision by the Lord, which would be, without a doubt, one of the most important Visions ever given to any man.

• He was given the responsibility of going to Paul and praying for him that he might receive his sight and be baptized with the Holy Spirit; consequently, this man, although of short duration, played a tremendous part in that which the Lord was doing with Paul. What an honor! What a privilege!

WHO WAS JUDAS?

The only information we have on this particular Judas is that which is given in Acts 9:11. The Lord simply said to Ananias, *"Go . . . and enquire in the house of Judas for one called Saul of Tarsus."* We know that he lived on the *"street which is called Straight."* In fact, that street still exists presently in Damascus.

Was this the man with whom Paul had originally planned to stay with while in Damascus? If so, he would have been in sympathy with Paul's persecution of the followers of Christ. But it's doubtful that this was the case. The Scripture being silent, we can only surmise that if the Holy Spirit had desired that we know more, He would have included more information in the Sacred Text.

THE ANSWER OF ANANIAS TO THE LORD

The Scripture says:

"Then Ananias answered, Lord, I have heard by many of this man *(how empty our fears often are! how ignorant we are of where our chief good lies hid! but God knows; let us trust Him)*, how much evil he has done to Your Saints at Jerusalem *(but yet, the Lord has changed this man, and he will become the greatest blessing to the Saints of anyone in history)*:

"And here he has authority from the Chief Priests to bind all who call on Your Name *(Paul's evil intentions had preceded him; but the Lord invaded those intentions, completely changing them)*" (Acts 9:13-14).

THE MISSION ASSIGNED TO ANANIAS

The phrase, *"Then Ananias answered, Lord, I have heard by many of this man, how much evil he has done to Your Saints at Jerusalem,"* proclaims the fact that the activity of Paul, then known as Saul, was well known. Paul's hatred for the followers of Christ, and especially of Christ, had preceded him to the city of Damascus. In fact, he was the talk, it seems, of not only those who were followers of Christ, but, as well, of those who did not believe in Christ. Ananias construed Saul's work as that of *"evil,"* and so it was! As well, he refers to the followers of Christ, of which he was one, as *"Saints."*

In some way, Paul's mission to Damascus had preceded him, with Ananias knowing, as well as many others, no doubt, that Paul was coming by the *"authority from the Chief Priests."* And here the Lord is telling Ananias to go pray for him and tells him where to go—to the house of Judas on the street called Straight.

What must Ananias have thought at this turn of events? Evidently, he was certain that it was the Lord speaking this to him, especially considering the danger involved if he were wrong. So, the Lord told him several things. They were:

- *"Go to the street called Straight."*
- Go to the *"house of Judas."*
- Ask for one *"called Saul of Tarsus."*
- He has been praying and will be praying when you arrive.
- I have already given him a Vision of you coming to him, so he will be expecting you.
- In this Vision I showed him that you would put your hand on him so that he might receive his sight.

THE LORD SAID TO ANANIAS

"But the Lord said unto him, Go your way *(presents an urgency which demands instant obedience by Ananias)*: for he is a chosen vessel unto Me *(it means, 'Divine Selection')*, to bear My Name before the Gentiles, and kings, and the Children of Israel *('Gentiles' are placed first; that was Paul's principal calling)*:

"For I will show him how great things he must suffer for My Name's sake *(this is altogether different from much of the modern gospel, which, in fact, is no Gospel at all!)*" (Acts 9:15-16).

THREE THINGS SAID BY THE LORD
THAT PAUL WOULD DO

1. *"He is a chosen vessel unto Me."* The idea is, Paul was chosen by the Lord before he was even born. He would be given the meaning of the New Covenant, which is the greatest Word that the Lord ever gave any human being. In fact, it was much greater than what was given to Moses on Mt. Sinai. As well, he would be the Masterbuilder of the Church. Also, the Lord would use him to write some fourteen Epistles as it

regards the Word of God. In other words, he wrote about one third of the New Testament. Truly, he was a *"chosen vessel unto the Lord."*

2. Jesus said, *"He will bear My Name before the Gentiles, and kings, and the Children of Israel."* As we stated in the notes, it is obvious that the word *"Gentiles"* comes first, because this was Paul's principal calling. He ministered to the *"Children of Israel,"* but his direction was always to the Gentiles. To be sure, he did minister to kings, but there is no record that any accepted Christ. At this moment, those to whom he ministered, unless they repented at the last moment, are in Hell. They have thought about Paul's Message to them untold numbers of times from then until now. They will think about it forever and forever.

3. Paul would be called upon by the Lord to suffer great things for Jesus' Name's sake. As is obvious, the Lord does not resort to very much diplomacy. He simply told Ananias what Paul would do. How does this measure up against much of the modern gospel? Not very favorably, I think!

Did Ananias relate these things to Paul?

While the Scripture gives no indication as to what type of conversation these two men had, it is certain that Ananias revealed to the Apostle exactly that which the Lord had spoken to him. I think he would have felt obligated to do so!

ANANIAS, USED OF GOD

"And Ananias went his way, and entered into the house *(he obeyed the Command of the Lord)*; and putting his hands on him *(on Paul)* said, Brother Saul *(he addressed Paul in this manner because Paul was already Saved, and had been so for the last three days and nights)*, the Lord, *even* Jesus, Who appeared unto you in the way as you came, has sent me, that you might receive your sight, and be filled with the Holy Spirit *(this proclaims the fact that one is not baptized with the Holy Spirit at conversion, as many teach; in fact, the Baptism with the Holy Spirit is a separate work of Grace, which takes place after conversion [Acts 2:4; 8:14-17; 19:1-7]).*

"And immediately there fell from his eyes as it had been scales: and he received sight forthwith, and arose, and was baptized *(was baptized with water, after he was baptized with the Holy Spirit)*" **(Acts 9:17-18).**

BROTHER SAUL

When Ananias was ushered in to the presence of Paul, his coming was expected by the Apostle. It is ironical that one of the very men whom he had come to Damascus to imprison will instead lay hands on him and pray for him. What a turn of events!

If it is to be noticed, Ananias addressed Saul (Paul) as *"Brother Saul."* He did this not to merely show respect but because Paul had already been Born-Again, which happened on the Road to Damascus. Therefore, he would address him as *"Brother Saul,"* and simply because he was indeed now his brother in the Lord.

FILLED WITH THE HOLY SPIRIT

Paul was Saved on the Road to Damascus, then three days later, baptized with the Holy Spirit, although nothing is said here about speaking with other Tongues and, in fact, no information is given whatsoever as to what happened. But, we do know that when Paul was baptized with the Spirit, he most definitely did speak with other Tongues. He said, as it regards his first Epistle to the Church at Corinth, *"I thank my God, I speak with Tongues more than you all"* (I Cor. 14:18).

THREE THINGS HAPPENED TO PAUL HERE

1. When Ananias prayed for him, *"immediately there fell from his eyes as it had been scales: and he received sight."*

2. He was *"filled with the Holy Spirit."*
3. He was then baptized in water.

PREACHING CHRIST

The Scripture says:

"And when he had received meat, he was strengthened *(refers to him ending his three-day fast)*. **Then was
Saul certain days with the Disciples which were at
Damascus** *(probably means that Ananias introduced him
to these followers of Christ; he had come to arrest them,
and now he joins them; what a mighty God we serve!)*.
"And straightway *(immediately)* **he preached Christ
in the Synagogues** *(these were the very Synagogues to
which letters of the High Priest were addressed, empow-
ering Paul to arrest any Jewish Believers who called
upon the Name of Jesus)*, **that He is the Son of God** *(the
first time in Acts that Jesus is referred to by this title)*"
(Acts 9:19-20).

JESUS IS THE SON OF GOD

Immediately, Paul begins to preach Christ in the Synagogues. The *"certain days"* does not tell us how long he
remained in Damascus. But the truth is, he was taking his life
in his hands by *"preaching Christ in the Synagogues,"* which
is exactly what he did. Using the Name *"Christ,"* in essence,
states that he was claiming Jesus as Israel's Messiah. Furthermore, he referred to Him as he preached as *"the Son of God."*
What happened to him on the road to Damascus, and with
Ananias, is very doubtful that it was revealed to the rulers of
the Synagogue where he ministered. So, when Paul is introduced, more than likely, they had no idea as to what had happened to him, therefore, had no idea as to what he was about
to say. They were expecting a diatribe against the followers of

Christ, all of them having heard of his reputation. But how surprised they were when he began to proclaim Jesus as the Messiah of Israel and, furthermore, referring to him as *"the Son of God,"* which meant that Jesus is God. How surprised they must have been! Actually, it would have been much more than surprise; they would have been shocked!

AMAZED

"But all who heard *him* were amazed, and said; Is not this he who destroyed them which called on this Name in Jerusalem, and came hither for that intent, that he might bring them bound unto the Chief Priests? *(This means that those in the Synagogues had been expecting him, but not what he is now saying.)*
"But Saul increased the more in strength *(refers to his greater understanding of the Word of God as the days wore on; in fact, for the first time, he understands the Word)*, and confounded the Jews which dwelt at Damascus, proving that this is very Christ *(proving from the Word of God that Jesus was the Messiah)*" (Acts 9:21-22).

PROVING FROM THE WORD OF GOD
THAT JESUS IS THE CHRIST

From the account of other Messages in the Book of Acts, we know what Paul's method was. When he preached in the Synagogues, and in whatever city he visited, he would prove from the Word of God that Jesus was the Messiah. He *"confounded the Jews"* because they could not answer his argument. Yet, most of them would not believe him, which he found to his dismay.

THE REACTION OF THE JEWS IN DAMASCUS

"And after that many days were fulfilled, the Jews took

counsel to kill him *(the persecutor is now persecuted)*:

"**But their laying await was known of Saul** *(presents Believers informing him of the proposed action of the Jews)*. **And they watched the gates day and night to kill him** *(which he was informed of as well; therefore, he will escape by a different route)*.

"**Then the Disciples** *(followers of Christ)* **took him by night, and let** *him* **down by the wall in a basket**" (Acts 9:23-25).

THE PERSECUTOR IS NOW THE PERSECUTED

It seems that his Ministry in the Synagogues was short lived. What he was preaching incensed the Jews; consequently, they *"took counsel to kill him."*

The Lord saw to the fact that word got to Paul as to what plans were being laid for his murder. Feeling that he must leave, the followers of Christ, who were Jews themselves, *"took him by night, and let him down by the wall in a basket."* They did this to foil those who would have murdered the Apostle.

"Teach me Your Way, O Lord;
"Teach me Your Way!
"Your guiding Grace afford;
"Teach me Your Way!
"Help me to walk aright,
"More by Faith, less by sight,
"Lead me with Heavenly Light;
"Teach me Your Way!"

"When I am sad at heart,
"Teach me Your Way!
"When earthly joys depart,
"Teach me Your Way!
"In hours of loneliness,
"In times of dire distress,

"In failure or success,
"Teach me Your Way!"

"When doubts and fears arise;
"Teach me Your Way!
"When storms o'er spread the sky;
"Teach me Your Way!
"Shine through the cloud and rain,
"Through sorrow, toil and pain,
"Make You my pathway plain;
"Teach me Your Way!"

"Long as my life shall last;
"Teach me Your Way!
"Wherever my lot be cast;
"Teach me Your Way!
"Until the race is run,
"Until the journey's done,
"Until the Crown is won;
"Teach me Your Way!"

PAUL
THE APOSTLE

CHAPTER THREE

The Silent Years

THE SILENT YEARS

This period known as the *"silent years,"* which spans the time from Paul's conversion on the road to Damascus to his first missionary journey, presents a time frame of about ten years. Although speculative, Paul's conversion probably happened in about A.D. 35, and his first missionary journey happened about A.D. 45, thus making a ten year time period. Luke's purpose, as the Holy Spirit Moved through him in giving us an account of these times, little had time frames in view, but rather what was taught and given as it regarded the New Covenant.

As it regards this time frame of approximately ten years, there has been an ongoing controversy for many centuries as to exactly what Paul did in that particular period of time, at least as it regards Ministry. Some think that he preached immediately in Damascus after his conversion, and others think not.

Luke gives no account of this personal phase of Paul's career, but he allows room for it between Acts 9:22 and 23. It is Paul who tells us of his sojourn into Arabia (Gal. 1:17) to prove his independence of the Apostles in Jerusalem.

He did not go to them for instruction or for ecclesiastical authority. He did not adopt the merely traditional view of Jesus as the Messiah. He knew the contention well enough, of course, for he had answered it often. But now his old arguments were gone, and he must work his way around to the other side and be able to declare his new Gospel with clearness and force.

He was done with calling Jesus anathematic (I Cor. 12:3); henceforth, to him Jesus is Lord.

We know nothing of Paul's sojourn into Arabia for the approximate three years, or in what part of Arabia he was. Some even contend that he may have gone to Mt. Sinai and thought out Grace in the atmosphere of Law, but there is no evidence of that.

But one thing is clear, Paul grew in apprehension of the things of Christ during these years as, indeed, he grew to the very end, and altogether, we might hastily say, by Revelation. However, he never pulled away from the first clear Vision of Jesus. He claimed that God had revealed His Son in him that he might preach to the Gentiles (Gal. 1:16). He claimed that from the first until the very last.

We will find that it is impossible to escape the conclusion that the significance and value of the Cross became clear to him at a point in time. This narrow Jew had surrendered to Christ Who died for the sins of the world.

We will also find that the universal Gospel had taken hold of his mind and heart, and that this great Gospel will work out its logical consequences in Paul and his life and living. The time in Arabia seems to be when he received from the Lord the New Covenant, but once again, that is speculation. We do know that by the time he began his first missionary journey, he then had a *"developed Faith"* that would bear, we might say, instant fruit. He is now the slave of Christ.

For him, henceforth, to live is Christ. He is crucified with Christ. He is in Christ. The union of Paul with Christ is the real key to his life. And more particularly, it is Jesus Christ and Him Crucified. We will find that the Cross of Christ was the Means by which the Doctrine of Christ was played out in his life. It was the Means of his real fellowship with Christ.

Thus it is that the man who probably never saw Christ in the flesh understands Him best, and because he understood the Cross.

Now Paul does not merely proclaim Christ as before, he *"proves Christ."*

As well, he does it with such marvelous skill that the Jews are first confounded and then enraged to the point of murder. Their former hero was now their foe.

TWO GREAT THINGS THAT HAPPENED TO PAUL DURING THE SILENT YEARS

1. The first thing that happened to Paul during the *"silent*

years" was his attempt to live for God by means of Law, which is all that was known at the time, and which account is given to us in the great Seventh Chapter of Romans. While this is one of the most misunderstood Chapters in the Bible, if properly understood, it is, to be sure, one of the most informative. We will see from our study of this Chapter how impossible it is for one to successfully live for God and not understand the Message of the Cross. While one can be a Believer and not understand this Message, one most definitely cannot live a successful life in Christ. The truth is, if Paul couldn't do it, and he definitely couldn't, then neither can we.

So, it is important that we understand this. In fact, it is very important! It will help us to learn some things about ourselves that we desperately need to know.

2. The second, and by far the most important thing that happened during this span of some ten years, was the Lord giving by Revelation to Paul the meaning of the New Covenant, which is the meaning of the Cross. This is the greatest Word that God ever gave to anyone. The meaning of the New Covenant is that to which the Old Covenant ever pointed. In fact, every word by every Sage, every word by every Patriarch, and every word by every Prophet of old pointed toward this time. And it was to Paul, the Jew from Tarsus, to whom the Lord entrusted the greatest Message that was ever known. Actually, the New Covenant is Jesus Christ. It can probably be summed up in one short phrase, *"Jesus Christ and Him Crucified"* (I Cor. 1:23).

We will first of all look at the great Seventh Chapter of Romans. The Apostle Paul was moved upon by the Holy Spirit to give us an account of these particular times in his life and living. They do not flatter the Apostle, as such can never flatter anyone; however, the teaching contained in this great Seventh Chapter is of vital significance to the Believer, and yet, regrettably and sadly, most Christians simply do not understand it. Hopefully, the following will let some light into this most important Word, and to be sure, it is that which the Lord desires that we know.

THE GREAT EXPERIENCES OF THE APOSTLE PAUL

I wish to make it clear and plain that the Cross of Christ and our Faith in that Finished Work is the only Means that God has given us that we may live a victorious life—Victory over the world, the flesh, and the Devil, a phrase coined by the Early Church Fathers. The Lord gave no other means of life and living, because no other means is needed. It is ever the Cross.

In the next few paragraphs I hope to show all and sundry that as important as experiences are, as should be overly obvious, and as Scriptural and wonderful as they might be, still, they do not give us the victory we must have in Christ. Jesus said, *"You shall know the Truth, and the Truth shall make you free"* (Jn. 8:32).

Most would say that the experiences, which Paul had, would guarantee victory in every capacity. While those experiences were absolutely phenomenal, to say the least, and were absolutely necessary, still, until Paul was given the Revelation of the meaning of the New Covenant, which is the meaning of the Cross, the truth is, Paul could not successfully live for the Lord. And, if he couldn't, how do you think we can?

• First of all, the great Apostle had the Vision of Christ on the road to Damascus, to which we have already addressed ourselves. He saw the Lord and talked with the Lord. Now, there cannot be an experience that could be much greater than that. It is so phenomenal as to defy all description. In fact, it was so phenomenal that Paul would never be the same again. In a few moments' time, his whole world changed. All of his arguments fell to the ground. He had seen the Lord Jesus Christ, and beyond the shadow of a doubt, he knew it was the Lord, and he knew that the One they crucified was actually the Messiah of Israel and the Saviour of the world. There was no doubt about that!

• The second thing that happened to Paul was him being baptized with the Holy Spirit as Ananias prayed for him (Acts 9:10-18). You see, there are many people who believe that the

Baptism with the Holy Spirit is, once again, the answer to all problems. While most definitely the Holy Spirit is, as should be obvious, a tremendous help in every capacity of our life and living, the truth is, a person can be baptized with the Holy Spirit, have all nine Gifts of the Spirit, be used mightily of God, and still not know how to live for the Lord. That may sound strange to most modern ears, but it happens to be the truth.

• Please understand, if anyone reads this and thinks we are denigrating the Baptism with the Holy Spirit, well, evidently that person does not know too very much about what we teach and preach. But again, while the Holy Spirit is most definitely the action figure in our life and living, it is the Cross of Christ, which Paul taught us, that is the key.

• Immediately after being Saved on the road to Damascus and baptized with the Holy Spirit, Paul began to preach (Acts 9:19-22). There is more that needs to be said about this.

Just because a man or a woman is called to preach the Gospel and used mightily of the Lord in this capacity, as it should be, still, that doesn't mean the preacher knows and understands God's Prescribed Order of Life and Living. As it regards the Ministry, these are Gifts, which means that not very much is required of the individual except to receive the Gift and allow the Lord to use him in respect to this Gift, whatever it might be. Some people have the erroneous thought that if the Lord is using somebody, that means he has all the answers. While that may be true in a few cases, most of the time, it isn't. Let me say it again, if the individual doesn't understand the Cross of Christ, not only as it regards our Salvation but, as well, as it regards our Sanctification, such a person, whomever that person might be, simply cannot successfully live for the Lord.

AN EXPERIENCE

Many years ago, when Frances and I were preaching in meetings at churches all over the U.S.A., we went any number of times to the great city of Dallas, Texas, preaching for H.C. Noah,

Pastor of one of the great churches in that city. Virtually every time we would go, Gordon Lindsay, who edited the *"Voice Of Healing"* Magazine, would invite Frances and me out for lunch.

In those days, the *"Voice Of Healing"* was one of the most influential magazines in the world. As the Lord had moved upon this nation and the balance of the world with great Divine Healing Revivals, the biggest the world had ever known other than the time of Christ, it was this magazine, and above all, the capabilities of Brother Lindsay, who helped spread it all over the world. To be brief, this magazine and Brother Lindsay were greatly used of God.

At any rate, Brother Lindsay took an interest in me, and I will never forget those times. I would ply him with question after question.

At a particular time, quite a number of the Evangelists who were being mightily used of God, drawing some of the biggest crowds in the world and seeing much done for the Lord Jesus Christ, had tremendous problems in their own lives, which seriously curtailed their Ministries and, as well, hurt the Cause of Christ, which would be obvious.

One particular day, while Frances and I were having a meal with Brother Lindsay, this particular subject came up. I asked him, *"Brother Lindsay, what is happening with these men? Why are they having these difficulties?"*

I'll never forget the answer of this dear Brother. He sat there for a few moments and said nothing, and finally he said, that is, if I remember his words correctly, *"Brother Swaggart, I simply don't know."*

And the truth was, as much as this man did know about the Bible, he did not understand, and neither did the Evangelists, what Paul taught us, even as the Lord had given it to him, as to how we as Believers are to face the powers of darkness and to successfully live for the Lord, in other words, to be victorious.

While the Bible does not teach sinless perfection, it most definitely does teach that *"sin is not to have dominion over us"*

(Rom. 6:14). So, what am I saying?

I'm saying that the preachers who were mightily used of God in the 1950's and early 1960's, despite the fact that they were being used of the Lord, and that it was genuine and real, still, they did not know how to live a victorious, Christian life.

I remember reading an article in a major Christian magazine about this very subject. The year was 1953.

The writer stated, and he was right, *"The deliverance preachers need Deliverance themselves."* Of course, he wrote an entire article in the magazine, but what he had to say could be summed up in the short statement just made. Their problem was, they did not understand, as stated, what Paul taught us in this respect. And even though they were used greatly of the Lord, still, unless a person understands what the great Apostle gave us, one cannot live a successful Christian life. And to be sure, even if one does understand what Paul taught, and understands it thoroughly, to be blunt, it's still not going to be easy. In fact, the Holy Spirit through Paul referred to this as *"war."* He said:

WARFARE

"For though we walk in the flesh *(refers to the fact that we do not yet have Glorified Bodies)*, we do not war after the flesh *(after our own ability, but rather by the Power of the Spirit)*:

"(For the weapons of our warfare *are* not carnal *(carnal weapons consist of those which are man-devised)*, but mighty through God *(the Cross of Christ [I Cor. 1:18])* to the pulling down of strongholds;)

"Casting down imaginations *(philosophic strongholds; every effort man makes outside of the Cross of Christ)*, and every high thing that exalts itself against the Knowledge of God *(all the pride of the human heart)*, and bringing into captivity every thought to the obedience of Christ *(can be done only by the Believer looking exclusively to the Cross, where all Victory is found; the Holy Spirit will then perform the task)*" **(II Cor. 10:3-5).**

• **As well, even at this time, which is at the beginning of his life lived for the Lord, Paul is an Apostle; however, it will take some years before the great Word is given to him by Revelation, and he is able to deliver it to the people.**

WHAT IS AN APOSTLE?

An Apostle is one who has been given a very special Message from the Lord as it concerns the Doctrine of the Church. In fact, as Prophets were the de facto leaders of the Nation of Israel in the Old Testament, Apostles are the de facto leaders in the church. The Holy Spirit knows the Message, which the church desperately needs, and correspondingly gives such a Message to the Apostle for it to be given to the church. Much of the time it is met with opposition, but the Holy Spirit has a way to make His Word felt.

But, despite all of this, until the Lord gave the Revelation of the meaning of the New Covenant to Paul, the great Apostle simply did not know how to live for God. In his defense, no one else at that time knew how to either. In fact, as stated, it would be to Paul that this great Word would be given, which is the meaning of the New Covenant.

To do a book about Paul, of which hundreds have been done, and to properly tell his story, one must at the same time proclaim what he taught. To not do that would be to not do this man justice. Paul suffered much, and it was the Message for which he suffered, the Message of the Cross. But, it ignited a flame in this world that has burned from then until now and, in effect, has changed the world and has done so in the face of the concentrated powers of darkness. By the Power of God, Paul ignited a light that not only has not been dimmed, but instead, has touched every corner of this Planet with untold millions of lives gloriously changed. As we said in the foreword of this Volume, every blessing and every good thing that has happened

anywhere in the world has been because of the Message of the Cross that the Lord gave to Paul, which is the meaning of the New Covenant. It would be very difficult to exaggerate its effect or to overstate its influence. One could say many things, but perhaps the following statement will capture the essence of this man: The Jew from Tarsus made a difference!

THE SEVENTH CHAPTER OF ROMANS

As we have stated, to deal with Paul and ignore his Message presents itself as missing the very core of what this man was and what he did. In 1997, the Lord gave me a Revelation of the Cross, which, in essence, is exactly that which Paul taught. It changed my life, and it's changed my Ministry. To be brief, the Revelation was given in three stages, and in the following manner:

1. The Lord took me to the Sixth Chapter of Romans and showed me the meaning of the sin nature. He showed me how the sin nature could control the Believer, forcing such a Believer into a course of action to which the Believer doesn't want to go. In fact, the Seventh Chapter of Romans portrays this in detail. After a period of time, I also learned that the sin nature was the very first thing that was shown to the Apostle Paul, that is, as it regards how we live for the Lord. Of course, Paul was first shown the great Doctrine of *"Justification by Faith"* (Rom., Chpts. 4 and 5). But when it came to living for God, how we order our behavior, how we conduct ourselves, and how we walk in Victory before the Lord, or the lack thereof, the understanding of the sin nature was given to Paul by the Lord as recorded in Chapter 6 of Romans.

2. Even though the Lord gave me some understanding respecting the sin nature on that memorable morning before daylight in 1997, He did not at the time give me any solution for this extremely important aspect of our life and living. That was to come several days later. It was in one of the morning prayer meetings.

That particular morning, along with several others present,

after seeking the Lord for a few minutes, I sensed the Presence of God come over me very heavily. The Lord then spoke to my heart, giving me the solution to the sin nature, etc. It was very simple and very much to the point, yet so revealing. He said to me:

A. The answer is found in the Cross of Christ.

B. The solution is found in the Cross of Christ.

C. The answer is found only in the Cross of Christ.

Once again, the Lord took me to the Sixth Chapter of Romans in giving me this tremendous Truth. This is what Jesus was talking about when He said, *"And you shall know the Truth, and the Truth shall make you free"* (Jn. 8:32).

But, in this, the Lord did not tell me how the Holy Spirit functions. I knew beyond the shadow of a doubt, that the Holy Spirit played a great part, yet, the Lord said nothing to me about this. I earnestly began to seek His Face as it regarded the answer to this question. By the Power of the Holy Spirit, the Lord had helped me to touch a great part of the world with the great and glorious Gospel of Jesus Christ, actually seeing hundreds of thousands brought to a Saving knowledge of Jesus and Him Crucified. But, the Lord said nothing to me that morning about the Holy Spirit. I thought in my mind if, in fact, the Cross of Christ is the only answer for the sin nature, once again, where does that leave the Holy Spirit?

3. The Lord was to give me the answer regarding how the Holy Spirit works in one of our teaching sessions over SonLife Radio, which we carry forth every morning Monday through Friday. But, to make it understandable, I must go back to March of 1988.

It was a terrible time for the Ministry, and the fault was mine. It was like my whole world had crashed, and I was to blame. The secular world was laughing at me, and the church world was referring to me as a hypocrite.

That particular morning, Frances and I stayed home from the office, where I was to seek the Lord much of that day. My only answer was the Lord. I could not find help anywhere else.

Our house, along with Donnie's, sits on 20 acres of land

outside the city limits of Baton Rouge, Louisiana. I was at the back of the compound seeking the Lord that morning. In all of my life, I've never felt the powers of darkness, I think, as I did that day. Satan kept saying to me, *"You have disgraced your family, your Church, and above all, the Work of God. Why don't you just take what money you have in the bank and disappear?"* I remember I had $800 in the bank.

I remember leaning up against the fence and saying to the Lord, *"You promised that You would not allow anything to come upon us any harder than we could bear, but, with every temptation that You would make a way of escape."* I then went on to say, *"Lord, no human being can stand this; I plead with You for Your Help."*

All of a sudden it happened, the Spirit of God came over me. One moment it was like a thousand pounds on my back, and I was being crushed. But, the next moment, as the Spirit of the Lord had His Way, that heaviness instantly lifted with everything changing, and I mean for the better. And then the Lord spoke to my heart. It was very simple and very much to the point. He said, *"I will show you things about the Holy Spirit you do not now know."*

As the Lord spoke that to my heart, I instantly reasoned, the Holy Spirit is God. And there are all types of things about Him that I do not know. But I knew that the Lord was speaking of the situation at hand.

As stated, that was in March of 1988. As the weeks and months passed, there was nothing that came from the Lord as it regarded that which He said to me. And then the years passed. I thought about this occasion many times, but still, I had received nothing from the Lord.

THE LORD SPOKE

As stated, that morning over our radio program, *"A Study In The Word"*, we were coming down to the end of the broadcast. I don't remember the month, but I do know it was 1997.

Loren Larson was on the program with me that morning.

Usually there are several, but that morning he was the only one other than me.

All of a sudden I made a statement that startled me. I did not really understand what I said. I had not read it anywhere, and it had not crossed my mind at any time. So, where did it come from? I stated:

"The Holy Spirit works exclusively within the parameters of the Finished Work of Christ, and will not work outside of those parameters." I'm not quoting verbatim what I said, but basically, that's what was said.

I paused, wondering how in the world that I knew that? Nothing like that has ever happened to me before or since. At any rate, I paused for a moment saying nothing, contemplating what had been said.

Then Loren spoke up and said, *"Can you give me Scripture for that?"*

How could I give him Scripture when I had not even thought of the situation and didn't even really understand what I had said? And then, as quickly as the Word had come to me about how the Holy Spirit works, the Lord gave me the Scripture to prove what was said. I quoted it:

"For the Law of the Spirit of Life in Christ Jesus, has made me free from the Law of Sin and Death" (Rom. 8:2).

I knew what I said was right, but other than the Lord, I had no idea as to where it came from.

A few minutes later the program ended. I got up from the table and turned to my right to walk out of the little studio. All of a sudden the Spirit of God came over me. The Lord then spoke to my heart and said:

"Do you remember when I told you back in 1988 that I would tell you things about the Holy Spirit that you did not then know?" Of course I remembered!

The Lord then said, *"I have just fulfilled that Promise that I made to you."*

I stood there totally overwhelmed by the Presence of the Lord. It took me a while to assimilate that which the Lord had given me, but ultimately, I came to realize how so very, very important it actually was. Tragically, most Believers, even those who are Spirit-filled, little know how the Holy Spirit works within their lives. Once again, to be brief, He works entirely within the framework of the Cross of Christ. It is what Jesus did at the Cross that gives the Holy Spirit the legal right and the legal means to do all that He does. In fact, this is so much the case that it is referred to as a *"Law"* (Rom. 8:2).

I've been very brief, but what I've given in the past few paragraphs is the gist of the Revelation that the Lord gave me in 1997. To be sure, it was nothing new. It was that which had already been given to the Apostle Paul and possibly many, many others down through the centuries. But, this I do know, this Revelation, which is based 100% on the Word of God, has changed everything about my life and living, for which we give the Lord all the praise and all the Glory.

LIVING A LIFE OF DEFEAT

From the first four Verses of Romans, Chapter 7, Paul tells us the following:

• We who are Born-Again are married to Christ.

• We are to be faithful to Him in every respect, for He alone can meet our every need.

• If we look to anything else other than Christ and the Cross, we are, in effect, committing spiritual adultery, which, as should be obvious, greatly hinders what the Holy Spirit can do within our lives.

• Ironically enough, to explain this tremendous Truth, the Holy Spirit through Paul gave us the following analogy. I copy directly from THE EXPOSITOR'S STUDY BIBLE both Text and notes.

THE LAW AND DOMINION

"Know you not, Brethren *(Paul is speaking to*

Believers), **(for I speak to them who know the Law,)** *(he is speaking of the Law of Moses, but it could refer to any type of religious Law)* **how that the Law has dominion over a man as long as he lives?** *(The Law has dominion as long as he tries to live by Law. Regrettably, not understanding the Cross regarding Sanctification, virtually the entirety of the church is presently trying to live for God by means of the Law. Let the Believer understand that there are only two places he can be, Grace or Law. If he doesn't understand the Cross as it refers to Sanctification, which is the only means of victory, he will automatically be under Law, which guarantees failure.)"*

THE ADULTERESS

"For the woman which has an husband is bound by the Law to *her* husband so long as he lives *(presents Paul using the analogy of the marriage bond)***; but if the husband be dead, she is loosed from the Law of *her* husband** *(meaning that she is free to marry again).*

"So then if, while *her* husband lives, she be married to another man, she shall be called an adulteress *(in effect, the woman now has two husbands, at least in the Eyes of God; following this analogy, the Holy Spirit through Paul will give us a great truth; many Christians are living a life of spiritual adultery; they are married to Christ, but they are, in effect, serving another husband, 'the Law'; it is quite an analogy!)***: but if her husband be dead** *(the Law is dead by virtue of Christ having fulfilled the Law in every respect)***, she is free from that Law** *(if the husband dies, the woman is free to marry and serve another; the Law of Moses, being satisfied in Christ, is now dead to the Believer and the Believer is free to serve Christ without the Law having any part or parcel in his life or living)***; so that she is no adulteress, though she be married to another man** *(presents the Believer as now married to Christ, and* *no longer under obligation to the Law)*."

WE ARE MARRIED TO CHRIST

"**Wherefore, my Brethren, you also are become dead to the Law** *(the Law is not dead per se, but we are dead to the Law because we are dead to its effects; this means that we are not to try to live for God by means of 'Law,' whether the Law of Moses, or Laws made up by other men or of ourselves; we are to be dead to all Law)* **by the Body of Christ** *(this refers to the Crucifixion of Christ, which satisfied the demands of the broken Law, which we could not satisfy; but Christ did it for us; having fulfilled the Law in every respect, the Christian is not obligated to Law in any fashion, only to Christ and what He did at the Cross)*; **that you should be married to another** *(speaking of Christ)*, *even* **to Him Who is raised from the dead** *(we are raised with Him in Newness of Life, and we should ever understand that Christ has met, does meet, and shall meet our every need; we look to Him exclusively, referring to what He did for us at the Cross)*, **that we should bring forth fruit unto God** *(proper fruit can only be brought forth by the Believer constantly looking to the Cross; in fact, Christ must never be separated from the Work of the Cross; to do so is to produce 'another Jesus' [II Cor. 11:4])*."

THE FLESH

"**For when we were in the flesh** *(can refer to the unsaved state or to the Believer who is attempting to overcome the powers of sin by his own efforts, i.e., 'the flesh')*, **the motions of sins** *(denotes being under the power of the sin nature, and refers to the 'passions of the sin nature')*, **which were by the Law** *(the effect of the Law is to reveal sin, which Law is designed to do whether it's the Law of God or Laws made up of ourselves; that doesn't mean it's* *evil, for it isn't; it just means that there is no victory in the Law, only the revelation of sin and its penalty),* **did work in our members to bring forth fruit unto death** *(when the Believer attempts to live for the Lord by means of Law, which regrettably most of the modern church does, the end result is going to be sin and failure; in fact, it can be no other way; let us say it again! if the Believer doesn't understand the Cross, as it refers to Sanctification, then the Believer is going to try to live for God by means of Law; the sadness is that most of the modern church thinks it is under Grace, when in reality it is living under Law because of not understanding the Cross)."*

NEWNESS OF THE SPIRIT

"But now we are delivered from the Law *(delivered from its just demands, meaning that Christ has paid its penalty),* **that being dead** *(dead to the Law by virtue of having died with Christ on the Cross)* **wherein we were held** *(we were once held down by the sin nature)***; that we should serve in newness of Spirit** *(refers to the Holy Spirit and not man's spirit; the Believer has a completely new way of living, which is Faith in Christ and what He did at the Cross on our behalf; this guarantees perpetual victory),* **and not *in* the oldness of the letter** *(this refers to the Law of Moses; most modern Believers would argue that they aren't living after the Law of Moses; but, as we have stated, the truth is if they do not understand the Cross as it refers to Sanctification, then in some way they are still living under that old Law)"* **(Rom. 7:1-6).**

THE GROUNDWORK LAID

In these first four Verses of Chapter 7 of Romans, Paul pictures the Believer serving the Law while at the same time married to Christ. It is an un-winnable situation. The Law of

Moses, or any type of religious law, laws we make up ourselves or others devise, are to be put away from us in totality. We, as Believers, are to look to Christ exclusively. As stated in the notes, we died with Him, were buried with Him, and raised with Him in Newness of Life (Rom. 6:3-5). Christ is our all-in-all. Everything we need is found in Him, and the Means by which He gives these things to us is the Cross. When we speak of the Cross, I'm sure it is understood that we aren't speaking of a wooden beam. We are rather speaking of what Jesus there did. And what He did was to atone for all sin, past, present, and future, at least for all who will believe (Jn. 3:16). If the individuals will avail themselves of all that Christ has done for us at the Cross, we will find that everything has been provided, and we will also find that the sin nature will no longer have dominion over us (Rom. 6:14). However, if the Believer places his or her faith in anything except the Cross of Christ, and it doesn't really matter what it is, such a Believer is putting himself under Law. This means that such a Believer is living in a state of spiritual adultery, which means that the Holy Spirit is greatly hindered as to what He can do for us. To be sure, the Spirit of God is not going to aid and abet the Believer to carry out spiritual adultery, which means being unfaithful to Christ. He's not going to do that, so that leaves us on our own, which guarantees defeat in every capacity. Unfortunately, most of the modern church, not understanding the Cross of Christ relative to Sanctification, is trying to live for God by the means of law. While it's not the Law of Moses, nevertheless, it is law, which, and as stated, we have devised out of our own minds, or others have devised, and we have borrowed. Unfortunately, preachers by the scores are over television presenting law as the means of living a victorious life. I would hope it would be understood from Paul's writings that such presents an impossibility.

THE LAW OF MOSES IS NOT AT FAULT

Paul continues, and he says:

"**What shall we say then?** *(In Verses 1 through 6 of this Chapter, Paul has shown that the Believer is no longer under Law; in the remainder of the Chapter, he shows that a Believer putting himself under Law, thus failing to avail himself of the resources of Grace, is a defeated Christian.)* **Is the Law sin? God forbid** *(man's condition is not caused by the Law of God, for the Law is Holy; rather it is exposed).* **No, I had not known sin, but by the Law** *(means that the Law of Moses defined what sin actually is, but gave no power to overcome sin)*: **for I had not known lust, except the Law had said, You shall not covet** *(tells us that the desire for what is forbidden is the first conscious form of sin; this is the sin nature at work!)*" (Rom. 7:7).

WE ARE NOT TO MISUNDERSTAND THE LAW

Paul is quick to explain in this Seventh Verse that the Law is not to blame for man's condition. In fact, one might say that the Law is like a mirror. Man looks into the mirror to see what he is, which the mirror will portray to him; however, all the mirror can do is show him what he is. It has no power to change him.

Why did the Lord give the Law to Israel, which is His Standard of Righteousness, demand that man keep the Law, with a severe penalty if he didn't, but gave man no power to do such? Some of the reasons are as follows:

• The Law portrays to us God's Standard of Righteousness and Holiness.

• Man will find that due to the Fall, despite the simplicity of the Law, he simply cannot keep it.

• The only recourse for the demands of the Law is the Cross of Christ. If it had not been for the Sacrificial system in Israel, which was a symbolism of the Cross of Christ, Israel would have been totally and completely destroyed. The Sacrificial system, portraying Christ, brought about a covering for their sin. It and it alone would suffice. We might say the following:

The Cross of Christ alone stands between man and eternal Hell. As well, the Cross of Christ alone is the dividing line between Righteousness and unrighteousness.

• Man was to see that he could not within himself obey the Law of God, therefore, he was to turn to Christ and the Cross.

• It must, as well, be understood, had the Lord given man the power to keep the Law, the end result would not have turned out to be victory but rather the opposite.

Man's problem is pride which culminates in self-righteousness. If he had been given power to keep the Law, and had done so, instead of giving the Lord credit for such, he would have given himself credit, which would have made his problem even worse.

Paul is quick to say that it is not the Law that is at fault, but rather man. Man has no recourse except in Christ and what Christ did for us at the Cross.

CONCUPISCENCE

"But sin *(the sin nature)*, taking occasion by the Commandment, wrought in me all manner of concupiscence *('concupiscence' is 'evil desire,' meaning, if the Believer attempts to live for God by means other than the Cross, he will be ruled by 'evil desires'; and no matter how dedicated he might be otherwise, he will not be able to stop the process in that manner, with it getting worse and worse)*. For without the Law sin *was* dead *(means that the Law of Moses fully exposed what was already in man's heart; that's one of the reasons God gave the Law)*" (Rom. 7:8).

TAKING OCCASION BY THE COMMANDMENT

The statement offered by Paul, *"taking occasion by the*

Commandment," presents a strange scenario. It is not the Commandment of God that's at fault, but rather man is at fault. When man tries to live by Commandments, this stops the Holy Spirit, Who functions entirely in the Finished Work of Christ, from helping us. Consequently, the sin nature begins to take control, and *"evil desires"* then become the natural course of events.

Through the years, I've had untold numbers of letters from men, and even women, stating that evil thoughts were crowding their minds, and they did not know how to stop it.

This is happening because the individual has his or her faith exclusively in the law and not the Cross of Christ, whether they realize it or not. And that's the sadness. The modern church has had such a paucity of teaching regarding the Cross of Christ respecting Sanctification that modern Christians simply do not know how to live for God. There is Victory only in the Cross of Christ and not at all in trying to keep some type of law that our church has made up, or we have devised ourselves, or someone else. The way the Believer is to live for God, and do so on a continuing basis, is to place his or her Faith exclusively in Christ, understanding that what the Lord did for us at the Cross guarantees total and complete victory. Please look at the following very abbreviated formula:

FOCUS: The Lord Jesus Christ (Jn. 1:1; 14:6).

THE OBJECT OF FAITH: The Cross of Christ (Rom. 6:3-5; I Cor. 1:17-18; 2:2).

POWER SOURCE: The Holy Spirit (Rom. 8:1-2, 11).

RESULTS: Victory (Rom. 6:14).

This very abbreviated formula that we've just given explains what we're trying to say. Now let's look at it, using the same formula, but in the manner in which it is presently being used by most Christians.

Focus: works.

Object of Faith: performance.

Power Source: self.

Results: defeat.

The Believer should look at both of these examples very, very closely, and ask himself in which formula is he functioning?

THE COMMANDMENT

"For I was alive without the Law once *(Paul is refer-ring to himself personally and his conversion to Christ; the Law, he states, had nothing to do with that conversion; nei-ther did it have anything to do with his life in Christ)*: but when the Commandment came *(having just been Saved, and not understanding the Cross of Christ, he tried to live for God by keeping the Commandments through his own strength and power; in his defense, no one else at that time understood the Cross; in fact, the meaning of the Cross, which is actually the meaning of the New Covenant, would be given to Paul)*, sin revived *(the sin nature will always, without exception, revive under such circumstances, which results in failure)*, and I died *(he was not meaning that he physically died, as would be obvious, but that he died to the Commandment; in other words, he failed to obey no matter how hard he tried; and let all Believers understand that if the Apostle Paul couldn't live for God in this man-ner, neither can you!)*" (Rom. 7:9).

THE APOSTLE PAUL

After Paul has had this wonderful experience with the Lord on the road to Damascus, and he is now Born-Again and even baptized with the Holy Spirit, he sets out to live for God by the only way that he knows, which is the keeping of Com-mandments. Now that he is Saved and Spirit-filled, he reasons that most definitely he can now live for the Lord and live a victorious life. He finds to his dismay that no matter how hard he tries, he cannot keep the Commandments. He rather finds that the sin nature, which he then did not understand, has a revival in his life and begins to control him. When he uses the words, as stated, *"and I died,"* he wasn't meaning that his heart quit beating, etc., but rather that he failed the Lord. We will find in Paul's writings that he ever links sin with death and death with sin. In other words, sin destroys everything that it touches.

Unfortunately, despite the passing of some 2,000 years, most in the modern church are trying to live for God by the same means that Paul attempted to do so those years of long, long ago. Let me say again what we said in the notes:

"If Paul couldn't do it in this manner, how do we think we can?"

THE COMMANDMENT AND DEATH

"And the Commandment, which *was ordained* to life *(refers to the Ten Commandments)*, I found *to be* unto death *(means that the Law revealed the sin, as it always does, and its wages which are death; in other words, there is no victory in trying to live by Law; we are to live by Faith, referring to Faith in Christ and the Cross)*" (Rom. 7:10).

This is hard for the Believer to understand. The idea that the Commandment of God, and we're speaking of the Ten Commandments, can fall out to one's defeat is strange to our thinking. But we find the modern church following suit. Let me explain:

I see preachers over television telling people that if they want victory over sin, they should fast twenty-one days, or some such number. Others state that if one wants victory in one's life, and healing, etc., one should take the Lord's Supper several times a week, if need be. Others claim that the way to victory is for the Believer to memorize two or three Scriptures and quote them over and over again, which will then bring God on the scene, etc.

All of these things are legitimate in their own right. But

when we try to use them in this manner, we turn them into a law and, in fact, it is possible to turn anything in Christendom into a law. We can even turn prayer into a law, meaning that if we pray so much, we think this will give us victory, etc. It won't!

Now, please understand. We are not speaking against fasting, or the Lord's Supper, or memorizing Scriptures, etc., what we are speaking against is the Believer using these things in the wrong manner. Let us say it again:

There is only one place of Victory and blessing, and that is the Cross of Christ. It's that simple (Lk. 9:23; 14:27). All of these other things have their place, but it is the Cross alone through which Christ works, and works exclusively. Paul said:

"Christ sent me not to baptize, but to preach the Gospel, not with wisdom of words, lest the Cross of Christ should be made of none effect" (I Cor. 1:17).

Was Paul knocking Water Baptism? Of course not! He was merely saying that neither Water Baptism nor anything else of this nature, even the things we have named, must be the object of our faith. The Cross alone must be the Object of our Faith, and that we must ever understand (Rom. 6:3-5; 8:1-2, 11; I Cor. 1:17-18, 23; 2:2; Gal., Chpt. 5; 6:14; Eph. 2:13-18; Col. 2:14-15).

THE SIN NATURE

"For sin *(the sin nature),* **taking occasion by the Commandment** *(in no way blames the Commandment, but that the Commandment actually did agitate the sin nature, and brought it to the fore, which it was designed to do),* **deceived me** *(Paul thought, now that he had accepted Christ, by that mere fact alone he could certainly obey the Lord in every respect; but he found he couldn't, and neither can you, at least in that fashion),* **and by it slew** *me (despite all of his efforts to live for the Lord by means of Law-keeping, he failed; and again, I say, so will you!)"* **(Rom. 7:11).**

DECEPTION

How can a Believer, who is sincere before the Lord, be deceived in this fashion?

That's a good question!

The idea is this: when the Believer attempts to live for God by the means of keeping Commandments, and whatever those Commandments might be, as we've already stated, the Holy Spirit cannot help a person in such circumstances and situations, which gives the sin nature occasion to then begin to function in one's life. This guarantees failure. In other words, the Believer, no matter how hard he tries otherwise, is going to sin. In fact, millions of Christians at this moment are struggling in this very area, meaning they are trying to live for God by the means of Commandments. They may not think of it in that fashion; however, let me say it this way.

If our faith is not exclusively in Christ and the Cross, and I mean exclusively, then whether we understand it or not, whether we believe it or not, it is in law, i.e., *"commandments."* This guarantees failure simply because the Holy Spirit will not and, in fact, cannot work in such an atmosphere. Once again we state, Faith must be in Christ and the Cross exclusively if we want the Holy Spirit to do that which He Alone can do.

Our Lord in His Life and Living kept the Commandments perfectly, never failing even one time in word, thought, or deed. And please understand, He did all of this for us.

He then addressed the broken Law, of which everyone was guilty, by going to the Cross and giving Himself as a Perfect Sacrifice, which was accepted by God. Again, He did all of that for us. When we place our Faith in Him and what He did for us at the Cross, then the Holy Spirit can function on our behalf and give us Victory in every capacity. But the problem is, most Christians don't know this, so their Faith is in something other than the Cross of Christ, which guarantees failure, even as Paul experienced. And once again let us state, all of this happened to Paul before he was given God's Prescribed

Order of Victory, which is Faith in Christ and the Cross.

THE LAW IS HOLY

"**Wherefore the Law** *is* **Holy** *(points to the fact that it is God's Revelation of Himself; the problem is not in the Law of God, the problem is in us)*, **and the Commandment Holy, and just, and good** *(the Law, as stated, is like a mirror which shows man what he is, but contains no power to change him)*" **(Rom. 7:12).**

Considering that Paul is writing to Gentiles, who knew next to nothing about the Law of God, why did he deal so much with this aspect of life and living?

He did it for an excellent reason. There is something in all of us, which thinks that now that we are Saved, and now that we are baptized with the Holy Spirit, surely we can keep the Ten Commandments, etc. And despite the fact of continuous failing, we keep trying and keep trying. To be sure, a whole system of self-righteousness is built up around trying to keep the Law of God. In today's climate, and probably then, as well, people do not think of it as law, but rather the common struggle that we all have in living for God. But that's incorrect!

As Paul said, the fault and the problem are not in the Law, but rather in us. It's that we think we can do something that we cannot do and, in fact, are not even meant to do.

THE WAY OF THE LORD

The Way of the Lord is Faith, and Faith exclusively; however, for it to be Faith that God will recognize, it must have the correct Object, which is always the Cross of Christ. That's the Way the Holy Spirit functions, and the only Way that He functions. But again we state, the modern Believer knows nothing about the Cross of Christ as it refers to our Sanctification. This means that the faith of most Believers is all over the map, and regardless of where it is, it's not in the Cross of Christ.

WORKING DEATH

"Was then that which is good made death unto me? God forbid *(once again, it is not the Law that is at fault, but rather the sin in man which is opposed to the Law)*. But sin *(the sin nature)*, that it might appear sin *(proclaims the Divine intention of the Law, namely that sin might show its true colors)*, working death in me by that which is good *(the Law was good, and is good, but if one attempts to keep its moral precepts by means other than constant Faith in the Cross, the end result will be the 'working of death' instead of life; all of this can be done, but only by Faith in Christ and the Cross)*; that sin *(the sin nature)* by the Commandment might become exceeding sinful *(this greatly confuses the Believer; he is trying to live for God, and trying with all of his strength and might, but continually fails; he doesn't understand why! the truth is that no one can live for God in this fashion; it is not God's Prescribed Order; that Order is the Cross)*" (Rom. 7:13).

WORKING DEATH IN ME BY THAT WHICH IS GOOD

This comes, as we have stated, as a great shock to most Believers. Trying to function in law, while it seems right, will not, in fact, turn out right. Always and without exception, when individuals try to live for God by any means other than Faith in Christ and what Christ has done for us at the Cross will conclude in failure. And the thing in which we place our faith other than the Cross, within itself, might be good, as the Law most definitely was. But the Believer trying to function in the manner of trying to obey and keep laws will find that the end result is not what he thought it would be. It will only bring failure. We have explained it again and again, but let us say it one more time.

In the Seventh Chapter of Romans we find a Believer, in this case Paul, trying to live for God by means of Law because that's all he knew. But despite the fact of being baptized with the Holy Spirit, the Holy Spirit would not help him in such a manner and, in fact, could not help him. And please understand, as it was then, so it is now.

The Believer places his faith in *"good things."* He is shocked then when he finds that instead of it bringing good things to him, it brings the very opposite. Again, it is because such a Believer doesn't have the help of the Holy Spirit and, in fact, cannot have the help of the Holy Spirit according to such a direction.

The Believer will find that the situation will get more and more sinful, *"exceeding sinful."* He now tells us why.

CARNALITY

"For we know that the Law is spiritual *(refers to the fact that the Law is totally of God, from God, and by God)*: but I am carnal, sold under sin *(refers to Adam's Fall, which has affected all of mankind and for all time; this means that no one, even Spirit-filled Believers, can keep the Law of God if they attempt to do so outside of Faith in the Cross; in other words, it is all in Christ)*."

I DO NOT UNDERSTAND

"For that which I do *(the failure)* I allow not *(should have been translated, 'I understand not'; these are not the words of an unsaved man, as some claim, but rather a Believer who is trying and failing)*: for what I would, that do I not *(refers to the obedience he wants to render to Christ, but rather fails; why? as Paul explained, the Believer is married to Christ, but is being unfaithful to Christ by spiritually cohabiting with the Law, which frustrates the Grace of God; that means the Holy Spirit will not*

help such a person, which guarantees failure [Gal. 2:21]);
but what I hate, that do I *(refers to sin in his life, which
he doesn't want to do and, in fact, hates, but finds himself
unable to stop; unfortunately, due to the fact of not understanding the Cross as it refers to Sanctification, this is the
plight of most modern Christians)"* **(Rom. 7:14-15).**

THE TERMINOLOGY OF A BELIEVER

Some have claimed that the Seventh Chapter of Romans
portrays Paul before his conversion; consequently, the Chapter is by and large ignored by those who believe that. The
truth is, this Chapter, as we've already stated, portrays Paul
right after he was Saved and filled with the Spirit, and actually for a period of several years, trying to live for God by the
wrong means. As we've already stated, in his defense, not only
did he not know God's Prescribed Order of Victory at that
time, no one else in the world knew it either. This great Truth
had not yet been given. In fact, it would be given to Paul.

But irrespective of the fact that he was in ignorance of this
great Truth, still, the results were the same, failure. Millions
presently do not know or understand God's Prescribed Order.
In fact, the Cross of Christ relative to our Sanctification is
taught almost not at all in the modern church. So, that means
that Faith for such is not present because such is not being
preached. Nevertheless, even as Paul found that he failed, and
no matter how hard he tried otherwise, modern Believers will
face the same thing.

There are millions of Believers right now who love the
Lord. They are not hypocrites. They are doing all they can to
serve God as they should, but their lives are not one of victory,
but rather of failure. And the sadness is, the failure is getting
worse and worse, with every intent to *"steal, kill, and destroy"*
(Jn. 10:10).

When Paul said, *"I don't understand,"* he said this with
purpose and reason. He was doing everything at the time he

knew to do to live for God, and to do so successfully. As a Child of God, he hated sin, as every true Child of God hates sin. But he found to his dismay that the thing he didn't want to do, which was to fail the Lord, that's what he found himself doing. And what he wanted to do, which is to live a life of obedience and Victory, he found he could not do, no matter how hard he tried. That is the state of most good Christians presently.

The truth is, every single Believer who has ever lived has had to go through the Seventh Chapter of Romans. There is no getting around it; however, the Lord most definitely does not intend for us to stay there. But the sad fact is, most Believers have been in the Seventh Chapter of Romans ever since they've been Saved, and they will stay there until they die.

While an individual can be Saved in such a state, he most definitely cannot live a victorious life. It doesn't matter if he is a Pastor pastoring the largest church in the world or the Evangelist drawing the biggest crowds. The failure will be the same! And the truth is, they will not really understand why they are failing. It is because the sin nature is ruling them, but they don't understand that, and they don't know God's Solution for the problem. It's tragic but true!

THE LAW IS GOOD

"**If then I do that which I would not** (*presents Paul doing something against his will; he doesn't want to do it, and is trying not to do it, whatever it might be, but finds himself doing it anyway*), **I consent unto the Law that *it is* good** (*simply means that the Law of God is working as it is supposed to work; it defines sin, portraying the fact that the sin nature will rule in man's heart if not addressed properly*)" **(Rom. 7:16).**

IS PAUL RESPONSIBLE?

If a person is forced to do something against his will, does that person remain responsible?

Most definitely yes!

The real problem is not in the sin committed, but rather in taking the wrong direction. Unfortunately, the modern church does little more than treat symptoms. It seldom goes to the heart of the problem.

For every Christian who fails, it can be said that most have failed because they do not understand the Cross of Christ relative to Sanctification. So, in such a climate, people jump on the sin committed, never really knowing why it was committed. And, if they try to give a reason as to why, it's almost always wrong.

Ninety percent of the time or more, the reason for failure is that the Believer has placed his Faith in something other than the Cross of Christ. This having been done, the end result is always going to be failure, no matter how hard the Believer tries otherwise.

THE INDWELLING SIN NATURE

"Now then it is no more I that do it *(this has been misconstrued by many! it means, 'I may be failing, but it's not what I want to do'; no true Christian, as stated, wants to sin because now the Divine Nature is in his life and it is supposed to rule, not the sin nature [II Pet. 1:4])*, but sin *(the sin nature)* that dwells in me *(despite the fact that some preachers claim the sin nature is gone from the Christian, Paul here plainly says that the sin nature is still in the Christian; however, if our Faith remains constant in the Cross, the sin nature will be dormant, causing us no problem; otherwise, it will cause us great problems; while the sin nature 'dwells' in us, it is not to 'rule' in us)*" (Rom. 7:17).

SCRIPTURAL PROOF OF THE SIN NATURE

Some seventeen times in the Sixth Chapter of Romans

alone, Paul mentions the word *"sin."* Sixteen of those times he is speaking of the sin nature and not acts of sin. He speaks of acts of sin only in the Fifteenth Verse.

How do we know this?

In the original Text as written by Paul, he has in front of the word sin, at least when he's talking about the sin nature, which is by far most of the time, what is referred to now as the *"definite article,"* making it read *"the sin."* This means that he is not speaking of acts of sin, but rather the root cause of sin, the reason for sin, in other words, the sin principle.

Now when the believing sinner comes to Christ, the sin nature is made dormant. It is not removed, but is rather made ineffective.

WHY IS THE SIN NATURE NOT REMOVED?

There are probably many reasons the sin nature is not removed; however, the main reason that the Lord allows it to remain is for disciplinarial reasons. In other words, knowing and understanding that the sin nature is there, it serves as a brake on things we do or don't do. The sin nature will remain dormant as long as the Believer keeps his Faith in Christ and the Cross. When the believing sinner comes to Christ and is Born-Again, everything changes. The sinful things he once loved, he now hates. And the good things he once hated, such as the Lord and His Work, he now loves. He thinks in his mind that he will never sin again. But he finds very shortly, despite all of his efforts otherwise, that he fails the Lord in some fashion.

It shocks such a Believer, and he determines to put things in force that will keep him from making this mistake again, whatever it might be. That's when the law comes in.

He begins to make up rules and regulations which he thinks will keep him from sinning. That's when the trouble begins.

The failure within itself does not cause a revival of the sin nature, but rather the Believer placing his faith in something other than Christ and the Cross. When he does such a thing, the sin nature begins to resurrect itself, and little by little begins to dominate such a Believer. And he will not get out from under this yoke until his Faith is properly placed. Listen again to Paul:

RULING IN THE MORTAL BODY

The Apostle said:

"**Let not sin** *(the sin nature)* **therefore reign** *(rule)* **in your mortal body** *(showing that the sin nature can once again rule in the heart and life of the Believer, if the Believer doesn't constantly look to Christ and the Cross; the 'mortal body' is neutral, which means it can be used for Righteousness, or unrighteousness)*, **that you should obey it in the lusts thereof** *(ungodly lusts are carried out through the mortal body, if Faith is not maintained in the Cross, which then gives us the help of the Holy Spirit, without which we cannot live the life we must live [I Cor. 1:17-18])*" **(Rom. 6:12).**

As we said in the above notes, *"While the sin nature 'dwells' in us, it is not to 'rule' in us."* Sadly, it does *"rule"* in most Christians' lives.

WILLPOWER IS NOT ENOUGH

Paul said:

"**For I know that in me (that is, in my flesh,) dwells no good thing** *(speaks of man's own ability, or rather the lack thereof in comparison to the Holy Spirit, at least when it comes to spiritual things)*: **for to will is present with me** *(Paul is speaking here of his willpower; regrettably, most modern Christians are trying to live for God by means of willpower, thinking falsely that since they have* *come to Christ, they are now free to say 'no' to sin; that is the wrong way to look at the situation; the Believer cannot live for God by the strength of willpower; while the will is definitely important, it alone is not enough; the Believer must exercise Faith in Christ and the Cross, and do so constantly; then he will have the ability and strength to say 'yes' to Christ, which automatically says, 'no' to the things of the world)*; **but *how* to perform that which is good I find not** *(outside of the Cross, it is impossible to find a way to do good)*" **(Rom. 7:18).**

CAN SATAN OVERRIDE THE WILL OF A BELIEVER?

Yes! Satan can override the will of a Believer.

In fact, Satan is doing such a thing millions of times each and every day. There are millions of Christians who do not understand God's Prescribed Order of Victory, who are struggling and fighting with all the strength that's within them, but doing so in the wrong way, and then finding themselves yielding to the sin, whatever the sin might be. They don't want to do it, even as Paul has carefully outlined in this Chapter, but they find themselves doing it anyhow.

Is such a person responsible?

Most definitely, yes!

As we've already stated, the responsibility is not so much in the wrong committed, whatever it might be, but in the direction that we have taken which is wrong. God has His Direction, and man has his direction; unfortunately, man's direction is not God's Direction. But I say it again:

The Cross of Christ and the Cross of Christ alone is God's Direction. If we do not function in that capacity as Believers, we will find ourselves struggling and fighting to try not to do something wrong, but doing it anyway. In fact, in the very next Verse, Paul will say the exact same thing.

As we stated in the notes, a person's will is most definitely important. The Scripture still says, *"Whosoever will . . ."*

(Rev. 22:17). But willpower alone is not enough, which millions of Believers find out each and every day. The sadness is, most Believers don't know what to do otherwise. So they keep trying, but all in the wrong way.

As we've already stated, no true Christian wants to sin. In fact, every true Christian hates sin. But despite the fact that sin is hated, such a Christian, nevertheless, will fail in the very thing he's trying not to do. Unfortunately, the modern church doesn't understand this. As we've already stated, the church deals with symptoms instead of the reality of what is actually happening.

Such Believers don't need punishment; they need for someone who is Spiritual enough to tell them why they went wrong, how they went wrong, and how it can be corrected. In fact, that's what Paul said in Galatians 6:1.

TRYING NOT TO FAIL

"For the good that I would I do not *(if I depend on self, and not the Cross)*: but the evil which I would not *(don't want to do)*, that I do *(which is exactly what every Believer will do no matter how hard he tries to do otherwise, if he tries to live this life outside of the Cross [Gal. 2:20-21])*" (Rom. 7:19).

As we've already stated in this very Passage, the Apostle Paul states that no matter how hard he tried to do the good, he found that he was unable to carry out his desires. And then again, the evil which he was trying not to do, in other words, struggling with all his strength, he found himself doing anyway.

Now again let us state that when sin is committed, the responsibility is with the perpetrator. In other words, if we fail, it is our fault. But again I wish to emphasize, it's not our fault as most people think. The fault is not really in the wrong act committed, whatever it might be, and as sinful as it might be, but rather in the wrong direction taken. As again we have stated, the modern church treats symptoms but very seldom treats the root cause of the problem.

What is that root cause?

The cause of sin in most Christians is that they do not understand God's Way, which is the Cross of Christ and, thereby, place their faith in something other than the Cross. Most do so out of ignorance, but still, the end result is the same—failure.

THE DOMINION OF THE SIN NATURE

"**Now if I do that I would not** *(which is exactly what will happen if the Believer tries to live this life outside of God's Prescribed Order)*, **it is no more I that do it, but sin** *(the sin nature)* **that dwells in me** *(this emphatically states that the Believer has a sin nature; in the original Greek Text, if it contains the definite article before the word 'sin,' which originally did read 'the sin,' it is not speaking of acts of sin, but rather the sin nature or the evil nature; the idea is not getting rid of the sin nature, which actually cannot be done, but rather controlling it, which the Apostle has told us how to do in Rom., Chpts. 6 and 8; when the Trump sounds, we shall be changed and there will be no more sin nature [Rom. 8:23])*" **(Rom. 7:20).**

WHAT IS THE SIN NATURE?

The *"sin nature"* is that which became Adam and Eve immediately after the Fall. In other words, their human nature, which had previously been controlled by the Divine Nature, is now controlled by the *"sin nature."* This means their very nature drives toward disobedience, sin, iniquity, and rebellion against God, in other words, all things which are wrong. Every human being is born with a human nature and with a sin nature.

If you will think back to your life before you came to Christ, you will have to admit that you were totally and completely controlled during that time by the sin nature. There was nothing in you that pertained to the Lord, nothing about the Lord, in fact, you were rather in rebellion against God and in every capacity.

When you came to Christ, while the sin nature was not removed, it was most definitely made ineffective. As previously stated, the Lord left it there in order that it may serve as a disciplinarial measure. In fact, the Scripture tells us that the sin nature will not be removed from Believers until the First Resurrection of life. Paul said:

> "For this corruptible *(sin nature)* must put on incorruption *(a Glorified Body with no sin nature)*, and this mortal *(subject to death)* *must* put on immortality *(will never die)*" (I Cor. 15:53).

That which is labeled *"corruptible"* in the heart and life of the Believer is, as stated, the sin nature.

There is only one way for the Believer to have victory, and constant victory, over the sin nature. We must place our Faith exclusively in Christ and the Cross and not allow it to be moved elsewhere. Then the sin nature will remain dormant (Rom. 6:1-3; I Cor. 1:17-18, 23; 2:2; Gal. 6:14).

Due to the fact that Jesus was virgin born, which means that man had nothing to do with His Conception, while He definitely was born with a human nature, He was not born with a sin nature.

HOW CAN I KNOW IF THE SIN NATURE IS ACTIVE WITHIN MY LIFE?

That's an excellent question!

If there is a habitual sin that you are struggling with and trying to quit, whatever it might be, and you have not been able to do so, that is the sin nature that is dominating you as a Believer. Such a situation can make life miserable, as would be obvious.

As previously stated, any true Believer hates sin. So, considering that sin is dominating such a person, life in that case is certainly not what it ought to be, and definitely not what it can be. But unfortunately, due to the modern church having little or no understanding whatsoever as it regards the Cross of Christ and Sanctification, most modern Christians, even those who truly love the Lord, are controlled more or less by the sin nature.

HOW CAN ONE MAINTAIN VICTORY OVER THE SIN NATURE?

As we've already stated, the Believer must place his or her Faith exclusively in Christ and the Cross and not allow it to be moved elsewhere. Then the Holy Spirit, Who works entirely within the framework of the Finished Work of Christ, will work mightily on our behalf, making us what we ought to be. That's the only way that we can live the life we ought to live. Jesus addressed this by saying:

"... **If any *man* will come after Me** *(the criteria for Discipleship)*, **let him deny himself** *(not asceticism as many think, but rather that one denies one's own will-power, self-will, strength, and ability, depending totally on Christ)*, **and take up his cross** *(the benefits of the Cross, looking exclusively to what Jesus did there to meet our every need)* **daily** *(this is so important, our looking to the Cross; that we must renew our Faith in what Christ has done for us, even on a daily basis, for Satan will ever try to move us away from the Cross as the Object of our Faith, which always spells disaster)*, **and follow Me** *(Christ can be followed only by the Believer looking to the Cross, understanding what it accomplished, and by that means alone [Rom. 6:3-5; Gal. 6:14; Col. 2:14-15])*" **(Lk. 9:23)**.

LAWS

"**I find then a Law** *(does not refer in this case to the Law of Moses, but rather to the 'Law of Sin and Death' [Rom. 8:2])*, **that, when I would do good, evil** *(the evil nature)* **is present with me** *(the idea is that the sin nature is always going to be with the Believer; there is no hint in the Greek that its stay is temporary, at least until the Trump sounds; we can successfully address the sin nature in only one way, and, as stated, that is by Faith in Christ and the Cross, which Paul will detail in Romans, Chapter 8)*" **(Rom. 7:21).**

Paul is now going to deal with four Laws, with three found in these last Verses of Romans 7, and the fourth one found in the Second Verse of the Eighth Chapter of Romans.

These are Laws which were designed by the Godhead in eternity past, and which in a sense either confront or govern our lives. Considering how important they are, we should desire to know everything we can about them. To be sure, they are active, and due to the fact that they are a *"Law,"* they will function exactly as designed. Of that one can be certain!

THE LAW OF GOD

"**For I delight in the Law of God** *(refers to the moral Law of God ensconced in the Ten Commandments)* **after the inward man** *(refers to the spirit and soul of man which has now been regenerated)*" **(Rom. 7:22).**

When the person comes to Christ, thereby, becoming a new creation, which happens to all when one is Born-Again, there is an instant delight created in the heart and life of such a person for the *"Law of God."* As stated, this refers to the Ten Commandments. We want to obey them. We want to walk clean and pure before the Lord. And to be sure, we must obey them. But the great question is, how? If we do it God's Way, it will be done without difficulty; otherwise, we will fail and fail miserably.

But the idea is the delight that one finds within one's heart for *"the Law of God,"* once that person comes to Christ.

THE INWARD MAN

The *"inward man"* refers to the soul and the spirit of the individual, which is indestructible. As well, such will last forever and forever. Man is a soul and has a spirit, with both living in a human body. The human body is perishable, while the soul and the spirit are eternal.

With the spirit of man we deal with God. With the soul of man we deal with the human body. With the human body we deal with the world.

When a person is Saved, at the very moment of coming to Christ, he is Saved holistically. This means he is Saved spirit, soul, and body. The idea that the spirit is Saved and the soul is being Saved is not taught in Scripture. The Holy Spirit through the Word of God always deals in one way or the other with the whole man, in other words, man's spirit, soul, and body. So there is no such thing as the spirit being Saved and the soul trying to be Saved.

As well, the physical body is neutral. Within itself, it is not holy or unholy. It is what we make it (Rom. 6:13).

THE LAW OF THE MIND AND
THE LAW OF SIN AND DEATH

"But I see another Law in my members *(the Law of Sin and Death desiring to use my physical body as an instrument of unrighteousness)*, warring against the Law of my mind *(this is the Law of desire and willpower)*, and bringing me into captivity to the Law of sin *(the Law of Sin and Death)* which is in my members *(which will function through my members, and make me a slave to the Law of Sin and Death; this will happen to the most consecrated Christian if that Christian doesn't constantly exercise Faith in Christ and the Cross, understanding that it is through the Cross that all powers of darkness were defeated [Col. 2:14-15])"* **(Rom. 7:23).**

LET'S FIRST LOOK AT THE LAW OF THE MIND

The moment the believing sinner comes to Christ, at that moment, the *"mind"* of such a person changes.
Paul said:

"Therefore if any man *be* **in Christ** *(Saved by the Blood),* ***he is*** **a new creature** *(a new creation):* **old things are passed away** *(what we were before Salvation);* **behold, all things are become new.** *(The old is no longer useable, with everything given to us now by Christ as 'new')"* **(II Cor. 5:17).**

At conversion the mind of the individual is renewed. That comes with the Born-Again experience. It involves the will of the individual, which, of course, is very important. *"Whosoever will . . ."* (Rev. 22:17).

While the will of the individual is definitely important, even as we have stated, still, within itself, it is not enough to bring the Believer to victory. But unfortunately, most people are trying to live for God solely by the means of the will, i.e., *"willpower."* As we've already stated in this Volume, in such a capacity, Satan can override the will of a Believer, forcing that Believer into a course of action which he is trying not to do. That's exactly what Paul said in the Nineteenth Verse. Such a Believer is left very confused. He is trying with all of his willpower to do what he ought to do and be what he ought to be, but failing. That's why Paul also said, *"For that which I do I understand not"* (Rom. 7:15).

Many Christians think that when they came to Christ, the Lord then gave them a superhuman will. He didn't. Your will is the same as it was before you came to Christ. To be frank, the answer is not found in your will, but rather in the Cross of Christ.

THE LAW OF SIN AND DEATH

Unfortunately, the *"Law of Sin and Death,"* is stronger than the *"Law of the Mind."* The *"Law of the Mind"* wants to obey the *"Law of God"* and, in fact, strives greatly to do so, but as we have stated, within itself, it is unable to fulfill this desire. It is because the *"Law of Sin and Death"* is more powerful than the *"Law of the Mind."*

In a moment we will look at the one Law that is greater and stronger than the *"Law of Sin and Death."* It is the *"Law of the Spirit of Life in Christ Jesus."* This Law is the most powerful Law in the universe.

Unfortunately, the *"Law of Sin and Death"* has made the Earth into a graveyard, and has brought untold suffering and pain into the hearts and lives of untold billions. But the tragedy is, the world not at all knows or understands the *"Law of the Spirit of Life in Christ Jesus."* And sadder still, most of the church doesn't understand it either. Let's look at the balance of this Seventh Chapter of Romans, and then we'll go to the *"Law of the Spirit of Life in Christ Jesus."*

WRETCHED MAN

"O wretched man that I am! *(Any Believer who attempts to live for God outside of God's Prescribed Order, which is 'Jesus Christ and Him Crucified,' will, in fact, live a wretched and miserable existence. This life can only be lived in one way, and that way is the Cross.)* **Who shall deliver me from the body of this death?** *(The minute he cries 'Who,' he finds the path to Victory, for he is now*

calling upon a Person for help, and that Person is Christ;
actually, the Greek Text is masculine, indicating a Person)"
(Rom. 7:24).

THE BODY OF DEATH

There was in Roman times, a method of execution that was horrible beyond compare. A dead body would be tied to a living victim, with the living victim gradually dying as the dead body putrefied and rotted, until the corruption spilled over on the victim and ultimately brought about death. But to be sure, before death came, the horror of such would know no bounds.

Whether the Apostle was thinking of this or not, we have no way of knowing. But this we do know, being dominated by sin made him, despite the fact that he was Saved and Spirit-filled, *"a wretched man."* And to be sure, it will have the same effect on modern Believers.

As we have stated, any true Believer hates sin. And when sin is dominating a Believer, as it will when the sin nature is dominating the person, this makes for a most miserable life.

To be sure, this is not what the Lord intends for His Children. However, He never promised that life would be uneventful with no problem at all. In fact, the Holy Spirit plainly tells us that it is a *"war"* in which we are engaged. And war is not pleasant! But whatever the difficulties, and there will be difficulties, and whatever the problems, and there will be problems, still, in the midst of it all, we can have a *"peace that passes all understanding."* The Lord promised such to us (Jn. 14:27).

The only way the Believer can live a victorious life, in other words, to be what the Lord intends that we be, is that our Faith be planted securely and completely in Christ and the Cross, and not in anything else. That being the case, the Holy Spirit, Who Alone can make us what we ought to be, will work mightily on our behalf; however, if we place our Faith in anything except Christ and the Cross, this greatly hinders the Holy Spirit, which means He cannot do with us and for us what He desires to do. He doesn't ask much of us, but He does ask one thing, and that is that we have the correct Object of Faith.

THE FLESH

"I thank God through Jesus Christ our Lord *(presents Paul revealing the answer to his own question; Deliverance comes through Jesus Christ and Christ Alone, and more particularly what Jesus did at Calvary and the Resurrection)*. So then with the mind I myself serve the Law of God *(the 'will' is the trigger, but it within itself can do nothing unless the gun is loaded with explosive power; that Power is the Cross)*; but with the flesh the Law of sin *(if the Believer resorts to the 'flesh,' [i.e., 'self-will, self-effort, religious effort'] which refers to his own ability outside of Christ and the Cross, he will not serve the Law of God, but rather the Law of sin)*" **(Rom. 7:25).**

What does Paul mean by this particular Verse?

THE MIND AND THE FLESH

In essence, Paul is saying that irrespective that the *"mind"* of the Believer desires, and strongly, to *"serve the Law of God,"* if it stops there, he will find himself, i.e., *"the flesh,"* serving the *"Law of Sin."* For the Law of the Mind to function as it should function, the Believer's Faith must without fail be anchored in Christ and the Cross. Then the Holy Spirit will begin to function and work within our lives. Otherwise, we're going to find the *"flesh,"* which refers to our own personal ability, strength, efforts, etc., trying to function but failing. Please understand, *"the flesh"* is incapable of doing what must be done.

The *"flesh"* was made ineffective at the Fall. So, if we try to live for God by that method, which speaks of our willpower, our own personal efforts and strength, every time we will fail.

A WARNING

Now Paul is also telling us that even though we understand God's Way, which is Christ and the Cross, still, if we lapse back into our own personal efforts, i.e., *"the flesh,"* we will be overcome by the *"Law of Sin and Death."* That's the reason that Jesus told us to *"take up the cross daily and follow Him"* (Lk. 9:23).

NO CONDEMNATION IN CHRIST JESUS

While this part belongs in the great Revelation given to Paul that tells us how to live for God, which is given to us in the Sixth Chapter of Romans, still, it would leave the teaching incomplete were it omitted here.

LIFE IN THE SPIRIT

Paul has now been given the great Revelation of the Lord, which tells the Believer how to live for God, how to be victorious, and how to be what we ought to be. One might label it as *"Life in the Spirit."*

It is easy to see the change of pace, so to speak, from the last Verse of Chapter 7, to the First Verse of Chapter 8. Paul now knows God's Way, and is walking therein, which we, as well, are to do. He said:

> *"There is* therefore now no condemnation *(guilt)* to them which are in Christ Jesus *(refers back to Rom. 6:3-5 and our being baptized into His Death, which speaks of the Crucifixion)*, who walk not after the flesh *(depending on one's personal strength and ability or great religious efforts in order to overcome sin)*, but after the Spirit *(the Holy Spirit works exclusively within the legal confines of the Finished Work of Christ; our Faith in that Finished Work, i.e., 'the Cross,' guarantees the help of the Holy*

Spirit, which guarantees Victory)."

THE LAW OF THE SPIRIT OF LIFE
IN CHRIST JESUS

"**For the Law** *(that which we are about to give is a Law of God, devised by the Godhead in eternity past [I Pet. 1:18-20]; this Law, in fact, is 'God's Prescribed Order of Victory')* **of the Spirit** *(Holy Spirit, i.e., 'the way the Spirit works')* **of Life** *(all life comes from Christ, but through the Holy Spirit [Jn. 16:13-14])* **in Christ Jesus** *(any time Paul uses this term or one of its derivatives, he is, without fail, referring to what Christ did at the Cross, which makes this 'life' possible)* **has made me free** *(given me total Victory)* **from the Law of Sin and Death** *(these are the two most powerful Laws in the Universe; the 'Law of the Spirit of Life in Christ Jesus' alone is stronger than the 'Law of Sin and Death'; this means that if the Believer attempts to live for God by any manner other than Faith in Christ and the Cross, he is doomed to failure)*" **(Rom. 8:1-2).**

As to how long Paul lived in this state of defeat as he describes for us in the Seventh Chapter of Romans, we aren't told; however, it was probably at least several years. It is believed that the entire span of time between his Salvation on the road to Damascus and his first missionary journey recorded in Acts, Chapter 13, spanned about ten years. Whether this Revelation was given to him at about the middle of this ten year period or along toward the end, we aren't told. If I had to venture a guess, I would say that probably it was given to him somewhere between the midpoint of the ten year period and the end of that time frame.

Irrespective that it was without a doubt the greatest Word, the greatest Revelation, ever given to a human being by God, still, we actually know very little about how it all took place. The following will be what Paul told us.

BY THE REVELATION OF JESUS CHRIST

The great Apostle, concerning this Revelation which proclaimed to Paul the meaning of the New Covenant, gave us the following words. He said:

"But I certify you, Brethren *(make known)*, that the Gospel which was preached of me *(the Message of the Cross)* is not after man. *(Any Message other than the Cross is definitely devised by man.)*

"For I neither received it of man *(Paul had not learned this great Truth from human teachers)*, neither was I taught *it* *(he denies instruction from other men)*, but by the Revelation of Jesus Christ. *(Revelation is the mighty Act of God whereby the Holy Spirit discloses to the human mind that which could not be understood without Divine Intervention.)*

"For you have heard of my conversation *(way of life)* in time past in the Jews' religion *(the practice of Judaism)*, how that beyond measure I persecuted the Church of God, and wasted it *(Acts 9:1-2)*:

"And profited in the Jews' religion above many my equals in my own nation *(he outstripped his Jewish contemporaries in Jewish culture, etc.)*, being more exceedingly zealous of the traditions of my fathers *(a zeal from his very boyhood)*.

THE GOSPEL

"But when it pleased God, Who separated me from my mother's womb *(presents the idea that God had set Paul apart, devoting him to a special purpose from before his birth)*, and called *me* by His Grace *(called, not because of any merit on his part, but rather because of the Grace of God)*,

"To reveal His Son in me *(the meaning of the New*

Covenant, which is the meaning of the Cross), **that I might preach Him among the heathen** *(Gentiles)***; immediately I conferred not with flesh and blood** *(his Commission and Message came to him from God, and neither was affected in any way by human intervention)***:"**

THE OTHER APOSTLES

"Neither went I up to Jerusalem to them who were Apostles before me *(did not get this Revelation from the original Twelve)***; but I went into Arabia** *(according to the Holy Spirit)***, and returned again unto Damascus.** *(There would not have been any Apostles in Damascus. There he preached the Message of the Cross.)*

"Then after three years I went up to Jerusalem to see Peter *(showing his independence from the Jerusalem Apostles)***, and abode with him fifteen days** *(when he, no doubt, revealed to Peter the Revelation of the Cross, which the Lord had given to him).*

"But other of the Apostles saw I none, save James the Lord's Brother. *(James didn't refer to himself as an Apostle, but Paul did.)*

"Now the things which I write unto you, behold, before God, I lie not.

"Afterwards I came into the regions of Syria and Cilicia;

"And was unknown by face unto the Churches of Judaea which were in Christ *(had he been a Disciple of the Twelve, the Churches in Judaea would have known him)***:**

"But they had heard only *(were constantly hearing)***, That he which persecuted us** *(Believers)* **in times past now preaches the Faith which once he destroyed** *(Faith in Christ)***.**

"And they Glorified God in me. *(As he had 'constantly persecuted,' and now was 'constantly preaching,' they were 'constantly glorifying.')***" (Gal. 1:11-24).**

WHY DID GOD CALL PAUL
RATHER THAN PETER OR JOHN?

I use Peter and John because they stand out relative to the original Twelve, with Matthias having taken the place of Judas.

Some claim that the original Apostles were not functioning in the Will of God when Matthias was chosen, claiming that Paul should have been the one. That is incorrect!

Paul wasn't even Saved at that time, and there is no record that the Lord desired such.

As to why the Lord did not choose Peter or John to whom the great Revelation of the New Covenant would be given, we aren't told. At best, we can only speculate. This we do know:

Receiving the Revelation was one thing; putting it into force was something else altogether. What people have believed all of their lives, they do not give up easily. And to be sure, the transition from the Law of Moses to the Message of Grace presented a leap that was insurmountable to most. In studying the Word of God, I'm not sure if any other person could have made this leap but the Apostle Paul. It took one with an iron will and an iron determination to proclaim the Message that the Law had finished its course, all of it completed in Christ, and now the great Message of Grace was paramount, typified by the Cross of Christ.

At that time the Jews were the only people on the face of the Earth who had any knowledge of God whatsoever. And, tragically, they had so perverted the Law of Moses that any more it little resembled what God had given at the beginning. In fact, for the most part, Israel did not know the Lord. I think that should be obvious considering that the religious leaders of Israel didn't even recognize their own Messiah, and actually crucified Him. While it was necessary that Jesus would go to the Cross, meaning that that is the reason He came, still, it was definitely not the Will of God that Israel would be the ones who put Him there. They did so because their hearts were evil. As stated, despite their religious claims, they did not know Jehovah. While, of course, there were some in Israel who were godly, regrettably, that number was small. But at any rate, what little was known of God was held by the Jews. The Gentiles were idol worshippers, having no knowledge of God whatsoever. As Jesus said to the Samaritan woman, *"You worship you know not what"* (Jn. 4:20-24). If it is to be remembered, one of the first things that the Lord said to Paul, which He did through Ananias, was:

"For he is a chosen vessel unto Me, to bear My Name before the Gentiles, and Kings, and the Children of Israel."

But then the Lord added, *"For I will show him how great things he must suffer for My Name's sake"* (Acts 9:15-16).

THE DIFFICULTIES

When Paul turned from his *"threatenings and slaughter,"* which occurred, of course, with the Damascus experience, then the Nation of Israel as a whole turned on him. Through the entirety of his life after his conversion, they tried their best to kill him. Only the Power of God spared him.

As well, because of his insistence that the Law was completed in Christ and, in effect, was no more, even the Christian Jews were not happy with him at all. In fact, for those who believe that Paul wrote Hebrews, as I do, it is believed that quite possibly he wrote this Book in order to warn the Church in Jerusalem, which was made up altogether of Jews. They could not hold to both. They could not keep putting new wine into old wineskins.

And then he had the problem of the Judaizers coming into the Churches which he had planted, or his associates, and trying to turn these Gentiles over to Law. In fact, much of what Paul wrote in his Epistles concerned this problem. In respect to this, he struggled constantly that there be no split in the Church, and we refer to the Church as a whole. He did all that he could do to ingratiate himself to the Church in Jerusalem, at least without compromising his Faith, but, in fact, it was a struggle that really never ended. He was looked at with suspicion with many not too very much unhappy when he was imprisoned.

But despite all of that, the Gospel which was given to him by the Lord Jesus Christ, and which, to his credit, he compromised not at all, changed the world. He was used of God, I believe, as no other man!

There is only one hint regarding this great Revelation as to how it was given. Whether the account pertained to the New Covenant, we actually have no way of knowing. But it's the closest thing in Paul's Epistles which deals with this all-important subject.

He gives us the following information from his second Epistle to the Corinthians. He said:

VISIONS AND REVELATIONS OF THE LORD

"It is not expedient for me doubtless to glory *(but necessary!)*. I will come to Visions and Revelations of the Lord *(refers to that given to Paul by the Lord)*.

"I knew a man in Christ above fourteen years ago *(speaking of himself)*, (whether in the body, I cannot tell; or whether out of the body, I cannot tell: God knows;) *(He doesn't know if he was actually taken to Heaven in his physical body, or only saw these things in a Vision.)* such an one caught up to the third Heaven. *(The first heaven is the clouds, etc. The second heaven is the starry space. The third Heaven is the Planet Heaven, the Abode of God.)*

"And I knew such a man, (whether in the body, or out of the body, I cannot tell: God knows;) *(This is the second time he said this, and not without purpose.)*

"How that he was caught up into Paradise *(presents the word 'Paradise' being used by Paul in a general manner)*, and heard unspeakable words *(it was not possible for the Apostle to properly put what he saw into words)*, which is not lawful for a man to utter *(not permissible)*.

"**Of such an one will I glory** *('of such a thing will I glory')*: **yet of myself I will not glory, but in my infirmities** *(that I was counted worthy to suffer for Christ)*.

"**For though I would desire to glory, I shall not be a fool** *(knowing that God knows all things, and we have nothing to glory about)*; **for I will say the truth: but *now* I forbear, lest any man should think of me above that which he sees me *to be*, or *that* he hears of me.** *(In effect, says, 'I will not relate more about this Vision, and for the obvious reasons.' He wanted the eyes of all Believers on Christ, and not on him at any time.)*"

THE THORN IN THE FLESH

"**And lest I should be exalted above measure through the abundance of the Revelations** *(presents the reasons for the thorn in the flesh)*, **there was given to me a thorn in the flesh** *(I think it was all the difficulties of II Cor. 11:23-27)*, **the messenger of Satan to buffet me** *(an angel of Satan)*, **lest I should be exalted above measure.** *(This has the Apostle concluding this sentence as it began.)*

"**For this thing I besought the Lord thrice, that it might depart from me.** *(The Apostle knew it was the Lord allowing this, but he didn't understand why.)*

"**And He said unto me** *(the Lord responded, but did not agree)*, **My Grace is sufficient for you** *(speaks of enabling Grace, which is really the Goodness of God carried out by the Holy Spirit)*: **for My Strength is made perfect in weakness.** *(All Believers are weak, but the Lord tends to make us weaker, with the intention being that we then depend solely upon Him, thereby, obtaining His Strength.)* **Most gladly therefore will I rather glory in my infirmities** *(because of the end result)*, **that the Power of Christ may rest upon me.** *(If Paul needed so humbling and painful an experience of what the carnal nature is,* *it is evident that all Christians need it. Whatever weakens, belittles, and humiliates that proud and willful nature should be regarded by the Believer as most worthwhile.)*

"Therefore I take pleasure in infirmities, in reproaches, in necessities, in persecutions, in distresses for Christ's sake: for when I am weak, then am I strong *(then the strength of Christ can be exhibited through me, but only when I know I am weak)*" **(II Cor. 12:1-10).**

CAN WE SAY THAT THESE VISIONS AND REVELATIONS WERE THE NEW COVENANT?

No, it cannot be said for certain that the Visions and Revelations of which Paul spoke in II Corinthians, Chapter 12, can be positively identified as the time when the great Apostle was given the meaning of the New Covenant. But personally, I think his statement in Verse 1 regarding *"Visions and Revelations of the Lord,"* lends credence to the idea that this indeed was the time, whenever it was, for no time frame is given, that the Apostle was given the meaning of the New Covenant. We do know that these Visions and Revelations were of such magnitude that the Apostle could not really tell whether he was physically taken to Heaven or went there in spirit. Something of that magnitude is powerful indeed!

Then he stated that he *"heard unspeakable words, which is not lawful for a man to utter,"* which proclaims something of phenomenal magnitude. And to be certain, there is nothing of any greater magnitude than what Jesus did at the Cross. In fact, what he saw was of such magnitude, what he heard was of such magnitude, and what he experienced was of such magnitude, *"lest he should be exalted above measure through the abundance of the Revelations, there was given to him a thorn in the flesh, the messenger of Satan to buffet him, lest he should be exalted above measure."* I am satisfied in my mind that at this time, whatever time frame it was in the ten year period referred to as the *"silent years,"* this was when the Lord gave to Paul the greatest Word that has ever been given to any mortal. The New Covenant is that to which the Prophets of old pointed. It is that of which the Patriarchs spoke. And yet, it was accompanied by no fanfare whatsoever, as was the giving of the Law on Mt. Sinai, when at that time the mountains shook, and fire played across its summit. The sign of the New Covenant is the Salvation of souls, and there have been untold millions who have said *"yes"* to Christ, and had their lives marvelously and gloriously changed. And yet, this marvelous Covenant, this New Covenant, this Eternal Covenant, this Covenant that is so profound as to beggar description, still can be summed up in the most simplistic of words, *"Jesus Christ and Him Crucified."* Faith evidenced in the Christ of the New Covenant and what He did on the Cross guarantees a New Life, and even above that, Eternal Life.

In the next Chapter we will look at the New Covenant even as Paul gave this great Truth, this great liberating factor, unto us.

"There's within my heart a melody,
"Jesus whispers sweet and low,
"Fear not, I Am with you, peace, be still,
"In all of life's ebb and flow."

"All my life was wrecked by sin and strife,
"Discord filled my heart with pain,
"Jesus swept across the broken strings,
"Stirred the slumbering chords again."

"Feasting on the riches of His Grace,
"Resting 'neath His sheltering Wing,
"Always looking on His smiling Face,
"That is why I shout and sing."

"Soon He's coming back to welcome me,
"Far beyond the starry sky;

"I shall wing my flight to worlds unknown,
"I shall reign with Him on high."

"Jesus, Jesus, Jesus,
"Sweetest Name I know;
"Fills my every longing,
"Keeps me singing as I go."

PAUL
THE APOSTLE

CHAPTER FOUR

The Book Of Romans

THE BOOK OF ROMANS

More than likely Paul wrote the great Book of Romans from the city of Corinth. It was written to Christians in Rome, where he at this time had never been. Actually, it is not known who founded the Church in Rome; nevertheless, due to the vast significance of Rome, the Church there was of great importance. As well, we have no knowledge of what prompted Paul to write this Epistle, other than the Holy Spirit. One thing is certain, as it regards the Benediction in the Sixteenth Chapter of Romans, Paul evidently knew many people there. Cenchrea was about nine miles from Corinth. It is believed that Phebe, a *"deaconess"* in the Church at Cenchrea, took this great Epistle with her to deliver there to the Church while on a trip to Rome. Someone has well said, *"I wonder if Phebe knew that she held in the robes of her skirt the theology of the Church."*

As it regards the Book of Romans, I think one can say without fear of contradiction that of all the Books of the Bible, Romans is the most important. And why would that be?

One could say that every Book in the Bible before Romans strained toward that Book. As well, one can say that every Book written after Romans strains back toward that Book. In this Book the great Plan of Salvation is recorded and, as well, the key to victory is given to us as it regards the Sanctification of the Saint recorded in Chapters 6, 7, and 8.

A DIAGRAM OF THE VARIOUS CHAPTERS

CHAPTER 1: In this Chapter Paul deals with the Gentile world. It is not a very pretty picture. With no exceptions, I think it can be said that every Gentile nation fell into the ranks of polytheism, meaning they worshipped many gods, in effect, demon spirits. So, one can easily conclude as to what they were. No matter that the great Apostle stated at the conclusion of that Chapter, *"Who knowing the Judgment of God, that they which commit such things are worthy of death, not only do the* *same, but have pleasure in them who do them"* (Rom. 1:32).

CHAPTERS 2 AND 3: In these two Chapters Paul deals with his own people, the Jews. They were the people of the Book, in fact, the only people on Earth who were monotheistic, meaning they worshipped one God, Jehovah. But, despite the privileges they had, he put them in the same category as the Gentiles, both classes of people desperately needing a Saviour. To be sure, Israel was not happy at all with his summation, and even Christian Jews were nonplussed at his conclusion. How could they be classified in the same category as the Gentile dogs? So, the Jewish segment of the Church, which at that time was very large, gave Paul little respect.

CHAPTERS 4 AND 5: Chapters 1 through 3 leave man in a terrible dilemma. He cannot save himself, and there is nothing he can do to earn Salvation. But Chapters 4 and 5 solve the problem. Paul makes his great argument, which we will address momentarily, of *"Justification by Faith."* That was and is man's answer. And it was and is man's only answer.

CHAPTERS 6, 7, AND 8: Now that believing man has come to God, these three Chapters tell us how to live for God. If one doesn't understand these three Chapters, then one doesn't understand God's Prescribed Order of Life and Living. In fact, the meaning of the sin nature and how to overcome it was the very first thing shown by the Lord to the great Apostle, as it regards Believers living for the Lord. Consequently, there are no Chapters in the Word of God more important, as it regards the Believer and his life and living, than these three Chapters. It is absolutely imperative that the Believer understand what the great Apostle was saying concerning this all-important subject.

CHAPTERS 9, 10, AND 11: Many Christians think that Paul has just abruptly changed the subject and is now dealing with Prophecy. While he does deal to a small degree with Prophecy, that's not the intent of these three Chapters. Actually, the intent of the Holy Spirit in giving this information regarding Israel, etc., is that if the church does what Israel did, which was to abandon God's Way of Righteousness and, thereby, substitute their own, which means to abandon the Cross, then the chilling word comes forth that the Lord will cut off the church exactly as He has cut off Israel. And if He wouldn't spare Israel, which was more important to Him than the church, why do we think that He would spare the church? The truth is, He cannot spare anything that ignores His Way.

CHAPTERS 12 THROUGH 16: The last five Chapters of this Epistle concern themselves with the practical side of Christianity, in other words, what the Believer will do, that is, if he is to be a good Christian.

ABRAHAM

Paul deals with the unconverted person coming to Christ, typified by Abraham. Then he deals with the Believer who fails the Lord in some way, and does so by addressing David. As stated, it is the greatest teaching on Salvation and Sanctification found anywhere in the Word of God.

THE PATRIARCH

"What shall we say then that Abraham our father, as pertaining to the flesh, has found? *(Having stated that the Old Testament teaches that God justifies the sinner on the Faith principle as opposed to the merit principle, the Holy Spirit now brings forward Abraham)*" (Rom. 4:1).

Why Abraham?

It was to Abraham that the Lord gave the meaning of *"Justification by Faith."*

When the Lord called Abraham out of Ur of the Chaldees, as far as we know, Abraham and Sarah were the only two people on Earth at that time living for God, with possibly the exception of Shem, Noah's son. Actually, we are not told how the Lord spoke to Abraham.

Some think that it was Shem, Noah's son, who witnessed to Abraham, which very well could have been the case. And then some years later, we come face-to-face with Melchizedek, who then was the king of Jerusalem, then called Salem (Gen. 14:18-20). As well, some think that Melchizedek may very well have been Shem, inasmuch as he was still alive at the time. But that is speculation at best. Incidentally, Abraham and Sarah lived about 2,000 years after Adam and Eve.

JUSTIFICATION BY WORKS?

"For if Abraham were justified by works *(which he wasn't)*, he has *whereof* to glory; but not before God *(the boasting of Salvation by works, which God will not accept)*" (Rom. 4:2).

There is no such thing as *"Justification by works."* In other words, there is nothing man can do that would earn him Salvation before God as far as works are concerned. So, immediately, Salvation by works is cast out. But yet, this is the greatest problem that all Believers face. Even without realizing it, we seek to be *"justified by works."*

I'm going to place before the reader a diagram which I have already used in this Volume, and possibly will use again. But I'm going to turn it upside down, so to speak. In other words, I will put the wrong way first and the right way last.

Focus: works.

Object of faith: one's performance regarding these works.

Power source: self.

Results: defeat.

Now, what you see in this little diagram is the way that most Christians are trying to live for God. In fact, if the Christian doesn't know and understand God's Prescribed Order of Life and Living, and I speak of the Cross of Christ relative to our Sanctification, then without fail, such a Believer is going to attempt to live for God by the little diagram listed above.

Most Christians have it in their minds that their works, whatever they might be, will produce Righteousness and Holiness. They won't! In fact, I think one can say without fear of contradiction that the modern church is buried up in works more than it ever has been in its history, at least since the Reformation. But no amount of works will develop Righteousness and Holiness in one's life. No amount of works will justify one before God. And we are presently seeing here exactly what Paul addressed in this Second Verse when he said, *"For if Abraham were justified by works, he has whereof to glory; but not before God."* In other words, the modern church is glorying in its works, but it is a glorying or boasting in which the Lord has no part. In fact, there is only one thing for which the Believer is allowed to glory or boast. It is the following:

"But God forbid that I should glory (boast), save in the Cross of our Lord Jesus Christ, by Whom the world is crucified unto me, and I unto the world" (Gal. 6:14).

Now let's look at the manner and the way in which the Believer Scripturally is to live for God.

FOCUS: The Lord Jesus Christ (Jn. 1:1-2; 14:6; Col. 2:10).

OBJECT OF FAITH: The Cross of Christ (Rom. 6:3-5; I Cor. 1:17-18, 23; 2:2).

POWER SOURCE: The Holy Spirit (Rom. 8:1-2, 11).

RESULTS: Victory (Rom. 6:14).

COUNTED UNTO HIM FOR RIGHTEOUSNESS

"For what says the Scripture? Abraham believed God, and it was counted unto him for Righteousness *([Gen. 15:6] if one properly understands this Verse, he properly understands the Bible; Abraham gained Righteousness by simple Faith in God, Who would send a Redeemer into the world [Jn. 8:56])*" **(Rom. 4:3).**

This which the lord taught Abraham is the only means,

the only way, in which one can gain the Righteousness of God. Immediately upon believing the Lord, a perfect, pure, spotless Righteousness is awarded to such an individual. It is not done by degrees, but instantly.

What does it mean, *"Abraham believed God?"* First, let's see what it didn't mean.

It didn't mean that Abraham merely believed there was a God. Millions do that and they aren't Saved. In fact, James said:

"You believe that there is one God; you do well: the devils also believe, and tremble" (James 2:19).

The idea is, Abraham believed what God told him. And what did God tell him?

In effect, the Lord told Abraham that through him, his seed, his progeny, One was coming Who would be God manifest in the flesh, Who would redeem fallen humanity (Gen. 15:1-6). Actually, Jesus referred to this when He said, *"Your father Abraham rejoiced to see My day: and he saw it, and was glad"* (Jn. 8:56).

In the great Revelation of Justification by Faith given to Abraham by God, he was made to understand that this great Redemption Plan was wrapped up, not in a philosophy, but rather a Man, the Man Christ Jesus, and what He would do at the Cross; the Patriarch rejoiced in that.

The moment that Abraham believed God in that respect, instantly, the Scripture says *"and it was counted unto him for Righteousness."*

The word *"counted"* in the Hebrew is *"chashab,"* and means, *"to plait or interpenetrate, to weave, to regard, to value, to compute."*

"Counted" in the Greek is *"logizomai,"* and means, *"to take an inventory, to impute, to reckon."*

GRACE AND DEBT

"Now to him who works *(tries to earn Salvation)* is the reward *(Righteousness)* not reckoned of Grace *(the*

Grace of God), **but of debt** *(claiming that God owes us something, which He doesn't!)*" **(Rom. 4:4).**

"Works" constitutes currency which will not spend in the economy of God.

"Works," as used here by Paul, in the Greek is *"ergon,"* and means, *"to toil as an effort of occupation, to labor, to do."* All of it refers to *"works"* as it regards earning one's Salvation, earning Righteousness, and earning Holiness.

Untold millions in the world are trying to earn Salvation by works, while untold millions of Christians are trying to earn Righteousness by works. Neither one is successful, as neither one can be successful. Please understand the following:

THE CROSS OF CHRIST

Unless the Believer understands the Cross of Christ as it regards our Sanctification, in other words, how we live for God on a daily basis, then such a Believer without fail is going to try to live for God by the means of works, which means he is not living by Faith. There aren't but two places that anyone can be, and that is *"law"* or *"Grace."* If one is functioning in works, this means that one is functioning in *"law,"* whether he understands such or not. If one is functioning in the Cross, one is functioning *"in Grace."*

But, the sadness is, virtually the entirety of the modern church is functioning in works simply because it doesn't know anything about the Cross relative to Sanctification. Satan has been very successful in steering the church in ways other than the Cross. And please understand, he doesn't too very much care what the other ways are, just as long as it's not the Cross of Christ.

WHAT DOES IT MEAN TO UNDERSTAND THE CROSS?

• **The Believer must understand that every single thing we** receive from God, and I mean every single thing, comes to us from Jesus Christ as our Source and the Cross as our Means. In other words, it is the Cross of Christ which makes everything possible, and I mean everything from Salvation to Sanctification. Every blessing comes through the Cross. Every answer to prayer comes because of the Cross. All healing comes by Means of the Cross. All prosperity comes as a result of the Cross. The Fruit of the Spirit, the Gifts of the Spirit and, in fact, all the Working of the Holy Spirit, all and without exception are made possible by what Jesus did for us at the Cross.

• The Believer must understand that, must believe that, must act upon that, and must make the Cross of Christ the Object of his Faith, and the Cross of Christ alone the Object of his Faith.

• But now we come to the offense of the Cross.

WHAT IS THE OFFENSE OF THE CROSS?

Paul said:

"And I, Brethren, if I yet preach Circumcision, why do I yet suffer persecution? *(Any message other than the Cross draws little opposition)* then is the offence of the Cross ceased" (Gal. 5:11).

The Greek word for *"offense"* is *"skandalon,"* and means, *"the thing that offends, a stumbling block."*
Why is it that?
The Cross of Christ lays waste all of religious man's religious efforts. In other words, it closes the door to every work of the flesh and to all allegiance to things other than the Cross. Let me use Abraham as an example.

Abraham and Sarah knew that a son had to be born to them as it regarded the coming Redeemer who would come through the human race. But yet, Sarah was barren. So they concocted a scheme that they thought would solve the problem. Abraham would go into their servant girl, Hagar, and the child that would be born to her would be looked at as that belonging to Sarah, which, in effect, was the custom of that time; however, this was not God's Way, as such could never be God's Way. God cannot use anything that man produces, even though it may seem that the motives are right.

In effect, all of this proclaims the impatience of unbelief; the *"flesh"* quickly tires of waiting for the Divine Promise. In fact, the path of Faith is full of dignity, the path of unbelief full of degradation. They grew tired of waiting, which means, whether they realized it or not, they no longer set their hopes upon God, but rather upon the Egyptian slave girl.

LAW AND GRACE

The Epistle to the Galatians declares that Sarah and Hagar represent the two principals of Law and Grace. Hagar represents Salvation by works; Sarah Salvation by Faith. These principals are opposed to one another. Ishmael is born as the result of man's planning and energy; Isaac would be born as the result of God's Planning and Energy. In the birth of Ishmael, God had nothing to do with it and, as it regards the birth of Isaac, man was dead. So it is today. Salvation by works entirely depends on man's capacity to produce them; Salvation by Faith depends upon God's Ability to perform them. Under a covenant of works, God stands still in order to see what man can do; under the Covenant of Grace, man stands still to see what God has done. The two covenants are opposed; it must be either Hagar or Sarah. If Hagar, God has nothing to do with it; if Sarah, man has nothing to do with it.

ISAAC AND ISHMAEL

Isaac and Ishmael symbolize the new and the old natures in the Believer. Hagar and Sarah typify the two covenants of works and Grace, of bondage and liberty (Gal., Chpt. 4). The birth of the new nature demands the expulsion of the old. It is impossible to improve the old nature. How foolish, therefore, appears the doctrine of moral evolution! Allowed to remain, Ishmael would murder Isaac; allowed to remain, the flesh will murder the Spirit. The Divine Way of Holiness is to *"put off the old man,"* just as Abraham *"put off"* Ishmael. Man's way of holiness is to improve the *"old man,"* that is, to improve Ishmael. The effort is both foolish and hopeless.

THE BONDWOMAN AND HER SON

There came an hour when the Lord told Abraham that the bondwoman (Hagar) and her son must go (Gen. 21:9-12).

It is always a struggle to cast out this element of bondage, that is, Salvation by works, of which this is a type. For legalism is dear to the heart. Ishmael was the fruit, and to Abraham, the fair fruit of his own energy and planning, which God can never accept. But the Believer must remember, it is labor lost to seek to make a crooked thing straight. Hence, all efforts after the improvement of nature are utterly futile, so far as God is concerned. The *"flesh"* must go, which typifies the personal ability, strength, and efforts of the Believer.

The Faith of the Believer must be entirely in Christ and what Christ has done at the Cross. Then, and then alone, can the Holy Spirit have latitude to work in our lives, bringing forth perpetual Victory (Rom. 6:14). It must ever be understood, *"in Isaac (in Christ) shall your seed be called."*

While it was difficult for Abraham to obey God and cast out the bondwoman and her son, still, the Patriarch obeyed. And the moment he did this, there marked a distinct advance in the Spiritual experience of this man. From this moment onwards, all is strength and Victory. He cast out the bondwoman and her son; he no longer fears the prince of this world (Abimelech), but reproves him; and now that the heir is come, Christ in Type, he knows himself to be the possessor of Heavenly as well as earthly Promises.

Religious man doesn't like to give up that which he has

conceived. Almost all of the time it is very, very religious. And that is the offense of the Cross. The Cross demands that everything be given up, and I mean everything, i.e. allegiance to particular denominations, or even to a particular church, or particular preachers, or works in which we engage ourselves, such as fasting, confession of Scripture, etc. In other words, the list is long.

Some of the things named are very right, at least within themselves; however, when we seek to make them the source of victory, such as fasting, the Lord's Supper, and even our prayer life, we then violate the Word and actually commit sin. Paul said:

EXAMINE YOURSELVES

"Examine yourselves, whether you be in the Faith; prove your own selves. Know you not your own selves, how that Jesus Christ is in you, except you be reprobates?" (II Cor. 13:5).

The words as used by Paul, *"the Faith,"* refer to *"Christ and Him Crucified,"* with the Cross ever being the Object of our Faith. The phrase, *"prove your own selves,"* means to make certain your Faith is actually in the Cross and not other things.

Was Paul opposed to Water Baptism when he said, *"For Christ sent me not to baptize, but to preach the Gospel: not with wisdom of words, lest the Cross of Christ should be made of none effect"* (I Cor. 1:17).

Of course not!

Are we opposed to fasting, to prayer, to memorizing Scriptures, etc., when we warn the Believer about placing our faith in those things, thinking that by doing them, such will guarantee victory within our lives? No, we aren't opposed to these things, not at all! We are just warning Believers of the wrong use of such.

PRAYER

Going back to the late 1980's, not knowing the meaning of the Cross of Christ as it refers to our Sanctification, which means I simply did not know how to live for God, the only thing I knew to do was pray. I thought I could pray so much each day, actually several hours, and this would guarantee me victory over the world, the flesh, and the Devil. I would get up in the wee hours of the morning, stagger around the house trying to pray, doing this until I almost drove myself to a nervous breakdown, but finding that my consecration to this particular effort did not bring victory.

Now, if you think we're talking against prayer, then you could not be more wrong. My grandmother taught me to pray when I was but a child. I have always had a strong prayer life, and I think, a stronger prayer life now than ever. But now it's done in the right way. Let me ask a question.

How much prayer each day will it take to guarantee victory within your heart and life? Thirty minutes? An hour? Two hours a day?

The truth is, one cannot gain victory in this manner. Every true Believer will most definitely have a prayer life. Without such, one really cannot have a relationship with Christ. But, if one understands the Cross as one should understand the Cross, then one will engage in prayer in the right manner. It will be to thank the Lord for what He has done and is doing for us. It will be to bring our petitions before Him. It will be to just simply express our love to Him, as we should perpetually do.

Yes, there is an offense to the Cross because it lays to waste all of man's ambitions, efforts, strength, personal ability, education, etc. In other words, it strips religious man bare. It leaves nothing but Faith, but Faith in Christ and what Christ has done for us at the Cross.

One can work all one desires, but it does not place God in our debt. We must ever understand that. In fact, God has nothing for sale. Everything He has is a free gift.

FAITH COUNTED FOR RIGHTEOUSNESS

"But to him who works not *(doesn't trust in works*

for Salvation), **but believes on Him Who Justifies the ungodly** *(through Christ and the Cross)*, **his Faith is counted for Righteousness** *(God awards Righteousness only on the basis of Faith in Christ and His Finished Work)*" **(Rom. 4:5).**

This is very difficult for the religious man to accept. The idea that one who is obviously guilty, and who has done no good works, done no good things, and has engaged in no penance for his wickedness, could simply exhibit Faith in Christ and immediately be justified before God, with *"his Faith counted for Righteousness,"* is preposterous to the religious mind.

The better way to define religion is that which is conceived by man, a means or a way to reach God or to better oneself in some way, which man has ever tried to do. Due to the Fall, God cannot accept anything that man conceives as it regards a supposed Righteousness or Holiness. He can, however, justify man, no matter how wicked that man might be, on the basis, and only on the basis, of Faith exhibited in Christ. God will not accept Faith exhibited in anything else. It must be Christ and Christ Alone. Of course, when the believing sinner accepts Christ, at the same time, even though he understands little about it, he is accepting Christ and what Christ has done for him at the Cross.

THE JEWS

The Jews exhibited a hatred for Paul to such an extent that they tried repeatedly to kill him, and we speak of the Nation of Israel as a whole. The very idea that this man could claim that Gentiles were as good as Jews when they accepted Christ was in their minds a gross insult. While Gentiles could be accepted, it was only after they had become a proselyte Jew, so to speak. Even Christian Jews found it difficult to accept Paul's teaching. The idea that their efforts to keep the Law gave them no standing with God was galling, to say the least. And to be frank, much of the modern church world still has a problem with Believers not doing penance.

PENANCE

"Penance" is *"an act of self-abasement, or devotion performed to show sorrow for sin."* The Bible does not teach penance. It does teach Repentance, but not penance. While this is a part of Catholic dogma and doctrine, regrettably, it is a part of most protestant doctrine as well.

While many, if not most, protestant preachers will proclaim the fact that the unconverted person can be Saved only by Faith in Christ with no works enjoined whatsoever, the same preacher will demand penance on the part of a Believer who fails. They don't call it penance, but that's what it is.

For instance, I'm thinking now of one particular Pentecostal denomination, and all of them are approximately the same. If one of their preachers commits a wrongdoing, he's not allowed to preach for two years, etc.

Now, they do state that he can preach in nursing homes, if he so desires, or even on a street corner, but he cannot preach behind a pulpit in one of their churches. I hope that one can see the foolishness of such a position. As well, he can join another group and preach in their churches, if he so desires, and then, when the two years are up, he can come back and be reinstated in the denomination in question. All of this is merely laws made up by men that have no basis in the Word of God. There is no such thing as a partial Justification.

AN ILLUSTRATION

At a particular meeting, a Preacher stood to his feet and gave an utterance in Tongues. It was interpreted by the visiting Minister who was an official in that particular denomination. After he interpreted the Message, the Spirit of the Lord came across the congregation, with people worshipping the Lord, etc., as they should have.

The next day, one of the Pastors called the District Superintendent. He asked him the question, *"Did you not know who it was who gave the utterance in Tongues, which was interpreted by our guest speaker?"*

The District Superintendent responded in the affirmative. Yes, he knew who the Brother was. The Preacher then said, *"Well, how could the Holy Spirit use this man to give the utterance in Tongues, when we have banned him from preaching for the next two years?"*

That's a good question!

The Holy Spirit used the Preacher, who had evidently done something wrong some months before, to give an utterance in Tongues. As stated, he was banned from preaching in that denomination for two years. With the visiting speaker interpreting the Message, and him being an official in the denomination, and considering that the Spirit of God had Moved over the building, no one could deny that it was the Lord Who engineered all of this.

When the question was put to the Superintendent, his only reply was, or words to this effect, *"Well that's our tradition."* Jesus had something to say about erroneous tradition. He said:

"You have made the Word of God of none effect through your tradition" (Mk. 7:13).

Religious men love to make up religious laws and then force other men to obey them.

THE IMPUTATION OF RIGHTEOUSNESS WITHOUT WORKS

"Even as David *(both Abraham and David were progenitors of the Promised Messiah, and as such they held a unique place in the Faith and veneration of the Work of God)* **also describes the blessedness of the man** *(a blessed man)*, **unto whom God imputes Righteousness without works** *(works will never gain the Righteousness of God)"* **(Rom. 4:6).**

As we previously mentioned, the Holy Spirit had Paul to use Abraham as a type of the unredeemed person coming to Christ, and David as a redeemed person who has failed and then been granted forgiveness by the Lord. Both situations are identical. In other words, the Lord doesn't have one way or method for the unsaved and something else for Believers.

WORKS

When Paul uses the word *"works,"* exactly what is he addressing?

To make it very simple to understand, it refers to anything other than Faith in Christ and what Christ did for us at the Cross. The Apostle is not demeaning works, but is showing us that our place and position in Christ are not attained by *"works,"* but rather by our Faith. And, as well, for Faith to be the Faith that God recognizes, it must ever have as its Object the Cross of Christ. That is God's Way (Rom. 6:3-5; 8:2, 11; I Cor. 1:17-18, 21, 23; 2:2).

The whole Jewish system was built on *"works,"* which referred to works as it regards the Law of Moses. They had conjured up all types of things, which they did or did not do that made them think they were right with God. The truth is, when Jesus came, the Law of Moses had been so perverted, so wasted, that anymore it hardly even resembled that which had been originally given. As a result, precious few in the Israel of Jesus' day were actually Saved. For example:

On the Sabbath Day, a woman could not put a brush or comb through her hair for fear there might be a speck of dust on her hair, and it would be moved by the brush and could be construed as plowing. The Law of Moses did say that it was wrong to plow on the Sabbath Day, etc. But this is how ridiculous the Jews in Jesus' Day had made the system.

HOW DO WORKS AFFECT THE MODERN CHURCH?

The principle is the same! If modern Believers do not

have their Faith in Christ and the Cross, and Christ and the Cross exclusively, then whatever it is in which they are trusting is defined by the Lord as *"works,"* which will justify no one. Now, the facts are, that in which they are placing their faith, whatever it might be, may be very good within itself and may be Scriptural. But when we put our faith in such an item or such a situation, in the Mind of God, it becomes *"works,"* which again, cannot bring us any place and position in Christ. Let me give an example:

When Frances and I first began in Evangelistic work in the late 1950's, a book came out on fasting. Now, fasting within itself is Scriptural and will bless the individual, that is, if done correctly. But those many years ago, every Believer was fasting because it was supposed to bring about some tremendous revolution in one's life, etc. It didn't because it was being used in the wrong way.

It has come full circle. As I dictate these notes, the same thing is being promoted all over the nation and around the world. Some are even saying, if you fast so many days, this will give you victory over sin, etc.

No, it won't!

When such is done, *"fasting"* is turned into *"works,"* which God can never accept. Let us say it again:

FAITH

The Lord works exclusively on the system of Faith. But, as we've already stated, and will continue to state, if it's not Faith exclusively in Christ and the Cross, then it's Faith that God will not recognize. In fact, the people who are fasting, thinking it's going to bring about victory in their lives, or whatever else they might be doing, are evidencing faith, but it's in the wrong object. Listen again to Paul:

"But God forbid that I should glory (boast), save in the Cross of our Lord Jesus Christ, by Whom the world is Crucified unto me, and I unto the world" (Gal. 6:14).

When the Believer boasts in the Cross of Christ, he is giving the glory to where it rightly belongs, the Lord. Whenever we do these other things, and I speak of works, then the glory goes to the individual. Even though that's not the prime reason it's wrong, it is one reason. In fact, Faith registered in anything except Christ and the Cross always ends up in self-righteousness. That's the reason, and I say it kindly, if such can be said kindly, the modern church is the most self-righteous church I personally think that has ever been, at least since the Reformation.

INIQUITIES FORGIVEN

"Saying, **Blessed** *are* **they whose iniquities are forgiven** *([Ps. 32:1-2] iniquities can only be forgiven by Faith in Christ)*, **and whose sins are covered** *(the Cross made this possible)"* **(Rom. 4:7).**

What is Paul saying here?

In effect, he is saying that the only way that sins can be forgiven and victory, thereby, brought about in such a life is by the individual registering Faith in Christ and the Cross. The person doing such can rejoice in iniquities forgiven. Listen again to Paul:

"So Christ was once offered to bear the sins of many" (Heb. 9:28). The Apostle also said, *"But this Man, after He had offered One Sacrifice for sins forever, sat down on the Right Hand of God"* (Heb. 10:12).

AN ILLUSTRATION

Sometime back I had a young preacher write to me, who had had a problem in his life. Regarding the group he was with, they assigned him to a particular church. These were the rules laid down:

He had to have a session with a psychologist once a week.

He had to spend at least thirty minutes, or some such time, in prayer each day. He also had to volunteer some manual labor for the church each day. In fact, there was a long list of rules. And, oh yes, he could not go further than thirty miles outside of the city.

I wrote him back and stated to him that, while I did not doubt the motives of the preachers who were assigning all of this to him, still, his one year of regimentation in this effort was not going to do any good.

He wrote me back and stated that he knew this was going to help him greatly, and it was the way that it should be done, etc.

He ultimately finished his regimen and fell right back into the same sin. How long does it take for us to learn? Man's problem, and it started with Adam, has always been that we aren't satisfied with God's Way, but rather feel like we have a better way. How foolish can we be? And yet, all of us have fallen into this trap.

THE BLESSED MAN

"**Blessed** *is* **the man to whom the Lord will not impute sin** *(the Lord will not impute sin to the person who places his Faith solely in Christ and what Christ did at the Cross)*" **(Rom. 4:8).**

The idea of this Verse is that if we do not go to the Lord in Faith, asking Him to forgive us of our sins when sins have been committed, understanding that it was the Cross of Christ that addressed all sin, then such an individual is still saddled, so to speak, with the sin. There is only one way that sin can be forgiven:

That one way is *"Jesus Christ and Him Crucified,"* and our Faith in that Finished Work. This is so serious that we must say it again:

For sin to be cleansed, it can only come about by the Means

of Christ and what He did for us at the Cross and our Faith in that Finished Work. If we attempt to rid ourselves of sin in any other way, to be blunt, the sin remains. When a person goes before the Lord, confessing his sin, understanding that we have forgiveness of sin simply because of what Jesus did at the Cross, such sin, whatever it might be, is instantly forgiven. In other words, such a person is blessed because now the Lord will not impute that sin to him any longer (I Jn. 1:9). But if man tries to address sin in any other way, and it doesn't matter what kind of way it is, pure and simple, the sin remains.

FAITH

"*Comes* this blessedness then upon the Circumcision *only*, or upon the uncircumcision also? *(It comes on all alike!)* for we say that Faith was reckoned to Abraham for Righteousness *(presents Faith alone as the ingredient)*" (Rom. 4:9).

Paul is saying in this Ninth Verse that since the Cross, "*this blessedness*" comes upon both Jew and Gentile alike. In other words, God doesn't have one method for the Jews and another for the Gentiles. Christ is Lord over all. Now, of course, this did not endear Paul to the Jews, even Christian Jews. They liked to think of themselves as being special in the Eyes of God. In fact, in a sense, they were; however, as it regarded the basis of Salvation, there was no difference, as there can be no difference. When the Lord died on the Cross, He died for the whole of mankind.

RECKONED FOR RIGHTEOUSNESS

Abraham did not engage in any religious works of any nature in order to reach God or have the Blessings of God. He simply evidenced Faith in the Lord, and the Scripture says, "*and it was counted unto him for Righteousness*" (Gen. 15:6).

In a sense, Abraham was the pattern. Now, why is it that modern Believers do not desire to accept that? Let's answer the question in this way.

Legalism (law i.e., works) is dear to the heart. These are things we do which make us feel religious.

The Believer is to understand that it is no longer a self-centered life that he lives but a Christ-centered one. His new life is a Person, the Lord Jesus, through the Person of the Holy Spirit, living in his heart and life. And through the Ministry of the Holy Spirit, the Lord Jesus is manifest in our lives. The new life is no longer, like the former one, dependent upon the ineffectual efforts of a man attempting to draw near to God by his own works. The new life is a Person, namely Christ, within a person, living out His Life in that person.

A SET OF RULES?

Instead of attempting to live our lives in obedience to a set of rules in the form of the legal enactments of the Mosaic Law, we are to now yield to the indwelling Holy Spirit and cooperate with Him in the production of a life pleasing to God, all energized by the Divine Life resident in us through the regenerating Work of the Spirit, all made possible by the Cross.

THE PROBLEM THAT MAN HAS

However, man, even believing man, somewhat balks at this position given by the Holy Spirit through Paul (Gal. 2:20). Man likes to have some credit and some position. He likes that which he can see and handle. He refuses to be treated as vile and incapable of good, and is angered that he and his religious efforts should be condemned to annihilation.

Oh yes! He will willingly practice efforts to annihilate himself, for that ministers to his own importance; but to accept the absolute judgment of death upon his nature, his religious energies, and his moral virtues, and to be commanded to be silent, and as a dead sinner, to trust the life-giving Saviour, finding in Him all that is needful for Righteousness and worship, is distasteful and repelling, hence, the offense of the Cross. But this is the Doctrine of Galatians, Chapter 2, Verse 20.

THE CROSS

When Paul mentioned in Galatians 2:20, *"Living by the Faith of the Son of God,"* he is once again taking the Believer to the Cross. With the first phrase of that Verse, *"I am Crucified with Christ,"* he takes the Believer back to Romans, Chapter 6, Verses 3 through 5. There the Believer was baptized into the Death of Christ, buried with Him by baptism into death, and raised with Him in Newness of Life. No! This is not speaking of Water Baptism but the Crucifixion of Christ. The Believer gains this place and position in Christ by simply having Faith in Christ and what Christ did at the Cross.

HOW WAS FAITH RECKONED TO ABRAHAM?

"How was it then reckoned? *(This may be the greatest question of all time.)* when he was in Circumcision, or in uncircumcision? Not in Circumcision, but in uncircumcision *(because of his Faith, Abraham was declared Righteous by God before the Covenant of Circumcision was ever given [Gen. 15:6])*" **(Rom. 4:10).**

Why is Paul dealing here with Circumcision, especially considering that his letter is actually to Gentiles? The reason was this:

In the Early Church there were among the Gentiles, Jews. And then, Judaizers were coming from Jerusalem into these Churches which Paul had founded, or ever how they came into being, telling the people that if they wanted to be a complete Christian, the Gentile men who had accepted Christ had to also be circumcised. Some were even teaching that if a person were to be Saved, he had to be circumcised.

One must remember that Circumcision was the physical seal of the Mosaic Covenant. In fact, the sign of this Covenant was even given to Abraham about 400 years before Moses. But Paul is making the case that Circumcision now doesn't really even enter into Salvation or serving God in any fashion. Now, how could he say that whenever Circumcision was, in fact, as stated, the physical seal of the Old Covenant (Ex. 12:48; Lev. 12:3)?

He could say that because the Lord had shown him that the entirety of the Law, including Circumcision, had been finished in Christ. The Scripture says concerning this:

"For Christ is the end of the Law for Righteousness to everyone who believes" (Rom. 10:4). This simply means that Jesus fulfilled the Law in every respect, doing so in His Life and Living, not failing even one time, and did it all for us. As well, He addressed the broken Law, of which all were guilty, by giving Himself in Sacrifice on the Cross, thereby, shedding His Life's Blood, which satisfied the demands of a thrice-Holy God (Col. 2:14). In fact, the Law was never meant to save anyway. It was given for other reasons. Some of them are:

• To exhibit to mankind God's Standard of Righteousness.

• To show man that because of the Fall, he was incapable of keeping the Law.

• He was then directed to the Sacrificial system, which typified Christ and the Cross, where there he could have forgiveness of sins.

Salvation has always been wrapped up entirely in Christ. It has never been in the Law or anything else of such nature. Admittedly, before the Cross, it wasn't easy for a person to be Saved. In fact, if Gentiles were to be Saved, they had to become a Proselyte Jew and then place their Faith unreservedly in that which the Sacrificial system represented, namely the coming Redeemer, the Lord Jesus Christ. Even though they would not have known Him by that name, they most definitely were to know that One was coming, which was what all of this was all about.

So, Paul is simply saying that Circumcision, and all Law-keeping for that matter, is out. It is now simple Faith in Christ and Christ alone!

THE FATHER OF THE FAITHFUL

"And he received the sign of Circumcision *(Gen. 17:9-14)*, a seal of the Righteousness of the Faith which *he had yet* being uncircumcised *(plainly states that his Righteousness was by Faith, and was received long before Circumcision)*: that he might be the father of all them who believe *(Jews and Gentiles)*, though they be not Circumcised *(places the ground or Foundation of Salvation squarely on Faith instead of works)*; that Righteousness might be imputed unto them also *(Righteousness has never been imputed on the ground of works, but always on the ground of Faith)*" **(Rom. 4:11).**

The idea of this Verse is that Abraham received the *"seal of the Righteousness of Faith,"* even before the Covenant of Circumcision was given to him by the Lord. In fact, it was about fifteen years from the time that the Lord declared Abraham as Righteous solely on the basis of his Faith (Gen. 15:6) until the time He gave him the Covenant of Circumcision (Gen. 17:9-14).

As it regards the Covenant of Circumcision given to Abraham, notes from Genesis 17:13 in THE EXPOSITOR'S STUDY BIBLE say:

"This Covenant is everlasting, but only in Christ; under the New Covenant, Paul stated that we are to experience the circumcision of the heart, which is a Spiritual work (Phil. 3:3); under the New Covenant, everything being fulfilled in Christ, of which Circumcision was a Type of His Sacrifice, the rite is no longer necessary; in fact, it carries no spiritual meaning now whatsoever."

Paul said:

"For in Jesus Christ neither Circumcision avails anything,

nor uncircumcision; but Faith which works by Love" (Gal. 5:6).

This Eleventh Verse of Romans, Chapter 4, tells us that Abraham, due to his Faith, is the father of us all in the sense that the pattern was established in him, as given to him by the Lord (Gen. 15:6). Paul is building on this fact.

FAITH IN CHRIST

"And the father of Circumcision to them who are not of the Circumcision only *(presents Abraham as being the father of all Believers, whether Jews or Gentiles)*, but who also walk in the steps of that Faith of our father Abraham *(refers to him simply believing God, and God accounting his Faith to him for Righteousness [Gen. 15:6])*, which *he had* being *yet* uncircumcised *(clenches the argument and opens up Salvation to all who come by Faith in Christ, irrespective as to whom they may be)*" **(Rom. 4:12).**

Paul is trying to show the Jewish Believers that the physical act of circumcision, while admittedly it was a physical sign of the Mosaic Covenant, still contained no Salvation. His argument is, and rightly so, that Abraham received Salvation before the Rite of Circumcision was introduced, which would be some fifteen years later. And Paul emphasizes the fact that this Salvation was received by Faith in the Lord, and Faith alone, which in reality was Faith in Christ. In fact, Salvation has always been on the basis of Faith alone. The problem is, man has tried to introduce other things into the Salvation mix, and it doesn't really matter what the other things are. Any addition nullifies Faith. And, as we have stated, for it to be Faith that God recognizes, it must be Faith in Christ and the Cross.

WHAT DID ABRAHAM KNOW ABOUT THE CROSS OF CHRIST?

Abraham knew far more about the Cross of Christ than we

realize. In fact, Jesus said of him, and speaking to the Jews:

"Your father Abraham rejoiced to see my day: and he saw it, and was glad" (Jn. 8:56). Notes from THE EXPOSITOR'S STUDY BIBLE regarding this Verse say, *"In the great Revelation of Justification by Faith given to Abraham by God, he was made to understand that this great Redemption Plan was wrapped up, not in a philosophy, but rather a Man, the Man Christ Jesus, and what He would do at the Cross; the Patriarch rejoiced in that."*

THE RIGHTEOUSNESS OF FAITH

"For the Promise, that he should be the heir of the world, *was* not to Abraham, or to his seed, through the Law *(the Law of Moses, which had not even been given during the time of Abraham)*, but through the Righteousness of Faith *(when Paul uses the word 'Faith,' without exception, he is speaking of Faith in Christ and what Christ did at the Cross; in fact, Christ must never be separated from the Cross, as it regards His Redemptive Work)"* (Rom. 4:13).

Paul is careful to say in this Thirteenth Verse that everything Abraham received, which is what we receive now, as well, was not through the Law, but rather *"through the Righteousness of Faith."*

This latter phrase tells us that true Righteousness can come only by the Means of Faith. But let us emphasize, it has to be Faith in Christ and the Cross. Everybody in the world has faith, but it's not faith that God recognizes. It is Faith in Christ and what He did for us at the Cross, which must ever be the Object of our Faith. God will always recognize that, honor that, and reward that. In fact, He imputes to the Believer upon such Faith, a perfect, spotless, pure *"Righteousness,"* called *"the Righteousness of God"* (Rom. 1:17; 3:5, 21-22; 10:3; II Pet. 1:1). Anything else leads to self-righteousness.

FAITH IS MADE VOID

"**For if they which are of the Law *be* heirs** *(only those in the Law)*, **faith is made void** *(Salvation cannot exist in both works and Faith; either one cancels out the other)*, **and the Promise made of none effect** *(faith in works cancels out Christ and all that He has done for us)*" **(Rom. 4:14).**

Paul is saying that if the Jews can be the heirs of Salvation through the Law, then *"faith is made void, and the Promise made of none effect."* As we stated in the notes in the Scriptural Text, either one, *"law or Faith,"* cancels out the other. When one functions in law, one is not functioning in Faith.

THE LAW

Most of the time when Paul was speaking of the *"Law of Moses,"* he would use what is referred to now as the definite article in front of the word *"Law,"* making it read, *"the Law."* This spoke of a specific Law, and in this case, the Law of Moses. However, when he was speaking of law in general, what we might call religious law that is made up by men, whatever it might be, he did not use the definite article, referring to it only as *"law."*

That problem is with us presently, and in a big way. Let us say it again, any faith exhibited in anything except Christ and the Cross makes it *"law."* Consequently, it is something God cannot recognize. Let's say it another way:

If a preacher says (or anyone, for that matter) that one has to be baptized in water to be Saved, along with accepting Christ, then he turns Water Baptism into law. If one says that one has to fast so many days in order to have victory over sin, as well, he has turned fasting into law. To be sure, these things, and many others not mentioned, are not actually law within themselves, but made so by erroneous usage.

The Believer has to understand, it is either law or Faith, i.e., *"Grace."* It cannot be by both. If one is going to place his faith in anything except Christ and the Cross, whatever it is he has chosen becomes law, and *"faith is made void, and the Promise made of none effect."* Now that's quite a powerful statement, but I didn't say it, the Holy Spirit said it through Paul.

WRATH

"Because the Law works wrath *(Law has a penalty, so it must work wrath)*: for where no Law is, *there is* no transgression *(Christ has satisfied the Law, thereby, taking away all transgression)*" (Rom. 4:15).

It should be remembered, there is no Salvation, no Victory, and no Blessing in Law, only *"wrath."* In other words, all law, that is, if it truly is law, has a penalty attached to it. If it is broken, the penalty goes into effect. That is the workings of law.

AN ILLUSTRATION

Quite a few individuals at this particular time, preachers included, have come up with the idea that if they wear a Jewish prayer shawl, they will get their prayers answered more readily, etc. What they do not seem to understand is, they have reverted back to law. Admittedly, it was not a part of the Law of Moses but only a custom developed by the Jews. But still, individuals who do that now are reverting to law, and instead of having prayers answered, they are rather inviting upon themselves *"wrath."* This makes this teaching extremely serious.

If the Believer resorts to law in any capacity, and I speak of religious laws made up by themselves, by preachers, by churches, or by church denominations, etc., instead of blessing, there will be wrath. This is a fact simply because such a person has stepped outside of God's Prescribed Order of Life and Living, which is the Cross of Christ and, thereby, to some other way. Let us say it again:

The unredeemed world has forever been trying to develop another god, while the church has ever been trying to develop another sacrifice. God help us!

WHAT DID PAUL MEAN BY THE STATEMENT, *"FOR WHERE NO LAW IS, THERE IS NO TRANSGRESSION"?*

He is meaning that the Law of Moses, which is the Law of God, with all of its transgressions, committed by every human being who has ever lived, was addressed at Calvary. Consequently, I can presently say, and because I am in Christ, there is no transgression whatsoever that is held against me by God, and so it can be said by every True Believer.

FAITH AND GRACE

"Therefore *it is* of Faith, that *it might be* by Grace *(Grace functions only on Faith, and we speak of Faith in Christ; otherwise, Grace stops)*; to the end the Promise might be sure to all the seed *(refers to the whole of humanity, at least those who will believe)*; not to that only which is of the Law *(Jews)*, but to that also which is of the Faith of Abraham *(everything is by Faith)*; who is the father of us all *(proclaims the Patriarch being used as an example of Faith [Gen. 15:6])*" **(Rom. 4:16).**

So, Paul is saying that everything we receive from God has to be received on the basis of Faith, *"that it might be by Grace."* What does he mean by that latter phrase?

Grace is simply the Goodness of God extended to undeserving people. When the Believer evidences Faith in Christ and the Cross, and not at all in himself or man-devised schemes, then the Lord, Who is the Giver of all good things, will abundantly give to us that which we need, whatever it might be, and much more besides. But it must be remembered, *"it must be by Faith."* And again we state, if it is Faith that God recognizes, which guarantees the constant flow of the Grace of God, then it must be Faith in Christ and the Cross.

ALL SEED

When Paul used the phrase, *"To the end the Promise might be sure to all the seed,"* he was speaking of the entirety of humanity, both Jew and Gentile, and wherever they might be. In other words, the *"Promise,"* which pertains to Salvation by Grace through Faith, is guaranteed to all who exhibit Faith in Christ and what He did for us at the Cross. As Paul, in one way or the other, says over and over, it is the same for the Jew and the Gentile.

". . . THE FATHER OF US ALL"?

What did Paul mean by the statement of our heading?

He meant that the Lord revealed to Abraham the Way and Means of Salvation, which is by Faith alone, and we might quickly add, Faith in Christ and the Cross. Him being the first one to whom this great Revelation was given makes him the *"father of us all."*

And, once again, it must be remembered that Abraham received Righteousness not on the basis of circumcision, or law, or works, but solely on the basis of Faith in Christ and the Finished Work of our Lord.

". . . CALLS THOSE THINGS WHICH BE NOT AS THOUGH THEY WERE."

"(As it is written, I have made you a father of many nations *[Gen. 12:1-3; 17:4-5]*,) before Him Whom he believed, *even* God *(refers to Abraham believing God)*, who quickens the dead *(makes spiritually alive those who are spiritually dead)*, and calls those things which

be not as though they were *(if God has said it to us personally, we can call it; otherwise, it is presumption)*"
(Rom. 4:17).

When the Lord told Abraham that he would be *"a father
of many nations,"* at that particular time, he was the father
only of Ishmael, who was a work of the flesh. Despite that,
which caused great problems, the Lord still made Abraham
the father of many nations. And yet, Ishmael, one might say,
was the birth seed of the religion of Islam, which has been a
scourge on this Earth, possibly more so now than ever. This
is what happens when we unlawfully involve ourselves in the
great Promises of God.

As it regarded Abraham being the *"father of many nations,"*
the Patriarch believed it and confessed it, even though he was
then the head only of one family.

But for the Lord to bring all of this to pass, he had to *"quicken
the dead,"* which is explained in the following Verses.

HOPE

"Who against hope believed in hope *(a description
of Abraham's Faith, as it regarded the birth of Isaac)*, that
he might become the father of many nations; according
to that which was spoken *(the Promise of God)*, So shall
your seed be *(Gen. 15:5)*" (Rom. 4:18).

How could Abraham become the father of many nations
when Sarah was barren? In fact, there was no *"hope"* in
her bringing forth the promised seed. But yet, the Patriarch
"believed in hope," which was a hope that he could not see.

In fact, at a point of great discouragement in Abraham's
life, the Lord told the Patriarch one night to leave out of his
tent, go outside, and:

". . . Look now toward Heaven, and tell the stars

(count the stars), **if you be able to number them: and He said unto him** *(to Abraham)*, **So shall your seed be"** **(Gen. 15:5).**

That's when it said that Abraham

". . . believed in the LORD; and He counted it to him for Righteousness" (Gen. 15:6).

In other words, the Lord was telling the Patriarch, *"Even though you do not now have any seed at all, (*referring to a baby boy*), and besides that, it looks impossible for such to be simply because Sarah is barren; nevertheless, if you will believe Me, your seed shall be as the stars for multitude."* **And that's when the Bible says that Abraham believed God, and that's when God counted it to him for Righteousness.**

I think it should be obvious that the Lord places great stock in Faith, and we speak of Faith anchored in His Word, which, in effect, is Christ and the Cross.

HE CONSIDERED NOT

"And being not weak in Faith *(strong Faith)*, **he considered not his own body now dead, when he was about an hundred years old** *(no longer able to have children)*, **neither yet the deadness of Sarah's womb** *(placed her in the same situation as her husband)*" **(Rom. 4:19).**

Several things are said regarding Abraham in this Nineteenth Verse. Some of them are:
• He was not weak in Faith: He believed these preposterous things that the Lord was saying to him, although there was no visible, outward evidence of what was promised. Regardless, he believed.
• *"He considered not his own body now dead, when he was about an hundred years old"*: In other words, at 100 years of

age, he was too old to father children, as should be overly obvious. But despite that, he continued to believe the Lord.

• *"Neither yet the deadness of Sarah's womb"*: Sarah had been trying to conceive for all of her productive years, but yet, without any success. The Holy Spirit through Paul says that her womb was *"dead."*

PRESUMPTION

There are all kinds of people claiming all kinds of things in the Lord, to whom the Lord has not promised anything. Or else, they have imagined that He did, when, in reality, He didn't. Such is not faith, but rather presumption.

The Lord had spoken to Abraham and had told him that his seed would be as the stars of the heavens. So he had the Word of God on which to base his position.

If the individual is absolutely certain that the Lord has said to him a certain thing, and no matter how preposterous it may seem to be at the outset, he can *"call those things which be not as though they were."* But only on that foundation.

Presumption is not Faith. It is merely the boasting of the flesh, which God will never accept. And yet, I'm afraid that so much of what passes for Faith presently is little more than presumption.

STRONG IN FAITH

"He staggered not at the Promise of God through unbelief *(he did not allow difficulties to deter him from the intended conclusion)*; but was strong in Faith, giving Glory to God *(his Faith came from the Word of God)*" (Rom. 4:20).

When the Lord revealed all the great Promises to Abraham as it regarded his seed, although it was beyond his scope of comprehension, still, *"he staggered not at the Promise of God through unbelief."* He might have done some other things wrong, but he never stopped believing in that which the Lord had spoken to him.

In other words, in his devotion on a daily basis, by, no doubt, quoting the Promises of God to himself, he kept his Faith strong, always *"giving Glory to God."*

The word *"staggered"* in the Greek is *"diakrino,"* and means, *"to doubt, to waver, to call in question."* Abraham did not know how the Lord would fulfill this which He was to do, especially considering that he was nearing 100 years old and Sarah 90; however, he continued to believe, never wavering. Of course, we know that the Lord at His Time performed a Miracle on both the physical bodies of Abraham and Sarah. Isaac was the result of that, and through him, the Redeemer would ultimately come.

FULLY PERSUADED

"And being fully persuaded *(no turning back)* that, what He *(God)* had Promised, He was able also to perform *(whatever it was, God could do it!)*" (Rom. 4:21).

Unbelief is one of the greatest problems in the church and, in fact, ever has been.

AN ILLUSTRATION

Some time back, I saw four men debate the Miracles of God over television. Two claimed to be atheists, and the other two claimed to be Believers. I found that the *"Believers"* were operating in about as much unbelief as the atheists.

For instance, they tried to explain away the three Hebrew children in the fiery furnace as having found a *"cool spot,"* whatever that is. And then two other Miracles addressed, the crossing of the Red Sea and the walls of Jericho falling down, were explained, according to these men, by natural methods such as earthquakes, etc. They were loath to admit that it was the Power of God that accomplished these things, whatever way the Lord used to get it done.

But, of course, when preachers claim that all Miracles stopped with the Early Church, with even Biblical Miracles called into question, exactly as we have just addressed, all of this, as stated, is caused by unbelief. What God can do must come under the label of *"anything."* What He will do is predicated on His Will. Abraham was fully persuaded that what the Lord had promised, *"He was also able to perform."*

RIGHTEOUSNESS

"And therefore it was imputed to him for Righteousness *(simple Faith in God brought Abraham a spotless Righteousness)*" (Rom. 4:22).

Righteousness, at least that which God recognizes, which is what He imputes upon Faith, actually is what all of this is all about. Sinful man can obtain the Righteousness of God in only one way. It has never changed from the beginning until now. That one way is Faith in the Lord, but that needs to be explained.

Then, Abraham and all who followed him up unto Christ could only have Faith in what the Lord said concerning that which was to come, namely Christ, and one might say, a Prophetic Jesus. God honored that!

Now, at least since the Cross, our Faith is in Christ and what He has done for us at the Cross, and Who might be described as a historical Jesus. Before the Cross, it was a Prophetic Jesus; since the Cross, it is a historical Jesus. But, whatever Dispensation, it was always Faith in Christ that granted one the Righteousness of God.

THE DOCTRINE OF IMPUTATION

"Now it was not written for his sake alone *(Abraham's*

struggle of Faith was meant to serve as an example), **that it was imputed to him** *(serves as the example of how we receive from God, whether it be Salvation or anything else);*

"**But for us also, to whom it shall be imputed** *(we can have that which Abraham had, a perfect Righteousness),* **if we believe on Him Who raised up Jesus our Lord from the dead** *(proclaims the condition for Salvation)*" **(Rom. 4:23-24).**

What did Paul mean when he used the term of Righteousness being *"imputed to Abraham"*?

The word *"impute"* or *"imputation"* means *"to attribute something to someone without cost or price;"* however, it doesn't mean that there hasn't been cost or price, but that someone else has paid it.

In the manner in which Paul uses the word, it means that the Lord imputes (freely gives) a perfect, pure, spotless Righteousness, actually, the Righteousness of God, to any person who evidences Faith in Christ and what He did at the Cross. It is given without works, or even merit, but simply on the basis of Faith.

WHY DID GOD CHOOSE THIS METHOD REGARDING RIGHTEOUSNESS?

As far as we know, there was no other way for it to be done. If man were obligated to pay the price, he simply could not do such. In fact, the idea of man qualifying himself for the Righteousness of God is so beyond our comprehension as to be incomprehensible. So, if man is to be Saved, God can only award Salvation on this basis. Paul said:

"**For by Grace** *(the Goodness of God)* **are you Saved through Faith** *(Faith in Christ, with the Cross ever as its Object);* **and that not of yourselves** *(none of this is of us,* *but all is of Him)*: *it is* **the Gift of God** *(anytime the word 'Gift' is used, God is speaking of His Son and His Substitutionary Work on the Cross, which makes all of this possible)*:

"Not of works *(man cannot merit Salvation, irrespective what he does)*, **lest any man should boast** *(boast in his own ability and strength; we are allowed to boast only in the Cross [Gal. 6:14])*" **(Eph. 2:8-9).**

The conclusion of all of this is that God declares the guilty righteous on the principal of Faith as opposed to works; and that He never Saved men on any other principal.

JUSTIFICATION BY WORKS AND JUSTIFICATION BY FAITH

The doctrine of Justification by works generates religious pride—that of Justification by Faith produces contrition and humility. In the matter of Justification, Faith and works are opposite and irreconcilable—as opposed as Grace and debt. Since God declares ungodly men righteous (Vs. 5), works cannot in any sense furnish a ground for Justification and, hence, the first step towards Salvation on the part of a sinner is to humble himself and accept the Divine pronouncement that he is *"ungodly."* Then, the second and concluding step is to repose Faith in Him Who justifies the ungodly. Nothing gives more glory to God than human beings simply believing Him. Justification is not necessarily a change in character but a declaration by God as to the Believer's standing before Him. It is objective. On the other hand, Sanctification affects character and is, in fact, subjective.

THE CROSS

"Who was delivered for our offences *(had to do with Jesus dying on the Cross for our sins; He had no sins)*, **and was raised again for our Justification** *(we were raised* *with Him in Newness of Life [Rom. 6:4-5])"* **(Rom. 4:25).**

Paul ascribes expiatory value to the Death and Blood of Christ: in the sense it is true the Work of Christ was finished on the Cross. But Paul never thought of that by itself: he always thought of Christ only as the Crucified Risen One Who had died, and Who had the virtue of His Atoning Death ever in Him. It should be obvious that without the Resurrection, there would have been no Atonement; however, the Resurrection was never in doubt. Satan, all of his demons, and all fallen Angels, were totally and completely defeated at the Cross (Col. 2:14-15). Sin was the legal right that Satan had to hold man captive; however, with all sin atoned, which Jesus did at the Cross, that legal right was removed from the Evil One. Now, if anyone remains in bondage to sin of any nature, it is because he isn't following Christ's Prescribed Order of Victory. If there had been left one sin unatoned, Jesus could not have been raised from the dead because the wages of sin is death (Rom. 6:23). But due to the fact that He atoned for all sin, past, present, and future, at least for all who will believe, this removed Satan's legal rights. Now, if he holds someone in bondage, it is by their consent, whether they understand such or not.

> **"Therefore being justified by Faith** *(this is the only way one can be justified; refers to Faith in Christ and what He did at the Cross)***, we have peace with God** *(justifying peace)* **through our Lord Jesus Christ** *(what He did at the Cross)***"** **(Rom. 5:1).**

In reading Verse 1, we must understand that there is a difference between having *"peace with God"* and having the *"peace of God"* in the heart. The first has to do with Justification, the second with Sanctification. The first is the result of a legal standing, the second, the result of the work of the Holy Spirit. The first is static, never fluctuates, never changes, the second changes from hour to hour. The first, every Christian has, the second, every Christian may have. The first, every Christian has as a result of Justification. What sense would there be in exhorting Christians to have peace when they already have it? The entire context is one of Justification. Paul does not preach the subject of Sanctification until Romans 5:12 where he speaks of positional Sanctification and Romans 6:1-8, where he deals with progressive Sanctification (Wuest[1]).

PEACE

The Greek word for peace is *"errene."* It means *"to bind together that which has been separated."* Our Lord made peace through the Blood of the Cross (Col. 1:20) in the sense that through His Atonement, He binds together again those, who by reason of their standing in the First Adam, had been separated from God, and who now through Faith in Him are bound again to God in their new standing in the *"Last Adam."* This is Justification.

Wuest said, *"The word 'with' is 'pros,' and means 'facing.' That is, a justified sinner has peace facing God. He stands in the Presence of God, guiltless and uncondemned and righteous in a Righteousness which God accepts, the Lord Jesus. Paul is here stating a fact, not exhorting the reader to do something. This 'Peace with God' comes 'through our Lord Jesus Christ,' meaning, 'what He did for us at the Cross.'"[2]*

ACCESS BY FAITH

"By Whom also we have access by Faith into this Grace *(we have access to the Goodness of God by Faith in Christ)* wherein we stand *(wherein alone we can stand)*, and rejoice in hope *(a hope that is guaranteed)* of the Glory of God *(our Faith in Christ always brings Glory to God; anything else brings glory to self, which God can never accept)*" (Rom. 5:2).

Williams says, *"The Grace wherein the Believer stands is that he is set before the Throne of God in a Righteousness that is spotless, in a life that is endless, and in a dignity that is glorious."*

Williams goes on to say, *"All the sins of the Believer are cancelled by God in the Death of Christ; God has consequently no sins to impute to the Believer. That matter has been eternally settled by Christ's sufficing Atonement; and His Resurrection attests the fact. There is, therefore, no longer any question as to the Believer's sins between him and God. That question was the one and only disturbing factor in relation to God, and Christ removed it according to the requirements of Divine Righteousness. He bore infinitely all the wrath of God due to sin and its fruit, and satisfied and vindicated all the claims of the Throne of God against man as a sinner, which He did at the Cross.*

"This great Salvation is, therefore, founded upon eternal Righteousness, and is the result of the Divine activity operating in Grace."[3]

Peace is the result of Justification and is consequently distinct from it. Faith enjoys this peace, and glories not only in Salvation and all that it embraces, but in its Divine Author, God Himself.

ACCESS AND THE CROSS

All of this given by the great Apostle presupposes the Cross of Christ. The Cross is what makes Justification possible, which in turn makes *"Peace with God"* an established fact. Let us say it again:

• The Lord Jesus Christ is the Source of all things we receive from God the Father (Jn. 14:6; Col. 2:10).

• The Cross of Christ is the Means, and the only Means, by which we receive all these good things from the Lord (Rom. 6:3-5; I Cor. 1:17-18, 23; 2:2).

• This demands that Who He is and What He has done, i.e., *"the Cross,"* ever be the Object of our Faith (Gal., Chpt. 5; 6:14).

• **The Holy Spirit superintends all of this and actually bars access to the Throne of God, if we try to come any way other than by the Cross of Christ (Eph. 2:13-18; Rom. 8:1-2, 11).**

THE LOVE OF GOD

"**And not only** *so*, **but we glory in tribulations also** *(in the fact that tribulations do not hurt us)*: **knowing that tribulation works patience** *(points to the characteristic of a man who is unswerved from his deliberate purpose and his loyalty to Faith, even by the greatest trials and sufferings)*;

"**And patience, experience** *(points to an end result)*; **and experience, hope** *(presents the natural product of an approved experience)*.

"**And hope makes not ashamed** *(in effect, tells us that this is not a false hope)*; **because the Love of God is shed abroad in our hearts** *(God's Love brings all of this about)* **by the Holy Spirit which is given unto us** *(all of this is wholly a work of the Holy Spirit)*" **(Rom. 5:3-5).**

WHAT DID PAUL MEAN?

Paul did not exult because of the tribulations themselves but because of their beneficial effect upon his Christian life. The idea is, the Saint of God must look at trials and difficulties as assets that develop our Christian character.

Of the words used, possibly *"experience"* **gives us a greater idea of what he is saying.**

The verbal form of experience is *"dokimazo,"* **and means** *"to put to the test for the purpose of approving, and finding that the person tested meets the specifications, to put one's approval upon him."* *"Patience"* **can be said to be the result of a Spiritual state, which has shown itself proven under trial.**

All of this is brought to bear in our Christian experience through and by the *"Love of God,"* **which has a set purpose in**

mind. In other words, the Lord is doing something with us and, therefore, every single thing that happens to a Believer is either caused by the Lord or allowed by the Lord. Of course, God most definitely does not cause one to sin, but, He does allow a Believer to do such, if the Believer is so foolish. But then, the Lord, if we allow Him to do so, will use that failure as an educational process in our lives, showing us why we went wrong and how we can benefit, not from the failure, but from Victory over the failure.

CHRIST DIED FOR THE UNGODLY

"For when we were yet without strength *(before we were Saved)*, in due time *(at the appointed time)* Christ died for the ungodly *(the entirety of humanity fell into this category)*.

"For scarcely for a Righteous man will one die *(not many would do such)*: yet peradventure for a good man some would even dare to die *(some few might)*.

"But God commend His Love toward us *(Christ dying for the ungodly is a proof of Love immeasurable)*, in that, while we were yet sinners, Christ died for us *(Jesus died for those who bitterly hate Him)*" **(Rom. 5:6-8).**

A DEMONSTRATION

All of this speaks of a demonstration of God's Love for mankind in that Christ died for the ungodly. It wasn't that man would have a difficult time addressing this problem, but rather that he could not address it at all. If God, Who Alone could do such, did not do this for man, man was forever doomed, and that meant not some, but rather all.

We must never forget that it was love that created man, therefore, love must redeem man.

Denney says, *"How greatly in these Passages is the utmost love of man surpassed by the Love of God."*

The phrase, *"But God commends His Love toward us,"* carries the idea of God *"continuously"* establishing His Love in that the Death of Christ remains as its most striking manifestation. The idea is, the Lord died for those who bitterly hated Him. That is beyond the comprehension of mankind. As the Holy Spirit through Paul said, there are some few times that one human being will die for another, and for various reasons; but there is no record of one human being dying for people who bitterly hated him.

JUSTIFIED BY HIS BLOOD

"Much more then *(if Christ died for us while we were yet sinners, how much more will He do for us now that we are Redeemed and, thereby, reconciled to Him!)*, **being now Justified by His Blood** *(we are justified now, and the Blood of Christ stands as the guarantee for that Justification)*, **we shall be saved from wrath through Him** *(the Wrath of God, which is always manifested against sin)*" **(Rom. 5:9).**

All of this tells us that our Salvation is based totally, not upon the pious emotion or personal moral merit of religious man, but upon the Person of Christ and His Atoning Sacrifice. This Divine Foundation is displayed in the words, *"His Blood,"* and *"Through Him."*

THE WRATH OF GOD

Modern Theology denies Christ's Atonement and God's Wrath. Both of these Foundation Truths of the Gospel are declared here to be fundamental. Those who believe there is no wrath to fear naturally seek no Saviour, and so cut themselves off from Salvation that is in Christ Alone.

The definite article appears before *"wrath"* in the original Text, making it read *"the wrath,"* which means it points out a particular wrath, which is that of the Lake of Fire, which is a manifestation of God's Wrath against sin.

RECONCILED TO GOD

"For if, when we were enemies, we were reconciled to God by the Death of His Son *(the only way we could be reconciled; this Verse shoots down the 'Jesus died spiritually' doctrine)*, much more, being reconciled, we shall be Saved by His Life *(does not speak of His Perfect Life, but rather the pouring out of His Life's Blood at Calvary)*.

"And not only *so*, but we also joy in God through our Lord Jesus Christ *(we are to boast of our Reconciliation to God, for it is a true confidence [I Cor. 1:31; II Cor. 10:17])*, by Whom we have now received the Atonement *(Reconciliation)*" (Rom. 5:10-11).

"Reconciled" in the Greek is *"katalasso,"* and means *"to change or exchange, meaning to reconcile those at variance."* It means, as it relates to the Lord, to change the relation of hostile parties into a relation of peace. In the Christian sense, the change in the relation of God and man is effected through Christ. Wuest[4] says this involves:

• *"A movement of God toward man with a view to break down man's hostility, to commend God's love and holiness to him, and to convince him of the enormity and the consequence of sin. It is God Who initiates this movement in the Person and Work of Jesus Christ.*

• *"There then has to be a corresponding movement on man's part toward God; yielding to the appeal of Christ's self-sacrificing love, laying aside man's enmity, renouncing his sin, and turning to God in Faith and Obedience.*

• *"There is then a consequent change of character in man: the covering, forgiving, cleansing of his sin; a thorough revolution in all of his dispositions and principles.*

• *"Then there is a corresponding change of relation on God's part, that being removed which alone rendered Him hostile to*

man, so that God can now receive him into fellowship and let
loose upon him all His fatherly love and Grace." (I Jn. 1:3, 7).
Thus, there is complete reconciliation.

Incidentally, when the word *"Atonement"* was used by the
King James translators, it then meant Reconciliation; however, the word *"Atonement"* presently carries the idea of satisfaction rather than of Reconciliation and, therefore, in the
manner in which it is presently understood, is inappropriate.

THE CENTRAL TRUTH OF THE GOSPEL

Christ's Obedience unto Death (Phil. 2:8), and that such
Death was a Sin-Offering (I Cor. 15:3), is the central Truth of
the Gospel. The effort to eliminate this Foundation Truth, or
to minimize it, or to substitute the Incarnation for it, is one of
the saddest features of what is presently termed *"a new way."*
The expiatory Sacrifice of Christ is the one and only and eternal ground upon which God can act in declaring ungodly men
righteous. Galatians 3:21, and many similar Divine declara-
tions, reveal the hopelessness of standing before God in a Righteousness, which He will not accept upon any other principal
than that of Faith in a Crucified Sin-Bearer.

Christ's Perfect Obedience to the Law of God formed His
Own Righteousness and gave virtue to His Sacrifice—for a
Sacrifice for sin must have neither spot nor blemish. It was not
the spotlessness of the Lamb, which made the Atonement, but
its outpoured Blood, i.e., it's surrendered Life, for the Blood is
the Life. The judgment pronounced upon sin being death, that
claim could only be vindicated and discharged by the suffering of death. Christ suffered that penalty, and in consequence,
saves the Believer from it.

THE DEATH OF CHRIST

If Christ's Obedience during His Life were man's obedience, then man stands as Christ stood, and consequently,
there was no reason man should die. In that case there was no

penalty, for if man fulfilled in Christ all Righteousness, there was no occasion for judgment. But the Scripture declares that Christ died for sinners, so that it is His Death that provides a spotless Righteousness for sinners who believe in Him; and it was His Obedience in life, which gave efficacy to His Suffering in death.

ADAM

"Wherefore, as by one man sin entered into the world *(by Adam)*, and death by sin *(both spiritual and physical death)*; and so death passed upon all men *(for all were in Adam)*, for that all have sinned *(all are born in sin, because of Adam's transgression)*:

"(For until the Law *(Law of Moses)* sin was in the world *(caused by Adam's Fall)*: but sin is not imputed when there is no Law *(before the Law was given, sin and its immediate Judgment were not imputed to the account of those who were then alive; but by the fact of Adam's Fall, they were still sinners)*.

"Nevertheless death reigned from Adam to Moses *(because of the sin nature that was in all men due to Adam's Fall)*, even over them who had not sinned after the similitude of Adam's transgression *(irrespective that all did not, in essence, commit high treason against God, as did Adam, they were still sinners)*, who is the figure of Him Who was to come *(Adam was the fountainhead of all sin and death, while Christ is the Fountainhead of all Redemption and Life)*" (Rom. 5:12-14).

Paul shows in these Passages that sin and death came from the First Adam, and Righteousness and Life, as stated, from the Last Adam.

SIN ORIGINATED WITH LUCIFER

In rebelling against God, sin originated with the Angel

Lucifer, who, due to his rebellion, contracted a sinful nature. Adam in his disobedience was the channel through which sin entered the human race. Through sin, death entered the race, physically and spiritually. In these Passages Adam is looked upon as the federal head of the human race, and that when he sinned, all of humanity sinned in him. It is Adam's initial sin that constituted him a sinner in which all human beings participated, and which brings death upon all. In other words, we could say, we are sinners, not because we have committed acts of sin, but because Adam sinned, and what he did was transferred to all of humanity.

DEATH

Now Paul proceeds to explain this. Until the Law of Moses was given, which defines sin, during that period between Adam and Moses, a time frame of about 2,500 years, sin was in the world. But, when there is no law, sin is not put to the account of the individual. Yet, people physically died from Adam to Moses just the same as they died after Moses, in other words, after the Law was given.

The idea is, irrespective of the fact that no sins were placed to the account of individuals during that time frame before Moses, still, individuals died, proving that this problem of death came about by reason of Adam's sin, meaning that when he sinned, all sinned. Adam is spoken of as *"the figure of Him Who was to come,"* namely Christ.

HOW IS ADAM A TYPE OF CHRIST?

He is a Type only in the sense that as all died in Adam, and because of Adam's sin, at the same time, all may live who exercise Faith in Christ and what He did for us at the Cross.

One might say that the one disobedience of the first man Adam assured death for all men, and the one obedience of the Second Man, the Lord Jesus Christ, secured life for all men, at least for all who will believe (Jn. 3:16).

THE OFFENCE

"But not as the offence, so also *is* the free gift *(would have probably been better translated, 'as the offence, much more the Free Gift'; the 'Free Gift' refers to Christ and what He did at the Cross, which addressed all that was lost at the Fall)*. For if through the offence of one *(Adam)* many be dead, much more the Grace of God *(proclaims the inexhaustible Power of this attribute)*, and the Gift by Grace *(presents Jesus as that 'Gift')*, *which is* by One Man, Jesus Christ *(what He did at the Cross)*, has abounded unto many *(this 'One Man,' the Lord Jesus Christ, nullified the offence of the 'one man' Adam)*" (Rom. 5:15).

"Offence" in the Greek is *"paraptoma,"* and means, *"a deviation from the right path."* Adam's original sin was the violation of the known Will of God.

Then Paul spoke of the *"free gift,"* which is *"a gift of Grace, a favor which one receives without merit of his own."* It refers here to the gift of Eternal Life, which comes solely through the Lord Jesus Christ.

Paul is introducing here a contrast. As Adam brought death by his failure into the entirety of the world, which passed to every human being, Grace is now introduced, which is the merit of Christ and, as well, is available to all. The idea is, as awful, as terrible, as horrifying, and as bad as was the sin that caused the downfall of man, Grace, the Grace of God, exhibited through Jesus Christ and what He did for us at the Cross, brought something about into this world infinitely better. While the *"better"* cannot be seen at present, most definitely it will ultimately come to pass.

The condemnation in Adam was for one sin, but the Justification in Christ is an absolution not only from all sins, but from the original germ of sin lodged in the nature of every child of Adam. Thus, Grace abounds in the abundance of the Gift of Righteousness—a Gift not only rich in character but rich in detail, for it leaves no one sin uncancelled and, not withstanding countless offences, sets the Believer before God in a Righteousness that is spotless.

THE FREE GIFT

"And not as *it was* by one who sinned, *so is* the Gift *(so much greater is the Gift)*: for the judgment *was* by one to condemnation *(by Adam)*, but the Free Gift *is* of many offences unto Justification *(cleanses from all sin)*" (Rom. 5:16).

Concerning this Verse, Wuest says, *"The contrast here is that of source. Out of the source of one sin, Adam's, God's judgment fell, resulting in the condemnation of all. Out of a source of many transgressions, as an occasion for the display of God's Grace, the free gift of Salvation came, resulting in Justification."[5]*

THE GIFT OF RIGHTEOUSNESS

"For if by one man's offence death reigned by one *(Adam's Fall)*; much more they which receive abundance of Grace *(not just 'Grace,' but 'Abundance of Grace'; all made possible by the Cross)* and of the Gift of Righteous-ness *(Righteousness is a Gift from God which comes solely through Jesus Christ, and is received by Faith)* shall reign in life by One, Jesus Christ.) *(This proclaims the Believer 'reigning,' even as death had reigned, but from a position of much greater power than that of death)*" (Rom. 5:17).

Death and life are contrasted here; but while it says *"death reigned"* over man, it does not say that life reigns over the Believer, for that would invest life with tyranny, but it says that the Believer reigns in life, and thus, the environment of freedom and liberty is preserved. This life is legally secured by the Life and Death of Christ.

JUSTIFICATION OF LIFE

"Therefore as by the offence of one *judgment came* upon all men to condemnation *(Judged by God to be lost)*; even so by the Righteousness of One *(Christ)* **the Free Gift came** upon all men unto Justification of Life *(received by simply believing in Christ and what He did at the Cross, which is the only answer for sin)*" **(Rom. 5:18).**

Once again, Paul uses contrast. Because of Adam's transgression, condemnation came upon all men, because in Adam, in a sense, was the procreation of all human beings.

To counteract what Adam had done, God would become Man, the Man Jesus Christ, and by His Righteousness, the Free Gift of Salvation, i.e., *"Justification of Life,"* comes upon all who believe.

THE OBEDIENCE OF ONE

"For as by one man's disobedience many were made sinners *(the 'many' referred to all)*, so by the obedience of One *(obedient unto death, even the death of the Cross [Phil. 2:8])* shall many be made Righteous *('many' refers to all who will believe)*" **(Rom. 5:19).**

Wuest says, *"Disobedience in the Greek is 'parakoe.' It is one of the nine words for sin in the New Testament. It describes the nature of Adam's first act of sin, the one act that plunged the entire race into sin with its accompanying degradation and misery."*[6] The word carries the idea of failing to listen when God is speaking. It need hardly be observed how continually in the Old Testament disobedience is described as a refusing to hear (Jer. 11:10; 35:17).

OBEDIENCE

On the other hand, *"obedience"* in the Greek is *"hupokoe,"* and means literally *"to hear."* The idea is that of a willing listening to authority. It implies obedience, compliance, and submission. The obedience here on the part of the Lord Jesus is spoken of in Hebrews 10:7, where He is quoted as saying to God the Father, *"Lo, I come, in the volume of the Book it is written of Me, to do Your will, O God."* The Father's Will was the Cross for the Son.

By the one act of Adam in disobeying God, the human race was constituted sinful, and this by the judicial act of God; likewise, by the one act of obedience of the Lord Jesus, all who believe are constituted Righteous, and this, as well, by the judicial act of God (Wuest[7]).

THE LAW OF MOSES

"Moreover the Law entered, that the offence might abound *(the Law of Moses, that the offence might be identified)*. But where sin abounded, Grace did much more abound *(where sin increased, Grace super-abounded, and then some on top of that)*" (Rom. 5:20).

The Law of Moses presented God's Standard of Righteousness. In fact, every righteous law in the world, and in every country, whatever it is, has as its source the *"Law of Moses,"* or referred to as the *"Law of God."* We speak of the moral part of the Law of Moses, i.e., *"the Ten Commandments"* (Ex., Chpt. 20).

The Law identified sin, declaring as to what kind of sin it was. When the Law was made available to the Jews, it encountered the flesh, which evoked its natural antagonism to God, and so, stimulated it into disobedience. It was meant to be this way in order to show man how depraved, how fallen, he actually was, which addressed his inability to properly serve God. So, as the offence multiplied, the need of Redemption, which was the purpose of allowing this by God, was intensified.

GRACE

What is Grace?

In simple terms, Grace is the Goodness of God extended to undeserving people. The idea of the phrase, *"but where sin abounded, Grace did much more abound,"* proclaims the fact that as bad as sin is, as destructive as sin is, it will not ultimately take best. The Grace of God, upon exhibited Faith by the individual, is greater than all sin. In other words, there is no sinner, and no matter how bad his sin, who cannot be Saved and, thereby, gloriously changed by the Power of God. Admittedly, the sinner doesn't deserve it and, in fact, can do nothing to deserve such, but upon simple Faith in Christ, this great super Grace will see to it that all sin is washed and cleansed by the precious shed Blood of the Lord Jesus Christ.

The Doctrine of Grace—especially that which declares Justification to be by Faith apart from works—excites the enmity of the natural heart, and this enmity expresses itself in rebellion against God's Ways.

The Bible declares that man is absolutely ruined by sin and wholly unable to restore himself to God's favor. Man's gospel teaches that man is not wholly ruined, that he can by self-culture merit God's Favor and secure his own happiness. Such is not to be because such cannot be.

ETERNAL LIFE

"That as sin has reigned unto death *(sin reigns as an absolute monarch in the being of the unredeemed),* even so might Grace reign through Righteousness unto Eternal Life by Jesus Christ our Lord. *(Grace reigns unto Life, but it reigns 'through Righteousness,' i.e., because of God's Righteous Judgment of sin at Calvary executed in the Person of His Son Jesus Christ)*" (Rom. 5:21).

Sin *"reigning unto death"* proclaims the total depravity of the human being. It speaks of the total depraved nature of the unsaved person. This means that sin reigns as an absolute monarch in his being.

All of this means that within himself, and I speak of fallen man, he cannot reach out for God, cannot know anything plausible about God, and cannot understand God's Word. So, if Salvation is to be effected, it must come from an outside source, which it most definitely does.

The Word of God is delivered in some form and through that Word, Holy Spirit conviction rests upon the individual who hears the Word and, thereby, opens the way of Salvation; however, still, such an individual must will to accept Christ. He will not be forced. It is always, *"whosoever will . . ."* (Rev. 22:17).

But, if the person says *"yes"* to the Lord, the Grace of God will immediately bestow Righteousness unto such a person, guaranteeing *"Eternal Life by Jesus Christ our Lord."*

Every person in the world, and irrespective as to whom they might be, or how deep in sin they might be, has the capacity to say *"yes"* or *"no"* to the Lord, upon Holy Spirit conviction being brought to bear.

If the answer of the ruined sinner is in the affirmative, Grace is then supplied in superabundance in order that it might reign as king through Righteousness, resulting in Eternal Life. This Eternal Life, in its application to the believing sinner, as stated, is made possible solely through the Lord Jesus' Work on the Cross.

Paul's great Gospel given to him by Jesus Christ can be wrapped up in the following, which we have already stated. It is:

• Jesus Christ is the Source of all things we receive from God (Jn. 1:1; 14:6; Col. 2:10).

• The Cross of Christ is the Means by which these good and wonderful things are given to us (Rom. 6:3-5; I Cor. 1:17-18, 23; 2:2).

• This demands our Faith exclusively in the Cross of Christ as its Object (Gal., Chpt. 5; 6:14).

* The Holy Spirit oversees and superintends all of this (Rom. 8:1-2, 11; Eph. 2:13-18).

"Jesus, Master, Whose I am,
"Purchased Thine Alone to be,
"By Your Blood, O spotless Lamb,
"Shed so willingly for me,
"Let my heart be all Your Own,
"Let me live to You Alone."

"Other lords have long held sway;
"Now, Your Name Alone to bear,
"Your dear Voice Alone obey,
"Is my daily, hourly prayer:
"Whom have I in Heaven but Thee?
"Nothing else my joy can be."

"Jesus, Master, Whom I serve,
"Though so feebly and so ill,
"Strengthen and in heart and nerve,
"All Your Bidding to fulfill;
"Open You my eyes to see,
"All the work You have for me."

"Jesus, Master, will You use,
"One who owes You more than all?
"As You will! I would not choose;
"Only let me hear Your Call.
"Jesus, let me always be,
"In Your Service, glad and free."

PAUL
THE APOSTLE

CHAPTER FIVE

What Is The New Covenant?

WHAT IS THE NEW COVENANT?

In point of reference, the New Covenant is Jesus Christ. More particularly, one might say it is *"Jesus Christ and Him Crucified"* (I Cor. 1:23).

Furthermore, the New Covenant, unlike any and every other Covenant that God has ever made with man, cannot be broken. It is absolutely impossible for it to be marred, weakened, or broken. So, how is this possible?

A Covenant, of necessity, is an agreement between two or more parties. In this case, it is between God and man. Every other Covenant which God has made with man, we find that man has broken it almost before the proverbial ink is dry. So, how is it possible that the New Covenant, which is a Covenant between God and man, cannot be broken? We can certainly understand how that God always keeps His Promises, but knowing the frailty of human flesh, the question looms large as to how this Covenant, considering that man is a part of it, cannot be broken?

JESUS CHRIST

The answer to this question, as complicated as it might seem, is actually very simple. It cannot be broken simply because it is all in Jesus Christ. He is both God and man. Paul referred to him as the *"Last Adam,"* and the *"Second Man."* In effect, Jesus Christ was and is our Representative Man. He did for us what we could not do for ourselves.

For instance, in His Life and Living, He kept the Law perfectly in every respect, not sinning even one time in word, thought, or deed. He did it all for us! And then when it came time to address the broken Law, of which all of us were guilty, He offered Himself as a Sacrifice, in effect, a Perfect Sacrifice, on the Cross of Calvary, shedding His Life's Blood, paying a price that we could not pay, and which was accepted in totality by God the Father. As it regards the broken Law, for all who will believe, the slate was wiped clean. Paul addressed this by saying:

THE FULLNESS OF THE GODHEAD BODILY

"Beware lest any man spoil you through philosophy and vain deceit *(anything that pulls the Believer away from the Cross is not of God)*, after the tradition of men *(anything that is not of the Cross if of men)*, after the rudiments of the world, and not after Christ. *(If it's truly after Christ, then it's after the Cross.)*

"For in Him *(Christ)* dwells all the fullness of the Godhead bodily. *(This is Godhead as to essence. Christ is the completion and the fullness of Deity, and in Him the Believer is complete.)*"

HE IS THE HEAD OF ALL
PRINCIPALITY AND POWER

"And you are complete in Him *(the satisfaction of every spiritual want is found in Christ, made possible by the Cross)*, which is the Head of all principality and power *(His Headship extends not only over the Church, which voluntarily serves Him, but over all forces that are opposed to Him as well [Phil. 2:10-11])*:

"In Whom also you are circumcised with the Circumcision made without hands *(that which is brought about by the Cross [Rom. 6:3-5])*, in putting off the body of the sins of the flesh by the Circumcision of Christ *(refers to the old carnal nature that is defeated by the Believer placing his Faith totally in the Cross, which gives the Holy Spirit latitude to work)*:

"Buried with Him in Baptism *(does not refer to Water Baptism, but rather to the Believer baptized into the death of Christ, which refers to the Crucifixion and Christ as our substitute [Rom. 6:3-4])*, wherein also you are risen with *Him* through the Faith of the operation of God, Who

has raised Him from the dead. *(This does not refer to our future physical Resurrection, but to that Spiritual Resurrection from a sinful state into Divine Life. We died with Him, we are buried with Him, and we rose with Him [Rom. 6:3-5], and herein lies the secret to all Spiritual Victory.)*"

THE LAW WAS SATISFIED

"**And you, being dead in your sins and the uncircumcision of your flesh** *(speaks of spiritual death [i.e., 'separation from God'], which sin does!)*, **has He quickened together with Him** *(refers to being made Spiritually alive, which is done through being 'Born-Again')*, **having forgiven you all trespasses** *(the Cross made it possible for all manner of sins to be forgiven and taken away)*;

"**Blotting out the handwriting of Ordinances that was against us** *(pertains to the Law of Moses, which was God's Standard of Righteousness that man could not reach)*, **which was contrary to us** *(Law is against us, simply because we are unable to keep its precepts, no matter how hard we try)*, **and took it out of the way** *(refers to the penalty of the Law being removed)*, **nailing it to His Cross** *(the Law with its decrees was abolished in Christ's Death, as if Crucified with Him)*;"

TRIUMPH

"***And* having spoiled principalities and powers** *(Satan and all of his henchmen were defeated at the Cross by Christ atoning for all sin; sin was the legal right Satan had to hold man in captivity; with all sin atoned, he has no more legal right to hold anyone in bondage)*, **He** *(Christ)* **made a show of them openly** *(what Jesus did at the Cross was in the face of the whole universe)*, **triumphing over them in it.** *(The triumph is complete and it was all done for us, meaning we can walk in power and perpetual Victory* *due to the Cross)"* **(Col. 2:8-15).**

WAS IT WHO HE WAS OR WHAT HE DID?

Generally those who ask the question, *"Was it Who He was or what He did?"* are in some way denigrating the Cross of Christ. They are claiming that it is insignificant. The answer to that question is simple!

It was both Who He was, and what He did!

There is no one else that could have carried out this great Sacrifice but the Lord Jesus Christ. No human being who has ever been born could have done such a thing. Man, due to Adam's Fall in the Garden of Eden, is born in original sin. He is born with the Adamic nature, which can be referred to as the *"sin nature."* As such, he is polluted, to say the least. And, as such, our Lord said, if man is to be Saved, he must be *"Born-Again"* (Jn. 3:3). Thus, man is shot down before he even begins.

So, if man were to be Saved, God would have to save man, because He Alone could perform this task. Therefore, God became Man, the Man Christ Jesus, and did so for the purpose of going to the Cross. Please understand this:

WHO HE WAS

Jesus Christ is God and, in fact, always has been God. As God, He had no beginning, was not created, was not born, was not made, and was not formed, but has always been. Admittedly, that is beyond the comprehension of a human being. When God became man, the Lord Jesus Christ, He never ceased to be God. As someone has capably said:

"While Jesus Christ laid aside the expression of His Deity, never for a moment did He lose possession of His Deity." He was very God and very Man. But yet, as the Man, Jesus Christ, He never used His Powers of Deity, not even one time, in the performing of Miracles and all the great things He did. He did

all of these things by the Power of the Holy Spirit. As God, no anointing was needed to do anything, but as a Man, the Man Christ Jesus, our Lord definitely needed the anointing to heal the sick, and to do all the great things that He did. The Scripture says:

"How God anointed Jesus of Nazareth with the Holy Spirit and with Power *(as a Man, Christ needed the Holy Spirit, as we certainly do as well! in fact, everything He did was by the Power of the Spirit)*: Who went about doing good *(everything He did was good)*, and healing all who were oppressed of the Devil *(only Christ could do this, and Believers can do such only as Christ empowers them by the Spirit)*; for God was with Him *(God is with us only as we are 'with Him')*" (Acts 10:38).

But, as we have stated, only as God, as glorious as that is, still, no souls were Saved, no lives were changed, and no Redemption was affected. To be sure, considering that God can do all things, He didn't have to go to the Cross; however, the Godhead definitely determined that the Cross was the Way in which man would be redeemed.

WHAT HE DID!

• While the Deity of Christ was absolutely necessary, that is if man were to be redeemed, still, had it ended there, not a single soul would have ever been Saved.

• While the Conception of Christ in the womb of Mary, without the benefit of man and decreed by the Holy Spirit, was absolutely necessary, still, had it stopped there, not a single soul would have been Saved.

• While the Perfect Life of Christ was absolutely necessary in that He did not sin one single time in word, thought, or deed, still, had it ended there, not a single soul would have been Saved.

• While the Miracles that Christ performed in healing all manner of diseases and even raising the dead were absolutely necessary, still, had it ended there, not a single soul would have been Saved.

• For man to be Saved, God had to become man, had to be born of the Virgin Mary, had to live a spotless, Perfect Life, and had to be a Miracle Worker, but for that which brought about Redemption, that which made it possible for man to be redeemed from sin and death, Jesus Christ had to go to the Cross. It was at the Cross that the sin debt was forever paid. It was at the Cross that all sin was atoned. It was at the Cross where Satan, demon spirits, and fallen Angels were totally and completely defeated, and done so by every sin being atoned. With sin being the legal means that Satan had to hold man captive, and with that legal means removed, which it was at the Cross, Satan has no more right to hold anyone in bondage.

All of this is why the Apostle Paul said to the Church at Corinth, and to all of us as well:

"For I determined not to know anything among you *(with purpose and design, Paul did not resort to the knowledge or philosophy of the world regarding the preaching of the Gospel)*, save Jesus Christ, and Him Crucified *(that and that alone is the Message, which will save the sinner, set the captive free, and give the Believer perpetual Victory)*" (I Cor. 2:2).

So, while it was Who He was, which was absolutely necessary, still, it was what He did, and we refer to the Cross, which set the captive free. Let me say it again!

Jesus Christ is God and, in fact, has always been God and ever will be God; however, it took the Cross with the price paid there for man to be redeemed and, thereby, given Eternal Life. If we denigrate the Cross in any way, if we belittle the Cross in any way, or if we make it secondary in any way, we blaspheme!

THE CROSS OF CHRIST,
THE VERY FIRST DOCTRINE

To begin with, it is perfectly proper to refer to the New Covenant as a *"Doctrine,"* inasmuch as it was referred to as such by the Holy Spirit. Through Paul the Spirit said:

> "But God be thanked, that you were the servants of sin *(slaves to the sin nature, what we were before we were Saved),* but you have obeyed from the heart that form of Doctrine *(Jesus Christ and Him Crucified; understanding that all things come to the Believer from God by the means of the Cross)* which was delivered you *(the Lord gave this 'form of Doctrine' to Paul, and he gave it to us in his Epistles)*" **(Rom. 6:17).**

FORM OF DOCTRINE

Incidentally, the word *"form"* in the Greek is *"tupos,"* and means, *"a shape, a model, a fashion, a figure, a pattern."*

To be sure, this is a pattern or form drawn off by the Holy Spirit, which means that it must not be tampered with, must not be changed, and must not be added to or taken from. This means it is an exact Doctrine, and in every respect.

In effect, it has to do with a *"blueprint."* If the Blueprint is followed, as it must be, the intended result will be achieved and done so 100%. The problem with the modern church, and actually, it is a problem that has always existed, man, and especially religious man, seeks to change the form, i.e., *"deviate from the blueprint."* Momentarily we will deal with that which is the blueprint, relating as to exactly what it means.

THE CROSS OF CHRIST,
THE VERY FIRST DOCTRINE

By the very first Doctrine, we are referring to that which

the Godhead has established first of all. Peter gave us this information:

"Forasmuch as you know that you were not redeemed with corruptible things, *as* silver and gold *(presents the fact that the most precious commodities [silver and gold] could not redeem fallen man)*, from your vain conversation *(vain lifestyle)* received by tradition from your fathers *(speaks of original sin that is passed on from father to child at conception)*;

THE CROSS OF CHRIST

"But with the Precious Blood of Christ *(presents the payment, which proclaims the poured out Life of Christ on behalf of sinners)*, as of a Lamb without blemish and without spot *(speaks of the lambs offered as substitutes in the Old Jewish economy; the Death of Christ was not an execution or assassination, but rather a Sacrifice; the Offering of Himself presented a Perfect Sacrifice, for He was Perfect in every respect [Ex. 12:5])*:"

FOREORDAINED BEFORE THE FOUNDATION OF THE WORLD

"Who verily was foreordained before the foundation of the world *(refers to the fact that God, in His Omniscience, knew He would create man, man would fall, and man would be redeemed by Christ going to the Cross; this was all done before the universe was created; this means the Cross of Christ is the Foundation Doctrine of all Doctrine, referring to the fact that all Doctrine must be built upon that Foundation, or else it is specious)*, but was manifest in these last times for you *(refers to the invisible God Who, in the Person of the Son, was made visible to human eyesight by assuming a human body and human limitations)*" (I Pet. 1:18-20).

ALL FALSE DOCTRINE HAS ITS ORIGIN IN
AN IMPROPER UNDERSTANDING OF THE CROSS

Due to the fact that it is so important, let us state it again:

Inasmuch, even as the Holy Spirit proclaimed through Peter, that the Doctrine of the Cross was actually formed in the Mind of the Godhead from before the foundation of the world, this tells us that as far as Redemption of mankind is concerned, the Doctrine of Christ Crucified is the very first Doctrine formed. That being the case, this means that it is the single most important Doctrine in the entirety of the Word of God. It also means that every Bible Doctrine is based squarely upon the Foundation of the Cross of Christ.

If men come up with a doctrine, any kind of doctrine, that is not based squarely on the Cross, this means that doctrine is spurious. In fact, this is the way all false doctrine begins. It is because the Doctrine of the Cross is ignored, or else denied, or else given an improper place. In other words, every false doctrine has its beginning because of a misinterpretation, a denial, or a misunderstanding of the Cross of Christ. Understanding that, we surely should understand how so very important this *"form of Doctrine"* actually is.

THE MEANING OF THE DOCTRINE OF THE CROSS

We find the core meaning of the Doctrine of the Cross in the Sixth Chapter of Romans. In the first two verses, even as we shall see, the Holy Spirit through Paul tells us that the problem is sin. Whatever label may be attached, whatever other types of claims may be made, still, the Holy Spirit has said that the problem is sin. It doesn't matter whether it's the redeemed or the unredeemed, the problem is sin.

And then, in Verses 3 through 5 of Romans, Chapter 6, we are given the solution to the sin problem, which is the Cross of Christ. But, more particularly, in these three verses, we are told how that we literally become a part of this *"form of Doctrine,"* which is probably explained better than ever by the words *"in Christ."* But it refers to being *"in Christ"* by virtue of His Death, Burial and Resurrection. In these three particulars, we are placed in Christ in His Death, in Christ in His Burial, and in Christ in His Resurrection. In fact, the entirety of the Sixth Chapter of Romans is given over by the Holy Spirit to inform us as Believers as to how to live for God. If one doesn't understand this great Sixth Chapter, then simply put, one doesn't understand how to live for the Lord. To be sure, such can cause all types of problems.

Now, let's go straight to the Text, and we will copy verbatim from THE EXPOSITOR'S STUDY BIBLE, Text and Notes.

THE PROBLEM IS SIN

"**What shall we say then?** *(This is meant to direct attention to Rom. 5:20.)* **Shall we continue in sin, that Grace may abound?** *(Just because Grace is greater than sin doesn't mean that the Believer has a license to sin.)*

"**God forbid** *(presents Paul's answer to the question, 'Away with the thought, let not such a thing occur')*. **How shall we, who are dead to sin** *(dead to the sin nature)*, **live any longer therein?** *(This portrays what the Believer is now in Christ)*" **(Rom. 6:1-2).**

In the Seeker Sensitive churches, so-called, sin is never mentioned. The same can be said for the Purpose Driven Life church as well. It is said that if sin is mentioned, this will be an offense to people. So, to keep from offending anyone, sin is never mentioned.

On the other side of the spectrum, the Word of Faith people, which in reality is no faith at all, claims that if sin is mentioned by the preacher, it will create a sin consciousness in the people, which will cause them to sin. So, according to what they say, if sin is never mentioned, then people won't sin.

It's strange that the Apostle Paul, and above all, the Holy Spirit, didn't have access to this great information. In fact, Paul mentioned sin 17 times in the Sixth Chapter of Romans alone. Let us say it again, the problem is sin! Denying it won't solve the problem, and neither will ignoring it solve the problem. Man is a sinner. As such, he desperately needs a Redeemer. There is only one Redeemer, and that is the Lord Jesus Christ. Let us put it in this fashion:

• The only way to God is through Jesus Christ (Jn. 14:6).
• The only way to Jesus Christ is through the Cross (Rom. 6:3-5).
• The only way to the Cross is a denial of self (Lk. 9:23).

THE CROSS OF CHRIST

"Know you not, that so many of us as were baptized into Jesus Christ *(plainly says that this Baptism is into Christ and not water [I Cor. 1:17; 12:13; Gal. 3:27; Eph. 4:5; Col. 2:11-13])* were baptized into His Death? *(When Christ died on the Cross, in the Mind of God, we died with Him; in other words, He became our Substitute, and our identification with Him in His Death gives us all the benefits for which He died; the idea is that He did it all for us!)"* (Rom. 6:3).

BAPTISM

Unfortunately, most Christians, even, by far, most preachers, think that Paul is speaking of Water Baptism in Romans 6:3; consequently, knowing they have already been baptized, most Christians discount this Chapter, which means they little understand what Paul is really saying. That is tragic considering that one could say that the Sixth Chapter of Romans is the central Chapter of the entirety of the Word of God.

Some 99% of the Bible or more is given over to telling Believers how to live for God. And this Sixth Chapter of Romans brings it all together. But due to misunderstanding the word *"baptize,"* most never understand the phenomenal Truth that is given to us in this particular Chapter.

If one looks in Strong's Concordance, one will see that the word *"baptize"* can be used in either a literal or figurative sense. Let me give you an example how the Word of God uses the word in both senses.

John the Baptist said, *"I indeed baptize you with water unto Repentance (here, the word 'baptize' is used in its literal sense): but He (Christ) Who comes after me is mightier than I, Whose Shoes I am not worthy to bear: He shall baptize you (here it is used in the figurative sense) with the Holy Spirit, and with fire"* (Mat. 3:11).

When the believing sinner accepts Christ, which is done by Faith in Christ, at that moment, in the Mind of God, such a person is placed in Christ *"into His Death."* It is like the person dies with Christ. At least that's the way the Lord sees it. This is the reason the Cross is so very, very important!

BURIED WITH HIM AND RAISED
IN NEWNESS OF LIFE

"Therefore we are buried with Him by baptism into death *(not only did we die with Him, but we were buried with Him as well, which means that all the sin and transgression of the past were buried; when they put Him in the Tomb, they put all of our sins into that Tomb as well):* that like as Christ was raised up from the dead by the Glory of the Father, even so we also should walk in newness of life *(we died with Him, we were buried with Him, and His Resurrection was our Resurrection to a 'Newness of Life')*" (Rom. 6:4).

LIVING FOR GOD

Whenever we accepted Christ, as stated, in the Mind of God,

we died with Christ, we were buried with Christ, and we were raised with Christ that *"we also should walk in Newness of Life."*

Even though we did not die physically on that Cross, and even though Jesus died in our place, still, Faith exhibited in Him and what He did for us at the Cross, gives us all for which He died, which was and is the intention of the Crucifixion. Now don't misunderstand, Christ is not still on a Cross. As well, He is not dying again and again. In fact, He is seated presently at the Right Hand of the Father, and Spiritually speaking, we are seated with Christ in heavenly places (Eph. 2:6).

But the one Sacrifice of Christ was of such magnitude that anyone and everyone who evidences Faith in Him receives the benefits for which He died. One must ever understand that everything Christ did, He did it for us. He did not do it for Himself, because He did not need such. He did not do it for Angels, or anything else, but only for sinners.

RESURRECTION LIFE

"For if we have been planted together *(with Christ)* in the likeness of His Death *(Paul proclaims the Cross as the instrument through which all Blessings come; consequently, the Cross must ever be the Object of our Faith, which gives the Holy Spirit latitude to work within our lives)*, we shall be also *in the likeness* of *His* Resurrection *(we can have the 'likeness of His Resurrection,' i.e., 'live this Resurrection Life,' only as long as we understand the 'likeness of His Death,' which refers to the Cross as the Means by which all of this is done)*" (Rom. 6:5).

WHAT DO WE MEAN BY RESURRECTION LIFE?

Paul is not speaking here of the Resurrection, which will take place when the Trump sounds. He is speaking of the Victory that we now have as a result of the Death of Christ and our Faith in His Finished Work. Every Believer is meant to have *"Resurrection Life,"* but it must be understood, this can only be had if we first of all understand that it has been made possible by His Death.

"If we have been planted together in the likeness of His Death," meaning that we understand why He died, then *"we shall be also in the likeness of His Resurrection."* However, this is all predicated on our understanding the veracity of the Cross of Christ.

Many Christians talk about Resurrection Life, but they don't understand that it is predicated solely on the Death of Christ. It is the Cross of Christ, and this we must ever understand, that makes everything possible.

THE SIN NATURE MADE INEFFECTIVE

"Knowing this, that our old man is Crucified with *Him (all that we were before conversion)*, that the body of sin might be destroyed *(the power of sin broken)*, that henceforth we should not serve sin *(the guilt of sin is removed at conversion, because the sin nature no longer rules within our hearts and lives)*" (Rom. 6:6).

A BETTER TRANSLATION

The phrase, *"That the body of sin might be destroyed,"* would have been better translated, *"that the body of sin might be made ineffective."*

The Greek word for *"destroyed"* is *"katargeo,"* and means, *"to destroy or to make of no effect."* We know from the way Paul addresses the sin nature in the balance of the Chapter that it is not destroyed, but rather made ineffective at conversion. If it were destroyed, it would not be possible for it to be revived again; however, if it is made ineffective, it can be revived, which, of course, is what Paul teaches.

The *"old man,"* as Paul uses the term, is what we were, our life and living before we came to Christ. That *"old man"* was

"Crucified with Him." In fact, it could be no other way.

The *"old man"* cannot be improved, it must die! The type of death it must die cannot be brought about by mankind, only by Christ, and only by what Christ did at the Cross. That's what Paul was talking about when he said we *"were baptized into His Death."*

Unfortunately, the greater pastime of modern America is self-improvement. It once was baseball, but now it's an emphasis on self. While we are a self, and will ever be a self, and while it is obvious that self definitely needs improvement, the truth is, self cannot improve self. There is no such thing as moral evolution. And yet, man keeps trying, and religious man most of all! In fact, the most popular preachers presently over television are those who constantly acclaim the improvement of self. In other words, they claim to know how to improve self by eliminating bad habits and developing good habits. Unfortunately, the problem is far worse than that. The *"old man"* is totally and completely corrupted. That's the reason when the believing sinner comes to Christ, *"he is made a new creation: old things are passed away; behold, all things are become new"* (II Cor. 5:17).

But even then, the Believer finds the *"old man"* trying to come alive again, trying to usurp authority over the *"new man."* The Believer will find this is a constant struggle never ending. There is only one solution for it, and we mean only one.

THE CROSS OF CHRIST

Jesus addressed this very thing by saying:

". . . If any man will come after Me (the criteria for Discipleship), let him deny himself (not asceticism as many think, but rather that one denies one's own will-power, self-will, strength, and ability, depending totally on Christ), and take up his cross (the benefits of the Cross, looking exclusively to what Jesus did there to meet our every need) daily (this is so important, our looking to the

Cross; that we must renew our Faith in what Christ has done for us, even on a daily basis, for Satan will ever try to move us away from the Cross as the Object of our Faith, which always spells disaster), **and follow Me** *(Christ can be followed only by the Believer looking to the Cross, understanding what it accomplished, and by that means alone [Rom. 6:3-5, 11, 14; 8:1-2, 11; I Cor. 1:17-18, 21, 23; 2:2; Gal. 6:14; Eph. 2:13-18; Col. 2:14-15])*.

"For whosoever will save his life shall lose it *(try to live one's life outside of Christ and the Cross)***: but whosoever will lose his life for My Sake, the same shall save it** *(when we place our Faith entirely in Christ and the Cross, looking exclusively to Him, we have just found 'more Abundant Life' [Jn. 10:10])***" (Lk. 9:23-24).**

THE HOLY SPIRIT

The Holy Spirit Alone can develop us, thereby, making us what we ought to be. And just because we are Born-Again, meaning that the Holy Spirit now lives within our physical and Spiritual lives, still, we hinder Him greatly, not understanding how He Works.

The Holy Spirit works exclusively within the parameters of the Finished Work of Christ (Rom. 8:2). In fact, He will not work outside of those parameters. He doesn't demand very much of us, but He most definitely does demand one thing, and that is that our Faith be exclusively in Christ and the Cross. This being done, it means that we understand that our Source is the Lord Jesus Christ, while the Means by which He gives us all things is the Cross. Only then can the Holy Spirit function as He desires to do within our hearts and lives, developing us as He so desires. It cannot be done any other way.

SERVING THE SIN NATURE

Paul said in Romans, Chapter 6, Verse 6, **"That henceforth** *we should not serve sin."* This refers to serving the sin nature. What did he mean by that?

If we do not function God's Way, which means that we place our Faith exclusively in Christ and the Cross, to be sure, the sin nature will have a revival in our lives, actually functioning somewhat as it did, or even worse, before we were Saved. At this very moment, there are millions of Christians all over the world who are struggling with something in their lives, and they are losing the struggle. As Paul said in Romans 7:15, they don't really understand what is happening to them. Many of these Believers are doing everything within their power to live for God to the best of their ability. But still, they are plagued by some vice over which they seemingly have no control. As someone once said, *"They rebuke the Devil, but he don't buke."*

The reason is, they are trying to defeat this thing by their own strength. They do not understand that, considering they're using the Name of Jesus, are quoting Scriptures, and doing anything and everything else they know, but, if the truth be known, it is all to no avail. By placing their faith in something other than Christ and the Cross, this limits, as stated, the Holy Spirit as to what He can do in their lives, which means they are failing and will continue to fail. In fact, the situation in such circumstances will continue to get worse and worse, no matter how much they love the Lord.

TREATING THE SYMPTOMS OF SIN

The modern church little knows what to do with these situations. They recommend a psychologist, who can only make the matter worse, or they rather treat the symptoms. In other words, what the individual has done and is doing that is wrong, no doubt, terribly wrong, is not the real cause of the problem. It's just a symptom of what the real problem is. And what is the real problem?

The real problem is a wrong Object of Faith. That Object must be the Cross of Christ. And, as well, our Faith must be maintained in the Cross of Christ. It must not move elsewhere. And please believe me, Satan will do everything within his power to move your faith to other things. And he doesn't too very much care what the other things are, just as long as it's not the Cross of Christ.

The reader must understand that everything we receive from the Lord, and I mean everything, comes from Christ as the Source and the Cross as the Means. If we divorce either one from the other, we are left with *"another Jesus"* (II Cor. 10:4).

DEAD

"For he who is dead *(He was our Substitute, and in the Mind of God, we died with Him upon Believing Faith)* is freed from sin *(set free from the bondage of the sin nature)*" (Rom. 6:7).

As we have stated, the *"old man"* cannot be improved. He had to die, and die he did, on the Cross of Calvary. Of course, and as is understood, this was all by Faith. This means it is not a physical thing, as should be obvious, but rather that which is Spiritual. The moment the *"old man"* died, he was set free from the dominion of the sin nature. In fact, before anyone gives his heart to Christ, looking back to his unsaved state, he was ruled by the sin nature 24 hours a day. But now, as stated, that dominion is broken. As long as we keep our Faith in Christ and the Cross, the dominion of the sin nature will remain broken. Now, this doesn't mean that Satan will cease all of his temptation, nor does it mean we'll never have another problem. Such as that does not exist.

Satan is going to continue, trying his best to come up with new means and ways to trip us up, but, above all, to get us to transfer our Faith from the Cross of Christ to other things. This is where the *"good fight of Faith"* comes in. Admittedly, it is a *"fight,"* but it is a *"good fight,"* because it is the *"right fight"* (I Tim. 6:12).

Most Christians, sad to say, are fighting the *"wrong fight."*

FIGHTING SIN?

There's really nothing in the Bible that tells us to fight sin per se. While it is a *"fight"* and, as well, *"war,"* still, as stated, the *"fight"* and the *"war"* are with our Faith. This is the battleground! If we are trying to fight sin, we are fighting a battle that's already been fought and won at the Cross of Calvary (Col. 2:14-15). Now that's a phenomenal truth, and one that we need to learn, seemingly, all over again. When Paul said, *"He made a show of them openly, triumphing over them in it,"* (Col. 2:15) he meant exactly what he said. Jesus triumphed over Satan, over every fallen Angel, and over every demon spirit. This means that by atoning for all sin, he took away Satan's legal right to hold man captive. Paul also said:

"**But this Man** *(this Priest, Christ Jesus)*, **after He had offered One Sacrifice for sins forever** *(speaks of the Cross)*, **sat down on the Right Hand of God** *(refers to the great contrast with the Priests under the Levitical system, who never sat down because their work was never completed; the Work of Christ was a 'Finished Work,' and needed no repetition)*" **(Heb. 10:12).**

This tells us that our Lord offered up *"one Sacrifice for sins,"* which was Himself in the shedding of His Life's Blood. Likewise, the word *"forever"* means that there will never be a need for another sacrifice. It is done forever.

The phrase, *"Sat down on the Right Hand of God,"* means that God accepted His Sacrifice, meaning that all sin has been atoned, and that the sin nature need not any longer dominate any Believer. So, fighting against sin of any nature is a fruitless exercise. It's a wasted effort! As stated, we are to *"fight the good fight of Faith,"* and never cease *"fighting that good fight of Faith."*

DEAD WITH CHRIST

"**Now if we be dead with Christ** *(once again pertains to the Cross, and our being baptized into His Death)*, **we believe that we shall also live with Him** *(have Resurrection Life, which is more Abundant Life [Jn. 10:10])*" (**Rom. 6:8**).

When Jesus died on the Cross, and when we evidence Faith in Him, whenever that was when we were Born-Again, at that moment, we *"died with Christ."* That's the way that God looked at the situation. As we've already stated, the *"old man"* had to die. And that we died with Him, Paul also said, *"We believe that we shall also live with Him."* Actually, the Eighth Verse is very similar to the Fifth Verse. Resurrection Life, for this is what it is speaking of, can be had by the Believer and, in fact, is meant to be had by the Believer, but, it can be had only by us understanding that the *"Resurrection Life"* is made possible by what Jesus did at the Cross and, in essence, our dying with Him. Unfortunately, far too many Believers attempt to have Resurrection Life while ignoring the Cross. Such is not to be, as such cannot be. It is the Cross of Christ that has made, and does make, all things possible.

DOMINION IS BROKEN

While the dominion of the sin nature is broken with the conversion of the believing sinner, still, for it to remain broken, the individual has to know and understand how it was broken to begin with. If Believers understand anything about this at all, and most don't, they know that the dominion of sin was broken in their lives by virtue of the Cross. However, most of the time, if any thought is given to it at all, which it seldom is, most do not understand that what got them in keeps them in. Not understanding that, faith is transferred to something else. When that happens, the sin nature, as we have stated, begins to have a revival, and once again begins to dominate the Child of God. And it doesn't matter how consecrated that person might be or how much he loves the Lord, it is impossible for such a Believer to properly live for God. They can be Saved and can make Heaven their Eternal Home; however, when it comes to Victory over the world, the flesh, and the Devil, when it comes to growing in Grace and the knowledge of the Lord, and when it comes to enjoying the *"more Abundant Life,"* which Christ spoke about, that they don't have. And the sadness is, due to the paucity of preaching and teaching from the Pulpit as it regards this all-important subject, these Believers, and I speak of those who truly love the Lord, are left in a quandary. And sadder yet, this is not speaking or addressing one here and there but virtually the entirety of the present body of Christ. Not understanding the Cross as it refers to Sanctification, how we live for God, such an individual is programmed, so to speak, for failure. There are no exceptions!

While many aren't controlled by vices, they are controlled by other types of sins. In fact, the Apostle Paul listed these *"works of the flesh."*

WORKS OF THE FLESH

"Now the works of the flesh are manifest, which are *these (if one attempts to function by means of law of any nature, the 'works of the flesh' will be manifested in one's life)*; Adultery, fornication, uncleanness, lasciviousness,

"Idolatry, witchcraft, hatred, variance, emulations, wrath, strife, seditions, heresies,

"Envyings, murders, drunkenness, revellings, and such like *(if one is walking after the flesh [Rom. 8:1], one or more of these sins will manifest themselves in one's life; the only way, and I mean the only way, one can walk in perpetual Victory is to understand that everything we receive from God comes to us by Means of the Cross; consequently, the Cross must ever be the Object of our Faith;*

this being the case, the Holy Spirit, Who works exclusively within the confines of the Sacrifice of Christ, will exert His mighty Power on our behalf, which will enable us to live a Holy life): **of the which I tell you before, as I have also told *you* in time past** *(refers to the fact that the Apostle was not afraid to name specific sins)*, **that they which do such things shall not inherit the Kingdom of God.** *(This tells us in no uncertain terms that if our Faith is not everlastingly in Christ and the Cross, we simply won't make it. God doesn't have two ways of Salvation and Victory, only one, and that is 'Jesus Christ and Him Crucified')*" **(Gal. 5:19-21).**

HERESIES

The word *"heresy"* means *"a departure from revealed truth."* So, while many Christians may not be involved in the vices, although many are, some are most definitely involved in heresy or idolatry. In fact, idolatry is rampant in the church, with untold millions putting their faith in their church denomination, etc. So, the *"works of the flesh"* run the gamut from the proverbial A to Z. The point is this:

If the Believer doesn't have his Faith anchored in Christ and the Cross, but rather in something else, without fail, one or more of the works of the flesh are going to manifest themselves in one's life. The Cross of Christ is God's Way. Unfortunately, most do not see that or know that.

The unredeemed world has forever tried to manufacture another god. The church, sadly and regrettably, has ever tried to manufacture another sacrifice. The next verse gives us the answer to that.

DIED UNTO SINS ONCE AND LIVES UNTO GOD

"For in that He died, He died unto sin *(the sin nature)* **once** *(actually means, 'He died unto the sin nature, once,* *for all')*: **but in that He lives** *(the Resurrection)*, **He lives unto God** *(refers to the fact that all life comes from God, and that we receive that life by virtue of the Cross and our Faith in that Finished Work)*" **(Rom. 6:10).**

ONE SACRIFICE FOR SIN

There was and there is only one Sacrifice for sin, and because only one Sacrifice was needed. The phrase, *"For in that He died, He died unto sin once,"* proclaims several things. Some of them are:

• He atoned for all sin, past, present, and future, at least for all who will believe (Jn. 3:16).

• The word *"once"* means that it will never have to be repeated.

• It means, as well, that God accepted the Sacrifice in totality.

• For someone, anyone, to propose another sacrifice is an insult to the Lord of the worst proportions.

LIFE

The phrase, *"But in that He lives, He lives unto God,"* tells us that Jesus Christ is the Source of all life. But, it also tells us in the first phrase of this verse that the Cross is the Means by which this life is given unto us.

The idea is, Jesus Christ has already won the Victory, and has done so in every capacity. He died, and He lives! Herein lies all life and living. Understand this and the pieces of life, so to speak, will fall into place. Ignore it, and there is no life.

FAITH

"**Likewise reckon** *(account)* **you also yourselves to be dead indeed unto** *(the)* **sin** *(while the sin nature is not dead, we are dead unto the sin nature by virtue of the*

Cross and our Faith in that Sacrifice, but only as long as our Faith continues in the Cross), **but alive unto God** *(living the Resurrection Life)* **through Jesus Christ our Lord** *(refers to what He did at the Cross, which is the means of this Resurrection Life)*" **(Rom. 6:11).**

The idea is, considering that we died with Christ on the Cross of Calvary, Spiritually speaking, and considering that that Victory is just as valid today as it was when we first accepted the Lord, we are to reckon ourselves as *"dead indeed unto the sin nature, and alive unto God through Jesus Christ our Lord."*

THE KEY TO VICTORY

It is not doing, but rather believing. It sounds easy, but actually, it is the hardest thing for a person to do. As a human being, we want to do something, when the truth is, it has already been done. When we believe that we died with Him, were buried with Him, and were raised with Him in Newness of Life, and that this is the key to all Victory, and I continue to speak of our simple Faith in what He did at the Cross, the Holy Spirit, Who Alone can make us what we ought to be, can then work mightily within our hearts and lives. It is all *"through Jesus Christ our Lord,"* and what He did at the Cross.

SANCTIFICATION

"**Let not sin** *(the sin nature)* **therefore reign** *(rule)* **in your mortal body** *(showing that the sin nature can once again rule in the heart and life of the Believer, if the Believer doesn't constantly look to Christ and the Cross; the 'mortal body' is neutral, which means it can be used for Righteousness or unrighteousness)*, **that you should obey it in the lusts thereof** *(ungodly lusts are carried out through the mortal body, if Faith is not maintained in the*

Cross [I Cor. 1:17-18])" **(Rom. 6:12).**

THE ORIGINAL TEXTS

When Paul wrote this particular sentence, he actually said, *"Let not* (the) *sin therefore reign in your mortal body. . . ."* The reason he wrote it that way is because he wasn't speaking of acts of sin, but rather the sin nature, or as some may say, *"the evil nature."*

The subject of the *"sin nature"* is one of the least understood subjects in the entirety of the New Testament. And yet, it is one of the most important.

The following are some of the ways the sin nature is addressed in the modern church. We will be brief. (For a more expanded treatment of this most important subject, I would advise the reader to secure for yourself our Study Guide under the name, "The Sin Nature, *The Cross Of Christ Series*".)

I have coined some five words to describe the way this subject is addressed by the modern church. They are *"ignorance, denial, license, struggle, and Grace."* Of the five, *"Grace"* is the only Scriptural way to address this subject. We'll look at *"ignorance"* first.

"IGNORANCE"

Actually the vast majority of the modern church world has no understanding whatsoever regarding the subject of the sin nature. Most have never heard a sermon preached on this subject, have never read any material about this subject and, therefore, have no knowledge whatsoever. In fact, I think one could probably say that most Christians have never even heard the term *"sin nature."* And if they did, it was only in passing, with little or no explanation given.

But, please understand, ignorance is not bliss in this area of one's life. In fact, what you don't know about the sin nature can kill you.

The *"sin nature"* can be referred to as the *"evil nature,"* the *"Adamic nature,"* or the *"carnal nature,"* etc.

WHAT IS THE SIN NATURE?

Even though we've already addressed this material in this Volume, let us briefly state, the sin nature has to do with the Fall of Adam and Eve in the Garden of Eden. Before the Fall, their human nature was controlled by the Divine Nature. But, once the Fall took place, then their human nature was controlled in totality by the sin nature. In other words, their very nature became that of disobedience, sin, rebellion, iniquity, transgression, etc. In fact, they were ruled by the sin nature 24 hours a day, 7 days a week. And like Adam, so it is with all who are born thereafter, for every one of us was born with the Adamic nature, i.e., *"the sin nature."*

When the believing sinner comes to Christ, the sin nature is made dormant, meaning that it's made ineffective. But when the Believer begins to place his or her faith in something other than Christ and the Cross, and no matter how religious the other thing might be, that's when the sin nature has a revival, and can become dominant in our lives, actually dominating us, which it is with most Believers. I say *"most"* simply because most Christians have no knowledge of the Cross of Christ relative to Sanctification, which means they simply do not know how to live for God. As such, the sin nature rules most Believers. It is tragic and sad, but true.

"DENIAL"

Some preachers claim that once the person comes to Christ, there is no more sin nature. My answer to that is simple:

If it is true that the Believer doesn't have a sin nature, then I wonder why the Holy Spirit took up so much time explaining something that doesn't exist? Almost the entirety of the Sixth Chapter of Romans deals with this very subject.

"LICENSE"

Some few Believers have a modicum of knowledge regarding the sin nature, in other words, they know they have a sin nature. Having this smattering of knowledge, they conclude that because they have a sin nature, they have to sin a little bit every day, etc.

The Holy Spirit answered this by saying, *"Shall we continue in sin, that Grace may abound? God forbid. How shall we, who are dead to sin, live any longer therein?"* (Rom. 6:1-2). The Lord does not save us in sin, but rather from sin.

"STRUGGLE"

Oddly enough, some Christians think that the Christian life is simply a life lived in a constant struggle with sin. Please understand, Jesus defeated all sin 2,000 years ago at Calvary's Cross. So, if the Believer is fighting sin, he is fighting the wrong fight. It's a fight that's already been fought and won. The only fight we are called upon to engage is the *"good fight of Faith"* (I Tim. 6:12).

If the Believer is struggling with sin, it is a struggle he is going to lose. While there is a struggle, as stated, it is with our Faith. This is where Satan attacks the Child of God, and where the real struggle commences.

"GRACE"

Out of all the things we've named, Grace is the only Scriptural way and means that we are to address the sin nature.

First of all, Grace is simply the Goodness of God extended to undeserving Believers. Secondly, when we place our Faith exclusively in Christ and the Cross, then the Holy Spirit can give us good things and can do good things for us, which amounts to the Grace of God, i.e., *"good things given to us."* While Grace comes from our Lord, it is the Holy Spirit Who superintends this. He doesn't demand much of us, as previously stated, but He does demand that our Faith be exclusively in Christ and the Cross. That being done, good things can be given to us, and to be sure, good things will be given unto us.

INSTRUMENTS OF RIGHTEOUSNESS UNTO GOD

"Neither yield you your members *(of your mortal body)* **as instruments of unrighteousness unto sin** *(the sin nature)*: **but yield yourselves unto God** *(we are to yield ourselves to Christ and the Cross; that alone guarantees Victory over the sin nature)*, **as those who are alive from the dead** *(we have been raised with Christ in 'Newness of Life')*, **and your members as instruments of Righteousness unto God** *(this can be done only by virtue of the Cross and our Faith in that Finished Work, and Faith which continues in that Finished Work from day-to-day [Lk. 9:23-24])*" **(Rom. 6:13).**

CAN SATAN OVERRIDE THE WILL OF BELIEVERS, FORCING THEM TO DO SOMETHING THEY DO NOT DESIRE TO DO?

Yes, that is, if the Believer has his faith in something other than Christ and the Cross, which then greatly hinders the Holy Spirit from helping us. Paul said as much in Romans 7:19, *"For the good that I would I do not: but the evil which I would not, that I do."* This plainly tells us that Satan can override the will of an individual if that, indeed, is what the Believer is depending on. Satan is stronger than our will, as should be obvious. Some Believers have the erroneous idea that the Lord gives Believers superhuman wills when they get Saved. That is not true! My will and your will are no stronger today than they were before we came to Christ. While the will is definitely important, the *"will"* is not God's Way of bringing about victory in our lives.

His Way is Christ and the Cross, and Christ and the Cross exclusively. Our Faith placed in the Finished Work of Christ guarantees us Victory, which then enables us to yield our body members to Righteousness. However, the Believer should understand, this is the only way it can be done.

SIN SHALL NOT HAVE DOMINION

"For sin shall not have dominion over you *(the sin nature will not have dominion over us if we as Believers continue to exercise Faith in the Cross of Christ; otherwise, the sin nature most definitely will have dominion over the Believer)***: for you are not under the Law** *(means that if we try to live this life by any type of law, no matter how good that law might be in its own right, we will conclude by the sin nature having dominion over us)***, but under Grace** *(the Grace of God flows to the Believer on an unending basis only as long as the Believer exercises Faith in Christ and what He did at the Cross; Grace is merely the Goodness of God exercised by and through the Holy Spirit, and given to undeserving Saints)*" **(Rom. 6:14).**

WHAT IS DOMINION?

While the Bible does not teach sinless perfection, it most definitely does teach that the sin nature is not to have dominion over the Believer.

What is dominion?

It is when a particular sin dominates a person, with that person unable to throw it off, unable to quit, unable to stop, and in a sense, with it dominating his life. And please believe me, this will happen if the Believer doesn't have his or her Faith exclusively in Christ and the Cross. Let the Believer ever understand, our Victory is in Christ and the Cross, and our Victory is in Christ and the Cross alone!

Are we saying that if the Believer doesn't have his Faith exclusively in Christ and the Cross that sin in some way (the sin nature) is going to have dominion over that person?

That's exactly what we are saying!

As I dictate these notes, there are millions upon millions of Christians around the world, and I speak of those who truly love the Lord, who are battling with some type of vice, or some type of sin and, in fact, are losing that battle. But if the truth be known, in any and every case, the problem is not getting better but rather worse. The church, regrettably, doesn't have any solution to these problems, because the church doesn't understand Christ and the Cross, at least as it regards our Sanctification, i.e., *"how we live for God."*

ONE WAY

The Lord has one Way, and only one Way, because only one Way is needed. That one Way is, *"Jesus Christ and Him Crucified"* (I Cor. 1:23). Please allow me to repeat the following:

• Jesus Christ is the Source of all things we receive from God (Jn. 1:1; 14:6; Col. 2:10).

• The Cross of Christ is the Means by which all of these things are given to us (Rom. 6:3-5; I Cor. 1:17-18, 23; 2:2).

• The Cross of Christ must be the Object of our Faith, and the Cross of Christ alone the Object of our Faith (Gal., Chpt. 5; 6:14; Eph. 2:13-18; Col. 2:14-15).

• The Holy Spirit superintends all of this (Rom. 8:1-2, 11; Eph. 2:13-18).

LAW OR GRACE

Every human being in the world is either under law or Grace. To break it down as follows, every unsaved person in the world is under the Law of God, and we speak of the Ten Commandments. They may not understand that, but nevertheless, it is true. As well, they have broken that Law countless times and are under its penalty of death, i.e., separation from God. The only way out is Jesus Christ.

THE DISPENSATION OF GRACE

Many Christians believe that because this is the Dispensation of Grace, and it most definitely is, then that means we are automatically under Grace. That isn't so!

For the Grace of God to flow uninterrupted to the Believer, the Believer's Faith has to be in Christ and the Cross. The Cross of Christ is the Means by which Grace is given to us.

The truth is, the Lord has no more Grace presently than He did 3,000 years ago or more. Due to the fact that the blood of bulls and goats could not take away sins, this meant the sin debt remained, which greatly hindered the Lord from giving good things to His Children. In fact, Grace is simply the Goodness of God extended to undeserving Saints.

If the Believer has his faith in anything except the Cross of Christ, such a direction will *"frustrate the Grace of God."* Paul said:

"I do not frustrate the Grace of God *(if we make anything other than the Cross of Christ the Object of our Faith, we frustrate the Grace of God, which means we stop its action, and the Holy Spirit will no longer help us)*: for if Righteousness *come* by the Law *(any type of religious Law)*, then Christ is dead in vain. *(If I can successfully live for the Lord by any means other than Faith in Christ and the Cross, then the Death of Christ was a waste)*" (Gal. 2:21).

As well, Paul said that if the Grace of God continues to be frustrated, such a Believer will *"fall from Grace."* The Apostle said:

"Christ is become of no effect unto you *(this is a*

chilling statement, and refers to anyone who makes any-thing other than Christ and the Cross the Object of his Faith), **whosoever of you are justified by the Law** *(seek to be justified by the Law)*; **you are fallen from Grace** *(fallen from the position of Grace, which means the Believer is trusting in something other than the Cross; it actually means, 'to apostatize')*" **(Gal. 5:4).**

While the Lord doesn't require very much of us, He does require one thing, and on that He will not bend. Our Faith must be in Christ and the Cross, and our Faith must be exclusively in Christ and the Cross (Rom. 6:3-5; 8:1-2, 11; I Cor. 1:17-18, 21, 23; 2:2).

GRACE

"**What then?** *(This presents Paul going back to the first question he asked in this Chapter.)* **shall we sin, because we are not under the Law, but under Grace?** *(If we think such a thing, then we're completely misun-derstanding Grace. The Grace of God gives us the liberty to live a Holy life, which we do through Faith in Christ and the Cross, and not license to sin as some think.)* **God forbid** *(every true Believer hates sin; so the idea of liv-ing under its dominion is abhorrent to say the least!)*" **(Rom. 6:15).**

"LICENSE"?

The Apostle is, in essence, saying, *"Don't get the idea that just because we are under Grace, it's alright to sin. Sin is deadly!"* And to be sure, no one engages in this terrible malady with-out coming away adversely affected. As we said in the notes above, every true Believer hates sin. While the flesh at times may want something that's wrong, the mind of the Believer wants to obey the Law of God (Rom. 7:25).

The only way, and I mean the only way, that one can have Victory over sin, i.e., Victory over the world, the flesh, and the Devil, is for one to place one's Faith exclusively in Christ and the Cross and maintain it there. This is God's Way, and His only Way, because it's the only Way that is needed.

SERVANTS

"Know you not, that to whom you yield yourselves servants to obey, his servants you are to whom you obey *(the Believer is either a slave to Christ, for that's what the word 'servant' means, or else a slave to sin, which he will be if he doesn't keep his Faith in Christ and the Cross)*; whether of sin unto death *(once again allow us to state the fact that if the Believer attempts to live for God by any method other than Faith in the Finished Work of Christ, the Believer will fail, no matter how hard he otherwise tries),* or of obedience unto Righteousness? *(The Believer is required to obey the Word of the Lord. He cannot do that within his own strength, but only by understanding that he receives all things through what Christ did at the Cross and his continued Faith in that Finished Work, even on a daily basis. Then the Holy Spirit, Who Alone can make us what we ought to be, can accomplish His Work within our lives)*" **(Rom. 6:16).**

SIN UNTO DEATH

All sin is linked with death in some way, as death is linked with sin in some way. At this moment, millions of marriages are dying simply because of sin. Talent and ability are being wasted and will never come to fruition because it is dying because of sin. Everything in this world is dying because of sin. There will come a day that there will be no more sin, and everything will then stay beautiful, new, and fresh forever. John said:

"**And I saw a New Heaven and a New Earth** *('New'* *in the Greek is 'kainos,' and means 'freshness with respect* *to age'; when it is finished, it will be new, as is obvious,* *but the idea is it will remain new and fresh forever and for-* *ever because there is no more sin)*: **for the first Heaven** **and the first Earth were passed away** *(refers to the origi-* *nal Creation, which was marred by sin; 'passed away' in* *the Greek is 'parerchomai,' and means 'to pass from one* *condition to another'; it never means annihilation) . . ."* **(Rev. 21:1).**

OBEDIENCE UNTO RIGHTEOUSNESS

The *"obedience"* mentioned here refers to obedience ren-
dered to God, or rather obeying His Word.
What is that Word?
That Word is the *"Cross."* That's what the entirety of this
Sixth Chapter of Romans is all about. Sin is the problem, and
the Cross of Christ is the solution to that problem and, in fact,
the only solution.
When the Lord began to open up to me the great Message
of the Cross, actually that which had been given to the Apostle
Paul, He said three things to me, three things which I will never
forget. They are:
• The answer for which you seek is found in the Cross.
• The solution for which you seek is found in the Cross.
• The answer for which you seek is found only in the Cross.
The next verse tells us emphatically what that obedience is.

THE FORM OF DOCTRINE

"**But God be thanked, that you were the servants of**
sin *(slaves to the sin nature, what we were before we were* *Saved)*, **but you have obeyed from the heart that form** **of Doctrine** *(Jesus Christ and Him Crucified; understand-* *ing that all things come to the Believer from God by the*

Means of the Cross) **which was delivered you** *(the Lord gave this 'form of Doctrine' to Paul, and he gave it to us in his Epistles)"* **(Rom. 6:17).**

THE DOCTRINE OF THE CROSS

The Doctrine of the Cross is the Foundation Doctrine of all doctrine. It was established by the Godhead from before the foundation of the world (I Pet. 1:18-20). This means that every single doctrine in the Bible is built squarely upon the Doctrine of the Cross. In fact, this is the way all false doctrine begins. If it's false, it means that it is built upon a foundation other than the Cross of Christ.

When Believers succumb to seducing spirits, it means they have shifted their faith from Christ and the Cross to something else.

FORM

The word *"form"* in the Greek is *"tupos,"* and means, *"a stamp, a shape, a style, a model, a pattern."*

As we have already stated, this form is a *"blueprint,"* and a *"blueprint"* designed by God. That *"form"* is the pattern of the Cross of Christ. If we deviate at all from the form, we have just added to or deleted from the Word of God. And what does the Bible say about that?

"And if any man shall take away from the words of the Book of this Prophecy, God shall take away his part out of the Book of Life, and out of the Holy City, and from the things which are written in this Book" **(Rev. 22:19).**

That has been man's problem from the dawn of time. He does not want to accept the Word of God at face value. In fact, ever since the dawn of time, man has been trying to invent another god, and regrettably and sadder still, the church has been trying to invent another sacrifice. Tragedy is the result of both accounts.

SERVANTS OF RIGHTEOUSNESS

"Being then made free from sin *(being made free from the sin nature; it has no more power over the Believer, but only as we continue to look to the Cross)*, **you became the servants of Righteousness** *(whereas you were formerly a slave to the sin nature, you are now a slave to Righteousness; if Faith is maintained in the Cross, there is a constant pull of the Believer toward Righteousness)*" **(Rom. 6:18).**

FREE FROM THE DOMINATION
OF THE SIN NATURE

There are millions of Christians right now around the world, people who truly love God, who long for freedom from the domination of the sin nature. Some of these individuals pastor large churches. Others are Evangelists being used of God, but still, the sin nature dominates them in some way.

They understand the Cross as it regards Salvation; however, as it regards Sanctification, how we live for God, how we order our behavior, and how we live this life, the part the Cross of Christ plays in all of this, of that they have no knowledge. As a result, most simply do not know how to be free from the domination of the sin nature.

SERVANTS OF RIGHTEOUSNESS

Irrespective of the knowledge or lack thereof as it regards the Cross of Christ respecting Sanctification, if anyone wills Righteousness, in other words, hungers and thirsts after Righteousness, the Lord will see to such that Righteousness in some way is imputed to them. Admittedly, it's not a simple journey, an easy journey, or a quick journey. But, if the person truly wants Righteousness, the Lord will see to it that that person comes in contact with the Message given to us by the Apostle Paul as it regards the Cross of Christ respecting Sanctification.

When the Lord said, *"Blessed are they who do hunger and thirst after Righteousness: for they shall be filled,"* He meant every word of it (Mat. 5:6).

THE INFIRMITY OF THE FLESH

"**I speak after the manner of men because of the infirmity of your flesh** *('the manner of men' pertains to the Fall, which has made the flesh weak; this speaks of our own personal strength and ability)*: **for as you have yielded your members servants to uncleanness** *(which the Believer will do, if the object of his Faith is anything but the Cross)* **and to iniquity unto iniquity** *(without constant Faith in the Cross, the Believer's situation regarding sin will get worse and worse)*; **even so now yield your members servants to Righteousness unto Holiness** *(which, as repeatedly stated, can only be done through constant Faith in the Cross; understanding that it is by and through the Cross that we receive all things, and that the Holy Spirit, Who Alone can develop Righteousness and Holiness in our lives, works exclusively through the Cross)*" **(Rom. 6:19).**

INIQUITY UNTO INIQUITY

When the sin nature dominates an individual, as it does any and every person whose faith is not exclusively in Christ and the Cross, the situation will go from bad to worse, i.e., *"iniquity unto iniquity."* Sin never remains static. It never improves itself. It always degenerates, with the ultimate idea of totally and completely destroying the individual involved.

When Paul said, *"Now yield your members servants to Righteousness unto Holiness,"* he was speaking of those who understood the Cross of Christ as it regards Sanctification, which now gives them the help of the Holy Spirit, Who will develop these great attributes within their hearts and lives. But, if the

Believer has his faith in something else other than the Cross of Christ, he may want to yield the members of his physical body to Righteousness and Holiness, but he will not be able to do so.

We must understand that living for God is serious business. The Devil doesn't want us to make it through; consequently, he will do everything within his power to hinder or even stop us. If we do things God's Way, we will be the beneficiary of the Power of the Holy Spirit, which Satan cannot overcome. Otherwise, the situation is hopeless!

DEATH

"For when you were the servants of sin *(slaves to sin)*, you were free from Righteousness *(speaking of our lives before conversion to Christ)*.

"What fruit had you then in those things whereof you are now ashamed? *(This means that absolutely nothing of any value can come out of the sinful experience. It is impossible for there to be any good fruit.)* **for the end of those things *is* death** *(if the Believer refuses to look to the Cross, but rather looks to something else regarding his Sanctification, domination by the sin nature is going to be the result, and spiritual death will be the conclusion; the Cross is the only answer for sin!)*" **(Rom. 6:20-21).**

As we've already stated, *"death"* is always attached to sin.

In essence, Paul is taking the Believers back to their unsaved experience. But yet, he is reminding them of the bondage of sin that held them in its death grip during those times. And, as well, he is saying that if the Believer did not function according to God's Manner and Way, then the Believer, even though Saved by the Blood of Jesus Christ, will once again find himself doing things that will make him grossly ashamed.

A Believer may read these words and claim that such could not happen to him or her; however, as we have repeatedly stated, God's Way, the Way of the Cross, is the only Way. Refuse that, and once again, the sin nature is going to dominate us and drag us down.

EVERLASTING LIFE

"**But now** *(since coming to Christ)* **being made free from sin** *(set free from the sin nature)*, **and become servants** *(slaves)* **to God** *(but this yoke is a light yoke [Mat. 11:28-30])*, **you have your fruit unto Holiness** *(which the Holy Spirit will bring about, providing the Cross is ever the Object of our Faith)*, **and the end Everlasting Life** *(so the Believer has the choice of 'death,' which is the end result of trusting something other than Christ and the Cross, or 'Everlasting Life,' which is the result of trusting Christ and the Cross)*.

"**For the wages of sin *is* death** *(speaks of spiritual death, which is eternal separation from God)*; **but the Gift of God *is* Eternal Life through Jesus Christ our Lord** *(as stated, all of this, without exception, comes to us by the Means of what Christ did at the Cross, which demands that the Cross ever be the Object of our Faith, thus giving the Holy Spirit latitude to work within our lives and bring forth His Fruit)*" **(Rom. 6:22-23).**

"O Thou, to Whose all-searching Sight,
"The darkness shines as the light,
"Search, prove my heart it pants for Thee;
"O, burst these bands, and set it free."

"Wash out its stains, refine its dross:
"Nail my affections to the Cross;
"Hallow each thought, let all within,
"Be clean, as You, my Lord, are clean."

"If in this darksome wild I stray,

"Be Thou my Light, be Thou my Way;
"No foes, no violence, I fear,
"No fraud, while You, my God, are near."

"Saviour, wherever Your Steps I see,
"Dauntless, untired, I follow Thee;
"Oh, let Your Hands support me still,
"And lead me to Your Holy Hill."

"If rough and thorny be the way,
"My strength proportion to the day;
"Till toil, and grief, and pain shall cease,
"Where all is calm, and joy, and peace."

PAUL
THE APOSTLE

CHAPTER SIX

Antioch

Paul's First Missionary Journey

ANTIOCH

The Early Church began, one might say, at Jerusalem. One might also say that it began on the Day of Pentecost. Simon Peter preached the inaugural message, and the Scripture says, *"And the same day there were added unto them about three thousand souls"* (Acts 2:41). And then the Scripture says, as it regards what took place on a daily basis, *"And the Lord added to the Church daily such as should be Saved"* (Acts 2:47). And then a few days later Peter preached once again, actually in the Temple, and the Scripture says, *"Howbeit many of them which heard the Word believed; and the number of the men was about five thousand"* (Acts 4:4).

If the number of men alone was about 5,000, more than likely, counting women and children, as well, the number Saved that day could have reached over 10,000 people. At any rate, it is believed there were between 40,000 and 50,000 people in Jerusalem who accepted Christ as their Saviour. And please understand, there were no church buildings in those days. The people worshipped mostly in homes, etc., during that time.

Rome came to look at Christianity as a part of Judaism. While, of course, it did have its roots in Judaism, that's about where the similarity ended. In fact, the time came that Paul and others were actually no longer welcome in the Jewish synagogues.

THE APOSTLES' DOCTRINE

What was the Apostles' Doctrine?
Acts 2:38 tells us! It says:

"Now when they heard *this*, they were pricked in their heart *(the convicting Power of the Holy Spirit)*, and said unto Peter and to the rest of the Apostles, Men *and* Brethren, what shall we do? *(This proclaims these people, whomever they may have been, desiring to get right with God.)*

"Then Peter said unto them, **Repent** *(admit that God is right, and we are wrong)*, **and be baptized every one of you in the Name of Jesus Christ** *(by the authority of that Name; there is no baptismal formula given in the Book of Acts; the only formula given was given by Christ in Mat. 28:19)* **for the Remission of sins** *(should have been translated, 'because of remission of sins'; one is baptized in water because one's sins have already been remitted due to Faith in Christ, and not that sins should be remitted)*, **and you shall receive the Gift of the Holy Spirit** *(Repentance guarantees Salvation, which makes the Believer ready to be baptized with the Holy Spirit; one is not baptized with the Spirit automatically at conversion; it is an experience that follows Salvation, and is always accompanied by speaking with other Tongues [Acts 2:4; 10:44-46; 19:1-7])*.

"**For the Promise** *(of the Baptism with the Holy Spirit)* **is unto you** *(directed toward the many Jews standing in the Temple listening to Peter that day)*, **and to your children** *(means that this great outpouring did not stop with the initial outpouring, but continues on)*, **and to all who are afar off** *(meaning that it's not only for those in Jerusalem, but the entirety of the world as well)*, *even* **as many as the Lord our God shall call** *(that 'Call' is 'whosoever will' [Jn. 7:37-39; Rev. 22:17])*" **(Acts 2:37-39).**

DID THE APOSTLES BEFORE PAUL PREACH THE CROSS?

No! Actually, they mostly preached the Resurrection of Christ (Acts 2:24-32; 3:15; 4:10). Of course, the Nation of Israel, which had crucified Christ at that time, was claiming that the Disciples had stolen away the Body of Christ, and that He had not really been raised from the dead.

That is an interesting concept when one realizes that four Roman soldiers stood guard at the tomb for three days and three nights, with the four soldiers being changed every three hours, meaning that their serving as guards was continuous. In fact, those guards did not leave until an Angel appeared at the tomb and so unnerved these guards that the Scripture says they ". . . *did shake, and became as dead men"* (Mat. 28:4). In fact, when the Angel came, that is the time they left and, ". . . *came into the city, and showed unto the Chief Priests all the things that were done"* (Mat. 28:11-15). So, the idea of the Disciples of Christ stealing away His Body can be construed as nothing less than preposterous.

Before the time of Paul the Disciples didn't preach the Cross because this great Revelation had not yet been given. In fact, it would be given to Paul, and then it would be preached mightily over the Roman world of that day.

JEWS AT JERUSALEM

The Jews in Jerusalem, which constituted the Mother Church, simply added Christ to their keeping of the Law of Moses. In those days there was no thought of the Law being set aside. At that time they simply did not understand at all that Jesus was the end of the Law for Righteousness, in other words, that He had fulfilled the Law in totality (Rom. 10:4).

Actually, the Jews in Jerusalem, under the leadership of James, the Lord's Brother, who was the senior Pastor of the Church, seemingly never did quite accept what Paul taught as it regarded Law and Grace. And yet, at the Council in Jerusalem recorded in Acts, Chapter 15, after hearing Peter, Barnabas, and Paul, the decree was made by James that the Gentile converts would not be bound by the Law of Moses (Acts 15:7-21).

I personally feel that James fell short of obeying the Lord in this respect in that he failed to include the Jews in this decision. In other words, it was still incumbent upon the Jews to keep the Law of Moses in conjunction with accepting Christ. Unfortunately, as stated, this caused Paul tremendous difficulties in the Churches he founded over the Roman Empire. Emissaries were constantly coming from the Church in Jerusalem, claiming the sanction of James, whether they had it or not, and trying to force Gentile converts into Law-keeping. Of course, they did these things after Paul had founded the Churches and gone on to other fields of endeavor. Because of this problem, the Holy Spirit quietly shifted His Headquarters, so to speak, from the Church at Jerusalem to the Church at Antioch, Syria. Concerning the beginning of the Church at Antioch, the following is said:

ANTIOCH

"Now they which were scattered abroad upon the persecution that arose about Stephen *(concerns that which happened in Acts, Chpt. 8, about six or seven years before)* traveled as far as Phenice *(Lebanon)*, and Cyprus, and Antioch *(a city of Syria)*, preaching the Word to none but unto the Jews only *(pertained basically to proclaiming Jesus as the Messiah of Israel and the Saviour of the world, and that He had risen from the dead)*.

"And some of them were men of Cyprus and Cyrene *(implies that they were latecomers to Antioch)*, which, when they were come to Antioch, spoke unto the Grecians *(pertains to Gentiles, not Greek-speaking Jews as some claim)*, preaching the Lord Jesus *(indicates that Jews who preached to them were not demanding that they also keep the Law of Moses)*."

THE HAND OF THE LORD

"And the Hand of the Lord was with them *(signifies that God was pleased with the Gospel being preached to these Gentiles)*: and a great number believed, and turned unto the Lord *(they gave their hearts and lives to the Lord Jesus Christ)*.

"Then tidings of these things came unto the ears of

the Church which was in Jerusalem *(which was then the headquarters Church; these 'tidings' spoke of good news)*: **and they sent forth Barnabas, that he should go as far as Antioch** *(Barnabas was the right man!; therefore, they were led by the Spirit in sending him)*."

BARNABAS

"**Who, when he came, and had seen the Grace of God** *(refers to the fact that Barnabas saw the changed lives of these Gentiles)*, **was glad, and exhorted them all, that with purpose of heart they would cleave unto the Lord** *(be led by the Holy Spirit)*.

"**For he was a good man** *(this is what the Holy Spirit said)*, **and full of the Holy Spirit and of Faith** *(describes Barnabas in the same manner as Stephen [Acts 6:5])*: **and much people was added unto the Lord** *(many Jews and Gentiles were coming to Christ)*."

SAUL

"**Then departed Barnabas to Tarsus, for to seek Saul** *(this is one of the single most important Verses in the entirety of the Word of God; the Holy Spirit led him to do this; as well, the Text implies that he had some difficulty in finding Paul; this was around the year A.D. 43, about ten years after the Crucifixion)*:

"**And when he had found him, he brought him unto Antioch. And it came to pass, that a whole year they assembled themselves with the Church, and taught much people** *(could well signal the beginning of teaching of the New Covenant as it had been given to Paul by Christ)*. **And the Disciples were called Christians first in Antioch** *(they received the name of 'Christians,' as followers of Christ, from the outside world and accepted it [Acts 26:28; I Pet. 4:16])*" **(Acts 11:19-26).**

WHAT TYPE OF CITY WAS ANTIOCH?

Antioch in Paul's time was the third greatest city in the Roman Empire with a population of approximately 500,000 people. It was no mere oriental town, but rather a Greek capital enriched and enlarged by Roman power. Through the city flowed the Orontes River, winding its way to the Sea, a distance of about 16 miles.

Farrar says concerning the place, *"Through the entire length of the city, from the Golden or Daphne gate on the west, ran for nearly five miles a beautiful street adorned with trees, colonnades, and statues. Originally constructed by Seleucus Nicator, it had been continued by Herod the Great, who, at once to gratify his passion for architecture, and to reward the people of Antioch for their goodwill toward the Jews, had paved the street for two miles and a half with blocks of white marble. As well, broad ridges spanned the river and its various affluents."*[1]

Also, an immense colony of Jews made their home in Antioch. It was here, it might be said, that Paul began his Ministry. To be sure, he had ministered in other places before this, but of that we have almost no information. When Barnabas personally went to Tarsus *"for to seek Saul,"* just how much that Barnabas knew at that time of the great Revelation given to Paul by the Lord Jesus Christ concerning the meaning of the New Covenant is anyone's guess; however, more than likely, he knew nothing of this Revelation at that time, but he did know that Paul claimed that his initial Commission was to the Gentiles (Acts 9:15). So, considering that scores of Gentiles were being Saved in Antioch, led by the Holy Spirit, Barnabas ferreted out Paul, and brought him to Antioch. He remained there a year, no doubt proclaiming the Gospel of Grace, which the Lord had given to him sometime in the intervening approximate 10 years from his conversion on the Damascus Road to his domicile now in Antioch.

If Paul preached in the marketplace at Antioch, which he more than likely did, his preaching probably would have evoked the whit and laughter of some of these citizens of Antioch.

How much less could they have conceived it possible that thence forward all the greatest art, all the greatest literature, all the greatest government, all the greatest philosophy, all the greatest eloquence, all the greatest science, all the greatest expansion of world empire, and more even than this, all of what is best, truest, purest, and loveliest in the possible achievements of man should be laid at the feet of the one referred to as the *"Jew from Tarsus."* Paul proclaimed the fact that Faith centered up not in some formula, but in historic realities, not in a dead system but in the Living Person of its Lord.

An ironic inscription on the Cross of Christ had been written in letters of Greek, of Latin, and of Hebrew; and that Cross, implement as it was of shame and torture, became the symbol, sad to say, of the national ruin of the Jew, but conversely, of the dearest hopes and the greatest gratitude of the world of civilization. In fact, it was at Antioch that the name or title *"Christian,"* which meant *"a follower of Christ,"* was coined, probably by Gentiles, and given more or less in derision. It could not have been given by the Jews, who preferred the scornful name of *"Galilean,"* nor was it in all probability a term invented by the Christians themselves. In the New Testament, as is well known, it occurs only three times. It was used once in the historical notice of its origin, and only in two other places as a name used by its enemies. In fact, during the lifetime of the Apostles, the name *"Christian"* does not seem to have acquired much favor among the Christians themselves, with them preferring the appellations of *"the Brethren," "the Disciples," "the Believers," "the Saints," "the Church of Christ," "those of the Way," "the elect," "the faithful,"* etc.

But, whatever may have been the spirit in which the name was given, the Disciples would not be long in welcoming so convenient a term. Bestowed as a stigma, it finally came to be accepted as a distinction.

For a whole year—and it may well have been the happiest year in the life of Paul—he worked in Antioch with Barnabas, preaching this great Gospel of Grace. And yet, the only recorded incident of this year of service is the visit of certain Brethren from Jerusalem, of whom one named Agabus prophesied the near occurrence of a general famine.

THE FIRST MISSIONARY JOURNEY

The following from the Word of God sets the tone for a journey, which will set things in motion that will literally change the world. The Scripture says, and I quote from THE EXPOSITOR'S STUDY BIBLE:

"Now there were in the Church that was at Antioch certain Prophets and Teachers *(the Holy Spirit, as we shall see, shifts the emphasis from Jerusalem to this Syrian city)*; as Barnabas, and Simeon who was called Niger, and Lucius of Cyrene, and Manaen, which had been brought up with Herod the Tetrarch, and Saul.

"As they ministered to the Lord, and fasted *(refers to worship)*, the Holy Spirit said *(the Holy Spirit still speaks, at least to all who have the right type of relationship, and anyone can who so desires)*, Separate Me Barnabas and Saul for the work whereunto I have called them *(expresses a strong Command; in other words, it is not a suggestion; the Lord does the calling, not man)*.

"And when they had fasted and prayed *(the Early Church was a praying Church; it is a shame that the same cannot be said for the modern church)*, and laid *their* hands on them *(it signified the Blessings of the Church upon Paul and Barnabas)*, they sent *them* away *(represents, as far as is known, the very first missionary trip to new places for the express purpose of planting new Churches)*."

SENT FORTH BY THE HOLY SPIRIT

"So they, being sent forth by the Holy Spirit *(presents the Spirit not only calling them, but sending them as well;*

*due to the Cross, the Holy Spirit now has far greater lati-
tude to work within our lives)*, **departing unto Seleucia;
and from thence they sailed to Cyprus** *(represented a
journey of approximately 100 miles; as well, Cyprus was
the boyhood home of Barnabas, where he, no doubt, still
had many friends [Acts 4:36])*" **(Acts 13:1-4).**

To which we have alluded, it is impossible for any mere
mortal to undertake a proper understanding of the vast significance of this first missionary journey. Using only the U.S.A.
as an example, and to be sure, many other countries could
likewise be named, every single blessing that we have, and
every freedom that we enjoy, can all be laid at the doorstep
of the great Gospel of Jesus Christ. But, it was to Paul that
the meaning of the New Covenant was entrusted. As we will
see in our study of this man, we will find that he made every
effort under the guidance of the Holy Spirit to take the Gospel
to ever more places. Accompanied by Barnabas and Mark, I
don't think it would have been possible even for the Jew from
Tarsus to understand the import of what they were doing.

One must wonder as to the thoughts that were in their minds
as they started out that first day, probably early in the morning. They would have walked the 16 miles from Antioch to the
port of Seleucia from where they would catch a boat to Cyprus.

THE MANNER OF THE HOLY SPIRIT

Perhaps this would be the best place to give a brief summation of the Plan of God as it regards world Evangelism. As
should be obvious, there were untold thousands in the city of
Antioch, from which Paul, Barnabas, and Mark had departed,
who had not accepted Christ as their Saviour. Actually, if the
truth be known, the Church in Antioch probably numbered
only several hundreds of people, if that! So, that being the
case, why would the Holy Spirit push Paul, Barnabas, and
Mark to other fields of endeavor?

236 Paul, The Apostle

There is a compulsion by the Holy Spirit that the opportunity of acceptance of the Gospel be given to all, whomever they may be, and wherever they may be. While it is certainly true, and that which He certainly knows, only a tiny percentage will truly accept Christ when the Gospel is offered; nevertheless, if there is a witness in a particular city, then the opportunity presents itself.

We know that most people ignore that witness, meaning they refuse to accept Christ, actually, with most not even giving it a second thought; nevertheless, the Holy Spirit insists that the opportunity be given. That's the reason that Paul, Barnabas, and Mark had to leave Antioch on their way to other regions. As well, it is the reason that untold scores of Missionaries have traveled all over the world to take the Gospel to every place on the face of the Earth. That's the reason that presently Jimmy Swaggart Ministries is doing everything we know to do by radio and television to take the grandest Story ever told to the ends of the Earth. We know that the far greater majority of people will reject the Message or, as stated, ignore it altogether, but still, the opportunity must present itself. There is nothing in the world more important than the Salvation of a soul. Just a few people accepting Christ has a profound effect of positive direction that changes everything. In fact, if even 10 Believers could have been found in Sodom and Gomorrah, which cities, no doubt, numbered tens of thousands of occupants, the twin cities would not have suffered destruction. But sadly, even 10 could not be found. Of course, the powers that be in most countries of the world give little or no credence at all to the Gospel of Jesus Christ; nevertheless, our Lord says that Believers are *"the salt of the Earth,"* and *"the Light of the world,"* and considering these are the Words of Christ, the Son of God, we should realize their vast significance (Mat. 5:13-14). Consequently, there must be a *"Light"* in every village, town, and city on the face of the Earth.

TELEVISION AND RADIO

I've had many newsmen ask me if Christ were living today,

would He utilize radio and television? In some weird way, they seem to think that preachers proclaiming the Gospel over television is something that should not be done. Of course, the answer to that question is overly obvious.

Jesus used every means at His Disposal in His First Advent to give the Gospel to a hurting, dying humanity. He preached on mountains, on boats, on the streets, in the Temple, in synagogues, and wherever opportunity presented itself.

To be sure, in the coming Kingdom Age when Christ will, in effect, be the King of the whole Earth, radio, television, and every other modern means of communication will be used on a worldwide basis to give to men and women the greatest Story ever told. That's the reason that modern television is so very, very important. While countries can build a wall around their respective boundaries, they cannot build a roof. So, by satellite, much of the entire world can presently be reached with the Gospel. That's the reason in 2010 we launched THE SONLIFE BROADCASTING NETWORK, which incorporates both radio and television; however, the primary purpose is for television because it reaches so many, many people. While I have personally been on television since 1972, the launching in 2010 of THE SONLIFE BROADCASTING NETWORK is our first effort into 24-hour programming. We believe the Lord, as we preach the Message of the Cross, beautifully enough, the same Message that Paul preached so long, long ago, is going to give us many, many souls. We have the Promise of the Lord on that. He said:

"**And I, if I be lifted up from the Earth** *(refers to His Death at Calvary; He was 'lifted up' on the Cross; the 'Cross' is the Foundation of all Victory)***, will draw all** *men* **unto Me** *(refers to the Salvation of all who come to Him, believing what He did, and trusting in its atoning Work).*

"**This He said, signifying what death He should die** *(Reynolds says, 'In these Words, we learn that the attraction of the Cross of Christ will prove to be the mightiest, and most sovereign motive ever brought to bear on the*

*human will, and, when wielded by the Holy Spirit as a
Revelation of the matchless Love of God, will involve the
most sweeping judicial sentence that can be pronounced
upon the world and its prince')"* **(Jn. 12:32-33).**

The Apostles embarked on a vessel that was bound for
Cyprus, thus began the first great planned proclamation of the
great and glorious Gospel of Jesus Christ. As the Apostles traveled this 100 or so miles to Cyprus, what were their thoughts?
Farrar said, *"They must have felt a deep emotion at the thought
that now for the first time the Faith, on which depended the hopes
of the world, was starting for fresh regions from its native Syria."*[2]

On this, Paul's first planned missionary journey, little did
he realize what lay in store for him in the next few years. I
speak of the scourgings, the stonings, the shipwrecks, and the
incessant toilings from one danger to the next. Had he foreseen all of this, could he have suffered it? How gracious is the
Lord to us that He keeps some things from us.

Some say that Paul was physically infirm, constitutionally
nervous, and painfully sensitive. They say his bodily presence
was weak, his speech despised, with his mind oftentimes overwhelmed with fear. But, they went on to say that despite the
feeble body and shrinking soul, *"there dominated a spirit so
dauntless that he was ready all his life long to brave torture,
to confront mobs, to quail as little before frowning tyrants as
before stormy seas."* And yet, there was the Perfect Faith, but
a Faith that continued to grow, and the self-sacrifice, even self-
annihilation, which rendered him willing, even eager, to pour
out his whole life as a libation, and as Farrar says, *"to be led in
triumph from city to city as a slave and a captive at the chariot-
wheels of Christ."*[3]

BARNABAS

And, as well, on this first missionary journey, the Lord
had provided for Paul one of, we think, the greatest souls that

could ever help anyone, and we speak of Barnabas. We must remember that up to this time, Barnabas, it might be said, held a higher rank and wielded a more authoritative influence. He enjoyed the confidence of the chiefest of the Apostles. Not long after Paul had come to Christ on the Damascus Road, he found himself in Jerusalem, but yet, most of the Believers in that city *"were all afraid of him, and believed not that he was a Disciple."* But then, the Scripture boldly, beautifully, and wondrously stated, *"But Barnabas took him, and brought him to the Apostles, and declared unto them how he had seen the Lord in the way, and that He (Jesus) had spoken to him, and how he (Paul) had preached boldly at Damascus in the Name of Jesus."* The idea is, Barnabas had heard this great report of Paul and now testifies to its veracity (Acts 9:26-27).

And then, it was Barnabas who was sent by the Church at Jerusalem to the Church at Antioch in order to deal with the Gentiles who were coming to Christ, which he did admirably so. Then it was Barnabas who was led by the Lord to go to Tarsus *"for to seek Saul,"* in order to be of service to the Church at Antioch. As it regarded the first missionary journey, it was the Holy Spirit Who said, *"Separate Me Barnabas and Saul for the work whereunto I have called them"* (Acts 13:2). But yet, as this first missionary journey progressed, Barnabas sank to a subordinate position regarding the ascendancy by the Holy Spirit of Paul. Please understand that this was not a detriment as it regarded Barnabas, but rather the Plan of God. Done by the Holy Spirit, Barnabas would not have felt slighted in the least, with him, no doubt, knowing and understanding, at least to a degree, that Paul was to play a special part in this great Plan of God.

JOHN MARK

Mark, who authored the Gospel, which bears his name, was the third member of this group. He was the youngest of the lot, probably in his twenties. He seems, at least at this time, to have been unmarried and a native of Jerusalem. His mother, named Mary, was related to Barnabas (Col. 4:10), which made Mark and Barnabas cousins.

Mary appears to have been a woman of wealth and position, as well as a Christian. Certainly her house was large enough to house a number of people, boasted at least one maidservant, and was used as a meeting place by the Apostolic Church even in time of persecution (Acts 12:12). It is significant that Peter, when he was released from prison by an Angel, had no doubt as to where he would find the Christians gathered. It would be at the house of John Mark.

Mark's father is nowhere mentioned in Scripture, and from the fact that the house of Acts 12:12 is referred to as belonging to Mary, it has been inferred, and probably correctly, that Mark's father was dead by that particular time, and his mother Mary then a widow.

It is believed that the Last Supper of our Lord, recorded in Mark, Chapter 14, actually took place in John Mark's house. The *"goodman of the house"* of Verse 14 could have been Mark's father, still alive then, although dead before the date of Acts 12:12.

Mark was brought to Antioch by Barnabas and Paul, who were returning from a relief mission to Jerusalem (Acts 12:25). When the two departed for Cyprus on their first missionary journey, Mark accompanied them (Acts 13:5). However, when the party reached Perga, which was on the mainland of Asia Minor (modern Turkey), Mark left them and returned to Jerusalem (Acts 13:13). This desertion by Mark, of which we will have more to say later, took its toll, not only at the present time, but later as well.

After Mark left Paul and Barnabas, he is lost to view in Acts but appears spasmodically in the Epistles. In fact, by the date of Colossians 4:10, he is in the company of Paul the prisoner, presumably at Rome, which signifies that the problems of the past had been worked out, with Paul now greatly admiring this young man, it seems.

THE FALSE PROPHET, BAR-JESUS

The first city on the island of Cyprus in which Paul and Barnabas ministered was Salamis. In fact, it was one of the principal cities of Cyprus. The Scripture just simply says, *"They preached the Word of God in the synagogues of the Jews,"* but gives no other information. Due to the fact that the word *"synagogues"* is plural, this tells us that they remained some weeks in Salamis.

They then left that city and went to Paphos, the Capital of Cyprus. And there, without Luke giving any more information, *". . . they found a certain sorcerer, a false prophet, a Jew, whose name was Bar-Jesus"* (Acts 13:6).

Luke tells us that this *"Bar-Jesus"* was *"with the deputy of the country, Sergius Paulus."* This man was the Roman Proconsul of the Island.

One would have to understand the culture of those times to conclude as to why Sergius Paulus had with him, apparently residing in his house, a Jewish imposter named Bar-Jesus, who had given himself also the title of *"Elymas or Wizard."*

Men have always had in their minds a belief in some personal power, which is the arbiter of their destiny. Evidently this false prophet had made Paulus believe that he was in touch with the spirit world, which he, no doubt, was, but the world of evil spirits. The Romans by this time had become cynical, hence, the cynical question asked by Pilate to Jesus, *"What is Truth?"* (Jn. 18:38). But, even though they had pretty much abandoned their supposed gods, which were derived out of Greek mythology, still, they continued to delve into the spirit world, not really understanding that they were contacting demon spirits, as with Bar-Jesus.

Even though Luke, as stated, gives us no information as to how Paul, Barnabas, and Mark came into contact with this sorcerer, he just tells us that they did. But the Holy Spirit through Luke does tell us that the *"deputy of the country, Sergius Paulus, was a prudent man."* Undoubtedly they had preached some services in the synagogues in Paphos, and this sorcerer had attended, and then conveyed to Sergius Paulus what he had seen and witnessed. At any rate, this deputy *"called for Barnabas and Saul, and desired to hear the Word of God"* (Acts 13:7).

The sorcerer, however, was not happy with these arrangements, feeling that his control over Paulus was slipping away, so he tried to contradict Paul in order to *"turn away the deputy from the Faith,"* even as our missionary party had witnessed to him.

PAUL

At this point, the Holy Spirit through Luke informs us that Saul will now go by the name of Paul (Acts 13:9).

It has been debated from then until now as to why Paul at this juncture in his life and Ministry would now go by the name of Paul instead of Saul? It is said that some of the ancient Christian writers have pointed out that the change of his name marks also a total change in all the conditions of his life. To use a play on words, they said, *"Paul suffers what Saul had inflicted; Saul stoned, and Paul was stoned; Saul inflicted scourgings on Christians, and Paul five times received forty stripes save one; Saul hunted the Church of God, Paul was let down in a basket; Saul bound, Paul was bound."*

Some have stated that *"Paul"* was the Greek derivative of *"Saul;"* however, that is not exactly correct. The Greek name for *"Saul"* is actually *"Saulos."* But, some say that *"Paul"* is the Roman derivative of the Hebrew *"Saul,"* which is probably the case.

At any rate, the Holy Spirit instructed Luke to write the words, *"then Saul, who also was called Paul,"* with the next phrase being, *"filled with the Holy Spirit,"* making us realize that the change of his name was determined by the Holy Spirit. We must remember that while he had a tremendous burden for the Jewish people and ministered to them through every door that was opened, still, his primary calling was to the *"Gentiles"* (Acts 9:15).

We should read these words and rejoice simply because, if you who hold this book in your hands are Saved by the Precious Blood of the Lord Jesus Christ, which I'm assuming you are, it is because of this Call laid on the life of Paul, which he faithfully administered, and which this Message of Redemption ultimately reached you and me.

THE SALVATION OF THE ROMAN PROCONSUL

As *"Elymas the Sorcerer"* attempted to *"turn away the deputy from the Faith,"* Paul confronted him saying, *"O full of all subtilty and all mischief, you child of the devil, you enemy of all Righteousness, will you not cease to pervert the Right Ways of the Lord?"* (Acts 13:10). In a sense, through this man, this Jew, this proclaims the sordid depths into which the entire Nation of Israel had fallen. Sadly and regrettably, the entire Nation, which crucified Christ, had now become a *"child of the devil, an enemy of all Righteousness,"* and instead of proclaiming the *"Ways of the Lord,"* were now seeking to *"pervert the Right Ways of the Lord."* How the mighty have fallen!

Paul spoke to this sorcerer and said, *"And now, behold, the Hand of the Lord is upon you, and you shall be blind, not seeing the sun for a season"* (Acts 13:11).

Actually, the phrase, *"Behold, the Hand of the Lord is upon you,"* would have been better translated, *"is against you."*

In the way the Holy Spirit phrased the words, there is indication that there was opportunity for Repentance; in other words, it was a remedial chastisement.

The Scripture says, *"And immediately there fell on him a mist and a darkness."* This was used by the Holy Spirit to teach this man that his message was *"darkness."*

At any rate, the Scripture says, *"Then the deputy, when he saw what was done, believed, being astonished at the Doctrine of the Lord"* (Acts 13:12).

And then, without giving any explanation, the Holy Spirit

through Luke informs us that John Mark departed from Paul and Barnabas, returning to Jerusalem (Acts 13:13). Even though the Holy Spirit is silent regarding why Mark did this, we do know that his departure caused hardship on this missionary team (Acts 15:37-39).

Some have ventured that Mark came from a wealthy family and was not accustomed to the hardships encountered on the missionary trail. It has also been suggested that Mark, at least at this stage, did not agree with Paul as it regarded the Law/Grace issue, in other words, the Message of the Cross. Inasmuch as the Holy Spirit did not desire to inform us as to the reason, anything conjectured is speculation at best.

PISIDIA

Paul and Barnabas now set sail from Cyprus to Perga in Pamphylia, a distance of approximately 200 miles. Incidentally, Pamphylia is a district that bordered Galatia where Churches were established by Paul with, no doubt, a Church established in Antioch in Pisidia.

There were 16 cities and towns named *"Antioch"* in that part of the Roman Empire, established by Seleucus in honor of his father. The Antioch of Syria, which was, one might say, the home Church of Paul, was by far the largest, actually the third largest city in the entirety of the empire. The Antioch that we will now address was in, as stated, Pisidia. It was, no doubt, here that the first Church in Galatia was established (please note the Epistle to the Galatians written by Paul sometime later, which was addressed to these very Churches).

THE FIRST RECORDED MESSAGE OF PAUL

It seems that Antioch in Pisidia possessed but a single synagogue, which must, therefore, have been a large one. If one walked inside a synagogue, one would have observed the women seated on one side and the men on the other. At the front was the reader's desk facing the congregation. The chief seats were close to the desk, where prominent Rabbis and Pharisees usually sat. The direction to which all prayer was offered was Jerusalem. There was a curtain behind the reader's desk, behind which was the Ark, in some ways a replica of the Ark of the Covenant, containing the Sacred Scrolls.

At the back of the auditorium was a space reserved for Gentiles, who were normally referred to as *"God-fearers."* In other words, they were not proselyte Jews, but still, even though Gentiles, desired to hear the Law explained. What they were hearing was of far greater substance than Greek mythology.

When prominent Jewish individuals came by, many times they were invited to address the congregation. Usually the Jewish speaker sat down during the delivery of his message, for that was the custom then; however, when Paul was invited to speak, the Scripture says that *"Paul stood up, and beckoning with his hand said, Men of Israel, and you who fear God..."* (Acts 13:16). As stated, the term *"fear God"* referred to the Gentile God-fearers.

Incidentally, Paul's custom was that when he went into a new area, he would always visit the synagogue, at least when there was one, and there usually was, ministering there first of all; however, the time finally came that he was no longer welcome in such.

WHAT DID PAUL PREACH IN THIS SYNAGOGUE?

Actually, referring to content, Paul's message was very similar to that of Stephen's those years before.

Did Paul preach the Cross to these Jews?

Not as he did to the Corinthians and others. It must be remembered, he's in a Jewish synagogue, with the greatest part of the congregation being Jews, and so the Holy Spirit impressed upon him to proclaim the Lord Jesus Christ as the Messiah of Israel. He did allude to the Death of Christ, but he never mentioned the Cross.

It must also be understood that the Jews considered anyone who had died on a Cross as being cursed by God (Deut.
21:22-23).

Paul, in concluding his Message, pulled no punches, plainly
stating that the Law of Moses could not justify, and yet, all who
believed on Christ, *"are justified from all things"* (Acts 13:39).
Every indication is that when the service ended, there were
many Jews who were angry with Paul.

In fact, when the next Sabbath came a week later, the indication is that Paul was not allowed to speak. The Jewish leaders in the synagogue the Scripture says, *"contradicted Paul and
blasphemed,"* meaning that they blasphemed Christ.

The Scripture then says:

"Then Paul and Barnabas waxed bold, and said, It
was necessary that the Word of God should first have
been spoken to you *(Jews)*: but seeing you put it from you,
and judge yourselves unworthy of Everlasting Life, lo, we
turn to the Gentiles *(proclaims a statement of far-reaching
magnitude; one might say this was the beginning of Western
Civilization)*.

"For so has the Lord Commanded us *(speaks not only
of His Personal Call, but of the Prophecy given by Isaiah as
well)*, **saying,** I have set you to be a Light of the Gentiles
(is taken from Isa. 49:6, and refers to the Messiah), that you
should be for Salvation unto the ends of the Earth *(the
Salvation afforded by Christ is intended for the entirety of
the world)*" (Acts 13:46-47).

The Scripture then says:

"And when the Gentiles heard this, they were glad,
and glorified the Word of the Lord *(they knew this meant
them, and it brought great joy, even as it should)*: and as
many as were ordained to Eternal Life believed *(means
that God has appointed and provided Eternal Life for all*

who will believe [Jn. 3:15-20; Rom. 1:16; 10:9-10; I Tim. 2:4; II Pet. 3:9; Rev. 22:17]).

"And the Word of the Lord was published throughout all the region *(it didn't say the Church, or some religious institution, etc., but 'the Word of the Lord'; this shows us where the emphasis must be)"* **(Acts 13:49).**

The Word of God then says:

"But the Jews *(those who opposed the Gospel)* **stirred up the devout and Honourable women** *(seems to indicate female Gentile Proselytes)*, **and the Chief men of the city, and raised persecution against Paul and Barnabas** *(means that these individuals believed the lies they were told about these two)*, **and expelled them out of their coasts** *(they were not merely requested to leave, but forcibly ejected; there is no evidence of physical violence, but definite evidence that physical violence was threatened).*
"But they shook off the dust of their feet against them *(presents that which Jesus Commanded His Disciples to do under these circumstances [Mat. 10:14; Mk. 6:11; Lk. 9:5; 10:11])*, **and came unto Iconium** *(a city in the southern part of the Roman Province of Galatia).*
"And the Disciples were filled with joy *(proclaims the fact that the Holy Spirit informed them that the problem in Antioch was not their fault; this brings them great joy)*, **and with the Holy Spirit** *(means that the Spirit of God was the Author of this 'joy')"* **(Acts 13:50-52).**

ICONIUM

The Jews of Antioch in Pisidia evidently were friends of powerful Roman administrators in the city and, as well, the Scripture says they *"stirred up the devout and Honourable women."* Evidently these were women who were quite possibly, as stated, female Gentile Proselytes. Some of them could very well have been wives of the *"chief men of the city."* They believed the lies told them about Paul and Barnabas, which shows how that even good people can be led astray.

So, they leave Antioch in Pisidia and go to Iconium, about 60 miles east of Antioch.

As was their custom, they went on the Sabbath Day to the synagogue and, as well, were given opportunity to speak. As a result, the Scripture says, *". . . that a great multitude both of the Jews and also of the Greeks believed"* (Acts 14:1). But as usual, there was opposition. The Scripture refers to these individuals as *"unbelieving Jews who stirred up the Gentiles."* Yet, they spent several weeks there, but whether they were able to continue in the synagogue each Sabbath, upon that, the Scripture is silent. At any rate, the Scripture also says, *". . . and granted signs and wonders to be done by their hands"* (Acts 14:3).

But the persecution became so forceful that plans were being made to stone them, with them then leaving and going to Lystra and Derbe. Lystra was about 10 miles west of Iconium, with Derbe being about 10 miles south of Lystra, all in the region of Galatia.

(There has been argument as to whether this was actually the Province of Galatia. Some say *"yes,"* and some say *"no."* This was due to the fact that particular districts changed names according to certain particulars. But according to the map that I have used, it shows these towns to be in the area that we presently refer to as Galatia.)

THE MIRACLE OF THE CRIPPLE BEING HEALED

Paul and Barnabas now leave Iconium and go to Lystra first and then to Derbe. The Scripture says, *"There they preached the Gospel,"* but, it doesn't tell us where. In other words, it seems that there was no synagogue in either place. This means, if, in fact, there was no synagogue there, they preached on the streets.

At any rate, hearing Paul preach about the Lord Jesus Christ, a cripple, who had been such from his mother's womb and had never walked and was known by all of the town people of Lystra, believed what Paul was preaching and evidenced Faith to be healed. Paul said, *"Stand upright on your feet. And he leaped and walked"* (Acts 14:10).

Most, if not all, of the townspeople of Lystra knew this crippled man. They saw this astounding Miracle, with him walking for the first time in his life. Because they were steeped in Greek mythology, they said of Paul and Barnabas, *"the gods are come down to us in the likeness of men."* They referred to Barnabas as Jupiter and Paul as Mercurius, two principal Greek gods. In fact, they were going to worship Paul and Barnabas, and when the two Apostles realized what was happening:

". . . they rent their clothes, and ran in among the people, crying out *(this was to show their disapproval of what was happening)*,

"And saying, Sirs, why do you these things? *(Why do people in India bathe in the filth of the Ganges River, thinking that such will guarantee them some type of eternal life? Why do many in Africa smear cow dung over their bodies, working themselves into a frenzy as someone beats a drum?)* We also are men of like passions with you *(Paul and Barnabas disavowed the ridiculous claims of these people that they are gods)*, and preach unto you that you should turn from these vanities unto the Living God *(other than the Living God Who can only be found through Jesus Christ, all is vanity)* . . ." (Acts 14:14-15).

At this stage, Paul preached a short message to them, directing them to the God of Heaven. But now, as quickly as they had wanted to crown Paul and Barnabas as gods, they turn the opposite way. But they had help in doing so.

PERSECUTION

The Scripture says:

"And there came thither *certain* Jews from Antioch and Iconium, who persuaded the people *(this evidently took place some days after the situation concerning the proposed sacrifice; these Jews persuaded the people to turn against Paul and Barnabas)*, and, having stoned Paul, drew *him* out of the city, supposing he had been dead *(they considered Paul to be the leader, with Barnabas, it seems, being spared from the stoning; Paul was near death)*" (Acts 14:19).

No doubt, one of the stones knocked Paul unconscious for a short period of time. While Believers stood around him thinking he was dead, he regained consciousness. To be sure, he most definitely was bruised badly. The Scripture says:

". . . he rose up *(indicates that however serious the situation was, there is some evidence that he was instantly healed)*, and came into the city *(means that Paul's detractors had now left, thinking he was dead)* . . ." (Acts 14:20).

Even though Luke doesn't mention it here, there is every evidence that Timothy found Christ as his Saviour in this particular meeting. In fact, it could well have been in the house of Eunice and Lois that accommodated Paul and Barnabas that night before they left the next day. This is the Timothy that Paul chose as his companion for future journeys, whom he sent on most confidential missions, and to whom he entrusted the oversight of his most important Churches. It was Timothy whom he summoned as the consolation of his last imprisonment, whom he always regarded as the son in the Faith who was nearest and dearest to his heart. How old Timothy was at this time has been conjectured to be anywhere from fifteen to twenty years old. In fact, Timothy was, no doubt, in the group that stood looking down at the body of Paul, thinking he was dead, when all of a sudden, he regained consciousness. He was, no doubt, touched greatly by the Lord. In fact, Timothy may very well have helped carry Paul to his mother's house, and there, it may be, not only bound his wounds, but showed to Paul at that time the responsibility, which reposed in him. The next morning Paul and Barnabas left for the town of Derbe, a distance of some 30 to 40 miles. It seems they had excellent success in Derbe as well (Acts 14:21). However we are given very little information except it says, *"And when they had preached the Gospel to that city, and had taught many. . . ."* The word *"many"* tells us they had good success.

They then returned to Lystra, Iconium, and Antioch. The Bible tells us that *"they ordained them Elders in every Church,"* which means that Paul and Barnabas, led by the Lord, from the midst of the congregation of each Church, selected those who felt the call to preach and, in effect, installed them as Pastors of these local Churches.

After ministering in Perga, they caught a ship for Antioch, their home Church, which concluded the first missionary journey. In fact, when they arrived home, they gave a report to the entirety of the Church at Antioch, telling *". . . all that God had done with them, and how He had opened the door of Faith unto the Gentiles"* (Acts 14:27).

The Scripture says that they *"abode long time with the Disciples"* at Antioch, which could have been as long as two years.

EPILOGUE

No doubt, Paul came to know any number of things regarding this first missionary journey. Up to a certain point, the Jews were willing to give him a hearing; but when they began to perceive that the Gospel was universal, and actually, that it was the Gospel of Jesus Christ Whom they had crucified, their anger burnt like a flame. One might say it was the scorn and indignation of the elder brother against the returning prodigal, and his refusal to enjoy privileges which, henceforth, he must share with others. In other words, the deep-seated pride of the Jews manifested itself. Who were these Preachers anyway who dared to run counter to the cherished hopes and traditional glories of nearly 2,000 years? Who were they to claim that all of this was by Faith alone, and above all, Faith in One Who had been branded an imposter?

THE REVELATION

It is almost positive that the great Apostle learned little by little the meaning of the great Revelation, which had been given to him concerning the meaning of the New Covenant. He, like us all, grew in Grace and in the knowledge of our Lord Jesus Christ. With experience, the Holy Spirit more and more brought his thinking into line with what he had been shown and given. And, in fact, that's the way the Lord works with most of us.

Obviously, in the great Revelation given to him, the Foundation of the Gospel was complete. As well, the framework was also developed, but it remained for the Holy Spirit to take the Apostle step by step into the greatest Word that had ever been given to a human being and, in fact, would ever be given. And when these great Truths were made clear to him, how that the Law had been finished in Christ, how that the rudiments of the Law, such as circumcision, etc., also had been finished in Christ, once that was known, and beyond the shadow of a doubt, the Apostle nailed it in his thinking, his preaching, and his writing.

And yet, as he ministered, as he continued to take this Gospel, there came a time in his spirit, even as Chapters 9, 10 and 11 of Romans bear out, that the Jews had closed the door on themselves, and yet, the Gentiles were evidently prepared to receive the Gospel. Being Jewish and knowing the Law as no other man on Earth at that time, this sorrow in his heart knew no bounds. I think the great Apostle sensed in his spirit the terrible tragedies, the horror, the unspeakable agonies, which this course would bring upon the Jews, and so it did! But yet, the great Apostle, along with the great Prophets of old, proclaimed by the Power of the Holy Spirit a restoration for Israel, which is even yet to come, but which most assuredly shall come!

"Soldier, soldier, fighting in the world's great strife,
"On yourself relying, battling for your life;
"Trust yourself no longer,
"Trust to Christ—He is Stronger:
"I can all things, all things do,
"Through Christ, which strengthens me."

"In your daily duty, standing up for right,
"Are you sometimes weary,
"Heart not always light?
"Doubt your Saviour never,
"This your motto ever:
"I can all things, all things do,
"Through Christ, which strengthens me."

"If your way be weary,
"He will help you through,
"Help you in your troubles,
"And your pleasures too;
"Say when Satan's by you;
"Say when all things try you:
"I can all things, all things do,
"Through Christ, which strengthens me."

"In a world of trouble, tempted oft to stray,
"You need never stumble, Satan cannot stay,
"Will but tempt you vainly,
"If you tell him plainly,
"I can all things, all things do,
"Through Christ, which strengthens me."

"Jesus' Power is boundless,

"Boundless as the sea;
"He is always able, able to keep me,
"Power bring from my weakness,
"Glory from my meekness:
"I can all things, all things do,
"Through Christ, which strengthens me."

PAUL

THE APOSTLE

CHAPTER SEVEN

The Council At Jerusalem

THE COUNCIL AT JERUSALEM

Upon arriving back at Antioch and giving a report to the Church in that city, the two Apostles experienced, no doubt, a much needed rest. They had been gone, it is believed, from twelve to eighteen months. Some also believe they were to stay approximately two years in Antioch before the second missionary journey, but with that time interrupted by the council in Jerusalem. It would be the Law/Grace issue.

While the Holy Spirit had, in effect, transferred His Base of Operations from Jerusalem to Antioch, still, the Church at Jerusalem, which was by far the largest anywhere, still held great sway, as would be obvious. James, the Lord's brother, was the senior Pastor, one might say, of that great Church. As well, when the original Twelve were in Jerusalem, which it seems was not too often, of course, this was their Church. So, due to this fact, and again as should be obvious, all of this held great sway. In fact, Paul felt, and rightly so, that he must have the approval of James, the Lord's brother, as well as the original Twelve. He would make the statement, *". . . lest by any means I should run, or had run, in vain"* (Gal. 2:2).

In fact, it has been argued for centuries as to whether the Jerusalem meeting described in Galatians, Chapter 2 is another meeting or the same meeting described in Acts, Chapter 15. I suppose the argument will never be settled, at least until we go to Glory, inasmuch as there seems to be evidence both ways. But, looking at what Paul said in the First Verse of Galatians, Chapter 2 leads me to believe that quite possibly Paul is describing the Acts, Chapter 15 meeting in Galatians, Chapter 2. I derive that from the phrase, *"Then fourteen years after I went up again to Jerusalem with Barnabas, and took Titus with me also"* (Gal. 2:1).

THE TIME FRAME

When Paul used the figure *"fourteen years,"* he was, no doubt, speaking of the time from his conversion on the road to Damascus. From the time of his conversion to his first missionary journey (Acts, Chpt. 13) was a time frame, it is believed, of about ten or eleven years. His first missionary journey took from one to two years. And then upon arriving back in Antioch, it could well have been a year or more before the trip to Jerusalem. So, to try to force the Galatians, Chapter 2 account into a separate meeting, which took place before Paul's first missionary journey, doesn't cover fourteen years. And yet, so much of this is speculative, as it regards time frames, that either way could be the case.

THE LAW/GRACE ISSUE

The Scripture says concerning this issue:

"And certain men which came down from Judaea taught the Brethren *(presents the greatest crisis of the Early Church)*, **and said,** Except you be circumcised after the manner of Moses, you cannot be Saved *(they were attempting to refute Paul's Message of Grace through Faith; in other words, they were attempting to circumvent the Cross, trying to add the Law of Moses to the Gospel of Grace).*

"When therefore Paul and Barnabas had no small dissension and disputation with them *(seems to indicate that these men came to Antioch not long after Paul and Barnabas had returned from their first Missions tour),* they *(the Elders of the Church at Antioch)* determined that Paul and Barnabas, and certain other of them, should go up to Jerusalem unto the Apostles and Elders about this question *(possibly refers to the trip mentioned by Paul in Gal. 2:1-10)*" (Acts 15:1-2).

WHAT WAS THE LAW/GRACE ISSUE?

In simple terminology, the Law/Grace issue consisted of

Jews from Jerusalem who insisted on attaching the Law of Moses to the Grace of God. Such, however, is impossible! Either one cancels out the other.

Salvation is by Grace through Faith alone. It must be Faith in Christ and what Christ has done at the Cross, which then allows the Goodness of God, i.e., *"the Grace of God,"* to flow unimpeded to the Believer. But, the moment that works are inserted, such as circumcision, Sabbath-keeping, etc., it cancels out Grace and does so immediately. That's what Paul was talking about when he said in his letter to the Galatians, *"that if you be circumcised, Christ shall profit you nothing"* (Gal. 5:2).

He then said, *"Christ is become of no effect unto you, whosoever of you are justified by the Law; you are fallen from Grace"* (Gal. 5:4).

And we must remember, Paul's Gospel is that which was given to him by the Lord Jesus Christ. It is the meaning of the New Covenant (Gal. 1:11-12). But some Christian Jews, evidently those of repute, whomever they may have been, were insisting upon Gentiles keeping the Law. In other words, every little Gentile boy baby who was born had to be circumcised on the eighth day, and every Gentile man who had given his heart to Christ had to also be circumcised, or so they claimed! As stated, Paul was adamant in his objection, stating that such was impossible! Let us say it again:

Either one cancels out the other. If law is inserted, it cancels out Grace. When Grace is inserted and Faith, thereby, evidenced, it cancels out all law. In other words, it is impossible to embrace both.

IS THE ISSUE OF LAW A PROBLEM PRESENTLY?

Yes!

In fact, it is just as much a problem now as it was then, and perhaps more so.

But now, it is more religious laws made up by preachers, or church denominations, or by individuals themselves, rather than Mosaic Law. But law is law and will have the same effect, irrespective of the time frame. Let me give some examples:

Paul teaches us the following:

• Jesus Christ is the Source of all things we receive from God (Col. 2:10).

• The Cross of Christ is the Means by which these things are given to us (Rom. 6:3-5; I Cor. 1:17-18, 23; 2:2).

• The Cross of Christ must ever be the Object of our Faith (Gal., Chpt. 5; 6:14).

• The Holy Spirit superintends all of this (Rom. 8:1-2, 11; Eph. 2:13-18).

This is the Gospel! Anything else is not the Gospel!

If the Believer says that if he will go on a *"fast"* for so many days, this will give him victory over sin, he's just made fasting into a *"law."* And God will not honor it. I heard one preacher say the other day that if we would get a buddy in whom we can confide, and we pray for each other, this is the answer to the sin question. While we appreciate very much the prayers of our fellow Believers, there's nothing in the Bible that lends any credence to that claim. I heard another one say that if healing is needed, or whatever, if one will take the Lord's Supper each day, or some such time frame, this will ensure healing and blessings, etc. Let everyone understand the following:

While these things mentioned are Scriptural and correct in their own right, still, if we take them out of their proper context, in other words, the manner in which they were originally given by the Lord, we then turn them into a law, which God will never honor. Laws always bring glory to the individual, who deserves no glory, and always and without fail, produce self-righteousness.

THE CROSS OF CHRIST

The Believer is to understand that every single thing we receive from the Lord; Salvation, the Baptism with the Holy Spirit, Divine Healing, answers to prayer, prosperity, blessings,

Fruit of the Spirit, Gifts of the Spirit, Righteousness, Holiness, everything, and I mean everything, comes strictly from Jesus Christ by and through the Cross. In other words, it's the Cross of Christ that has made everything possible. Without the Cross, there is no remission of sins, there is no way to approach God.

WHAT JESUS DID AT THE CROSS

At the Cross our Lord atoned for all sin, past, present, and future, at least for all who will believe (Jn. 3:16). Sin is the legal right that Satan has to hold man captive. With that legal right removed, which it was at the Cross, this leaves the Evil One with no legal right to hold anyone in bondage. So, if anyone, the unbeliever or the Believer, is not enjoying the freedom that comes only in Christ, it's because we have substituted law for Grace. When we do that, we nullify Grace, which is the Goodness of God, and which stops all blessings. If you want to read the plight of the Believer who loves the Lord but is still struggling and failing, simply read the Seventh Chapter of Romans. This Chapter gives us a page out of Paul's life before he understood God's Prescribed Order of Victory.

To be sure, Paul was Saved, and in that Salvation experience, the great Apostle saw the Lord and talked with Him, which had to be one of the greatest events in history. Three days later he was baptized with the Holy Spirit as Ananias laid hands on him (Acts 9:17). Immediately, he began to preach the Gospel, but still, not knowing God's Prescribed Order of Life and Living, the great Apostle, and no matter how hard he tried, could not live a victorious life. And please understand, if he couldn't, neither can you!

In fact, the meaning of the New Covenant, which is the meaning of the Cross, and is the key to all Victory, had not yet been given to anyone. It would very soon be given to the Apostle Paul, which he gave to us in his fourteen Epistles. The Lord has only one Way of Salvation, and that is *"Jesus Christ and Him Crucified"* (I Cor. 1:23). As well, the Lord has only one Way of Life and Living for the Believer, and that is *"Jesus*

Christ and Him Crucified" (I Cor. 1:23). This Gospel is a simple affair. It is strictly Christ and the Cross.

WHAT ARE WE MEANING WHEN WE SPEAK OF THE CROSS?

We aren't speaking of a wooden beam. We are speaking of what Jesus did there. And, as we have already stated, He atoned for all sin at the Cross, which totally and completely defeated Satan, and all demon spirits and fallen Angels (Col. 2:14-15). The Holy Spirit said so:

"**Blotting out the handwriting of Ordinances that was against us** *(pertains to the Law of Moses, which was God's Standard of Righteousness that man could not reach)*, **which was contrary to us** *(Law is against us, simply because we are unable to keep its precepts, no matter how hard we try)*, **and took it out of the way** *(refers to the penalty of the Law being removed)*, **nailing it to His Cross** *(the Law with its decrees was abolished in Christ's Death, as if Crucified with Him)*;"

TRIUMPH

"*And* **having spoiled principalities and powers** *(Satan and all of his henchmen were defeated at the Cross by Christ atoning for all sin; sin was the legal right Satan had, as stated, to hold man in captivity; with all sin atoned, he has no more legal right to hold anyone in bondage)*, **He** *(Christ)* **made a show of them openly** *(what Jesus did at the Cross was in the face of the whole universe)*, **triumphing over them in it.** *(The triumph is complete and it was all done for us, meaning we can walk in power and perpetual Victory due to the Cross)*" (Col. 2:14-15).

So, when we speak of the Cross, as stated, we aren't speaking of a wooden beam, but rather what Jesus did there. In fact, Paul used the Cross as a synonym for the entirety of the Gospel (I Cor. 1:17-18, 23; 2:2).

If the Judaizers had been successful in winning over James, the Lord's brother, and the Apostles (the original Twelve with Matthias taking the place of Judas), this would have effectively destroyed the great Word, the greatest known to mankind, that the Lord had given to Paul, which was the meaning of the New Covenant. So, that's what this meeting in Jerusalem was all about.

Would the Gentiles, who were coming to Christ by the thousands, be forced to embrace the Jewish Law, or would they be exempt, simply accepting Christ by Faith?

JERUSALEM

One can well imagine the thoughts that must have been in Paul's heart! This systematic attempt to undo all that had been done, and to render impossible all the progress, meant everything was at stake. Was the living and life-giving Spirit to be thus sacrificed to the dead letter? Were these new Pharisees to compass sea and land to make one proselyte, only that they might add the pride of the Jew to the vice of the Gentile and make him ten times narrower than themselves?

Farrar says, *"Was the superstitious adoration of dead ordinances to dominate over the heaven-sent liberty of the Children of God? So it boiled down to the following;*

"Was a Titus, young and manly, free and pure, with the love of Christ burning in his heart, to be held at arms length, while some unregenerate Pharisee, who while he wore the correct garments with exactly the right number of threads and knots, was yet an utter stranger to the love of Christ, and ignorant as a child of His free salvation?"[1]

DID THIS MEAN THAT THE LAW OF MOSES WAS BAD?

No!

In fact, Paul would later write:

"**Wherefore the Law *is* Holy** *(points to the fact that it is God's Revelation of Himself; the problem is not in the Law of God, the problem is in us)*, **and the Commandment Holy, and just, and good**" (Rom. 7:12).

But there were two things about the Law that should be readily known. They are:

1. The Law, which was God's Standard of Righteousness, was presented by God as the moral standard. And yet, because of the Fall, man was incapable of keeping the Law, even though it had a terrible penalty attached to its demands. Consequently, the sacrificial system, which symbolized Christ, was given in order that man could be forgiven for his trespasses respecting the Law.

2. By the time of Christ, however, the Law of Moses had been so polluted, so diluted, and so perverted that it anymore resembled not at all that which had been originally given. In fact, the Jews had added 613 oral laws to the original Law of Moses, which made the whole thing a hodgepodge of foolishness. Anyway, the Law, except for the moral part (the Ten Commandments), was always meant to be temporary. It pointed to the One Who was to come, namely the Lord Jesus, Who in man's place, as man's substitute, would keep the Law perfectly in word, thought, and deed. He did it all for us! As well, when He went to the Cross, He satisfied the demands of the broken Law, which God demanded, by the giving of Himself in Sacrifice, actually, a Perfect Sacrifice, which the Lord readily accepted. Everything about the Law pointed to Christ Who was to come and now, in fact, had come. But the Jews did not want to give up their Law, and so they were trying to force it onto the Gentiles who were now coming to Christ.

THE CONVERSION OF THE GENTILES

"**And being brought on their way by the Church**

(means that the Church at Antioch paid the expenses of the Brethren respecting this trip), **they passed through Phenice and Samaria, declaring the conversion of the Gentiles** *(indicates that they stopped to visit Churches all along the way)*: **and they caused great joy unto all the Brethren** *(seems to indicate that the Judaizers had not brought their false doctrine to these Churches)*.

"And when they had come to Jerusalem, they were received of the Church *(indicates they were received with open arms)*, **and** *of* **the Apostles** *(refers to the Twelve, minus James the brother of John who had been martyred)* **and Elders** *(other Preachers)*, **and they declared all things that God had done with them** *(gave a report of their recent Missions trip)*.**"**

THE PHARISEES

"But there rose up certain of the sect of the Pharisees which believed *(refers to them as having accepted Christ as their Saviour; they were in the Church at Jerusalem)*, **saying, That it was needful to circumcise them, and to command** *them* **to keep the Law of Moses** *(speaking of new converts; this was the great controversy; even though this was a different group, it was the same erroneous message)*.

"And the Apostles and Elders came together for to consider of this matter *(this was not a closed meeting, but was rather played out before many Believers)***" (Acts 15:3-6).**

These Christian Pharisees demanded obedience to the Law of Moses, especially the immediate acceptance of Circumcision as its most typical Rite. In fact, it denied the possibility of Salvation on any other terms. Of course, if this view were accepted, then Salvation by Grace through Faith was out the window, so to speak.

One can well imagine the thoughts of the Apostle Paul as

he observed these goings on, this systematic attempt to undo all that had been done, and to render impossible all further progress, at least, if such would be adopted.

Farrar said, *"They did not yet understand that Christ's fulfillment of the Law was its abrogation, and that to maintain the type in the presence of the antitype was to hold up superfluous candles to the sun."*[2]

SIMON PETER

The Scripture says:

"And when there had been much disputing *(much questioning and discussion)*, Peter rose up, and said unto them *(portrays the Apostle, at least now and at this particular meeting, in the position of Leadership)*, Men *and* Brethren, you know how that a good while ago God made choice among us, that the Gentiles by my mouth should hear the Word of the Gospel, and believe *(harks back some ten to twelve years earlier to Peter's experience with Cornelius [Acts, Chpt. 10])*.

"And God, Who knows the hearts *(speaks of this action concerning Cornelius being of the Lord and not of Peter)*, bear them witness *(witnessed to the validity of their conversion)*, giving them the Holy Spirit, even as *He did* unto us *(all of this without Circumcision and Law-keeping)*;

"And put no difference between us and them *(in other words, these Gentiles were just as Saved as Jews, and without all of the Laws of the Jews)*, purifying their hearts by Faith *(Faith in Christ and Faith in Christ alone, not by Law-keeping)*.

"Now therefore why do you tempt God *(calls into question that which God has done)*, to put a yoke upon the neck of the Disciples *(followers of Christ)*, which neither our Fathers nor we were able to bear? *(Peter*

*was not speaking disparagingly of the Law of Moses, but
stating that its demands were beyond the ability of human
beings to meet because of man's fallen condition.)*

"**But we** *(the Apostles)* **believe that through the
Grace of the Lord Jesus Christ we shall be Saved** *(with-
out Law-keeping)*, **even as they** *(even as the Gentiles)*"
(Acts 15:7-11).

THE SITUATION AT THAT TIME

Looking back over nearly twenty centuries and understanding that it was to Paul that the meaning of the New Covenant
was given, most presently, and rightly so, place Paul in the
position of leadership as it regards the Early Church. In fact,
the Holy Spirit allowed Paul to refer to himself as the *"masterbuilder of the Church"* (I Cor. 3:10). But during the time of
the Early Church, Simon Peter was looked at as the Prince of
the Apostles. He had walked with Christ personally for some
three and a half years. He had been chosen by the Holy Spirit
to preach the inaugural Message of the Church, so to speak, on
the Day of Pentecost. As well, the Lord had used him mightily
regarding the first months, and at least the first weeks after that
particular time, in seeing phenomenal healings and Miracles
take place (Acts 5:15-16). So, Paul announcing to the Church
of that day as to how the Lord had given him the meaning of
the New Covenant, which is the meaning of the Cross, didn't
sit exactly well with many people, even though every indication is that the original Twelve, with Matthias taking the place
of Judas, acquiesced to Paul's Message.

This particular day, Peter, to his credit, gave a ringing declaration of the Gospel of Grace.

He first of all reminded all the leaders of the Early Church
how that the Lord had used him to take the Message of Grace
to the Gentiles, as it regarded the household of Cornelius. And
he proclaimed it graphically so as to how that the Lord Saved
them and baptized them with the Holy Spirit without any

rudiments of the Law of Moses. In fact, the Apostle stated that the Lord *"put no difference between us and them, purifying their hearts by Faith."*

And now, he states that if this is denied, this great Message of Grace, that whoever does such would be *"tempting God."* And then, he closed his Message by stating, *"But we believe that through the Grace of the Lord Jesus Christ we shall be Saved, even as they,"* meaning that there was no Salvation in the Law, and if any Jew were to be Saved, he was going to have to come exactly as these Gentiles had come, with Faith in Christ, and Faith in Christ alone!

BARNABAS AND PAUL

If it is to be noticed in Verse 12, the Holy Spirit placed Barnabas at the forefront while in Jerusalem, because Barnabas was much better known there than Paul. And then, the Holy Spirit reverts back to putting Paul in the first place when they arrive back at Antioch (Acts 15:35).

The Scripture doesn't tell us as to exactly what Paul and Barnabas said to the leaders that day, simply saying that they *"declared what Miracles and Wonders God had wrought among the Gentiles by them"* (Acts 15:12).

Peter had spelled out the situation exactly as it should have been said, and I think that Paul felt that it was not wise at that time to add anything to Peter's Message. That would have been the wise course of action.

As it regards the Council of Acts, Chapter 15 and the account given of a Jerusalem visit by Paul in Galatians, Chapter 2, arguments have raged for centuries as to whether the Galatians, Chapter 2 account was the same as Acts, Chapter 15 or a different visit altogether?

I'll be honest with the reader, I have vacillated back and forth any number of times.

There are in the Acts of the Apostles five visits of Paul to Jerusalem. The following is, I believe, the order of those visits.

1. The evidence is that Paul visited Jerusalem almost immediately after his conversion (Acts 9:26-29).

2. The trip made to Jerusalem by both Paul and Barnabas to bring financial relief to that city, took place during the approximate two years that Paul was in Antioch, before his first missionary journey (11:29-30).

3. The General Council at Jerusalem, which we are now studying (Acts 15:2), I think, as well, is the Galatians, Chapter 2 account. Both accounts speak of the same visit.

4. The trip to Jerusalem after his second missionary journey, of which, almost no information is given (Acts 18:21-22).

5. His last visit, which was immediately before his imprisonment at Caesarea (Acts, Chpt. 21).

And yet, the above time frames that I have just given are not cast in concrete. Luke did not see fit to give much information as it regarded particulars, time frames being one of them. I suppose the Holy Spirit was telling us that those things are not that important.

PAUL'S MESSAGE TO THE GALATIANS

If, in fact, and I lay heavy emphasis on the word *"if,"* Galatians, Chapter 2 is an account given by Paul of the same meeting of Acts, Chapter 15, we then have some indication as to at least some of the things which happened in the Acts, Chapter 15 meeting.

The Apostle states that he *"went up by Revelation"* to Jerusalem. This means that the Lord told him to do so. He mentions that he *"communicated unto them that Gospel which I preach among the Gentiles, but privately to them which were of reputation"* (Gal. 2:2). It seems that when Paul was called upon to speak, he gave a ringing declaration of the Gospel of Grace to the congregation but, as well, had a private meeting with the Apostles, which included James, the Lord's Brother.

By the phrase, *"Lest by any means I should run, or had run, in vain,"* this tells us that he very well knew if the Church would split over this issue, the Kingdom of God would be set back many decades, if not destroyed altogether.

As a test case, he took Titus with him, who was a Gentile, and who had not been circumcised. If the right hand of fellowship, so to speak, were not given to Titus, thereby, recognizing his Salvation, the split would then commence. But, all the evidence is that Titus was greeted warmly and was not compelled at all to embrace any of the Law of Moses. But it didn't come easily.

Paul mentions *"False brethren unawares brought in, who came in privily to spy out our liberty which we have in Christ Jesus, that they might bring us into bondage"* (Gal. 2:4). But whatever ensued that day, the Apostle strongly proclaims the fact that neither he nor those with him by any means subjected themselves to the demands of these *"false brethren"* that the *"Truth of the Gospel might continue with you"* (Gal. 2:5).

He goes on to state to the Galatians that the meeting ended with James, the Lord's Brother, and Peter, along with John, giving Paul and Barnabas *"the right hands of fellowship"* (Gal. 2:9).

To be sure, this meeting recorded in Acts, Chapter 15, which was possibly the same meeting mentioned by Paul in Galatians, Chapter 2, was one of the most important meetings in the history of mankind. As stated, if Paul's Message of Grace had been repudiated by James, the Lord's Brother, or anyone of the original Twelve, it would have set the Kingdom of God back many years, if not destroy it altogether. But, as we shall see, the Evil One did not take best at this time.

JAMES, THE LORD'S BROTHER

James, along with Joseph, Simon, and Jude were, one might say, the half brothers of our Lord (Mat. 13:55). They did not accept His Ministry at all until His Crucifixion and Resurrection (Mk. 3:21; Jn. 7:5). It is hard to understand that! Yet, our Lord appeared to James after His Resurrection (I Cor. 15:7), which changed him completely. In fact, he became a leader of the Jewish-Christian Church at Jerusalem (Gal. 1:19; 2:9; Acts 12:17).

Tradition states that he was appointed the leader of the Church in Jerusalem by the Lord Himself; however, that is at best mere speculation.

This we do know, he presided at the first Council at Jerusalem, which we are now studying, which considered the terms of admission of Gentiles into the Church. He formulated the decree which was spread among all the Churches (Acts 15:19-23).

A few years after this Jerusalem Council, James suffered martyrdom by being stoned at the instigation of the High Priest Ananus. Tradition says that he was known as *"James the Just,"* because of his piety. As well, he is the author of the Epistle which bears his name. He described himself as *"a servant of God and of the Lord Jesus Christ"* (James 1:1). He never referred to himself as an Apostle, but Paul did refer to him as such (Gal. 1:19).

THE MESSAGE GIVEN BY JAMES

The Scripture says:

"And after they had held their peace *(Paul and Barnabas concluded their remarks)*, James answered, saying, Men *and* Brethren, hearken unto me *(presents the Lord's Brother as the presiding Elder of the Church in Jerusalem)*:

"Simeon has *(Peter)* declared how God at the first did visit the Gentiles *(refers to the conversion of Cornelius and his household)*, to take out of them a people for His Name *(presents this as the Plan of God, which it surely was!)*.

"And to this agree the words of the Prophets *(James now appeals directly to the Word of God, which verifies all that has been said)*; as it is written *(Amos 9:11)*,

"**After this I will return** *(speaks of the Church Age and the Second Coming of the Lord)*, **and will build again the Tabernacle of David, which is fallen down; and I will build again the ruins thereof, and I will set it up** *(speaks of the Restoration of Israel and the coming Kingdom Age, in which all the Prophets declare [Isa. 9:6-7; Dan. 7:13-14; Hos. 3:4-5; Lk. 1:32-33; Rom., Chpts. 9-11; Rev. 11:15; 20:1-10; 22:4-5])*:

"**That the residue of men might seek after the Lord, and all the Gentiles** *(a worldwide harvest of souls during the Kingdom Age)*, **upon whom My Name is called, says the Lord** *(refers to the Gentile world which has been favorable toward the Lord to a degree)*, **Who does all these things** *(refers to the Power of God in performing all of this)*.

"**Known unto God are all His Works from the beginning of the world** *(the Plan of God regarding the human family was known from 'the beginning of the world' [Gen., Chpt. 4])*" **(Acts 15:13-18).**

THE SENTENCE AS GIVEN BY JAMES

As James spoke that day, I think that Paul and all with him felt by the tenor of his Message that he was going to make the right decision. It would seem to be obvious from the introduction remarks of his Message. Now he comes to the conclusion.

"**Wherefore my sentence is** *(would have been better translated, 'I think it good')*, **that we trouble not them, which from among the Gentiles are turned to God** *(carries the idea that it does not make any sense to demand certain other things of them, claiming such things are needed in order to be Saved, when in fact the people are already Saved!)*:

"**But that we write unto them, that they abstain from pollutions of idols** *(this was common in the heathen world of that day)*, **and** *from* **fornication** *(all forms of* *immorality)*, **and** *from* **things strangled** *(which refers to the blood not being properly drained from the flesh)*, **and** *from* **blood** *(not to eat blood, which was somewhat common among the heathen during those days; in any case, blood was not to be imbibed, but this did not refer to transfusion; man is Saved by the shed Blood of Christ, so blood must be treated accordingly)*.

"**For Moses of old time has in every city them who preach him, being read in the synagogues every Sabbath Day** *(the idea is that Gentiles who desire to know more about the Law of Moses need only to go to one of the synagogues on the Sabbath, which was every Saturday)*" **(Acts 15:19-21).**

THE DECISION

The statement given by James was most everything that Paul had hoped for. No doubt, at least in that which was given, James was definitely led by the Lord. However, there is a nagging question that I personally think begs to be asked.

The decision rendered by James was solely for Gentiles. It was the right decision; however, should James have taken this opportunity to have included the Jews in his decision?

I realize that such a position at that time, at least as it regarded the Jews, would have created a phenomenal furor and uproar. But, we must remember, there aren't two Gospels, only one. And that one Gospel can be summed up in this Passage:

"*For by Grace are you Saved through Faith; and that not of yourselves: it is the Gift of God: not of works, lest any man should boast*" (Eph. 2:8-9).

While the Law of Moses within itself was not "*works,*" and was never meant by God to be "*works,*" still, the Jews had long since turned it into "*works.*" In their minds, keeping the Law, which Jesus plainly said none of them ever did, constituted Salvation. So, the Gospel of Grace, i.e., "*the Cross,*" comes up against the gospel of Law.

THE GREATEST TROUBLE FOR PAUL

If you study Paul's writings, and knowing that the Holy Spirit gave him all that he wrote, it is quickly obvious that the Law/Grace issue presented itself as the greatest problem. Satan used this as he used nothing else.

Individuals came out of Jerusalem who claimed to profess Christ but, insisted upon Gentiles also keeping the Law. They insisted that all Gentile men who had come to Christ now be circumcised, in other words, made a part of the old Mosaic Covenant. They refused to admit that all of this was finished in Christ, and was meant to be finished in Christ. Considering that these individuals came from Jerusalem, and maybe even from the Mother Church, this gave them a form of legitimacy, enabling them to make inroads into these Churches. To be sure, the perverted gospel of the Law could not win anybody to Christ, so they had to parasite off of those whom Paul and his associates had won to the Lord. In fact, the entirety of the Epistle to the Galatians was written to counter this effort by the Judaizers. Paul bluntly told the Galatians, and all others, as well, *"Christ is become of no effect unto you, whosoever of you are justified by the Law; you are fallen from Grace"* (Gal. 5:4).

After studying the Book of Acts and the Epistles of the New Testament for many, many years, it is my feeling that James was wrong in not including the Jews as it regarded the issue at hand. I do not at all mean to cast any reflection on James who, no doubt, was a godly Brother. And, had I been there in his shoes, I might have seen things differently then than I do now. But we do know the following:

The Holy Spirit shifted the center of world Evangelism from Jerusalem to the city of Antioch, Syria. And yet, Satan did his best there to override the great Gospel of Grace.

SIMON PETER AND PAUL

At least one of the greatest attacks against the New Covenant, and perhaps the greatest, was what happened regarding Peter and Barnabas at Antioch. If Paul had not taken the stand he took, even facing down the Prince of the Apostles, the Work of God could have suffered irreparable harm. And, if Peter had not taken the rebuke as he did, with humility, which must have been difficult, still, the harm could have been stupendous.

As well, the argument has raged for centuries as to whether this occurrence took place before the Jerusalem Council or after the Jerusalem Council. I think one could say without much fear of contradiction that it could have taken place either time.

The Word of God says concerning this situation:

> "But when Peter was come to Antioch *(Antioch Syria, the city used by God to spearhead world Evangelism)*, I withstood him to the face *(means Paul openly opposed and reproved him, even though Peter was the eldest)*, because he was to be blamed *(for abandoning the Cross and resorting to Law)*.
>
> "For before that certain came from James *(gives us all too well another example as to why Apostles, or anyone else for that matter, are not to be the final word, but rather the Word of God itself)*, he *(Peter)* did eat with the Gentiles *(Peter knew the Gospel of Grace)*: but when they were come *(those from James in Jerusalem)*, he withdrew and separated himself, fearing them which were of the Circumcision. *(The problem was 'man fear.' Some of the Jewish Christians were still trying to hold to the Law of Moses, which means they accepted Jesus as the Messiah, but gave no credence to the Cross whatsoever. This ultimately occasioned the necessity of Paul writing the Epistle to the Hebrews.)*"

BARNABAS

> "And the other Jews *(in the Church at Antioch)* dissembled likewise with him *(with Peter)*; insomuch that

Barnabas also was carried away with their dissimulation *(hypocrisy)*.

"**But when I saw that they walked not uprightly according to the Truth of the Gospel** *(they were forsaking the Cross)*, **I said unto Peter before** *them* **all** *(Paul's rebuke was in the presence of everybody, the whole Antioch Church)*, **If you, being a Jew, live after the manner of Gentiles, and not as do the Jews, why do you compel the Gentiles to live as do the Jews?** *(Hypocrisy)*" (**Gal. 2:11-14**).

Let's look at the particulars of what took place here.

THE EFFORTS OF SATAN

• **This, I believe, was one of the greatest attacks leveled against the New Covenant by Satan. Had it succeeded, it could have set back the Gospel for many years, or destroyed it altogether.**

• **We find Satan using some of the strongest stanchions of the Faith, showing that even the greatest among us, whomever that might be, can go astray if we do not keep our eyes on Christ and the Cross.**

• **Considering who Peter was and Barnabas, as well, their departure from Faith, if allowed to continue, could have stopped the great Gospel of Grace in its tracks.**

• **Even though Peter was older than Paul, still, Paul did what was necessary as it regarded the stand he took.**

• **The phrase,** *"I withstood him to the face, because he was to be blamed,"* **places the blame where it rightly belonged, in the lap of Simon Peter, so to speak.**

• **Paul emphatically stated that these Judaizers** *"came from James"* **in Jerusalem, which, of course, gave them credibility. This is one of the reasons I say that James should have included the Jews in the sentence he gave freeing the Gentiles from the Law.**

• **We find that fear on the part of Peter is what caused him** to do what he did. The moment the Believer, preacher, or otherwise, places what people think ahead of what God knows, we have just failed the Lord. It's what the Lord knows instead of what people think.

• What Peter did carried such weight that even *"Barnabas also was carried away with their hypocrisy."* Now think about this! No one in the world other than Paul knew the great Gospel of Grace as did Barnabas, and yet, he loses his way, which could have been permanent had it not been for Paul.

• When Paul rebuked Peter, he didn't do it behind closed doors, but rather before the entirety of the Church. This hypocrisy of not eating with Gentiles was carried out before all, so Paul felt he had to address the problem before all, which he did.

• Knowing now that there was neither Jew nor Gentile, Peter conducted himself accordingly; however, now that these individuals had come from Jerusalem, afraid of what they might say back at Jerusalem, he cut himself off from the Gentiles, refusing to eat with them, which, in effect, reverted back to legalism and a denial of the great Gospel of Grace. In other words, by his action, Peter was actually denying the Salvation of these Gentiles. That's how serious that it was.

• Even though Paul does not give any indication here, every evidence is that Peter took this rebuke, even though given publicly, admitted his wrong, and then proceeded to conduct himself as he should. It took a big man to do that!

WAS THE GOSPEL PREACHED BY OUR LORD THE SAME AS THE GOSPEL PREACHED BY PAUL?

No!

But, neither Gospel contradicted the other.

Jesus was the last Preacher under the Law; consequently, He came to proclaim the Law as it had originally been given and was meant to be given to the people. As stated, the Jews had so changed the Law, so perverted the Law, and so polluted the Law that it anymore little resembled that which was originally given.

Jesus did not preach the Gospel of Grace, even though He is the One Who made it totally possible. The Scripture says:

"For the Law was given by Moses, but Grace and Truth came by Jesus Christ" (Jn. 1:17). The Lord could not rightly preach something that had not yet been given. The Cross had to be a fact before the new Dispensation of Grace could be brought in.

With the Cross now a fact, the Lord gave to Paul the meaning of the New Covenant, which was wrapped up in the Cross of Christ. In fact, Jesus Christ is the New Covenant, but it was what He did at the Cross that constituted the New Covenant, which was to atone for all sin, past, present, and future, at least for all who will believe (Jn. 3:16). In fact, Jesus did two things at the Cross.

1. He satisfied the demands of the broken Law by giving Himself in Sacrifice, and did so by the shedding of His Own Precious Blood, which was accepted by God (Col. 2:14-15).

2. As stated, He atoned for all sin, which removed the legal right that Satan had to hold man captive. So, when we talk about the Cross, we, as already stated several times, are not talking about a wooden beam; we are speaking of what Jesus did there, the price He paid there, the Victory He won there, and a Victory, I might quickly add, which was and is Eternal (Heb. 13:20).

THE RESULTS OF THE JERUSALEM COUNCIL

Considering the edict or sentence handed down by James, the Scripture says:

"Then pleased it the Apostles and Elders, with the whole Church, to send chosen men of their own company to Antioch with Paul and Barnabas *(proclaims the fact that all of the Church at Jerusalem, or at least the greater majority, totally agreed with what James had said respecting Gentiles and the Law of Moses)*; ***namely*, Judas surnamed Barsabas, and Silas, Chief men among the Brethren** *(Silas was to play a very important part regarding his help to Paul with respect to future Evangelism):*"

LETTERS

"**And they wrote *letters* by them after this manner; The Apostles and Elders and Brethren *send* greeting unto the Brethren which are of the Gentiles in Antioch and Syria and Cilicia:**

"**Forasmuch as we have heard, that certain which went out from us have troubled you with words, subverting your souls** *(evidently speaks of those mentioned in Verse 1 of this Chapter)*, **saying, *You must* be circumcised, and keep the Law; to whom we gave no *such* Commandment** *(specifies exactly what the error was; these individuals, whomever they may have been, were not sent by the Church in Jerusalem, nor were they given any commandment to teach any type of false doctrine)*:

"**It seemed good unto us, being assembled with one accord** *(proclaims the unity of the Brethren in Jerusalem)*, **to send chosen men unto you with our beloved Barnabas and Paul** *(places a gracious and kind endearment toward Paul and Barnabas, which spoke volumes as well)*,

"**Men who have hazarded their lives for the Name of our Lord Jesus Christ** *(tells us for Whom it was done!)*.

"**We have sent therefore Judas and Silas, who shall also tell *you* the same things by mouth** *(with these two men accompanying this letter, and verifying its contents, no false prophet could claim that the letter was forged, etc.).*"

THE HOLY SPIRIT

"**For it seemed good to the Holy Spirit, and to us**

(proclaims without a doubt that the Holy Spirit led and guided these proceedings), **to lay upon you no greater burden than these necessary things** *(when men leave the Word of God, they get into a lot of 'unnecessary things')*;

"**That you abstain from meats offered to idols, and from blood, and from things strangled, and from fornication: from which if you keep yourselves, you shall do well. Fare you well.**

"**So when they** *(possibly six or seven Brethren)* **were dismissed** *(sent away with great love)*, **they came to Antioch: and when they had gathered the multitude together, they delivered the Epistle** *(we aren't told how large the Church was in Antioch; however, it could have numbered several hundred; that being the case, they would have met outdoors for this Epistle to be read to them)*:"

REJOICING

"*Which* **when they had read, they rejoiced for the consolation** *(tells us that the Law/Grace issue had been very serious; now this settles the dispute, at least for the time being)*.

"**And Judas and Silas, being Prophets also themselves** *(means that they stood in the Office of the Prophet [Eph. 4:11])*, **exhorted the Brethren with many words, and confirmed** *them* *(they addressed the multitude with words of great encouragement)*.

"**And after they** *(Judas and Silas)* **had tarried** *there* **a space, they were let go in peace from the Brethren unto the Apostles** *(refers to Judas returning to Jerusalem, but not Silas)*.

"**Notwithstanding it pleased Silas to abide there still** *(it was the Holy Spirit Who moved on him to remain in Antioch)*" **(Acts 15:22-34).**

"Shine on me, O Lord Jesus,

"And let me ever know,
"The Grace that shone from Calvary,
"Where You did love me so.
"My Child, I am your Saviour.
"'Tis not what you do feel,
"But My Own gracious Promise,
"Which does your pardon seal."

"Shine in me, O Lord Jesus,
"And let Your searching Light,
"Reveal each hidden purpose,
"Each thought as in Your Sight.
"My Child, I am your Searcher,
"I try each loving heart,
"For I would have most holy,
"All who in Me have part."

PAUL
THE APOSTLE

CHAPTER EIGHT

*The Second
Missionary Journey*

Paul's Second Missionary Journey

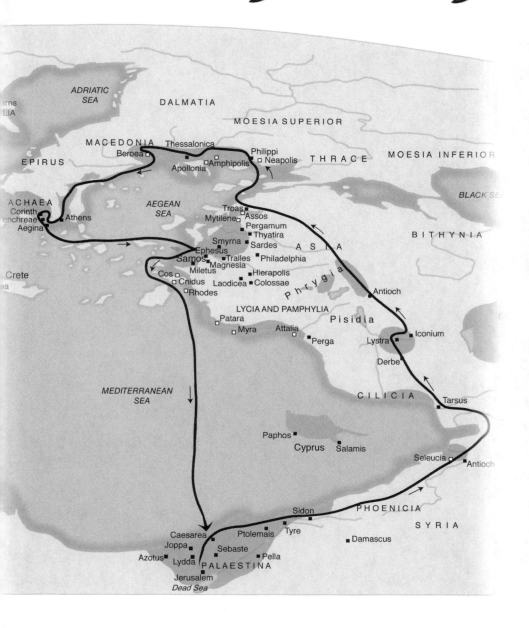

THE SECOND MISSIONARY JOURNEY

This journey will prove to be the most fruitful, in fact beyond comprehension, undertaken by the great Apostle. The Gospel, as we will soon see, will now go to the west, in other words, to Europe, the first country being Greece, the first city being Philippi. There is no way that the human mind can comprehend the significance of the Gospel going in this direction, which was westward. Why was the Lord so adamant about the Gospel going in this direction instead of other directions?

We as human beings, even as the Holy Spirit through Paul said, *"see through a glass, darkly"* (I Cor. 13:12). But God sees the past, the present, and the future. He had in mind the fact that the Gospel would be better received westward, with it eventually going to Spain, then to England, and then to North, Central and South America. So, we in the west owe our Salvation, as well as our prosperity and freedom, in totality, in a sense, to the Macedonian Call.

Concerning the beginning of the second missionary journey, the Scripture says:

"Paul also and Barnabas continued in Antioch, teaching and preaching the Word of the Lord, with many others also *(this Church was blessed, to say the least!).*

"And some days after *(could have been as much as a year)* Paul said unto Barnabas, Let us go again and visit our Brethren in every city where we have preached the Word of the Lord, *and see* how they do *(refers to the Churches they had planted on the first missionary journey)*" (Acts 15:35-36).

THE DISPUTE BETWEEN PAUL AND BARNABAS

The Scripture says:

"And Barnabas determined to take with them John,

whose surname was Mark *(the word 'determined' implies a 'deliberate action,' which means that Barnabas was adamant on the subject).*

"**But Paul thought not good to take him with them, who departed from them from Pamphylia** *(suggests a rupture)*, **and went not with them to the work** *(he did not go with them to the work to which God called them, as he ought to have done).*

"**And the contention was so sharp between them** *(means to dispute to the point of anger)*, **that they departed asunder one from the other** *(it created an abrupt and severe rupture; it is my feeling that Barnabas should have acquiesced to Paul; the Holy Spirit had said 'separate Me Barnabas and Paul for the work whereunto I have called them'; the Holy Spirit didn't mention Mark)*: **and so Barnabas took Mark, and sailed unto Cyprus** *(Barnabas will not be mentioned again in the great Book of Acts, and yet, we dare not take away from the godliness of this man)*" (Acts 15:37-39).

We see several things here in this episode given to us by Luke. Some of them are:

• There can be, as here, disputes between godly people; however, we learn elsewhere from Paul's writings that the situation was ultimately rectified, with Paul seeing in Mark the qualities that Barnabas had previously seen and, thereby, recommending him highly regarding the Gospel (II Tim. 4:11). As well, it seems that things were made right between Paul and Barnabas also (Col. 4:10).

• The facts are, I think, that Barnabas was right about Mark, but yet, Barnabas should not have taken it as far as he did. He should have acquiesced to Paul. The reason is, as stated, the Holy Spirit had said, *"Separate Me Barnabas and Saul for the work whereunto I have called them"* (Acts 13:2). While Barnabas was greatly used of the Lord, still, I think his contribution to the Work of God would have been much greater had he continued with Paul.

• **Paul was partly wrong in this episode, as well, I think!** Time would prove that there were excellent qualities in Mark. Incidentally, this is the same Mark who wrote the Gospel which bears his name. But Barnabas, as stated, should have acquiesced to Paul simply because Paul was now in the position of leadership, and a position accorded by the Holy Spirit.

• Evidently, Mark's defection from them almost at the beginning of their first missionary journey caused great hardship. Fearing that such might happen again, the Apostle was very reluctant to give Mark a second chance. As stated, He would rectify that later on in his Ministry.

PAUL AND SILAS

The Scripture says:

"**And Paul chose Silas, and departed** *(proclaims the beginning of the second missionary journey; this is the reason the Holy Spirit had Silas remain behind in Antioch),* **being recommended by the Brethren unto the Grace of God** *(he wholeheartedly approved of the great Covenant of Grace, which was absolutely necessary if he was to be of help to Paul).*

"**And he** *(Paul)* **went through Syria and Cilicia, confirming the Churches** *(teaching in each Church, which obviously was so very much needed)*" **(Acts 15:40-41).**

WHO IS SILAS?

Silas was evidently one of the Elders in the Church at Jerusalem. He was thought of so highly that he was chosen as one of the emissaries to confirm the genuineness of the letter sent by James to all the Churches as it regarded the Law/Grace issue. The last notice of him which occurs in Scripture, we find him still in the company of Peter, who sends him from Babylon with a letter to some of the very Churches which he had visited with Paul (I Pet. 5:12). His adherence to the Ministry of Paul, despite the close bonds which united him with the Jewish Christians, is a sufficient proof that he was a man of large stature, spiritually speaking.

Incidentally, his Roman name was *"Silvanus,"* which may prove that he was, as well, a Roman citizen. In every respect it was the Grace of God which provided Paul with so valuable a companion. Farrar said, *"And as they began the second great journey, carrying with them the hopes and fortunes of Christianity, they were especially commended by the Brethren to the Grace of God."*[1]

As we shall see, he accompanied Paul through Syria, Asia Minor, Macedonia and Thessalonica. When Paul left for Athens, Silas stayed at Berea and then joined Paul at Corinth (Acts 16-18). Paul mentions his work there in II Corinthians 1:19. As well, he was associated with Paul in the letters written from Corinth (I Thess. 1:1; II Thess. 1:1), but is not named again until the reference to him in I Peter.

The Scripture says:

> "And Paul chose Silas, and departed *(proclaims the beginning of the second missionary journey; this is the reason the Holy Spirit had Silas remain behind in Antioch)*, being recommended by the Brethren unto the Grace of God *(he wholeheartedly approved of the great Covenant of Grace, which was absolutely necessary if he was to be of help to Paul)*.
>
> "And he *(Paul)* went through Syria and Cilicia, confirming the Churches *(teaching in each Church, which obviously was so very much needed)*" **(Acts 15:40-41).**

TIMOTHY

The Scripture says:

> "Then came he *(Paul)* to Derbe and Lystra *(the*

second missionary journey will have a greater effect on civilization than anything that has ever happened, other than the First Advent of Christ): **and, behold, a certain Disciple was there, named Timothy, the son of a certain woman, which was a Jewess, and believed** *(speaks of Timothy and his mother as being followers of Christ)*; **but his father *was* a Greek** *(it seems he was not a Believer)*:

"**Which was well reported of by the Brethren who were at Lystra and Iconium** *(Timothy's consecration is obvious here)*.

"**Him would Paul have to go forth with him** *(which was undoubtedly a leading of the Spirit)*; **and took and circumcised him because of the Jews which were in those quarters** *(this was wisdom on Paul's part, which he felt led by the Holy Spirit to do)*: **for they knew all that his father was a Greek** *(Paul would do all he could to appease people, but not at the expense of compromising the Gospel)*" **(Acts 16:1-3).**

Not able in those days to inform cities of distance that they would be arriving, one can well imagine the delight of the Christians in Derbe and Lystra, as well as other areas, upon the arrival of Paul and Silas. Also, one can well imagine that one of the first questions asked was, *"And where is Barnabas?"* About all that Paul could say in answer to that question, and it was, no doubt, asked many times, was that Barnabas was elsewhere preaching the Gospel.

Paul would find that these Churches were thriving. How that must have gladdened his heart.

As well, he once again sees Timothy who had come to Christ respecting Paul's former visit to this area. More than likely, he and Silas stayed at the home of Timothy's mother Eunice, with his grandmother Lois more than likely living with them. These two pious women were Jewesses who had now accepted the Christian Faith.

It is believed by some that Eunice may have been a widow,

with her husband having already passed away. At any rate, Paul wanted to take on Timothy as a helper, which refers to traveling with him and Silas, which would have been a self-sacrifice on the part of Timothy's mother.

Timothy was to become one of the closest confidants of the Apostle Paul. Of the many whom Paul loved, none was dearer to him, it seems, than this young Disciple of Lystra. In some ways, one might say that he adopted Timothy and regarded him as a son in all affectionate nearness.

In fact, no name is so closely associated with Paul's as that of Timothy. Not only were two Epistles addressed to him, the last two written by Paul, he is associated with Paul in the superscription of five. He was with Paul during the greater part of this second missionary journey. As well, he was with him at Ephesus. He accompanied him in his last voyage to Jerusalem, doing what he could, as well, to help him regarding his first imprisonment at Rome. He is urged in the last Epistle, which was addressed to him, to hasten from Ephesus, to bring with him the cloak, books, and parchments which Paul had left with Carpus at Troas, and to join him in his second imprisonment before it was too late to see him alive.

Going back to their time at Lystra, more than likely the whole church was assembled, with the Elders and Paul laying their hands upon Timothy, giving him their blessing as he would depart with the great Apostle.

That day when Paul and Silas left Lystra with Timothy now in their company, who was probably at the time about twenty years old, little did his mother realize how eternal this mission would be. She probably never imagined that Timothy would be spoken of thousands of years in the future, and in strange lands of which she had never even heard, for such is the Power of the Gospel.

No, it would not have been possible for her to even remotely have understood the significance of what was happening that day when her son left. No doubt there was pain in her heart at seeing him leave, and yet, at the same time, I think that she knew and understood this was the Will of God.

After the death of Paul, tradition says that Timothy became the Pastor of the Church at Ephesus. In a sense, when Paul suffered martyrdom in Rome, the reins of this great Gospel of Grace, in many ways, were turned over to Timothy, then in his prime.

FORBIDDEN OF THE HOLY SPIRIT

"And as they went through the cities, they delivered them the decrees for to keep, that were ordained of the Apostles and Elders which were at Jerusalem *(pertained to copies of the decision concerning the Law/Grace issue, which came out of the Council at Jerusalem).*

"And so were the Churches established in the Faith *(Jesus Christ and Him Crucified),* and increased in number daily *(many were being Saved).*

"Now when they had gone throughout Phrygia and the region of Galatia *(implies a time frame of probably several months),* and were forbidden of the Holy Spirit to preach the Word in Asia *(refers to the area now known as northwestern Turkey; while the Holy Spirit definitely wanted the Gospel to go to this area, there was another place He desired first),*

"After they were come to Mysia, they assayed to go into Bithynia *(represented an area east of the Ephesus area)*: but the Spirit suffered them not *(proclaims the door being closed to this area as well!).*

"And they passing by Mysia came down to Troas *(this area would be closed for the time being also)*" (Acts 16:4-8).

THE LEADING OF THE LORD

It is not always easy to ascertain the leading and guidance of the Holy Spirit, even by someone as close to the Lord as Paul. No doubt, when they began this second missionary journey, they had planned to go to the Churches founded on the first journey and, as well, to push on further in Asia Minor, which would have been in modern northwestern and north central Turkey.

Paul and Silas, along with the Church at Antioch, thought surely they had the Mind of the Lord as it regarded these places to which they intended to go. So, the question begs to be asked as to why the Lord did not inform them of the change of plans. In other words, the Holy Spirit had plans other than those of the Apostles. Let us say it again:

It's not always easy to ascertain the Mind of God. Sometimes He informs us many years ahead of time as to what will take place, and sometimes He informs us at the last minute. There are reasons for all of that, which are known only by the Lord.

First of all, they went to Mysia, which is located in northwestern Turkey, but *"were forbidden of the Holy Spirit to preach the Word in Asia."*

As to exactly how the Holy Spirit informed them that they were not to make any effort at the Gospel in this particular area, at least at this time, we aren't told. At any rate, they planned to go from Mysia to Bithynia, but again, *"The Spirit suffered them not."* No doubt, very confused, they then went to Troas, which was located on the Mediterranean, actually, the opposite direction of Bithynia. As well, there is no record that they ministered in Troas at this time. And then something happened that was so great as to defy all description.

THE MACEDONIAN CALL

One can well imagine the consternation that must have filled the hearts of Paul and Silas as it regarded this second missionary journey. As we've already stated, no doubt thinking they had the Mind of the Lord regarding their destination, and now to find out that this was not the case, this left them somewhat in spiritual limbo. The Holy Spirit, and by what means we do not know, had made it very clear to them that they were not to then preach the Word in Asia. Neither were they to go to Bithynia, but at the time the Lord did not tell them what they were to do.

Many times the Lord conducts Himself toward us in the same exact manner. While the situation may not be nearly as important as their situation was, still, as far as the Lord is concerned, it is the same. I have learned through the years that He does what He does for many and varied reasons. Perhaps the following will be of some small help:

- He wants us to never take Him for granted.
- We are meant to seek the Lord earnestly about everything we do, seeking His Help, Leading and Guidance.
- He wants us to trust Him, which is a great part of the Christian process.
- He always has a Plan for us, meaning that He is never at a loss as to what to do next. It's up to us to find out what that Plan is. And sometimes, it doesn't come easily.
- If we earnestly desire His Will in all things, and we ardently seek His Will, we can be certain that He will ultimately give us His Will.

And now the Lord will make His Will known to Paul and Silas. As well, Luke will now join them. Concerning the Macedonian Call, the Scripture says:

> "And a Vision appeared to Paul in the night *(proclaims the Holy Spirit now telling the Apostle exactly where He wanted him to go)*; there stood a man of Macedonia *(the northern part of modern Greece, from the Adriatic to the Hebrus River)*, and prayed him, saying, Come over into Macedonia, and help us *(thus was ushered in the most momentous event in the history of the world, the going forth of Paul to take the Gospel to the nations of the West)*.
>
> "And after he had seen the Vision, immediately we endeavored to go into Macedonia *(by the use of the pronoun 'we,' we know that Luke, the writer of this Book of Acts, now joins Paul here at Troas)*, assuredly gathering

that the Lord had called us for to preach the Gospel unto them *(they knew they now had the Mind of the Lord)"* (Acts 16:9-10).

Now, as far as we know, there are four traveling to Macedonia, Paul, Silas, Timothy, and Luke.

WHY WAS THIS MISSION'S DIRECTION SO IMPORTANT?

One could well ask as to why the Holy Spirit was so insistent as it regarded the Gospel going to Europe at this time? For this was the first foray of Paul into Europe.

As we have previously stated, the Plans of our Lord so far exceed our plans, simply because He knows the beginning from the end and the end from the beginning. We only know in part. The Holy Spirit knew that the Gospel would be more received in the west than it was the east. In fact, Paul, at a later date, did go to these very areas in Asia that he had originally planned. I think we can see now that the east has never been too very much favorable toward the Gospel of Jesus Christ, rather at a later time, embracing Buddhism, Hinduism, Islam, etc. Of course, Biblical Christianity has made some inroads in the east, but not nearly as it has in the west. The Holy Spirit knew all of this would happen and, as well, even though Paul had absolutely no knowledge of what would come to be known as the *"new world,"* the Lord knew that nearly 2,000 years later, North America would be the greatest propagator of the Gospel that history has ever known. In fact, our Ministry by television and Crusades had and has a large part to play in all of this, for which we give the Lord all the Praise and Glory. So, when Paul and Silas were directed west, little could they realize the impact all of this would have.

PHILIPPI

Whenever Paul and his party left the port of Troas, they

knew they now had the Mind of the Lord. They anchored in the port of Neapolis, which would now be in modern Bulgaria, and which served as the port of the Macedonian Philippi. Even though there is no record that the Holy Spirit told them what city that they should first go to, for whatever reason, they chose Philippi. In fact, it was the leading city of the district of Macedonia. Philip, the father of Alexander the Great, had put it on the map, so to speak. But Augustus made it a Roman colony, which gave it great prestige.

While Philippi at that time was a military and agricultural town, which meant it was not really a commercial city as such, the Jews were very few there and did not even possess a synagogue.

Concerning this, the Scripture says:

"Therefore loosing from Troas, we came with a straight course to Samothracia, and the next *day* to Neapolis *(this would be the very first presentation of the Gospel on European soil, which would have such a bearing on what is presently referred to as 'Western Civilization')*;

"And from thence to Philippi, which is the chief city of that part of Macedonia *(Paul's destination)*, *and* a colony *(was a colony of Rome)*: and we were in that city abiding certain days *(represents tremendous hardships, but a Church was established here)*" (Acts 16:11-12).

THE FIRST CONVERT

The Scripture says:

"And on the Sabbath we went out of the city by a river side, where prayer was wont to be made *(evidently meant there was no synagogue in the city; what few Jews were there met by the riverside)*; and we sat down, and spoke unto the women which resorted *thither* *(seems to tell us that no men were present other than Paul and his party).*

"And a certain woman named Lydia, a seller of purple, of the city of Thyatira *(she was a businesswoman),*
which worshipped God *(proclaims her as a Gentile
who had probably begun visiting a Jewish synagogue in
Thyatira),* heard us *(Paul evidently was asked to speak to
these women, thus proclaiming the story of Jesus Christ
and His Redemption afforded by the Cross of Calvary):*
whose heart the Lord opened *(presents her hungry for
God),* that she attended unto the things which were
spoken of Paul *(she gave her heart to Christ, and was,
thereby, the first convert on European soil).*

"And when she was baptized *(evidently took place
some days later),* and her household *(refers to the fact
that all of those with her accepted the Lord as well, and
were baptized),* she besought *us,* saying, If you have
judged me to be faithful to the Lord, come into my
house, and abide *there (as well, her house was probably
the first Church on European soil).* And she constrained
us *(means they did not acquiesce at first, feeling perhaps
that it may be an imposition on her; but she would not take
no for an answer)*" (Acts 16:13-15).

LYDIA

As Paul and his party went into Philippi, knowing that the
Lord had sent them there, and of that it was unmistakable, still,
there seemed to be no open door. There wasn't even a Jewish
synagogue in the city, so on the Sabbath, they went down by
the river, knowing that if there were any type of gathering of
the Jews, it would take place in this particular area.

When they reached the place in question, they found only a
few women assembled. Obviously, they sat down among them
and entered into the conversation with the small group.

Among the women sat a Lydian proselytess, obviously a
Gentile, who had embraced the God of the Old Testament. She

was a native of the city of Thyatira. She was a businesswoman, who was a seller of purple.

It is said that the luxurious extravagance of the age created a large demand for purple in the market of Rome, and Lydia found room for her profitable trade among the citizens at Philippi. She was evidently a woman who was somewhat well-fixed financially. As she sat listening as Paul began to proclaim the Miracle of Christ and Him dying on the Cross of Calvary, and then being raised from the dead, and, as well, fulfilling all of the Scriptures regarding Who He was, the Son of God, the arrow of conviction pierced her heart. She accepted the Faith, and over the next few days, it seems that her entire household gave their hearts to Christ as well.

She then asked Paul and his party to stay at her house, making it their headquarters, and, as well, it serving as the first Church on European soil. She was the first convert, and her house was the first Church. Little did she know, or even Paul for that matter, as to what all of this meant. This meeting would change the world. In fact, there is evidence that this Church at Philippi continued to support Paul throughout his Ministry with, no doubt, Lydia taking the lead in this matter. In fact, Paul's Letter to the Philippians was actually a thank you note for the help they sent him while he was in prison in Rome (Phil. 4:10-19).

As stated, there were almost no Jews in Philippi, so most all the converts would have been Gentiles. As a result, there was almost a total absence of persecution from this source, even though, even as we shall see, Satan would use other means. Philippi was, as stated, a military city. Rome ruled in this area with all of its military precision. In effect, Philippi was looked at as a colony of Rome, which it actually was. So a Church was established here first of all in the house of Lydia.

Some ten years later when Paul wrote his Epistle to the Philippians, every evidence is that the Church had become quite large. In his introduction he said:

"Paul and Timothy, the servants of Jesus Christ, to all the

Saints in Christ Jesus which are at Philippi, with the Bishops (Pastors) and Deacons" (Phil. 1:1). And yet, the Apostle in his Epistle did not mention Lydia unless she had a second name, which could have been *"Euodias"* or *"Syntyche"* (Phil. 4:2). However, that is doubtful. So by now, she may have moved back to her native city, or considering that it's been approximately ten years, she may have passed away. At any rate, Lydia, the very first convert on European soil, was used mightily of the Lord to begin what would prove to be the great thrust made by the Holy Spirit, which would result in the Salvation of untold millions of souls, and even be the key to all freedom and prosperity. This dear sister could not have known any of these things that morning when she was seated by the riverbank with a few other ladies, there to discuss the Scriptures, when all of a sudden Paul and Silas joined their little group. We must ever understand, if the Lord be in something, always and without fail, great things will come about as a result.

THE DEMON SPIRIT

The Scripture says:

"And it came to pass, as we went to prayer *(does not tell us exactly where this was, but does specify that it was a certain place, more than likely the home of Lydia)*, a certain damsel possessed with a spirit of divination met us *(speaks of the girl being demon possessed)*, which brought her masters much gain by soothsaying *(claiming to give advice and counsel from the spirit world, which brought quite a sum of money to her owners)*:

"The same followed Paul and us, and cried, saying *(implies that this went on for some time, possibly several days)*, These men are the servants of the Most High God, which show unto us the way of Salvation *(should have been translated, 'a way of Salvation,' because that's the way it is in the original Text)*" **(Acts 16:16-17)**.

DIVINATION

The word *"divination"* was translated from the Greek *"Puthon,"* which was derived from *"Putho,"* the name of the region where Delphi, the seat of the famous oracle, was located. This *"oracle"* had to do with the *"Python,"* a serpent. So, this girl, possessed by this evil spirit, was able through the powers of darkness to discern some things in the future, which brought her masters or handlers, the Scripture says, *"much gain."* Evidently she occasionally got some things right, which could have been done by the means of a *"familiar spirit."*

Various types of fortune-telling, astrology, and spiritism, or spiritualism, were common in all the ancient heathen religions of the Middle East and Europe.

These things, as should be obvious, are part of the powers of darkness and must never, under any circumstances, be a part of anything which pertains to Believers in the Lord.

Believers are to receive guidance through the Spirit of God, Who will always guide us according to the Word of God. If it's not according to the Word of God, irrespective as to how religious it may be, it is not of God but of the Evil One.

SIGHTINGS OF MARY, THE MOTHER OF OUR LORD

For instance, all the many alleged sightings of Mary by Catholics constitute a case in point.

Is this really Mary who is being seen?

No! It is a familiar spirit imitating Mary, which is quite common respecting such spirits of darkness. There is no foundation in the Word of God for communicating with the dead. As well, the Mary-worship of the Catholics, being totally unscriptural, fosters and nurtures operations by demon spirits, which is always the case in such unscriptural circumstances.

POPE JOHN PAUL II

If one is to notice, Mary-worship and sightings exacerbated greatly upon Pope John Paul II gaining that highest office. One of the reasons is that he claimed Mary appeared to him many years ago, telling him that he would be Pope, etc. Actually, this situation had become so acute that feelers were put out from the Vatican to various Catholic Bishops and Cardinals all over the world respecting this Pope speaking ex cathedra, thereby, proclaiming Mary as a co-redemptress with her Son, the Lord Jesus Christ. The answer came back that the Pope and the powers that be should not pursue this course, inasmuch as the Bishops and Cardinals thought it to be extreme.

THE WORLD OF RELIGION

It should be understood that demon spirits operate far more in the world of religion than any place else. In fact, there are millions of Christians (so-called), who are supporting with their money what they think is of God and is actually nothing more than demon spirits. That's the reason that Jesus said:

"Not everyone who says unto Me, Lord, Lord, shall enter into the Kingdom of Heaven; but he who does the Will of My Father which is in Heaven" (Mat. 7:21).

DELIVERANCE

The Scripture says:

"And this did she many days *(for some reason, the Holy Spirit didn't give Paul latitude to pray for the girl until now)*. But Paul, being grieved, turned and said to the Spirit *(addressed himself to the evil spirit, and not directly to the girl)*, I command you in the Name of Jesus Christ to come out of her. And he *(the evil spirit)* came out the same hour *(means that the spirit came out instantly)*" (Acts 16:18).

The first thing we must understand is, there are demon spirits in this world, even untold millions of them.

Where do they come from?

We know that the Lord did not create them in this fashion, meaning that they became the way they are at a point in time. God has never created anything but that it is good, and to be sure, demon spirits aren't good.

Some scholars believe there was a pre-Adamic creation on this Earth before the Fall of Lucifer. In fact, it is believed that he was in charge of this creation on Earth, whatever it was. When he led a revolution against God as is described in Isaiah 14:12-15 and Ezekiel 28:13-15, the creation that then was threw in their lot with Lucifer, which became demon spirits. Actually, in Revelation 9, we have the account of demon locusts which will be released upon the Earth during the coming Great Tribulation, which will have shapes like horses, with faces like men, and hair like women. They will sting the inhabitants of the Earth but will not be able to be seen with the naked eye. The Lord, to be sure, didn't make these things this way; they became this way as a result of the Fall of Lucifer, when about a third of the Angelic host joined in with him (Rev. 12:4).

Demons seek to inhabit men, women, children, and even animals. There is no medical defense against them. The only Power that can overcome them is *"the Name of Jesus."*

PERSECUTION

"And when her masters saw that the hope of their gains was gone *(meaning that the girl could no longer function as she had previously done)*, they caught Paul and Silas, and drew *them* into the marketplace unto the Rulers *(these men evidently had some sway with these Rulers)*,

"And brought them to the Magistrates *(pertained to Romans appointed by Rome)*, saying, These men, being Jews, do exceedingly trouble our city *(the manner in which the word 'Jews' is used implies contempt)*,

"And teach customs, which are not lawful for us to receive, neither to observe *(a gross untruth! actually, Judaism was a legal religion in the Roman Empire; even though Paul and Silas were not actually teaching Judaism, but rather proclaiming Jesus, still the Romans would not have been able to distinguish the difference)*, being Romans *(implying superiority)*.

"And the multitude rose up together against them *(presents a stacked audience against Paul and Silas)*: and the Magistrates rent off their clothes *(took off Paul and Silas' clothes, at least to the waist)*, and commanded to beat *them (Paul recalls this in I Thess. 2:2; scourging under Roman Law was a most brutal and cruel punishment)*.

"And when they had laid many stripes upon them *(the lictors were egged on by the mob, with the Apostles being beaten almost to death)*, they cast *them* into prison *(prisons then were far worse than anything we can now imagine)*, charging the jailor to keep them safely *(contains the implication that Paul and Silas were desperados)*:

"Who, having received such a charge *(means that he could punish them even more if he so desired, which he did)*, thrust them into the inner prison *(reserved for the most violent of criminals)*, and made their feet fast in the stocks *(the legs were pulled wide apart, with the individual laying on their back on the floor; after a short time, the muscles in the legs would begin to constrict, causing severe pain)*" (Acts 16:19-24).

SLAVE-MASTERS

These men who owned this girl, for every evidence is that she was their slave, were touched in their pockets, and this filled them with fury. At first, it is more than likely that they were non-plussed as to how to take vengeance on Paul and Silas. They could hardly, indeed, go before the Magistrates and tell them that Paul by a single word had cast out a powerful demon; but they were determined to have vengeance somehow. So they went to the Magistrates and accused Paul and Silas of *"teaching customs, which are not lawful for us to receive, neither to observe."*

It seemed strange that Paul and Silas could not at this time inform their accusers that they were Romans, which would have stopped the beating. It may very well have been that they tried to get the attention of those that mattered, but the crowd had become a mob, and more than likely, their voices could not be heard.

Whereas the Jews by the Law of Moses could not inflict but thirty-nine stripes on the back of an individual, the Romans had no such law. They could beat one as long as they desired, and oftentimes, people did not survive such beatings.

Before they could utter one word in their own defense, or as stated, possibly they were trying to inform their accusers that they were Romans, they were seized, their garments rudely torn from their backs, with the *"cat"* then applied.

It is believed that this was the first of three such scourgings by the Romans which Paul endured. Coupled with the beatings that he received at the hands of the Jews, it is believed that if he had experienced one more beating of this nature, it would have paralyzed him for life, unable even to walk.

THE WILL OF GOD?

Some people have the erroneous idea that if one is in the Will of God, then everything is going to be beautiful, in other words, downhill with the wind at our backs; however, generally the opposite is true! Satan little opposes that which is not the direct Will of God, rather saving his venom for those who are assigned a task by the Holy Spirit, even as were Paul and Silas.

Why would the Lord, Who is able to do anything, allow His choice Servants to be beaten almost to death, suffering unimaginable pain, when He could easily have stopped it, and in any number of ways?

These were two of the choicest men on Earth used by the Lord at that time. In fact, in my personal opinion, I do not think that any have ever been able to equal the Apostle Paul. As someone has well said, *"Paul was the greatest example for Christianity that Christ ever produced."* But yet, the Lord allowed all kinds of troubles, difficulties, and problems, to constantly dog Paul's footsteps. In fact, several years later he would write to the Church at Corinth, *"in labours more abundant, in stripes above measure, in prisons more frequent, in deaths oft."*

"Of the Jews five times received I forty stripes save one.

"Thrice was I beaten with rods, once was I stoned, thrice I suffered shipwreck, a night and a day I have been in the deep;

"In journeyings often, in perils of waters, in perils of robbers, in perils by mine own countrymen, in perils by the heathen, in perils in the city, in perils in the wilderness, in perils in the sea, in perils among false brethren" (II Cor. 11:23-26).

THE THORN IN THE FLESH

Even though the Scripture does not say, it is my personal belief that the *"thorn in the flesh,"* which Paul mentioned, was actually all of these difficulties and problems that he constantly had to go through. Knowing that the Lord could stop the situation at any time, he asked the Lord to remove these difficulties, which he referred to as *"a thorn in the flesh,"* but to no avail. The Lord informed him, *"My Grace is sufficient for you: for My Strength is made perfect in weakness"* (II Cor. 12:9).

But none of that answers the question as to why the Lord allowed these things to be done to His choice Apostle?

I feel that Paul probably answered that question when he said, *"And lest I should be exalted above measure . . . there was given to me a thorn in the flesh, the messenger of Satan to buffet me, lest I should be exalted above measure"* (II Cor. 12:7).

BUT WHY WOULD PAUL NEED SUCH?

Out of his own mouth, we know that he did need such, but why?

In every one of us there is the tendency to get *"self"* involved. Self is always too forward or too backward. It is impossible for it to be right. About the only way it can be rightly treated is that it be constantly weakened. The sufferings that Paul endured, and which the Lord allowed, serve the purpose to accomplish the desired work.

MIDNIGHT

"And at midnight Paul and Silas prayed *(doesn't mean they began to pray at midnight, but rather that they were still praying at midnight having begun some time earlier)*, and sang praises unto God *(the Greek Text suggests that bursts of song broke out from time to time as they prayed; their song was probably one of the Psalms)*: and the prisoners heard them *(means they prayed and sang so loud that other prisoners heard them)*.

"And suddenly there was a great earthquake *(this was no ordinary earthquake)*, so that the foundations of the prison were shaken *(presents the Lord as the Instigator of this upheaval, not a normal force of nature)*: and immediately all the doors were opened, and every one's bands were loosed *(this implies no normal earthquake, but rather something supernatural)*" (Acts 16:25-26).

THE EARTHQUAKE

More than likely the scene that here presents itself had never occurred before in the world's history. Farrar says, *"And this perfect triumph of the spirit of peace and joy over shame and agony was an omen of what Christianity would afterwards affect."*[2] Picture this if you will:

Paul and Silas, although in excruciating pain, still began to *"pray and sing praises unto God."* No doubt the other prisoners in this dungeon, having never witnessed such before, and having never heard such before, were struck speechless by what was taking place. And then, there was an earthquake which shook the very foundations of the prison. The prison doors burst open, and the prisoners' chains were loosed from the staples in the wall. There is no evidence that the earthquake touched any other building in the city. So, and beyond the shadow of a doubt, this was a supernatural occurrence.

THE CONVERSION

"And the keeper of the prison awaking out of his sleep, and seeing the prison doors open *(automatically causes him to assume that all the prisoners had fled)*, he drew out his sword, and would have killed himself, supposing that the prisoners had been fled *(meaning that under the penalty of death, he was responsible for the prisoners)*.

"But Paul cried with a loud voice *(Paul sees what the jailer is about to do to himself)*, saying, Do yourself no harm: for we are all here *(tells us that none of the prisoners, ever how many there were, took the opportunity to escape; this also tells us that quite possibly some, if not all, had given their hearts to the Lord)*.

"Then he called for a light, and sprang in, and came trembling *(proclaims that something powerful was happening to this man, over and above the shock of the earthquake and his thoughts of suicide)*, and fell down before Paul and Silas *(the jailer treated Paul with great brutality, but Paul treated him with great humanity)*,

"And brought them out *(brought Paul and Silas out of the prison)*, and said, Sirs, what must I do to be Saved? *(This presents terminology that shows some familiarity with the Gospel; quite possibly before the arrest of the Apostle, the jailer had heard him preach.)*

"**And they said, Believe on the Lord Jesus Christ, and you shall be Saved** *(presents the most beautiful explanation of Salvation that could ever be given),* **and your house** *(means that Salvation is not limited merely to the jailer, but is available to the entirety of his family as well, that is if they will meet the conditions of Faith in Christ required of them).*

"**And they spoke unto him the Word of the Lord** *(pertained to a fleshing out of the answer given in the previous Verse, explaining what believing in Christ really meant),* **and to all that were in his house** *(presents this service being conducted sometime after midnight, which resulted in all of his family giving their hearts to Christ; what a beautiful night it turned out to be!)*" **(Acts 16:27-32).**

THAT WHICH THE GOSPEL CAN DO!

What can turn hate to love but the Gospel of Jesus Christ? What can turn a dreaded midnight hour filled with pain and sorrow into a night of Salvation, life, and rejoicing? Nothing but the Gospel of Jesus Christ! What can change men's hearts until, in a moment's time, they are no longer what they were, but have experienced a change called *"Born-Again?"* Nothing but the Gospel of Jesus Christ!

From the terminology used by the jailer, it seems that he may have heard Paul preach before now. Other than that, where could he have gotten the terminology, *"Sirs, what must I do to be Saved?"*

The answer that Paul and Silas gave was oh so simple, but yet, so profound, *"Believe on the Lord Jesus Christ, and you shall be Saved, and your house."*

It doesn't take much to be Saved, simply to believe, and to believe on the Lord Jesus Christ. In fact, Paul, in writing the great Book of Romans, would say, *"For whosoever shall call upon the Name of the Lord shall be Saved"* (Rom. 10:13). It's a matter of believing on Jesus Christ, which refers to Who He is, the Son of God, and What He did, which refers to Calvary's Cross. That is the entirety of the requirement for Salvation! This jailer would begin the day a lost sinner on his way to Hell, but the Lord would perform a Miracle, and shortly after midnight, his entire world, along with the entirety of his family, would change.

"What the world needs is Jesus,
"Just a glimpse of Him,
"What the world needs is Jesus,
"Just a glimpse of Him.
"He will bring joy and gladness,
"Take away sin and sadness,
"What the world needs is Jesus,
"Just a glimpse of Him."

A CHANGED MAN

"And he *(the jailer)* took them *(Paul and Silas)* the same hour of the night, and washed *their* stripes *(speaks of the terrible beating they had suffered a short time before)*; and was baptized, he and all his, straightway *(immediately)*.

"And when he had brought them into his house, he set meat before them *(proclaims, as obvious, a meal prepared for them)*, and rejoiced, believing in God with all his house *(a night of misery turned into a night of great joy, and joy which would last forever for this jailer and his family)*" (Acts 16:33-34).

POWER OF THE GOSPEL

Before this night, Paul and Silas were just two other prisoners, of whom he had no regard. But now, everything has changed. He has found Jesus as his eternal Saviour, and it means that his family had a brand new husband and father, and he had a brand new family.

When Paul and Silas with his family gathered around the table that early morning hour, there was joy in that house. He set a table before them, and in that high Hour of Visitation from the Living God, though he had but heard words and had been told of a Hope to come, he and his whole house felt that flow of elevated joy which sprang naturally from a new and inspiring Faith. Let me say it again!

Only Jesus Christ can instantly and immediately change a person to where they are no longer what they once were. That is the Power of the Gospel, and that is the Power of the Gospel alone!

THE AUTHORITIES

Concerning what had happened, Paul and Silas being submitted to the lictor's lash, and considering that they were Romans, what now will happen? The Scripture says:

"And when it was day, the Magistrates sent the serjeants *(probably refers to the same men who had administered the beating to Paul and Silas)*, saying, Let those men go *(the Codex Bezae says that the Magistrates came into court that morning feeling that their treatment of Paul and Silas had brought on the earthquake; they were right!)*.

"And the keeper of the prison told this saying to Paul, The Magistrates have sent to let you go: now therefore depart, and go in peace.

"But Paul said unto them, They have beaten us openly uncondemned, being Romans *(presents a scenario which puts an entirely different complexion on the matter; it was against Roman Law for Romans to be beaten; so, in beating them, the Magistrates had broken the law, evidently not realizing they were Romans)*, and have cast *us* into prison; and now do they thrust us out privily? *(They were treated as common criminals.)* **No verily; but let them come themselves and fetch us out** *(in this way, the city of Philippi would know that the charges were false)."*

ROMANS

"And the serjeants told these words unto the Magistrates: and they feared, when they heard that they were Romans** *(if Paul and Silas so desired, they could have brought charges against these individuals, which could have resulted in severe consequences).*

"And they came and besought them, and brought** *them* **out** *(refers to the fact that the 'Magistrates' now came to Paul and Silas),* **and desired** *them* **to depart out of the city** *(has reference to the fact that they were pleading with the Apostles not to bring charges against them, but rather depart in peace).*

"And they went out of the prison, and entered into** *the house* **of Lydia** *(they were somewhat the worse for wear in the physical sense, but greatly encouraged in the spiritual sense)*: **and when they had seen the Brethren, they comforted them, and departed** *(these were new converts in the Philippian Church)"* **(Acts 16:35-40).**

WE ARE ROMANS

As to what happened with the authorities the next morning after the earthquake that they *"sent the serjeants, saying, Let those men go,"* is anyone's guess. It is not known whether the earthquake was localized with the prison, or over the entire area, but at any rate, the ones who had ordered the beatings of Paul and Silas now were greatly troubled. Who were these men they had beaten? Did the startling events of the previous night, which might have reached their ears early that morning, have anything to do with the beating of these men? Whatever happened, whatever caused their feelings, they felt they had to quickly hush up the whole matter and get rid of these prisoners as quickly as possible. Accordingly, they sent certain ones to inform the prison warden to *"set these people free."*

When the keeper of the prison, who had recently been Saved, was given this message, he hurried to Paul with that which he thought would be heartily welcomed. But Paul felt that a lesson should be taught these men that they be not so ready to prostitute their authority at the howling of a mob. Paul instead sent back a message to them, stating, *"They have beaten us openly uncondemned, being Romans, and have cast us into prison; and now do they thrust us out privily?"*

When the message was returned to the authorities, it filled them with no small alarm. Farrar said, *"They had been hurried by ignorance, prejudice, and pride of office into glaring offenses against Roman Law. They had condemned two Roman citizens without giving them their chartered right to a fair trial; and, on condemning them, had further outraged the birthright and privilege of citizenship by having them bound and scourged; and they had thus violated, grossly so, Roman law, and in the sight of everyone."*[3]

But Paul and Silas were not going to be treated as common criminals and rushed out of the city under the cloak of an early morning hour. Instead, from the prison they went straight to the house of Lydia, and there they called all the converts together in order to give a last exhortation to this newly formed Church. There is a possibility that the jailer and his family were among them.

Luke, who wrote this account, was with Paul and Silas in Philippi. Due to the fact that he used the pronoun *"they"* in Acts 17:1, it indicates that Paul may have left Luke behind in Philippi to further season the Church. Or possibly, he was sent somewhere else. It is not until Acts 20:5 that Luke uses himself in the first person, indicating that he is now with Paul again. Between Philippi and Acts 20:5, there is a time frame of nearly seven years, meaning that Luke was not with Paul during that particular time.

THESSALONICA

As Paul and Silas now continue along with Timothy on their second missionary journey, the Scripture says:

"Now when they had passed through Amphipolis and Apollonia, they came to Thessalonica *(presents Paul's destination evidently directed here by the Holy Spirit)*, where was a Synagogue of the Jews *(presents Paul once again taking the Gospel first of all to the Jews)*:

"And Paul, as his manner was, went in unto them *(should have been translated, 'as his custom was')*, and three Sabbath Days reasoned with them out of the Scriptures *(the Old Testament, and concerning Christ)*,

"Opening and alleging *(to expound and present)*, that Christ must needs have suffered *(had to go to the Cross in order that all sin might be atoned [Gen. 3:15; Ex. 12:13; Isa., Chpt. 53])*, and risen again from the dead *(Lev. 14:1-7; Ps. 16:10)*; and that this Jesus, whom I preach unto you, is Christ *(is the Messiah, the One pointed to in the Scriptures)*" (Acts 17:1-3).

THE CITY OF THESSALONICA

No doubt Paul sought the Lord earnestly as to where he should go next in all of these missionary journeys. Leaving Philippi, he went through Amphipolis and Apollonia but did not stop there. Leaving Apollonia, they went about 40 miles to the city of Thessalonica, which was the capital of all Macedonia. It was an important seat of commerce. Cassander had changed its name from Therma to Thessalonica in honor of his wife, who was a daughter of Philip of Macedon, the father of Alexander the Great.

There was a large synagogue in Thessalonica, meaning there was also a sizeable presentation of Jews in the city. Paul went to this synagogue for three weeks and was asked to speak, which he did, *"reasoning with them out of the Scriptures."* His entire Message had to do with the Scriptures of the Old Testament presenting Christ Who died on the Cross and rose from the dead on the third day. And then, he bluntly, clearly, and plainly states to these assembled Jews and what Gentiles were present, *"that this Jesus, Whom I preach unto you, is Christ,"* meaning that Jesus is Israel's Messiah.

Paul most definitely knew what the reaction would be regarding his Message as it pertained to most of the Jews. By this time, some 20 years after the Crucifixion of Christ, the news had made it, no doubt, to every single synagogue in the Roman world, as it regarded Jesus Christ. More than likely, had the leaders of the synagogue known what Paul was going to address, they probably would not have even given him any opportunity to speak. But at any rate, he was able to minister to them for three weeks. That they allowed him to go beyond the first Sabbath is somewhat of a Miracle within itself, considering that he preached Christ so strongly, and above all that, He most definitely was the Jewish Messiah.

A GREAT MULTITUDE

"And some of them believed *(some Jews)*, and consorted with Paul and Silas *(wanted to hear more about Jesus)*; and of the devout Greeks a great multitude *(many Gentiles were Saved)*, and of the chief women not a few *(could have referred to the wives of some of the Civil Rulers in the city, or at least wives of influential men)*" (Acts 17:4).

Did Paul relate his personal experiences regarding his road to Damascus conversion? At times he did (Acts 26), but whether he did in Thessalonica and other places, we aren't told. But personally, I feel, especially in the synagogues, his conversion experience was so much a part of his proclamation concerning the Lord Jesus Christ, Who He was and What

He did, that it would have to be related. In fact, it is such an integral part of the Gospel, and something that would give pause to any Jew, or Gentile for that matter, I cannot see Paul ignoring, at least in most cases, that which was pertinent to his Message.

At any rate, it seems that Paul saw tremendous results in Thessalonica as it regarded the Salvation of some Jews, and it seems a multitude of Gentiles.

In fact, there were goodly numbers of Gentiles who frequented the Jewish synagogues constantly. The reason was simple! While the Jewish Law proclaimed Jehovah and, thereby, raised all Believers to a height of moral superiority above the Gentile contemporaries, the truth is, the Gentiles of that particular time, had no faith at all. The Greeks had taken the mind of man as far as it could be taken, but which satisfied nothing. In fact, the Gentile world of that day had sunk into the slough of cynicism, hence, the sarcastic question of Pilate to our Lord, *"What is Truth?"* (Jn. 18:38).

Gentiles that did not become outright proselytes, but yet attended the synagogues, were known as *"God-fearers."* It seems that many of these heard Paul gladly!

PERSECUTION FROM THE JEWS

The Scripture says:

"But the Jews which believed not, moved with envy *(presents a perfect example of religious people who refuse the Light of the Gospel, and then set about to stop the propagation of that Light)*, took unto them certain lewd fellows of the baser sort, and gathered a company, and set all the city on an uproar *(presents these Jews as being unable to Scripturally counter Paul's Message, so they now resort to other measures)*, and assaulted the house of Jason, and sought to bring them out to the people *(evidently refers to where Paul and his associates were staying).*

"**And when they found them not** *(evidently Paul and Silas were not there at the time)*, **they drew Jason and certain Brethren unto the Rulers of the city** *(proclaims the mob determined to take their anger out on someone, if not Paul!)*, **crying, These who have turned the world upside down are come hither also** *(tells us that the Jews had prepped certain people in this mob thoroughly)*;

"**Whom Jason has received** *(charges Jason as being a part of the alleged conspiracy)*: **and these all do contrary to the decrees of Caesar, saying that there is another King,** *One* **Jesus** *(presents that which is blatantly false, and the Jews knew it was false).*

"**And they troubled the people and the Rulers of the city, when they heard these things** *(by their lies, they created a commotion).*

"**And when they had taken security of Jason** *(probably means that Jason put up a security bond of some sorts)*, **and of the other** *(probably refers to a guarantee on the part of Jason and others that Paul and his party would leave the city, even though they were not to blame)*, **they let them go** *(implies that the authorities were now satisfied)*" **(Acts 17:5-9).**

JEALOUSY AND HATRED

Few indeed were the untroubled periods of Ministry in the life of Paul. The jealousy and hatred which had chased him from city to city, pursued him here at Thessalonica as well. It was the Jews who were the plague and misery of his suffering life. And yet, he loved these people enough to bear their venom to try to tell them about Christ. It was always the Jews who contradicted and blasphemed the Holy Name which he was preaching. In the planting of Churches, he had to fear their deadly opposition. Farrar says, *"The Jews who hated Christ sought the life of Paul; the Jews who professed to love*

Him undermined his efforts. The one faction endangered his existence, the other ruined his peace. Never, till death released him, was he wholly free from their violent conspiracies or their insidious calumnies. Without, they sprang upon him at every opportunity like a pack of wolves; within, they hid themselves in sheep's clothing to worry and tear his flocks."[4]

The Jews at Thessalonica were jealous that Paul had won more people to the Cause of Christ in a few weeks of preaching than they had won during their many years to the Doctrines of Moses.

Unable to get to Paul and Silas at the moment, they secured the help of the rowdies of the city, probably paying them a few shekels, to attack the house of Jason because he had supplied quarters for Paul and Silas, but who were absent at the time. Unable to get to Paul and Silas, they seized Jason and one or two others whom they recognized as Christians, and dragged them before the authorities. They were accused of being agitators and opposed Caesar, of course, which was ridiculous. On the face of it, it was ridiculous to suppose that people like Jason and his friends could be seriously contemplating revolutionary measures. In fact, a very short hearing proclaimed the fact that the entire uproar was over religious matters. So the authorities, with some type of security measure given, dismissed Jason and those with him.

But again, if Paul and Silas had been brought before these individuals, only the Lord knows what the end result might have been. In any case, it was best that they leave town, which they did. Possibly Timothy remained behind to continue teaching and the organization of the Church.

BEREA

"And the Brethren immediately sent away Paul and Silas by night unto Berea *(this town is about fifty miles from Thessalonica; they left by night, because to remain longer could have caused more problems)*: who coming *thither* **went into the Synagogue of the Jews** *(presents, as stated, Paul's custom, but which this time will turn out better, for a change).*

"These were more noble than those in Thessalonica *(we now learn God's definition of 'noble')*, **in that they received the Word with all readiness of mind** *(this is the meaning of the word 'noble')*, **and searched the Scriptures daily, whether those things were so** *(tells us why they so eagerly accepted the Message of Jesus Christ).*

"Therefore many of them believed *(speaks of Jews who accepted Christ as Saviour)*; **also of Honourable women which were Greeks, and of men, not a few** *(speaks of Gentiles who had been attending the Jewish synagogue and, as well, accepted Christ)*" **(Acts 17:10-12).**

THE NOBLE ONES OF BEREA

Why is it that the Jews hated Paul so much?

They hated him because of what he preached. They had crucified Christ, with His Disciples claiming that He had risen from the dead on the third day. As well, despite how hard they tried, they could not prove that He had not risen from the dead. And now Paul, who had been the darling of the Pharisees, the one destined to take the place of the great scholar of the Law, Gamaliel, and who, as well, had hated Christ, now claimed that Jesus Christ had appeared to him on the road to Damascus, which vision so mightily changed him that he became a most ardent Disciple of Christ. Consequently, the Jews hated Paul. They had crucified Christ, and here this one claims that Jesus is alive and, in fact, is the Messiah of Israel and the Saviour of men.

They hated Paul simply because they were wrong, dead wrong! They were not content to let him go his way and they go theirs, but they felt they had to kill him and definitely would have done so, had not the Lord watched over him.

It is no different presently. They who have compromised

the Gospel, they who have deserted the Gospel, they who preach a gospel of man instead of a Gospel of the Word of God, hate, and with a passion, those who adhere to the Truth. This problem goes all the way back to Cain and Abel. Cain was not content to go his way and let Abel, his brother, go his way. The one on whom God had laid His Hand had to be stopped. So Cain murdered his brother. That is the spirit, the Cain spirit, which has characterized false religions from then until now.

Please remember, Cain did not deny there was a God, did not deny that He was due a sacrifice, but rejected the type of Sacrifice demanded by God.

Why?

That's a good question! Since that day, man has ever been trying to manufacture another god, and the church has ever been trying to manufacture another sacrifice. Always remember, if the Sacrifice is accepted, that means the one offering the Sacrifice is accepted. If it is rejected, then the one offering the sacrifice is rejected as well. This means that the Lord really did not look too very much at Cain and Abel, for it was obvious as to what they were. He looked at their sacrifices. And to be sure, it hasn't changed from then until now.

It's not what church we attend, or with which we are associated, or how good we might think we are, but once again and forever, our Salvation, that is, if we have Salvation, is always registered in the Sacrifice (Jn. 3:16).

So, the spirit that rejected Paul and Silas, the religious spirit, I might quickly add, is alive and well today.

A PERSONAL EXPERIENCE

I have wondered many times as to why the Lord would be so gracious and kind to give me the Revelation of the Cross, which is that which was given to the Apostle Paul. I thought that if it had been given to someone else, maybe it might be more readily acceptable by the church. But late one night, the Lord spoke to my heart about this thing.

He said to me, *"It's not you they are rejecting, it's the Message. If I had given this Message, the Message of the Cross, to anyone else, the rejection would have been the same."*

WHY IS THERE AN OFFENSE TO THE CROSS?

Another good question!

The Holy Spirit through Paul said that the Cross is an offense (Gal. 5:11).

The Cross lays waste all of man's efforts, ability, talents, education, motivation, intellectualism, etc. The idea is, the Believer is to place his Faith exclusively in Christ and what Christ has done for us at the Cross (Rom. 6:3-5; Lk. 9:23-24; 14:26-27).

The only way that believing man can be what he is intended to be, can grow in Grace and the Knowledge of the Lord, and can have the Fruit of the Spirit evident in his life, is by and through Jesus Christ and what He has done for us at the Cross. The Cross of Christ must ever be the Object of one's Faith. That being done, the Holy Spirit, Who works exclusively within the parameters, so to speak, of the Cross of Christ, meaning that this is what gives Him the legal means to do all that He does, will then work mightily on our behalf (Rom. 8:1-2, 11; Eph. 2:13-18; Gal. 6:14). All of this is derived from Paul.

PAUL AND SILAS MUST LEAVE THESSALONICA

From Philippi, the virtual capital of Macedonia Prima, they had been driven to Thessalonica, the capital of Macedonia Secunda. Now, where will they go?

Farrar said, *"The Jewish Synagogues of the dispersion were in close connection with each other, and the watch word would now be evidently given to hound Paul and Silas from place to place, and especially to silence Paul as the arch-apostate who was persuading all men everywhere, as they falsely asserted, to forsake the Law of Moses.* "⁵

The town which they had in view, where no doubt the Holy Spirit led them, was Berea. Maybe it was because Berea was in such a secluded position that the Holy Spirit chose the place for Paul and Silas as being safer than certain other cities in the general area.

When they arrived, they made their way, first of all, into the Synagogue of the Jews. They were to find there a different situation than they had found in other places.

Paul expounded to them the Beauty of Christ, and did so from the Psalms, from Isaiah, etc., how He would die and rise again, which He did on the third day, and that Jesus and what He did at Calvary was the sole Means of Justification. The Jews in this little city, instead of turning upon him as soon as they understood the full scope and logical conclusions of his message, proved themselves to be *"nobler"* than those of Thessalonica. Instead of angrily rejecting this great Gospel, they daily and diligently searched the Scriptures to judge Paul's arguments and references by the Word and the Testimony. The results were that many Jews believed, as well as Greeks, i.e., *"Gentiles."*

As to how long they spent there, the Scripture doesn't say; but it must have been several weeks; however, the peaceful calm which they enjoyed, no doubt, so very much, was soon to be interrupted. The Scripture says:

THE JEWS OF THESSALONICA

"But when the Jews of Thessalonica had knowledge that the Word of God was preached of Paul at Berea *(these Jews in Thessalonica, not content with what they had done in their city, now attempt to stop that which is happening in Berea)*, they came thither also, and stirred up the people *(shows how effective a lie can be)*.

"And then immediately the Brethren sent away Paul to go as it were to the Sea *(speaks of the Aegean, which was about seventeen miles from Berea)*: but Silas and

Timotheus abode there still *(remained in Berea)*.

"And they who conducted Paul brought him unto Athens *(presents the chief city of Greece, famed for its learning)*: and receiving a commandment unto Silas and Timotheus for to come to him with all speed, they departed *(Paul sends the Message back with these men that Silas and Timothy are to come to Athens as soon as possible)*" (Acts 17:13-15).

CONTINUED PERSECUTION

The news of Paul's great success in Berea was soon reported to the Synagogue of Thessalonica.

Farrar says, *"The hated name of Paul acted like a spark on their inflammable rage, they instantly dispatched emissaries to stir up storms among the Jews and others in Berea."*[6]

It seems that Paul and not Silas was the main object of the persecution, so it was arranged that Paul would go elsewhere, namely Athens, and Silas and Timothy would remain behind in order to help solidify the Church in Berea, which they did. Those who had been Saved in Berea under his Ministry in the last few days would go with him the 16 miles to the colony of Dium, where he, with several of those who were with him, would sail for Athens.

ATHENS

"Now while Paul waited for them at Athens, his spirit was stirred in him, when he saw the city wholly given to idolatry *(means it was full of idols)*.

"Therefore disputed he in the synagogue with the Jews *(from the Scriptures, he would preach Jesus; the Scriptures then, at least as far as the Jews were concerned, were the Old Testament)*, and with the devout persons *(singles out the Jews who really seemed to be devoted to the Scriptures)*, and in the market daily with them that met with him *(this was a place in Athens, where speakers generally gave forth).*

"Then certain philosophers of the Epicureans *(those who claimed that gratification of the appetites and pleasures was the only end in life),* and of the Stoics *(they taught that man was not to be moved by either joy or grief),* encountered him *(challenged his statements about Christ).* And some said, What will this babbler say? *(This presents the highest insult of which they could think.)* other some, He seems to be a setter forth of strange gods *(in their minds, anything outside of Greek philosophy was of no consequence):* because he preached unto them Jesus, and the Resurrection *(they didn't want a Resurrection, simply because they did not desire the idea of living this life over again; this shows they totally misunderstood what Paul said)*" (Acts 17:16-18).

GREEK PHILOSOPHY

Even though Athens was now past its prime, actually by several hundreds of years, still, it was a place of note in the world of that day.

The Greeks had taken the mind of man as far as was humanly possible. I speak of philosophers such as Socrates, Plato, and Aristotle. In fact, Plato was the disciple, so to speak, of Socrates, as Socrates had been the disciple of Aristotle.

These philosophers, as brilliant as they may have been, did not start with God because they had no knowledge of Him, therefore, their ideas had to be formed out of pre-existing matter, which, in reality, gave them no answers at all.

Socrates raised the problems of morality and knowledge to the position of first importance.

Plato, the disciple of Socrates, took it a little further into one supreme principal or idea which he called *"The Good"* or *"God."* Of course, his thinking, as it regarded God, had no basis of reality.

Aristotle took it all a little further, recognizing the evil, but the problem was how to stop the evil. Actually, Aristotle created the science of logic, which in the Christian Middle Ages became the chief instrument of the great systematic theologians of the Church; however, it was earthly wisdom, and therefore devilish, which was almost the ruin of the Church.

Probably one could say that the following statement pretty well sums up their great wisdom, as it regards the understanding of the reason of things.

Socrates, in essence, said, *"There is good and there is evil."*

His disciple Plato said, *"There is bad and there is good, but there is a great gulf between the bad and the good."*

Aristotle took it further, saying, *"There is bad and there is good, but we don't know how to cross the chasm that separates the bad from the good."*

So, in this atmosphere came the Apostle Paul.

Farrar said, *"Had it been possible for the world by its own wisdom to know God; had it been in the power of man to turn into bread the stones of the wilderness; had permanent happiness lain within the grasp of sense, or been among the rewards of culture; had it been granted to man's unaided power to win salvation by the gifts and qualities of his own nature, and to make for himself a new Paradise in lieu of the lost Eden, then such ends would have been achieved at Athens in the day of her glory."*[7]

While Athens was greatly impressed with herself, Paul would not have been impressed at all, knowing the futility of human wisdom—for human wisdom was the highest attainment to which the Athenians could propel themselves. This was a wisdom, incidentally, which God labeled as *"foolishness"* (I Cor. 3:19).

THE BANE OF THE MODERN CHURCH

The twin evils that plague the church are:
- The wisdom of the world and
- The legalism of religion

In a sense, Athens had both. Their forte was the wisdom of the world, which, as already stated, God described as foolishness. And yet, they had made a religion out of all of these manufactured gods. The modern church is plagued no less.

Humanistic psychology, pure and simple, and in totality, is the wisdom of the world. It has no semblance of God and no semblance of His Word in its confines. It is totally of man, which means it is useless. And yet, the modern church has embraced it in totality.

The legalism of religion is just as lethal as the wisdom of the world. And to be sure, legalism is dear to the heart. As the wisdom of the world, legalism, as well, portrays the ability of man. Man is caught up in rules and regulations, in works, and in his own ability to perform these works. Paul said:

"For as many as are of the works of the Law are under the curse" (Gal. 3:10).

THE CROSS OF CHRIST

God's way is, *"Jesus Christ and Him Crucified"* (Rom. 6:3-5; I Cor. 1:17, 18, 21, 23; 2:2). In fact, when the Cross of Christ is embraced, this automatically cancels out the wisdom of the world and the legalism of religion. Those two things cannot coexist with the Message of the Cross. In fact, that is the Offense of the Cross (Gal. 5:11).

God's Way is not man's way, and, in fact, if man tries to insert his way at all into this great Plan of Redemption, the results aren't good.

DAVID AS AN EXAMPLE

The Lord told David, after he had been made King of the great nation of Israel, to bring the Ark of the Covenant back into the city of Jerusalem. In fact, for many years it had been discarded and ignored.

As all Bible students know, David was bringing the Ark

into Jerusalem with great fanfare, etc.; however, he was bringing it in, in an unscriptural way. It was being carried on a cart whenever it should have been on the shoulders of Priests, who, in effect, were types of Christ.

A man died as a result of that. The point is this:

It didn't matter that David was the king of Israel, a man after God's Own Heart, the writer of over half the Psalms, and the man through whose lineage the Messiah would come. In fact, David was the greatest Type of Christ in the Old Testament.

Despite all of that, his departure from the Word of God brought death. Let me make the following statement and please read it carefully:

There are tens of thousands of Preachers in this nation and all over the world who love God and sincerely want to do His Will; however, these Preachers are preaching about the Gospel instead of preaching the Gospel. Unless one understands that the Gospel of Jesus Christ is the Message of the Cross, as it refers to Salvation and also to Sanctification, then it's impossible to properly preach the Cross. As a result, their hearers, at the very best, aren't experiencing Spiritual Growth, and at the worst, could be causing untold problems and difficulties. And, if the Lord would demand such of David, to be sure, He demands such presently.

Please understand that if the Cross of Christ is eliminated from Christianity, then what is left is no more than an empty, vapid philosophy, which will help no one and will even bring hurt and harm to those who hear it.

THE GOSPEL OF JESUS CHRIST

"And they took him, and brought him unto Areopagus *(refers to Mars' Hill which faces the Acropolis; this was the Supreme Court of Athens)*, saying, May we know what this new doctrine, whereof you speak, *is?* *(This presents Paul facing this Supreme Court Justices of Athens.)*

"For you bring certain strange things to our ears

(it's strange that those who brought Paul to this place labeled what he said as mere babblings, but yet think it important enough to be taken to the highest Court in Athens): **we would know therefore what these things mean** *(presents a noble request to Paul, and an unparalleled opportunity).*

"(For all the Athenians and strangers which were there spent their time in nothing else, but either to tell, or to hear some new thing.) *(With the great philosophers now dead, Athens was attempting to live off the glory of former times)*" **(Acts 17:19-21).**

THE TEMPLES AND STATUES OF ATHENS

Athens was the city of statues. It was said that there were more statues in Athens than in all the rest of Greece put together. Farrar said, *"Their number would be all the more startling, and even shocking to Paul, because, during the long youthful years of his study at Jerusalem, he had never seen so much as one representation of the human form, and had been trained to regard it as apostasy to give the faintest sanction to such violations of God's express command."*[8]

When Paul looked at Athens, it is hardly likely that he would have admired anything there which he saw, simply because that which he saw was but a corpse. The Greece of old was dead, even as all religions of the world, no matter how fanciful, ultimately steals, kills, and destroys.

Farrar said, *"Greece was but repeating with dead lips the echo of old philosophies which had never been sufficient to satisfy the yearnings of the world. Her splendor was no longer the envy of the world, but rather a lingering reflex. In fact, centuries had elapsed since all that was grand and heroic in her history had 'gone glimmering down the dream of things that were.'"*[9]

And now all of that is gone, only the shadows are left! And so it is with the very best that man can produce, which is never enough to satisfy the craving of the soul.

As we said in the notes, it was strange that these would-be philosophers referred to Paul merely as *"this babbler,"* but yet, wanted to hear more of what he had to say. Evidently, from day to day in the marketplace, he with other speakers had held forth as it regarded the Gospel of Jesus Christ. It was a Message they had never heard before.

Here was an unparalleled opportunity that these men had. As they listened to Paul, did they have an inkling that the Message he was portraying to them, this Message of Jesus Christ and His Power to Save, would ultimately change the entirety of the world, doing a thousand times over what these vapid philosophies of Greek culture had failed to do?

They did not know it then, but they know it now; however, it is now too late.

MARS' HILL

"Then Paul stood in the midst of Mars' Hill, and said, *You* men of Athens, I perceive that in all things you are too superstitious *(in this one sentence, he debunks all of their philosophies; they are guided by superstition, which is no way to live).*

"For as I passed by, and beheld your devotions *(has reference to their objects of worship)*, I found an altar with this inscription, TO THE UNKNOWN GOD *(by addressing the situation in this way, he could not be accused of preaching a foreign god to them)*. Whom therefore you ignorantly worship, Him declare I unto you *(refers to them acknowledging that maybe they did not have the last word on gods! actually, they did not have any word at all)*" (Acts 17:22-23).

THE UNKNOWN GOD

As is obvious, Paul was not at all overpowered by the sense

of Athenian greatness. He knew it was *"greatness"* only in the eyes of man, not at all in the Eyes of God. These people were heathen. They had no knowledge of the True God; they were only worshippers of idols.

Knowing that Paul was praying and searching in his spirit as to how he should address these individuals, then he saw *"an altar with the inscription, 'TO THE UNKNOWN GOD.'"* And yet, as later events will bear out, I think, even though his Message was absolutely phenomenal, still, when it was all over, he wasn't certain if he had really had the Mind of the Holy Spirit regarding that which he gave to these Athenians. He did not preach the Cross, in fact, he never mentioned the Cross. I think from what he later told the Church at Corinth, he felt that this was a mistake. We will address that to a greater degree at a later time.

THE LORD OF HEAVEN AND EARTH

"God Who made the world and all things therein *(presents God as the Creator)*, seeing that He is Lord of Heaven and Earth *(proclaims Him not only as Creator, but the constant Manager of all that He has created as well)*, dwells not in Temples made with hands *(He is bigger than that!)*;

"Neither is worshipped with men's hands *(the Second Commandment forbids the making of any graven image of God, or the worship of any type of statue, etc.)*, as though He needed anything *(God needs nothing!)*, seeing He gives to all life, and breath, and all things *(presents His Creation needing what He provides, which is provided by no other source)*;

"And has made of one blood all nations of men for to dwell on all the face of the earth *(proclaims all having their origin in Adam)*, and has determined the times before appointed, and the bounds of their habitation *(pertains to particular parts of the world, and those who occupy these areas; however, the statement, 'one blood all nations of men,' eliminates any type of racial superiority)*;

"That they should seek the Lord *(presents the chief end of all God's dealings with men [I Pet. 2:24; II Pet. 3:9; Jn. 3:15-20; Rev. 22:17])*, **if haply they might feel after Him, and find Him** *(Paul is appealing to the action of logic and common sense in trying to address these Pagans)*, **though He be not far from every one of us** *(speaks of the Creator being very close to His Creation)*" **(Acts 17:24-27).**

FINDING THE LORD

First of all, Paul placed God as the Creator of both Heaven and Earth. He went on to state that God was so large, so all-encompassing, and so great that He did not dwell in temples or buildings. Neither would He allow statues or graven images to be made of Him, or at least what men thought He might look like. Paul went on to say that God needs nothing, but yet, all need Him.

As well, Paul placed all men on the face of the Earth to be of one blood. How well this set with the Greeks is anyone's guess. They considered themselves to be superior to most anyone else, even though they then were ruled by Rome.

He then begins to tell these Athenians that if they would then seek the Lord, they would find Him.

To try to get into the mind of Paul as to what he thought of his Message after it had been delivered, presents thin ice. But yet, at the same time, if I had to venture a guess, and again, noting what he would later say to the Church at Corinth and with, more than likely, this scene in his mind (I Cor. 2:2), I feel that he may have thought that he presented to these Athenians too much of what he knew about God, rather than what God could do for them. Despite all of their boasting, they were but poor pagans, who were totally ignorant of Jehovah and His Power to Save. They knew nothing of Jesus Christ, God's Son, and what He had done at the Cross in order that man could be Saved. Paul didn't tell them that, and I personally feel he ever regretted it.

REPENTANCE

"For in Him we live, and move, and have our being *(proclaims God as the Source of all life [Heb. 1:3])*; as certain also of your own poets have said, For we are also His offspring *(presents a direct quote from Aratus of Tarsus, Paul's own country)*.

"Forasmuch then as we are the offspring of God *(is offered by Paul in the sense of Creation; it does not mean the 'Fatherhood of God, and the Brotherhood of Man,' as many contend)*, we ought not to think that the Godhead is like unto gold, or silver, or stone, graven by art and man's devise *(Paul is saying that God is not a devise of man, as all the Greek gods in fact were)*.

"And the times of this ignorance God winked at *(does not reflect that such ignorance was Salvation, for it was not! before the Cross, there was very little Light in the world, so God withheld Judgment)*; but now commands all men everywhere to repent *(but since the Cross, the 'Way' is open to all; it's up to us Believers to make that 'Way' known to all men)*:

"Because He has appointed a day *(refers to the coming of the Great White Throne Judgment [Rev. 20:11-15])*, in the which He will Judge the world in Righteousness by *that* Man Whom He has ordained *(this Righteousness is exclusively in Christ Jesus and what He has done for us at the Cross, and can be gained only by Faith in Him [Eph. 2:8-9; Rom. 10:9-10, 13; Rev. 22:17])*; *whereof* He has given assurance unto all *men*, in that He has raised Him from the dead *(refers to the Resurrection ratifying that which was done at Calvary, and is applicable to all men, at least all who will believe!)*" (Acts 17:28-31).

TO JUDGE THE WORLD IN RIGHTEOUSNESS

As Paul framed his words, he addressed himself to points in which they seemed to be in agreement, but yet, at the same time, rebuked in every direction their natural and intellectual self-complacency. His Epicurean auditors, for instance, believed that the universe had resulted from a chance combination of atoms; he tells them that it was their unknown God Who, by His Fiat, had created the universe and all therein. While they believed there were many gods, he told them that there was but one God, the Lord of Heaven and Earth.

Surrounded by temples that day, some of them the most beautiful in the world, he told the crowd that the God of Heaven did not and does not dwell in temples made by hands, but in the Eternal Temple of His Own Creation.

He then tells these Athenians, the brightest in the city of Athens as far as worldly wisdom was concerned, that the Lord was at once the Creator and the Preserver of all of the material universe, and that every man at a point in time will answer to Him. He tells them that they must repent, and yet, I'm not so sure that they understood what repentance actually meant. But then he mentioned the Resurrection, how that God raised Jesus from the dead. As we shall see, they totally misunderstood what he said.

THE RESURRECTION OF THE DEAD

"And when they heard of the Resurrection of the Dead, some mocked *(the 'mocking' was caused by sheer unbelief)*: and others said, We will hear you again of this *matter (many were touched by Paul's Message, but regrettably procrastinated)*.

"So Paul departed from among them *(they ascertained that he had broken none of their laws, so he was free to go, which he did!)*.

"Howbeit certain men clave unto him, and believed

(these believed wholeheartedly, recognizing in Paul the true Words of Life): **among the which** *was* **Dionysius the Areopagite** *(he was a member of the Great Court of Athens; tradition says that he became the Pastor of the Church in Athens)*, **and a woman named Damaris** *(a person of prominence)*, **and others with them"** **(Acts 17:32-34).**

CERTAIN ONES BELIEVED

When they heard Paul mention the Resurrection of Christ from the dead, as stated, they totally misunderstood what he said. They thought, evidently, that he was teaching some type of reincarnation, and the idea was, life was so hard, they didn't want to come back and do this thing all over again. As stated, they misunderstood the whole idea of Resurrection. So, they jeered him down.

At this very moment, in the darkened pits of a place called Hell, those individuals that mocked him that day are there reliving for the millionth time that scene of Paul ministering to them. They could have had Eternal Life! In fact, some few that day did believe and did receive Eternal Life, and they are now in Heaven.

Some claim that a Church was founded in Athens, and that Dionysius the Areopagite became its Pastor. But others say no church was founded in Athens. We do know this, to Athens he wrote no Epistle, and in Athens, as often as he passed its neighborhood, we have no record of his going there again.

Farrar says, and probably right, *"Paul's Message, so far as any immediate effects were concerned, was an all but total failure, and Luke does not conceal its ineffectiveness."*[10]

The truth is, he left Athens as he had visited it, a despised and lonely man. And yet, his visit was not in vain. In fact, that one Service may very well have been the springboard the Holy Spirit needed in order to push Paul ever deeper into a greater understanding of the great Revelation of the Cross which he had been given. Sometimes we learn more from our mistakes than we do our victories, and yet, I'm not saying with certitude that Paul's Message was a mistake. We'll have to leave that to the Lord. But yet, I think if the Apostle stood before us today, he would not be happy with the course that was taken. As we've already said several times, future statements lead us to believe that he learned something from that Service, something of extreme significance. From then on, he would be *"determined not to know anything, save Jesus Christ, and Him Crucified"* (I Cor. 2:2).

CORINTH

The Scripture says:

"**After these things Paul departed from Athens** *(seems to imply that he departed alone, with Silas and Timothy joining him later at Corinth)*, **and came to Corinth** *(one of the great cities of the Roman Empire)*;

"**And found a certain Jew named Aquila, born in Pontus, lately come from Italy, with his wife Priscilla** *(pertains to a husband and wife who became very close friends to Paul)*; **(because that Claudius had commanded all Jews to depart from Rome:)** *(believed to have occurred in about A.D. 49 or 50)* **and came unto them** *(Paul came to them)*.

"**And because he was of the same craft, he abode with them, and wrought** *(evidently means that Paul had enquired concerning those involved in this occupation)*: **for by their occupation they were tentmakers** *(tentmakers wove the black cloth of goat or camel's hair with which tents were made)*.

"**And he reasoned in the synagogue every Sabbath** *(preached Christ from the Old Testament)*, **and persuaded the Jews and the Greeks** *(his argument was ironclad)*" (Acts 18:1-4).

PREACHING IN THE SYNAGOGUE

Chapter 18 begins with the words, *"After these things Paul departed from Athens, and came to Corinth."* Paul left Athens and only mentioned it one other time (I Thess. 1:3). This was his only recorded experience with the Gentile pharisaism of a pompous philosophy. Concerning this, Farrar said, *"There was more hope of raging Jews, more hope of ignorant barbarians, more hope of degraded slaves, than of those who have become fools because in their own conceit they were exceptionally wise; who were alienated by a spiritual ignorance born of moral blindness; who, because conscience had lost its power over them, had become vain in their imaginations, and their foolish heart was darkened."*[11]

Paul sailed to Corinth, then the capital of southern Greece, which formed the Roman Province of Achaia. The evidence is that his ship dropped anchor at Cenchrea. This was the harbor for Corinth. He then walked the distance of approximately eight miles into Corinth. Walking the eight miles probably took several hours, with the Apostle engaged heavily in thought. As we have stated, I don't think Paul was at all pleased with what had taken place at Athens. And now he's going into Corinth, the most jaded city in the Roman Empire at that time. The city was so corrupt, morally speaking, with its hundreds and hundreds of temple prostitutes, that the more jaded was a person, they were said to be *"corinthianized."* And then on the other side of the proverbial coin, the city looked at itself as a center of philosophy. So, the twin evils of Satan were awaiting Paul, vice and the wisdom of man, which latter was nearly as bad as Athens. No doubt the Apostle asked himself the question as to how this twin shell could be penetrated. If anything, Corinth was worse than Athens. But, as stated, sometimes we learn more from our failures than we do our victories.

The Holy Spirit may have whispered to him as these thoughts flooded his mind, saying, *"Preach the Cross!"* And then the Holy Spirit may have added, *"If the Cross will crack this twin citadel of evil, then it will work anywhere."* At any rate, the Apostle did say to the Corinthians, *"For I determined not to know anything among you, save Jesus Christ, and Him Crucified"* (I Cor. 2:2). I don't personally think that Paul would have made such a statement, especially using the word *"determined,"* without the Holy Spirit having taught him some lessons.

The word *"determined"* in the Greek is *"krino,"* and it means *"to decide mentally or judicially."* In other words, he didn't come to this position by chance. As it regarded the great Revelation given to him by the Lord concerning the meaning of the New Covenant, which, in effect, is the meaning of the Cross, he had now passed with the help of the Holy Spirit a great milestone, which, in effect, constituted the very core of what the Lord had shown him.

How little did the wealthy magnates of Corinth suspect that a Jew entering their city that day would change the entire thought concerning Corinth, and do so over the entirety of the world. How true it is that the living world often knows nothing of its greatest men!

AQUILA AND PRISCILLA

Aquila was a leather worker, which was the craft of Paul as well. Every Jewish boy was taught a trade as it regarded work with his hands. Paul was taught the craft of repairing tents, etc.

It is believed that Aquila and Priscilla were already Christians when they met Paul at Corinth. In fact, he stayed with them for a period of time and, as well, worked at the repairing of tents in order to provide sustenance.

When Paul left Corinth, Aquila and Priscilla accompanied him as far as Ephesus, where they received and assisted to a fuller Faith, the very influential Apollos (Acts 18:18-28). They were still in Ephesus, and a Church was meeting in their house when First Corinthians was written. Not long afterwards, perhaps taking advantage of relaxations toward Jews after the death of the Roman Caesar Claudius, it seems they went back to Rome (Rom. 16:3). They were much beloved by Paul, and, as well, they rendered extraordinary services to the cause of Christianity.

SILAS AND TIMOTHY

"And when Silas and Timothy were come from Macedonia *(probably means that Silas had come from Berea, with Timothy coming from Thessalonica; Macedonia was a Province which included both places)*, Paul was pressed in the spirit, and testified to the Jews *that* Jesus *was* Christ *(the Holy Spirit told him to bear down even harder!)*.

"And when they opposed themselves, and blasphemed *(proclaims the response of some of these Jews to Paul's claim that Christ was the Messiah)*, he shook *his* raiment, and said unto them, Your blood *be* upon your own heads; I *am* clean *(in other words, he had delivered his soul)*: from henceforth I will go unto the Gentiles *(does not mean that he would no longer minister to Jews if given the opportunity, which he did do at Ephesus [Acts 19:8], but that the thrust would be toward the Gentiles)*" (Acts 18:5-6).

PRESSED IN HIS SPIRIT

It is obvious that at this time, due to the fact that he worked daily helping to repair tents, Paul's resources were slim. But this was alleviated when Silas and Timothy came from Macedonia to join him, and even more helpful yet in that Timothy had brought him a sizeable offering from the Philippians, which was sorely needed. As well, and as should be obvious, he was so very, very happy to have their company.

At about this time, it seems that Paul was impressed greatly by the Holy Spirit to bear down even harder in his ministering in the synagogue every Sabbath, proving that Jesus was Christ and, thereby, the Jewish Messiah, and that He had died on the Cross for our sins and had been raised from the dead on the third day. Evidently, when he began to spell it out clearly, in effect, doing what the Holy Spirit had told him to do, the Jews rose up against him. The outcome was, he no longer could minister in the synagogue.

No one can say that the Lord didn't try to reach the Jews over and over again, despite the fact that they had crucified their Messiah and our Saviour, the Lord Jesus Christ.

THE VISION

"And he departed thence *(out of the synagogue)*, and entered into a certain *man's* house *(a meeting place for Church)*, named Justus, *one* who worshipped God, whose house joined hard to the synagogue *(evidently points to Justus in the recent past as having accepted Christ under Paul's Ministry)*.

"And Crispus, the Chief Ruler of the synagogue, believed on the Lord with all his house *(this must have been galling to the Jews to have their Chief Ruler of the synagogue converted to Christ)*; and many of the Corinthians hearing believed, and were baptized *(speaks of many Gentiles now being Saved)*.

"Then spoke the Lord to Paul in the night by a Vision *(does not clarify whether Paul saw the Lord, or only heard Him speak, it being a 'Vision' implies that he was awake)*, Be not afraid, but speak, and hold not your peace *(there evidently was fear in Paul's heart regarding the tremendous opposition against him; he was told by the Lord to speak with boldness)*:

"For I am with you, and no man shall set on you to hurt you *(speaks to the idea that Paul had threats on his life, threats which were not empty, but rather deadly serious)*: for I have much people in this city *(concerns the great Church which will be raised up at Corinth).*

"**And he continued *there* a year and six months, teaching the Word of God among them** *(records the longest time that Paul spent in any place other than Ephesus, where he spent some three years)*" **(Acts 18:7-11).**

MUCH PEOPLE IN THIS CITY

Paul, now driven from the synagogue, uses the house of Justus as a meeting place. It seems that this man's house was next door to the synagogue.

As well, the Scripture says that *"Crispus, the Chief Ruler of the synagogue,"* also accepted the Lord with all of his family.

We are also told that many Corinthians, i.e., *"Gentiles,"* also accepted the Lord.

At any rate, the Jews did not take kindly to this. Especially considering that the Chief Ruler of the synagogue had given his heart to Christ, and considering that they were holding church in a house right next to the synagogue, it was like rubbing salt in the wound. Apparently, they threatened Paul's life, and these were not idle threats, they were deadly serious.

Considering all of this, there is a possibility that Paul was considering leaving Corinth and going elsewhere, or at least, tempering his Message. But at this juncture, the Scripture says, *"Then spoke the Lord to Paul in the night by a Vision."* The Lord said several things to him. Some of them are:

• Don't be afraid. This tells us that he was afraid, and rightly so. But now, he has the Lord telling him, in effect, not to worry about the situation.

• *"But speak:"* it meant speak with boldness. Don't hold back on the Message. Proclaim the fact that Jesus Christ, Whom they crucified, was and is the Son of the Living God, and He died for the sins of man, and rose from the dead on the third day. Furthermore, tell them that unless they accept the Lord Jesus Christ as their Saviour, they cannot be Saved.

• *"Hold not your peace:"* meant, *"don't hold anything back."*

Give them My Word and do so with boldness and power.

• *"For I am with you:"* there can be nothing greater than the Lord being with us. And if He is with us, who can be against us, at least who will matter?

• *"No man shall set on you to hurt you:"* no doubt many plans were made to cause Paul great harm, but the Lord saw to it that they never matured to completion.

• *"For I have much people in this city:"* many of these people of whom the Lord speaks had not yet been Saved. They would be Saved shortly!

THE OPPOSITION

The Scripture says:

"And when Gallio was the deputy of Achaia *(it is believed that he was Proconsul in A.D. 52-53)*, the Jews made insurrection with one accord against Paul, and brought him to the judgment seat *(Jews had no power to punish any person in a Roman Province, so they were obliged to bring Paul before the Roman Governor)*,

"Saying, This *fellow* persuades men to worship God contrary to the Law *(does not pertain to Roman Law as some claim, but rather the Law of Moses)*.

"And when Paul was now about to open *his* mouth *(refers to him waiting for his accusers to cease their tirade against him)*, Gallio said unto the Jews *(proclaims the Proconsul interrupting Paul)*, If it were a matter of wrong or wicked lewdness, O *you* Jews, reason would that I should bear with you *(proclaims the Governor putting everything in its proper perspective immediately!)*:

"But if it be a question of words and names, and *of* your Law, look ye *to it* *(in effect, tells them to settle this thing themselves because it had no place in a Roman Court)*; for I will be no judge of such *matters* *(in essence says, 'you will not use a Roman Court to carry forth your personal schemes!').*

"And he drove them from the judgment seat *(implies the humiliating dismissal of the case, without even being tried or further heard).*

"Then all the Greeks took Sosthenes, the Chief Ruler of the synagogue *(presents the man who took the place of Crispus, with the latter having given his heart to the Lord),* and beat *him* before the judgment seat *(gives us little clue as to why this was done, unless they had refused to dissemble).* And Gallio cared for none of those things *(means that he considered the whole matter outside his jurisdiction)*" (Acts 18:12-17).

GALLIO

At Athens Paul had adopted a poetic and finished style, and it had almost wholly failed to make any deep impression. At Corinth, accordingly, and no doubt by the guidance of the Holy Spirit, he adopted a wholly different method. He had made the decision not to avoid, as he had done at Athens, the topic of the Cross. From Corinth he could, no doubt, see the snowy summits of nearby mountains, but he determined never again to adorn his teaching and preaching with poetic quotations or persuasive words of human wisdom, but to trust solely to the simple and unadorned grandeur of his Message, the Message of the Cross, which would always be coupled by the outpouring of the Holy Spirit. There was, indeed, wisdom in his words, but it was not the wisdom of this world, nor the kind of wisdom after which the Greeks sought. It was a Spiritual Wisdom of which he could merely reveal to them the elements. He aimed at nothing but the clear, simple annunciation of the Doctrine of Christ Crucified (I Cor. 2:2). Paul had determined that if converts were won, they would be won, not by human eloquence, but by the Power of God. He would preach the Cross, and he would preach nothing but the Cross. Never mind that it was a stumblingblock to the Jews and foolishness to the Greeks, he would preach the Cross because it was the answer and, in fact, the only answer.

To be sure, the Jews in the synagogue did not at all enjoy hearing about the Death of Christ, especially considering that their religious leaders were the ones who had crucified Him. So now, they surmise a way in which they think they will rid themselves of this man once and for all. They would haul him up before Gallio, the Roman Proconsul. Their charge? He persuaded men to worship God contrary to the Law, they claimed! But what they meant for harm would turn out to be one of the greatest things that happened at that particular time to Paul, and for the furtherance of the Gospel. And, as well, the Lord had told him in a Vision, *"Fear not, but speak, and hold not your peace; for I am with you, and no man shall set on you to hurt you; for I have much people in this city."*

WHO WAS GALLIO?

The Proconsul of Achaia had just ended his term of office, and the Emperor now appointed Lucius Junius Gallio to that office. It is said that he was one of the most genial and gracious men who could be known. Seneca wrote of him, *"No mortal man is so sweet to any single person as he is to all mankind."* It was also said that he was the very flower of pagan courtesy and pagan culture—a Roman with all a Roman's dignity and seriousness, and yet, with all the Grace and versatility of a polished Greek.

Farrar said, *"Such was the man on whose decision the fortunes of Paul were to depend. Whoever the former Proconsul had been, he had not been one with whom the Jews could venture to trifle, nor had they once attempted to get rid of their opponent by handing him over to the secular arm. But now that a new Proconsul had arrived, who was perhaps unfamiliar with the duties of his office, and whose desire for popularity at the beginning of his government might have made him complacent to prosperous Jews, they thought that they could with impunity excite a tumult. They rose in a body, took Paul, and dragged him before the tessellated pavement on which was set the chair of the Proconsul."*[12]

Before this man, Gallio, they charged Paul with *"persuading men to worship God contrary to the Law."*

Knowing that the religion of Judaism was licensed by the State, the religion of *"this fellow,"* they argued, though it might try to pass itself off under the name of Judaism, was not Judaism at all. It was a spurious counterfeit, they claimed!

Such was the charge urged by the mob of voices, and now, when their ugly charges died down, Paul was on the point of making his defense. But Gallio was not going to trouble himself by listening to any defense. He took no notice whatsoever of Paul, and disregarding him as completely as though he had been non-existent, replied to the Jews by instantly dismissing their charges.

He shocked the Jews thereby, in essence, saying that their accusation against Paul as a violator of any Law, Mosaic or otherwise, was utterly baseless. In essence his answer was:

"Had this been a matter of civil wrong or moral outrage, it would have been but right for me to put up with you and listen to these charges of yours; but, if it be a number of questions about an opinion, and about mere names, and your Law, see to it yourselves; for a judge of these matters I do not choose to be."

He ordered the guards to clear the court, which they instantly did. As deep as was the ignorance of Gallio of the issues which were at stake, his conduct was in accordance with the strictest justice when *"he drove them from his judgment seat."*

A MOST WORTHY DECREE

Whether he understood it or not, and to be sure, he didn't, the decision he made that day was without a doubt the most important decision made in the entire Roman world at that time. The decision made by Gallio to not entertain any of these charges made by the Jews against Paul would open the door for quite some time, actually several years, for Paul to preach the Gospel, with the word at hand that a Roman Court, and under the distinguished Lucius Junius Gallio, had ruled in his favor and against the Jews. Very little could have been done at that time that would have been any more important to the Work of God and the spread of the Gospel. How so much the Lord took a planned scheme by the Jews and turned it on their own heads, and at the same time under Roman Law, provided an open door for the spread of the Gospel.

THE GREEKS

But the scene did not end there. Whatever their thoughts, once the highest authority had pronounced the charge against Paul to be frivolous, the Greeks seized the opportunity to exact some punishment of their own.

It seems that the ringleader of the Jewish faction had been a certain Sosthenes, who had succeeded Crispus in the function of Ruler of the synagogue, and whose zeal may have been all the more violently stimulated by the defection of his predecessor. Whatever their ideas, they seized Sosthenes and gave him a beating in front of the tribunal, and under the very eyes of the Proconsul.

An ancient gloss says that he pretended not to see what they were doing, but the Text implies that he looked on at the entire proceeding with indifference. So long as they were not guilty of any serious infraction of the peace, it was nothing to him how they amused themselves. Evidently he thought that it would be so much the better if they taught this Sosthenes, and any number more of these Jews, a severe lesson. They would be more likely (he thought) to keep order in the future and less likely to trouble him again with their riots and their rancors.

Gallio, the brother of Seneca, the Proconsul of Achaia, one of the most popular men of his day, would have been amazed had anyone told him that this occurrence at which he had officiated would be forever recorded in history; that it would be the only scene in his life in which posterity would feel a moment's interest. Little did he realize that this Jew from Tarsus named Paul would be regarded as so much more important than all the Emperors of Rome. Little did he realize that these questions about a mere opinion, and names, and a matter of Jewish Law, which he had so disdainfully refused to hear, should hereafter become the most prominent of questions to the whole civilized world.

EPHESUS

"And Paul *after this* tarried *there* yet a good while *(could have referred to several months)*, and then took his leave of the Brethren *(was done strictly according to the timing of the Lord)*, and sailed thence into Syria, and with him Priscilla and Aquila *(they had now become fast friends of Paul)*; having shorn *his* head in Cenchrea: for he had a vow *(Cenchrea was the Port of Corinth; there was a Church there as well; we aren't told what this 'vow' was)*.

"And he came to Ephesus *(Ephesus was the most important city in the Roman Province of Asia)*, and left them there *(has to do with Priscilla and Aquila remaining in Ephesus when Paul left some days later)*: but he himself entered into the synagogue, and reasoned with the Jews *(has no reference to the previous phrase; no doubt, Priscilla and Aquila were with him during this meeting)*.

"When they *(the Jews in the Synagogue)* desired *him* to tarry longer time with them, he consented not *(Paul left, but Priscilla and Aquila remained and, no doubt, continued teaching these Jews about Christ)*" (Acts 18:18-20).

THE VOW

The verdict of Gallio had given Paul a respite for the balance of the time he spent at Corinth. It had been even as the Lord had promised. In fact, he ministered there for several months before leaving and saw a great Church founded. But yet, even as his Epistles would bear out, many problems in the future would arise in Corinth.

But at a particular period of time, he left, determined to visit Jerusalem once more. He took with him Priscilla and Aquila, who by now had become close friends of the Apostle.

The Scripture says that he had *"shorn his head in Cenchrea for he had a vow."* It was without a doubt the temporary vow of the Nazarite. Regarding this vow, he was to abstain from anything pertaining to grapes, whether grapes on the vine, grape juice, wine, etc. As well, he was to let his hair grow long. Supposedly, he was to shave his head at Jerusalem, but that not being possible because of the distance, he would cut his own hair, and do so, it seems, at Cenchrea.

Incidentally, there was a church at Cenchrea, of which Phoebe was a deaconess. Later on she would take the scroll containing the Epistle to the Romans to the city of Rome.

Paul was to keep the shorn locks of his hair until he offered a Burnt-Offering, and Sin-Offering, and Peace-Offering at the Temple in Jerusalem. The hair was to be burnt in the fire under the sacrifice of the Peace-Offering.

WHY THIS VOW?

For Paul, knowing that the Law was finished in Christ, what was the purpose of such a vow? Why did he engage himself in an Old Testament practice? What was the point?

When Paul was given the meaning of the New Covenant, which, as we have stated, was the greatest Word that God had ever given to any human being, he did not effect an understanding of all of this immediately. There was a growing process as it regarded the great Apostle. Little by little, the great Apostle came to understand more and more the meaning of all that which had been given to him. By degrees, it seems, he came to know and understand the all inclusiveness of the New Covenant, and how that Jesus had fulfilled the Law in every respect and, in fact, other than the moral part of the Law, the Ten Commandments, the Law was no more. But as stated, he did not come to this place and position overnight. It seems that he did not come into the full realization of the Cross until his service at Athens. There he had not mentioned the Cross of Christ, and I think he realized after the effort in Athens, that he had made a mistake. As we have previously stated, he more so told the Athenians how much he knew about the Lord, instead of what the Lord could do for them. As a result, he saw few results. Every evidence is, when he came to Corinth, which was immediately after Athens, he came preaching the Cross. In fact, he had stated, *"I determined not to know anything among you, save Jesus Christ, and Him Crucified"* (I Cor. 2:2).

Not being given any information at this time by the Holy Spirit as to the purpose of this vow, or what he thought it would accomplish, the Holy Spirit being silent, we had best be silent as well!

Coming to Ephesus, as was his custom, he went to the synagogue there, and *"reasoned with the Jews."* Miracle of Miracles, they did not rise up against him as they normally did in other places but *"desired him to tarry longer time with them."* Needing to go to Jerusalem, or so he thought, he did not consent to stay with them any longer at this particular time. But he would be back.

ANTIOCH

"But bade them farewell *(speaks of Priscilla and Aquila, and possibly some few Jews who had accepted Christ)*, saying, I must by all means keep this Feast that comes in Jerusalem *(probably was the Passover, although some say it was the Feast of Pentecost)*: but I will return again unto you, if God will *(portrays the manner in which all Believers should conduct everything)*. And he sailed from

Ephesus *(places him on his way to Jerusalem).*

"**And when he had landed at Caesarea** *(puts him about sixty-five miles northwest of Jerusalem)*, **and gone up, and saluted the Church** *(refers to the Mother Church at Jerusalem)*, **he went down to Antioch** *(refers to Antioch, Syria)*" **(Acts 18:21-22).**

HE SALUTED THE CHURCH

Luke gives us almost no information on this visit to Jerusalem. In fact, he merely stated that when Paul arrived in Jerusalem, he *"saluted the Church,"* and that's all that was said.

Luke was not with Paul at this time, so that may be the reason for the lack of information. But yet, there are some scholars who feel that because of Paul's Doctrine of Grace, the possibility of a split was ever present. In fact, Paul labored mightily that no split occur, and in that he was successful. The problem was the Law/Grace issue.

To be brief, Paul stated that Jesus Christ had fulfilled the Law in every respect, and it was no more. In other words, trying to keep the Law of Moses at this stage was not necessary. And, in fact, such an effort would prove to be detrimental to any Believer simply because Grace and Law could not mix. Men were Saved simply by trusting Christ and what Christ did for us at the Cross. It was a matter of Faith in Christ and not at all in keeping Law.

But the Jews, at least as a whole, did not desire that particular direction. Many were insisting that they continue to keep the Law, so this proved to be a problem in the Early Church.

About four years had now elapsed since his last visit to Jerusalem. He had, no doubt, much to relate to the Church, the Mother Church, in Jerusalem. The Gospel, above all things, had first of all been taken to Europe, and even at places so important as Philippi, Thessalonica, and Corinth.

Farrar said, and concerning this very thing, *"Had James, and the circle of which he was the center, only understood how vast for the future of Christianity would be the issues of these perilous and toilsome journeys – had they but seen how insignificant, compared with the labors of Paul, would be the part which they themselves were playing in furthering the universality of the Church – with what affection and admiration would they have welcomed him! How would they have striven, by every form of kindness, of encouragement, of honor, of heartfelt prayer, to arm and strengthen him, and to fire into yet brighter luster his grand enthusiasm, so as to prepare him in the future for sacrifices yet more heroic, for efforts yet more immense! Had anything of the kind occurred, Luke, in the interest of Christianity – Paul himself, in his account to the Galatians of his relations to the twelve – could hardly have failed to tell us about it. So far from this, Luke hurries over the brief visit in the three words they 'saluted the Church,' not even pausing to inform us that he fulfilled his vow, or whether any favorable impression as to his Judaic orthodoxy was created by the fact that he had undertaken it."* Farrar went on to say, *"There is too much reason to fear that his reception was cold and ungracious; that even if James received him with courtesy, the Jewish Christians who surrounded 'the Lord's brother' it seems, did not."*[13]

Now, it is quite possible that Farrar has read more into the silence than was intended by the Holy Spirit. I hope so, and I'm sure that Dr. Farrar hopes so as well! But yet, the silence regarding his visit seems to whisper to us, if nothing else, that the Law/Grace issue definitely was not dead.

From Jerusalem, the Scripture says that he went to Antioch, and we can well imagine that all there were so very eager for Paul to give an account of the great victories won on this last missionary journey. And so this second journey now ends.

At Jerusalem, Christianity was born in the cradle of Judaism; Antioch, however, had been the starting point of the Church of the Gentiles.

While Luke did not tell us as to exactly how long Paul remained at Antioch, it was probably several months. He no doubt very much needed the rest and, as well, the encouragement that the Believers in Antioch no doubt gave to him.

"Name of Jesus! Highest Name!
"Name that Earth and Heaven adore!
"From the Heart of God it came,
"Leads me to God's Heart once more."

"Name of Jesus! Living tide!
"Days of drought for me are past;
"How much more than satisfied,
"Are the thirsty lips at last!"

"Name of Jesus! Dearest Name!
"Bread of Heaven, and Balm of Love;
"Oil of Gladness, surest claim,
"To the treasures stored above."

"Jesus gives forgiveness free,
"Jesus cleanses all my stains;
"Jesus gives His Life to me,
"Jesus always He remains."

"Only Jesus! Fairest Name!
"Life and rest, and peace, and bliss;
"Jesus, evermore the same,
"He is mine, and I am His."

PAUL
THE APOSTLE

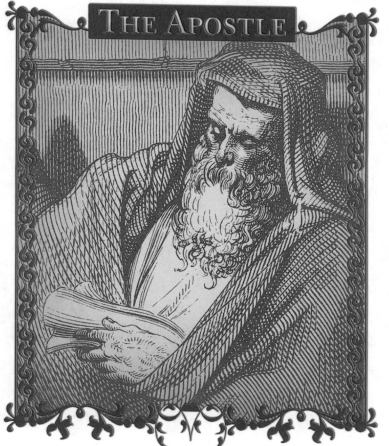

CHAPTER NINE

The Third
Missionary Journey

Paul's Third Missionary Journey

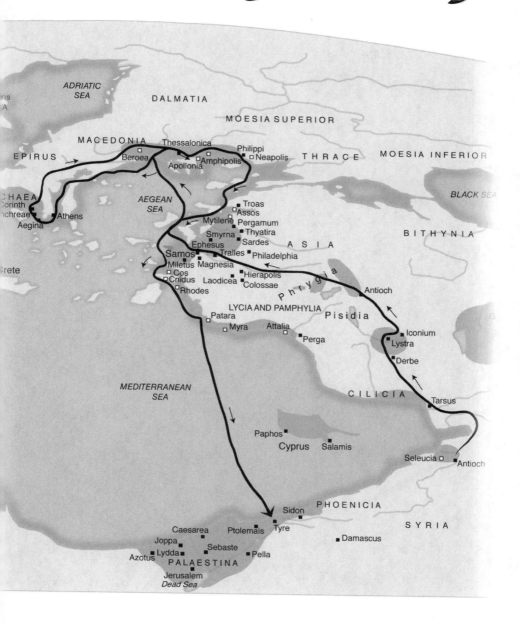

THE THIRD MISSIONARY JOURNEY

"And after he had spent some time *there*, he departed *(portrays the beginning of his third missionary journey)*, and went over *all* the country of Galatia and Phrygia in order, strengthening all the Disciples *(probably lasted about six months; it is believed that Timothy, Erastus, Gaius, and Aristarchus may have been traveling with Paul at this time; Titus may have been included as well)*" (Acts 18:23).

STRENGTHENING THE CHURCHES

One can well imagine with what joy the Believers in the Churches in the area of Galatia and Phrygia greeted Paul. Incidentally, this area is in what is now modern Turkey. Galatia seemed to be the largest of these areas. It bordered Pamphylia, Cilicia, which was on the south, and Bithynia and Pontus on the north, and Cappadocia on the east. Phrygia would have been to the west. It seemed to have been the largest region; however, due to particulars, those borders seemed to change at the whim of Rome. Just how many Churches were in these areas, of course, we have no way of knowing. As well, and as previously stated, when we say *"Churches,"* the reader should understand that there were no such things then as Church buildings. Rome would not allow such. Almost all Churches at that time were located in people's houses, so most were probably were very small, but yet, there is evidence that some were quite large.

Pastors had to be raised up, as should be obvious, out of the local congregation. So, the teaching that Paul would provide was sorely needed, again, as should be obvious.

Sadly, over a period of time, actually several hundreds of years, the Churches went into spiritual decline, little by little morphing into what we presently refer to as the Catholic Church. The Churches seemed to stay true to the Message

of *"Jesus Christ and Him Crucified,"* which is the Foundation of *"Justification by Faith,"* through the life of the original
Apostles and those who sat under them; however, when the
first generation after the Apostles died off, spiritual declension
began to set in. While it wasn't until the early 600's that the
Bishop of Rome was first referred to as *"Pope,"* the declension
set in long before that. Now this area is occupied by Muslims,
with not much trace of Bible Christianity left in those areas.
Nevertheless, they served as a springboard for the Gospel of
Jesus Christ, which ultimately morphed into the Reformation.
Actually, the Reformation was built entirely on the Epistles
of St. Paul. It took time for the entire story to unfold, but I
personally believe what is taking place presently, as it regards
the Message of the Cross, has brought and is bringing Paul's
Gospel into full bloom.

THE REVELATION THE LORD GAVE ME IN 1997

In the 1500's, when the Reformation began under Martin
Luther, which ultimately became the strength of England and
the United States, as well as other parts of the world, it only
incorporated part of Paul's teaching. And we must understand, the entirety of the meaning of the New Covenant was
given to Paul, which he gave to us in his fourteen Epistles, that
is, if he wrote Hebrews, and I believe he did. The Reformation
began, even as it should have, with the understanding as Paul
taught it of *"Justification by Faith."* This was totally contrary
to Roman Catholic doctrine, and opened the door for Salvation
to *"whosoever will."*

Following on the heels of this great Message of Justification
by Faith, the great Holiness movement sprang up in the 1700's
and 1800's. And then at the turn of the Twentieth Century,
the Holy Spirit took this Message even further, with the outpouring of the Holy Spirit with the evidence of speaking with
other Tongues, which, since that time, has swept the world.
In fact, it is believed that from the beginning of the Twentieth

Century, over 500 million people have been baptized with the Holy Spirit with the evidence of speaking with other Tongues.

The Revelation the Lord gave me in 1997, I personally feel, brought the teaching of Paul to full bloom once again.

The Lord gave me this Revelation in three stages:

1. An understanding of the sin nature as it regards Romans, Chapter 6.

2. The solution to the sin nature, which is the Cross of Christ and the Cross of Christ Alone, once again, found in the Sixth Chapter of Romans.

3. The manner and way in which the Holy Spirit works in all of this, found in Romans Chapter 8.

An understanding of the sin nature has been known all along by a few, and quite possibly, as well, an understanding of the Cross as the only solution. However, as it regards the manner and way in which the Holy Spirit works within our lives, even as Paul taught us, as far as I know, this has not been previously known. With the understanding as to how the Holy Spirit works, I personally feel that this rounds out, so to speak, that which was given to us by the Lord through the Apostle Paul. Paul said, and I quote from THE EXPOSITOR'S STUDY BIBLE:

> "*There is* therefore now no condemnation *(guilt)* to them which are in Christ Jesus *(refers back to Rom. 6:3-5 and our being baptized into His Death, which speaks of the Crucifixion)*, who walk not after the flesh *(depending on one's personal strength and ability or great religious efforts in order to overcome sin)*, but after the Spirit *(the Holy Spirit works exclusively within the legal confines of the Finished Work of Christ; our Faith in that Finished Work, i.e., 'the Cross,' guarantees the help of the Holy Spirit which guarantees Victory).*

THE LAW OF THE SPIRIT OF LIFE IN CHRIST JESUS

> "**For the Law** *(that which we are about to give is a Law*

of God, devised by the Godhead in eternity past [I Pet. 1:18-20]; this Law, in fact, is 'God's Prescribed Order of Victory') **of the Spirit** *(Holy Spirit, i.e., 'the way the Spirit works')* **of Life** *(all life comes from Christ, but through the Holy Spirit [Jn. 16:13-14])* **in Christ Jesus** *(anytime Paul uses this term or one of its derivatives, he is, without fail, referring to what Christ did at the Cross, which makes this 'life' possible)* **has made me free** *(given me total Victory)* **from the Law of Sin and Death** *(these are the two most powerful Laws in the universe; the 'Law of the Spirit of Life in Christ Jesus' alone is stronger than the 'Law of Sin and Death'; this means that if the Believer attempts to live for God by any manner other than Faith in Christ and the Cross, he is doomed to failure)"* **(Rom. 8:1-2).**

THE MEANING

The Cross of Christ has given the Holy Spirit the legal means to do all that He does within our hearts and lives. What do we mean by that?

Before the Cross, and due to the fact that the blood of bulls and goats could not take away sins (Heb. 10:4), the Holy Spirit was limited as to what He could do in the hearts and lives of Believers. It was because the sin debt remained, due to the ineffectiveness of animal blood. While the animal sacrifices served as a stopgap measure, so to speak, until Christ would come, they were very limited as to their effectiveness.

While the Holy Spirit could come into the hearts and lives of a select few, such as Prophets, etc., to help them carry out their task, there is no evidence in the Old Testament of the Holy Spirit helping them with Sanctification, etc. Whenever the task was completed, the evidence is, the Holy Spirit would withdraw.

When Jesus died on the Cross of Calvary, thereby, atoning for all sin, this satisfied the Righteousness of a Thrice-holy God, and removed the sin debt, so to speak, from every individual who believed. Then, since the Cross, the Holy Spirit immediately at conversion comes into the hearts and lives of Believers, there to abide permanently (Jn. 14:16-17). The Cross of Christ made all of this possible (Eph. 2:13-18).

THE HELP OF THE HOLY SPIRIT

To have the full help of the Holy Spirit, He doesn't require very much of us, but He does require one thing, and on that He will not bend. He demands that our Faith rest exclusively in Christ and what Christ did for us at the Cross. In other words, the Cross of Christ must ever be the Object of our Faith (Lk. 9:23; 14:27; Rom. 6:3-14; I Cor. 1:17, 18, 21, 23; 2:2; Gal. 6:14; Col. 2:10-14).

APOLLOS

"And a certain Jew named Apollos, born at Alexandria, an eloquent man, *and* mighty in the Scriptures, came to Ephesus *(introduces a man whom Paul came to hold in high esteem)*.

"This man was instructed in the Way of the Lord *(however, his knowledge was greatly limited respecting Grace and the Baptism with the Holy Spirit)*; and being fervent in the spirit *(spoke of his own spirit and not the Holy Spirit)*, he spoke and taught diligently the things of the Lord, knowing only the Baptism of John *(speaks of Repentance and Water Baptism)*.

"And he began to speak boldly in the synagogue: whom when Aquila and Priscilla had heard *(presents that which was all in the providence of God)*, they took him unto *them*, and expounded unto him the Way of God more perfectly *(no doubt pertained to the full complement of Salvation by the Grace of God exclusively, correct Water Baptism, and the Baptism with the Holy Spirit with the evidence of speaking with other Tongues)*.

"And when he *(Apollos)* was disposed to pass into

Achaia *(refers to Greece, across the Aegean Sea, and Corinth in particular),* **the Brethren wrote, exhorting the Disciples to receive him: who, when he was come, helped them much which had believed through Grace** *(he is now proficient in this most excellent Message of the Grace of God that comes through the Cross)***:**

"**For he mightily convinced the Jews,** *and that* **publickly, showing by the Scriptures that Jesus was Christ** *(had reference more than likely to ministering in their synagogue)*" **(Acts 18:24-28).**

THE HUMILITY OF APOLLOS

Apollos came into the life and ministry of Paul, and proved to be a tremendous boon to the Cause of Christ.

He was a Jew born in Alexandria, and from what little information is given, seemed to be a man who was very educated, not only as it regarded secular education, but also the Scripture says, *"mighty in the Scriptures."* Of course, at this time this was speaking of the Law of Moses, i.e., *"the Old Testament."*

It seems that Apollos had a rudimentary knowledge of the Lord Jesus Christ, but had no knowledge at all of the meaning of the New Covenant as it had been given to the Apostle Paul. So, even though his knowledge was great, to say the least, concerning Old Testament Doctrine, still, he was deficient in what the Lord was now doing.

When Aquila and Priscilla heard him, evidently he was holding forth in the synagogue. They were impressed by what they heard, even though his knowledge of the Lord Jesus Christ was elementary, to say the least.

These two people, Aquila and Priscilla, were repairers of tents, a most humble occupation. But despite that, every evidence is that Apollos accepted readily that which this couple told him. The Scripture says, *"they took him unto them, and expounded unto him the Way of God more perfectly."*

The truth is, considering how educated Apollos was, and

that Aquila and Priscilla more than likely did not at all match him in such training, it took a man of humility, even deep humility, to be corrected as he was and, thereby, be greatly benefited. Most, I think, would little have taken the correction given by this godly couple, but Apollos did!

There were three powerful lessons learned by Apollos that day. They were:

1. He was given full instruction as to what Paul taught as it regarded the meaning of the New Covenant, in other words, what Jesus did for us at the Cross of Calvary.

2. He was taken beyond the Baptism of John, which was a Baptism of Repentance, and into Water Baptism, as it regarded the Lord Jesus Christ. The phrase, *"Baptism of John,"* tells us, as well, that Apollos did not understand Justification by Faith, which they, no doubt, explained to him.

3. Undoubtedly, he was also taught the Baptism with the Holy Spirit with the evidence of speaking with other Tongues. As to exactly when he was filled, the Scripture doesn't say, but every evidence is that he was.

MODERN PREACHERS

There are, as well, untold numbers of modern Preachers who love the Lord exactly as did Apollos but have little or no knowledge at all of the Message of the Cross, in other words, that which Paul gave to us. They understand the Cross of Christ relative to Salvation but not at all relative to Sanctification. As a result, they cannot properly live for God, and at the same time, those who sit under their ministries are left lacking as well.

I would pray that these many, many thousands of Preachers, and I speak of Preachers all over the world, would be as receptive to the Message of the Cross as was Apollos.

After Aquila and Priscilla dealt with Apollos, he was then able to go into the synagogue, which he did, *"mightily convincing the Jews, and that publickly, showing by the Scriptures that Jesus was Christ."* When he finished his ministry in Ephesus, which greatly paved the way for Paul, who came to this city a little later, Apollos then went to Corinth, greatly recommended by the Brethren.

EPHESUS

"And it came to pass, that, while Apollos was at Corinth *(pertains to Acts 18:27)*, **Paul having passed through the upper coasts came to Ephesus** *(refers back to Acts 18:23)*: **and finding certain Disciples** *(they were followers of Christ, but deficient in their understanding)*,

"**He said unto them, Have you received the Holy Spirit since you believed?** *(In the Greek, this is literally, 'having believed, did you receive?' We know these men were already Saved because every time the word 'Disciples' is used in the Book of Acts, it refers to individuals who have accepted Christ. Paul could tell that these individuals, although Saved, had not yet been baptized with the Holy Spirit.)* **And they said unto him, We have not so much as heard whether there be any Holy Spirit** *(doesn't mean that they didn't know of the existence of the Holy Spirit, but they were not aware that the Age of the Spirit had come, and that Believers could literally be baptized with Him; at Salvation, the Holy Spirit baptizes Believing sinners into Christ; at the Spirit Baptism, Jesus baptizes Believers into the Holy Spirit [Mat. 3:11])*" **(Acts 19:1-2).**

THE BAPTISM WITH THE HOLY SPIRIT

Let it be settled that these twelve men addressed by Paul at Ephesus were Saved men. Anytime the word *"Disciples"* is used in the Book of Acts, it always, and without exception, refers to followers of Christ. In other words, people who are Saved.

In speaking with them, he ascertained that while they were Saved, they had not yet been baptized with the Holy Spirit.

This tells us, as should be obvious, that there is a vast

difference in being *"born of the Spirit,"* and being *"Baptized with the Spirit."* Every person who comes to Christ is *"born of the Spirit,"* which definitely does mean that the Holy Spirit comes into their hearts and lives, and there to abide permanently; however, every person who is Born-Again is not at the same time baptized with the Holy Spirit, the latter being a separate and distinct Work of Grace (Acts 2:4; 8:14-17; 9:17).

The Baptism with the Holy Spirit is for Power. That's why Jesus had much to say about this just before His Ascension. The Scripture says, which constituted the last word that He would give to His Followers:

> "And, being assembled together with *them* (*speaks of the time He ascended back to the Father; this was probably the time of the 'above five hundred' [I Cor. 15:6]*), **Commanded them** (*not a suggestion*) **that they should not depart from Jerusalem** (*the site of the Temple where the Holy Spirit would descend*), **but wait for the Promise of the Father** (*spoke of the Holy Spirit which had been promised by the Father [Lk. 24:49; Joel, Chpt. 2]*), **which, said *He*, you have heard of Me** (*you have also heard Me say these things [Jn. 7:37-39; 14:12-17, 26; 15:26; 16:7-15]*)" **(Acts 1:4).**

The command that our Lord gave to His Followers just before His Ascension is incumbent upon Believers presently as much now as it was then. In essence, His Followers, plus His chosen Apostles, were, in effect, commanded not to go testify of Him, not to go work for Him, or do anything for Him, until they were first baptized with the Holy Spirit. And this is exactly what they did. Let me emphasize it:

This command is just as binding presently as it was then. Without the Baptism with the Holy Spirit, which is always accompanied, and without exception, by speaking with other Tongues, while a lot of religious machinery may be involved, there will, in fact, be very little done for Christ. It is absolutely imperative that every Believer be baptized with the Holy Spirit.

JOHN'S BAPTISM OF REPENTANCE

"And he said unto them, Unto what then were you baptized? *(After asking about the Holy Spirit Baptism, Paul was met with a blank stare, so to speak.)* And they said, Unto John's Baptism *(this was the Baptism of Repentance).*

"Then said Paul, John verily baptized with the Baptism of Repentance *(which, in effect, was all that could be done at that particular time)*, saying unto the people, that they should believe on Him which should come after him, that is, on Christ Jesus *(proclaims John the Baptist lifting up Jesus as the Saviour of mankind).*

"When they heard *this (no doubt, Paul said much more; however, the evidence is they instantly believed and accepted what Paul said, and they then desired what he said)*, they were baptized in the Name of the Lord Jesus *(means, 'by the authority of the Lord Jesus'; the only Baptismal formula in the Word of God is Mat. 28:19).*

"And when Paul had laid *his* hands upon them *(constitutes a Biblical principle [Acts 8:17; 9:17-18])*, the Holy Spirit came on them *(refers to them being baptized with the Holy Spirit)*; and they spoke with tongues, and prophesied *(proclaims Tongues as the initial physical evidence that one has been baptized with the Holy Spirit; sometimes there is prophesying at that time, and sometimes not [Acts 8:17; 9:17; 10:46]).*

"And all the men were about twelve *(it seems that no women were involved at this particular time)*" (Acts 19:3-7).

THEY SPOKE WITH TONGUES AND PROPHESIED

These twelve men, or so, were somewhat in the same state as Apollos had been. They had some knowledge of the Lord but were not at all cognizant of the New Covenant, much less what it meant.

It is almost positive that the account given to us in this Nineteenth Chapter of Acts concerning these men is extremely abbreviated.

When Paul explained to them the Ministry of our Lord, and the price that He paid at Calvary's Cross, and that Faith must be exhibited in Him, and Him Alone, evidently, this they believed. Paul then laid hands on them, and the Bible says, *"the Holy Spirit came on them; and they spoke with tongues, and prophesied."*

There are five accounts in the Book of Acts as it regards Believers being baptized with the Holy Spirit. In all of these accounts it either plainly says the recipients spoke with other Tongues, or it strongly implies such (Acts 2:4; 8:14-16; 9:17; 10:44-46; 19:1-7).

While speaking with other Tongues is definitely not the only evidence that one has been baptized with the Holy Spirit, it most definitely is the initial physical evidence. In fact, all who are baptized with the Holy Spirit speak with other Tongues, with no exceptions. While individuals may have grand experiences with the Lord, which certainly are a blessing, still, if they haven't spoken with other Tongues, they haven't been baptized with the Holy Spirit. Unfortunately, there are some who erroneously think that certain experiences constitute the Baptism with the Spirit. Within itself, it doesn't. Speaking with other Tongues, as stated, is the initial physical evidence that one has been filled.

From then on, such a Believer should praise and worship the Lord in Tongues every day of his life. Of course, such is not demanded, but such is most definitely a tremendous blessing.

WHAT GOOD ARE TONGUES?

Many have asked that question, mostly those who opposed this grand and glorious experience given to us by the Lord. Let's see what the Word of God says about the value of speaking with other Tongues:

• If the infilling of the Holy Spirit is accompanied by speaking with other Tongues, then it is most valuable. In fact, anything from God is valuable!

• If it is the Holy Spirit Who gives such utterance, and He most definitely does, then it is valuable indeed (Acts 2:4).

• When individuals speak in Tongues, they are declaring *"the Wonderful Works of God"* (Acts 2:11). The Scripture says that those who speak with Tongues, *"speak not unto men, but unto God."* Such is a profound blessing (I Cor. 14:2).

• Those who speak with other Tongues *"edify themselves,"* which we all need (I Cor. 14:4).

• The Scripture says that *"Tongues are for a sign, not to them who believe, but to them who believe not"* (I Cor. 14:22).

• The Lord uses the Gift of Tongues to give a Message at times to His People (I Cor. 14:27).

• The great Prophet Isaiah said nearly 800 years before Christ that speaking in other Tongues would provide a *"rest"* for the people of God (Isa. 28:12).

• The great Prophet also said that it would be a *"refreshing,"* which we all need (Isa. 28:12).

THE SYNAGOGUE

"And he *(Paul)* went into the synagogue, and spoke boldly for the space of three months *(it seems that he lasted longer here than he had in most synagogues)*, disputing and persuading the things concerning the Kingdom of God *(he would have brought reasonable proofs from the Old Testament Scriptures to show that the Kingdom [ruled authority] of God is revealed in Jesus, Who is now Ascended to the Right Hand of the Father and seated at the Father's Throne [2:30-33])*" (Acts 19:8).

BOLD PREACHING

After dealing with the twelve men concerning the Baptism

of John, etc., the Scripture says that Paul *"went into the synagogue, where he debated the Jews for a space of some three months."* That he was able to remain there for three months ministering every Sabbath Day (Saturday) is a Miracle within itself. One can well imagine the repartee and the exchanges between Paul and the students of Moses.

We must remember, though Paul was Christian in every capacity, as should be overly obvious, as well, he was an Israelite. As such, he knew and understood the Law of Moses, more than likely, more than anyone else in the world of that day. As well, knowing what Christ had given to him as it concerned the meaning of the New Covenant, it had to hurt deeply for him to see his fellow Israelites miss in totality that which the Lord was doing. He knew that despite all their claims, this direction, the rejection of Jesus Christ, would take them to spiritual oblivion. Please let the following be understood:

ONE WAY

Some have claimed that the Jews, and from then until now, have a different way of Salvation other than the Lord Jesus Christ. Please let it be understood, there is only one Way, and that Way is the Lord Jesus Christ. He plainly said Himself:

"I am the Way, the Truth, and the Life: no man comes unto the Father, but by Me" (Jn. 14:6). That means that every Jew who rejects Jesus Christ, as well as every other person in the world, dies eternally lost. It is Christ and Christ Alone Who paid the price at Calvary's Cross for man's Redemption. No one else paid that price, only our Lord. So, one might say the following:

• The only way to God is through Jesus Christ (Jn. 14:6; Col. 2:10).

• The only way to Jesus Christ is through the Cross of Christ (Rom. 6:3-5; I Cor. 1:17, 18; 2:2; Col. 2:14-15).

• The only way to the Cross is a denial of self (Lk. 9:23; 14:27).

THE CHURCH

"But when divers were hardened, and believed not, but spoke evil of that Way before the multitude *(they rebelled against the Gospel of Christ)*, he departed from them, and separated the Disciples *(proclaims the break with the synagogue)*, disputing daily in the school of one Tyrannus *(is thought to be the Lecture Hall of a Greek philosopher)*.

"And this continued by the space of two years *(probably referred to most every night and, at times, during the day as well; he spent a total of three years in Ephesus [Acts 20:31])*; so that all they which dwelt in Asia heard the Word of the Lord Jesus, both Jews and Greeks *(does not refer to every single person, but rather to people from all walks of life, and from all surrounding areas)*" (Acts 19:9-10).

THEY HEARD THE WORD OF THE LORD

Paul stayed in the synagogue ministering to both Jews and Gentiles as long as he could. But there came a time that the Jews made a decision to reject what he was preaching, which and Who was the Lord Jesus Christ, and so the time came that he had to separate from them. This must have hurt him deeply because, as stated, he loved his people very, very much.

Consequently, Paul did something in Ephesus that he really had not done in other places. He rented a lecture hall of one who was thought to be a philosopher by the name of Tyrannus. Evidently, he conducted services there, more than likely every night, and possibly even during the day as well. This new place of worship gave him the advantage of being able to meet the Brethren, whereas in the synagogue, that was possible only two or three times a week. As a result, he stayed in Ephesus longer than anywhere else, a space of some three years total (Acts 20:31). How blessed the Church at Ephesus was, and how much benefit was accorded them, in that they had Paul to preach to them and to teach them all of this time. As a result, the Gospel of Jesus Christ went out all over that part of the country with possibly thousands accepting Christ as their Saviour.

The Gospel of Jesus Christ alone can change things and change them evermore for the good. Nothing else in the world has that kind of Power, not even close!

MIRACLES

"And God wrought special Miracles by the hands of Paul *(the Lord did these things, not Paul)*:

"So that from his body were brought unto the sick handkerchiefs or aprons *(there is no indication in the Text that he purposely sent these things out, although he definitely may have, but rather that people on their own simply picked them up; they took them to the diseased or demon-possessed, evidently placing the cloth on the person, with them receiving healing and/or deliverance)*, and the diseases departed from them, and the evil spirits went out of them *(it was not the pieces of cloth which did this, but rather the Power of God using these cloths as a point of contact regarding Faith)*" (Acts 19:11-12).

HEALING THE SICK AND CASTING OUT DEMONS

As many, many people were hearing the Gospel and accepting Christ, the Scripture says that the Lord *"wrought special Miracles by the hands of Paul;"* this, no doubt, included healings and Miracles of every nature. As well, those who could not get to the services, for whatever reason, the Scripture informs us that their loved ones took pieces of cloth which Paul had handled, and when these cloths were applied to the individuals with the diseases and sicknesses, not only were they healed, but, as well, *"evil spirits went out of them."*

As the Lord did those things then, to be sure, He is still doing the same thing presently. While Luke doesn't give us any particular testimonies at this time, he does allude to the fact that the Lord did mighty things, which, no doubt, greatly increased the Power of the Gospel over that part of the world.

In the Early Church this was the Gospel. Jesus Christ was the Saviour, the Baptizer with the Holy Spirit, the Healer, and demons were cast out in His Name. As stated, that was the Early Church. The modern church has so watered down the Gospel that, any more, unbelief rules. All of this, they say, passed away with the Apostles, or some such excuse.

No, the truth is, Jesus Christ is the same, yesterday, today, and forever. What was then, should be now! And it is in some circles.

WHO ARE YOU?

"Then certain of the vagabond Jews, exorcists *(speaks of individuals who practiced divination, and who were not of God, but rather of Satan)*, took upon them to call over them which had evil spirits the Name of the Lord Jesus *(apparently these people had heard Paul minister and observed him praying for the sick and casting out demons; they evidently noted that he used 'The Name of Jesus,' which had a powerful effect)*, saying, We adjure you by Jesus Whom Paul preaches *(seems to be their own formula or incantation they cooked up by observing Paul)*.

"And there were seven sons of *one* Sceva, a Jew, *and* Chief of the Priests, which did so *(infers that this man may have been a member of the Jewish Council at Ephesus)*.

"And the evil spirit answered and said *(points to a man who was demon-possessed, and that some or all of these seven sons had been hired to exorcise this spirit)*, Jesus I know, and Paul I know; but who are you? *(This represents two different and distinct Greek verbs regarding the word 'know.' Referring to Jesus, it implied fear!*

Referring to Paul, there was much less action.)

"And the man in whom the evil spirit was leaped on them, and overcame them, and prevailed against them *(probably involved all seven sons being soundly whipped by the demon-possessed man)*, **so that they fled out of that house naked and wounded** *(the Greek Text indicates that they suffered wounds severe enough to effect them for a while)*.

"And this was known to all the Jews and Greeks also dwelling at Ephesus *('all' does not mean every single person, but rather quite a number)*; **and fear fell on them all** *(they now knew not to trifle with the Name of Jesus)*, **and the Name of the Lord Jesus was magnified** *(presents the constant idea of the Holy Spirit that Jesus will always be Glorified [Jn. 16:14])*" **(Acts 19:13-17).**

THE NAME OF JESUS

We learn several things from these Passages. Some are:
• **The Name of Jesus carries tremendous Power in the spirit world, as should be obvious!**
• **However, the Name of Jesus cannot be used with any positive results by those who do not really know Christ as their Saviour, with possibly some few exceptions.**
• **Used by a Spirit-filled individual, this great Name, the Name of Jesus, carries great Power.**

Evidently, Paul was praying for the sick and casting out demons and doing so by the use of the Name of Jesus, which every true Preacher of the Gospel should do. A Jew named Sceva, and his seven sons, evidently observed Paul at some juncture praying for the sick, etc., and seeing tremendous results.

Evidently, they thought there was some type of magic incantation by the use of this Name, not understanding at all that it really could be used, for the most part, only by those who knew Christ as Saviour and Lord. So, we learn from that that the use of the Name and its effectiveness has a lot to do

with the person using it. These evil spirits instantly knew Who Jesus was, and, as well, they knew Paul, but *"Jesus"* was the Name that they feared greatly, and rightly so. So, the exorcism practiced by these Jews did not materialize, and not only that, the demons almost killed them.

A PERSONAL EXPERIENCE

If I remember correctly, the year was 1953. Actually, Donnie would be born just a few months later.

Frances and I had been married nearly two years at this stage, and were just starting to preach the Gospel. After she went to bed, I stayed up that night, studying the Word for awhile. We lived in a little 32-foot house trailer.

At any rate, that night, as I began to study the Word, I felt a powerful oppressive spirit come into the room. I remember leaving out of the little trailer and walking up and down a road that was immediately beside our domicile, which afforded some privacy, trying to pray, but to no avail. The powers of darkness seemed to be just as strong then, or stronger, than previously. At that time I knew this was the powers of darkness, but beyond that, I had precious little knowledge.

I came back inside, went to bed, and finally drifted off to sleep.

THE DREAM

It must not have been too long before daylight when the Lord gave me a dream pertaining to some things which were in store for me in the future. Of course, at that time I did not realize such, or even understand such, but it would begin to unfold in later years.

I dreamed that I was in a house, a place, incidentally, with which I was not acquainted. The dream began with me in the front room of the house, looking around, wondering why I was there. There were no windows in the room and no furniture in the room, only a door that led outside. In the dream I stood there wondering why I was there and where it was, and thinking to myself, wherever it was, it was a place to which I did not belong.

The front door was open, which led outside, and I turned to go in that direction. All of a sudden, there appeared in the doorway the most hideous looking creature that I had ever seen. It must have stood six or seven feet tall, with the body of a bear and the face of a man.

It seemed like all the evil in the universe was registered on its face, and especially its eyes. It was slowly coming toward me with its paws outstretched as if to say, *"I have you now."*

As it lumbered toward me, I became so weak that I could not stand, actually falling to the floor. I began to feel around, trying to find something with which to defend myself.

THE WEAPONS OF OUR WARFARE

I was so weak that even if I had found something, I could not have defended myself against this huge demon power, for that's what it was. And besides that, Paul plainly told us the following:

"**For though we walk in the flesh** *(refers to the fact that we do not yet have Glorified Bodies)*, **we do not war after the flesh** *(after our own ability, but rather by the Power of the Spirit)*:

"**(For the weapons of our warfare** *are* **not carnal** *(carnal weapons consist of those which are man-devised)*, **but mighty through God** *(the Cross of Christ [I Cor. 1:18])* **to the pulling down of strongholds;)**

"**Casting down imaginations** *(philosophic strongholds; every effort man makes outside of the Cross of Christ)*, **and every high thing that exalts itself against the Knowledge of God** *(all the pride of the human heart)*, **and bringing into captivity every thought to the obedience of Christ** *(can be done only by the Believer looking* *exclusively to the Cross, where all Victory is found; the Holy Spirit will then perform the task)*" **(II Cor. 10:3-5).**

THE NAME OF JESUS

Without premeditation and without forethought, one even might say, subconsciously, I shouted as loud as I could, *"In the Name of Jesus."* Even though I shouted with all of my strength, still, I was so weak that my voice was barely above a whisper. But yet, when I used that mighty Name, even as weak as I was, it had a powerful effect upon that demon spirit that was ascending on me.

It screamed and grabbed its head as if in mortal agony, which, no doubt, it was. It began to stagger back and forth across the floor, continuing to hold its head, and continuing to scream.

THE POWER OF THAT NAME WAS NOT PREDICATED ON MY PERSONAL STRENGTH

In the dream I learned that lesson. As weak as I was, in fact, with no personal strength at all, when I cried out that Name, the Name of Jesus, even though my voice was little more than a whisper, still, that demon spirit began to scream in mortal agony, continuing to hold its head.

When Jesus died on the Cross, His Death atoned for all sin, past, present and future, at least for those who will believe (Col. 2:10-15). In fact, the Power of that Name in the spirit world causes Satan and all his cohorts to tremble.

I BEGAN TO GATHER STRENGTH

In the dream I now began to arise. And as I stood up, I cried again, my voice much stronger this time, *"In the Name of Jesus."* As I said that Name the second time, that thing fell to the floor, still clutching its head and screaming, and writhing like a snake that had just received a death blow. And now, instead of it towering over me, I was towering over it.

I said it the third time, *"In the Name of Jesus!"* This time my voice, even though I exerted myself not at all, sounded like it was attached to a powerful public address system. It literally reverberated off the walls. And then I heard it:

THE SOUND OF A RUSHING MIGHTY WIND

As I used that Name of Jesus the third time, I then distinctly heard the sound of a mighty rushing wind. I didn't see anything, but I could hear it plainly, as it came toward that room. I knew it was the Holy Spirit. It hit that demon spirit writhing on the floor, brushing it out the front door and into the distance. I ran to the door, opened it and stood outside, looking at it disappear into the distance. Despite the power of that spirit, despite its bulk, it was nothing to the Power of the Holy Spirit as it hit this thing, sweeping it out the door, and far away.

WORSHIPPING IN OTHER TONGUES

The dream ended, and I literally woke myself up praising the Lord in other Tongues. In fact, lying there in the bed beside Frances, the Power of the Lord was all over me. It was now early morning just immediately after daylight. I laid there for quite some time, worshipping the Lord, knowing that the Lord had shown me something very special. But yet, at that time, I really did not know exactly what it meant.

I was to learn in later years that Satan would come against me with such power, making every effort to destroy me. But I learned from that dream that he would not succeed. I also learned the Power of the Name of Jesus. I saw in the dream what that Name could do. I also saw, as stated, that its Power was not predicated on my personal strength, because, in fact, I had no personal strength at that time.

As all know, the Name of Jesus means *"Saviour."* And as we well know, He is Saviour by virtue of the Cross. Before the Cross, one might say that He was the Healer, the Miracle Worker, the Prophet, the Priest, the King, in fact, the Creator of the ages, but after the Cross, He became the greatest of all, the Saviour of man.

Admittedly, every soul that was Saved before the Cross was Saved by trusting in Christ, whether they understood such very much or not. But one might say, and I think be theologically correct, that they were then Saved on credit. But when the Cross became a fact, it was no more on credit, but now an eternal reality. In other words, it is a Finished Work, meaning that nothing will ever have to be added to that which Jesus did at Calvary. And remember, every Believer on Earth, no matter how weak that Believer might be, has the privilege of being able to use the Name of Jesus against the powers of darkness. And to be sure, that Name is just as effective now as it was on the lips of Paul nearly 2,000 years ago, and as it was with me in that dream over a half century ago, and its effectiveness will never weaken or die.

MIGHTILY GREW THE WORD OF GOD AND PREVAILED

"And many who believed came (*speaks of those who had trusted the Lord for Salvation, but as of yet had not given up particular sins*), and confessed, and showed their deeds (*concerns the Holy Spirit now leading these Believers to Holiness and Righteousness, even as He had led them to Salvation previously*).

"Many of them also which used curious arts brought their books together, and burned them before all *men* (*'curious arts' refers to the practicing of magic; so the Holy Spirit was mightily working in people's lives, just as He desires to do always; if we will allow Him, He will clean us up; He does it through our Faith in Christ and the Cross [Rom. 8:2]*): and they counted the price of them, and found *it* fifty thousand *pieces* of silver (*it must have* *been many, many books, etc., for the amount in 2003 dollars would be approximately $2,000,000).*

"**So mightily grew the Word of God and prevailed** *(it doesn't say that the Church grew mightily, but rather the 'Word of God . . .')*" **(Acts 19:18-20).**

CLEANED UP LIVES

These Passages tell us that many of those who had come to Christ under the ministry of Paul still had things in their lives which were not right. In fact, Ephesus was a hot bed of idol worship, which, in reality, was demon worship. In fact, the great Temple at Ephesus, it is said, reeked with the congregated pollutions of Asia.

Farrar said, *"The Temple, which was the chief glory of the city and one of the wonders of the world, stood in full view of the crowded haven. Ephesus was the most magnificent of what Ovid calls 'the magnificent cities of Asia,' and the temple was its most splendid ornament. Actually, the ancient temple had been burnt down by Herostratus – an Ephesian fanatic who wished his name to be recorded in history – on the night of the birth of Alexander the Great. It had been rebuilt with ungrudging magnificence out of contributions furnished by all Asia – the very women contributing to it their jewels, as the Jewish women had done of old for the Tabernacle of the Wilderness. To avoid the danger of earthquakes, its foundations were built at vast cost on artificial foundations of skin and charcoal laid over the marsh. It gleamed far off with a star-like radiance. Its portico consisted of 120 pillars of the Ionic order hewn out of Parian marble."*[1]

At the end of this temple stood the great altar and behind it, the most sacred idol of classic heathendom. It was said to be the *"image that fell from heaven."* In reality, it was a hideous figure swathed like a mummy, covered with monstrous breasts, and holding in one hand a trident and in the other a club. And this is what, among many other idols, the Ephesians worshipped. In this superstitious power of darkness, the Apostle

Paul preached the Gospel of Jesus Christ, which resulted in thousands giving their hearts and lives to the Lord. But still, it seems, some of them had continued to hold on to these idols, with all their books of magic incantations. But as the Spirit of God moved upon them, at a particular time, hundreds, if not thousands, of people brought these *"curious arts"* and *"books,"* which catered to demon spirits, and burned them. When the Lord Saves us, if we allow the Holy Spirit to have His Way, He, and no doubt about it, will clean us up. As He did with these Ephesians, so will He now with any and all who accept Him as Saviour and Lord of their lives.

EVANGELISM

"After these things were ended, Paul purposed in the Spirit *(refers to the Holy Spirit)*, when he had passed through Macedonia and Achaia, to go to Jerusalem *(he wanted to be there for the Feast of Pentecost [Acts 20:16])*, saying, After I have been there, I must also see Rome *(the Greek Text indicates a Divine Hand laid upon Paul)*.

"So he sent into Macedonia two of them who ministered unto him, Timothy and Erastus *(concerned preparations they would make in the Churches for Paul's visit a short time later)*; but he himself stayed in Asia for a season *(stayed in Ephesus a little longer, maybe two or three months)*" **(Acts 19:21-22).**

CARE OF THE CHURCHES

Paul would go to Jerusalem, and, as well, he would go to Rome; however, it most definitely would not be in the manner which he probably at the beginning had planned. It would be through many dangers, toils and snares. Considering how much space that the Holy Spirit allotted to this, as we will ultimately see, lets us know how important it all was in the Mind of God.

At this time, the Apostle sends Timothy and Erastus into Macedonia with instructions that they would ultimately meet with him at Corinth. Paul will stay in Ephesus a while longer and will meet, as we shall see, with the situation which could have caused great difficulties for him, with Satan, no doubt, planning to take his life. The Evil One did not succeed, as we know, but it was not from a lack of trying.

It is believed that it was now the month of May, and this month was especially dedicated by the Ephesians to the goddess Diana, which Greek name was Artemis.

THE GODDESS DIANA

The Scripture says:

"And the same time there arose no small stir about that Way *('that Way' is the 'Pentecostal Way,' which characterizes the entirety of the Book of Acts)*.

"For a certain *man* named Demetrius, a silversmith *(he was probably the guild-master of the silversmith guild or trade union)*, which made silver shrines for Diana *(speaks of miniatures of the Temple of Diana with the goddess in the middle of the Temple background)*, brought no small gain unto the craftsmen *(speaks of those who made their living by this particular craft)*;

"Whom he called together with the workmen of like occupation *(whom Demetrius called together)*, and said, Sirs, you know that by this craft we have our wealth *(tells us that their chief concern was not really the worship or the honor of this goddess, but their own prosperity)*.

"Moreover you see and hear, that not alone at Ephesus, but almost throughout all Asia *(presents a powerful Testimony, from an enemy no less, to the power and effectiveness of Paul's labors and his Message)*, this Paul has persuaded and turned away much people, saying that they be no gods, which are made with hands *(proclaims that which Paul had preached, and which many people had come to believe, and rightly so)*:

"**So that not only this our craft is in danger to be set at nought** *(follows the idea that it would fall in disrepute)*; **but also that the Temple of the great goddess Diana should be despised, and her magnificence should be destroyed, whom all Asia and the world worships** *(there was quite a bit of exaggeration here)*" **(Acts 19:23-27).**

THE LOVE OF MONEY THE ROOT OF ALL EVIL

Now, Paul will be attacked, and above all, the Gospel which he preaches. Many people in Ephesus and all surrounding areas were coming to Christ as a result of his Ministry. And when these people came to Christ, they were giving up their idol worship, which affected several occupations, especially those who made the silver shrines of the goddess Diana and sold them for great profit. Their business had been hit enough that they will now rise up and protest.

WHAT WAS THIS GODDESS DIANA?

Every country in the world, other than Israel, at that time worshipped idols, i.e., *"many gods,"* which actually were demon spirits. Diana first appears in Greek literature as mistress and protectress of wildlife. In Greece proper she was worshipped as the daughter of Zeus and Leto and was the twin sister of Apollo. Horror at the pains her mother endured at her birth is supposed to have made her averse to marriage. As we have stated, her temple at Ephesus was one of the seven wonders of the world, and here worship of the *'virgin goddess'* appears to have been fused with some kind of fertility-cult of the mother-goddess of Asia Minor. Archeologists have discovered statues depicting her with many breasts.

The silversmiths, who would be greatly opposed to Paul, made all types of figures of her, some in the Temple, and some out of the Temple.

In the shadow of such worship, it is obvious that superstition was rampant. Ephesus differed from other cities which Paul had visited mainly in this respect, that it was preeminently the city of astrology, sorcery, incantations, amulets, exorcisms, and every form of magical imposture. Stories, which elsewhere would have been received with ridicule, at Ephesus found ready credence.

This month of May, to which we have already alluded, was especially dedicated to this goddess of the Ephesians. The great fair held during this month called *"Ephesia,"* attracted an immense number of people from all parts of Asia and was kept with all possible splendor and revelry.

THE APOSTLE PAUL

It is very probable that in this worship of Diana this particular month, Paul became an obvious target as one who opposed such worship, and whose preaching had caused many to cease their worship, which enraged the craftsmen who made these figurines of Diana and made great profit from them. Paul had readily preached that there were no gods which were made with hands.

And in the midst of all of this, there was a certain silversmith named Demetrius, who sold possibly thousands of these little figurines to the great crowds that visited Ephesus at this time of the year. Demetrius found that his trade was not as brisk as it had once been due to the preaching of Paul. So he addresses all of those who were in his particular craft, and any others who might be interested as well.

Farrar said, *"Demetrius first stirred up their passions by warning them of the impending ruin of their interests, and then appealed to their fanaticism to avenge the despised greatness of their temple, and the waning magnificence of the goddess whom all Asia and the world worshipped."*[2]

The answer to the speech of Demetrius was a unanimous shout of the watchword of Ephesus, *"Great is Diana of the*

Ephesians!" In fact, the whole city was thrown into a state of riot, and a rush was made for the Jewish quarter and the shop of Aquila. Paul at that time was either not in Aquila's home, or else he had been successfully hidden by Priscilla and her husband, who themselves ran great risk of being killed in their efforts to protect him.

GAIUS AND ARISTARCHUS

"And when they heard *these sayings*, they were full of wrath *(the accusations of Demetrius had the desired effect)*, and cried out, saying, Great *is* Diana of the Ephesians *(actually, the great wealth and prominence of the city of Ephesus were largely due to its great Temple of Diana, but it was basically localized to that city)*.

"And the whole city was filled with confusion *(the mob is forming)*: and having caught Gaius and Aristarchus, men of Macedonia, Paul's companions in travel, they rushed with one accord into the theatre *(recognizing these two men as Paul's associates, they dragged them into the amphitheater)*.

"And when Paul would have entered in unto the people *(Paul was determined to go into the theater and address the mob)*, the Disciples suffered him not *(these were the Believers who were a part of the Church at Ephesus, and who knew the danger that awaited Paul)*.

"And certain of the chief of Asia, which were his friends *(these were men of high rank and great wealth, which presents another striking proof of the enormous influence of Paul's preaching in Asia)*, sent unto him, desiring *him* that he would not adventure himself into the theatre *(seems to mean that they sent Paul word, but did not come to him in person)*" (Acts 19:28-31).

ALL BECAUSE OF PAUL'S PREACHING

They couldn't find Paul, so they forcibly took Gaius and

Aristarchus, Paul's associates. With these two men in their custody, the crowd rushed wildly into the vast space of the theater, an area, we are told, that could easily have accommodated some 30,000 people.

Knowing that Gaius and Aristarchus were in danger, Paul desired to go into the theater himself and address the people. But wiser heads prevailed, in effect, telling him this would be the worst thing that he could do. And then, several very influential men of the city, men of high rank, who evidently were Paul's friends, heard what he was about to do and quickly sent unto him, in effect, telling him that under no circumstances must he enter into this theater. As stated, wiser heads prevailed, and Paul held back, and rightly so.

THE EFFORT OF THE JEWS

"Some therefore cried one thing, and some another *(presents the actions and mannerisms of a mob)*: for the assembly was confused; and the more part knew not wherefore they were come together *(means that a few were agitating the many)*.

"And they drew Alexander out of the multitude, the Jews putting him forward *(exactly as to who this Alexander was is not clear)*. And Alexander beckoned with the hand, and would have made his defence unto the people *(presents that which is to no avail)*.

"But when they knew that he was a Jew *(proclaims the reason for their outburst which followed)*, all with one voice about the space of two hours cried out, Great *is* Diana of the Ephesians *(despite all of this, history records that the Gospel, which Paul preached, had such an effect that the worshipers of the goddess Diana came in ever fewer numbers, while the Church in Ephesus continued to flourish)*" (Acts 19:32-34).

As to who exactly this Alexander was, we aren't told. Some

think that he may very well have been Alexander the copper-smith who caused Paul great difficulties (II Tim. 4:14).

The Jews here saw an opportunity where they thought they might cause Paul great trouble. They wanted to inform the Greeks and the Romans that while some Christians might be Jews, the Jews actually were not Christians. They wanted Alexander to speak for them and to explain how matters really stood. But he never was able to do so.

When the crowd ascertained that he was a Jew, they had no desire to hear from him, and with *"one voice about the space of two hours cried out, 'Great is Diana of the Ephesians.'"*

As we stated in the notes, the great Gospel preached by the Apostle Paul grew in intensity and power, and through the years that followed, while the Church in Ephesus gained ground constantly, the worshippers of the Goddess Diana became ever fewer in numbers. Truly, what the world needs is Jesus, just a glimpse of Him.

THE MOB IS APPEASED

The Scripture says:

"And when the townclerk had appeased the people *(presents an office of influence)*, he said, *You* men of Ephesus, what man is there who knows not how that the city of the Ephesians is a worshipper of the great goddess Diana, and of the *image* which fell down from Jupiter? *(The idea is that Ephesus is the proud possessor of this goddess, of which no other city could boast.)*

"Seeing then that these things cannot be spoken against *(appeals to the pride of these individuals, as to Diana being so great)*, you ought to be quiet, and to do nothing rashly *(represents good advice, although coming from a heathen)*.

"For you have brought hither these men *(speaking of Gaius and Aristarchus)*, which are neither robbers of

Churches, nor yet blasphemers of your goddess *(means that Paul had not directed attention to this particular idol, but had, no doubt, referred to idols made by men's hands [Vs. 26]).*

"Wherefore if Demetrius, and the craftsmen which are with him, have a matter against any man, the law is open *(reflects the common sense of the town clerk),* **and there are deputies: let them implead one another** *(he was saying that if Demetrius really had a case against Paul and those with him, he should pursue it in open court).*

"But if you inquire any thing concerning other matters *(in effect, is saying, if there are other complaints against Paul than that mentioned, it should be addressed correctly, and not by mob action),* **it shall be determined in a lawful assembly** *(open Court).*

"For we are in danger to be called in question for this day's uproar *(refers to Roman peace being disturbed for no good reason),* **there being no cause whereby we may give an account of this concourse** *(proclaims the town clerk wondering how this mob action could be explained to Roman authorities, if called to account).*

"And when he had thus spoken, he dismissed the assembly *(common sense prevailed, and Gaius and Aristarchus were released forthwith)"* **(Acts 19:35-41).**

THE HOLY SPIRIT USES A HEATHEN

After the uproar, which lasted for some two hours, with this mob all the time screaming, *"Great is Diana of the Ephesians,"* finally the town clerk was able to bring silence and reason to the vast crowd.

He first of all bragged on the Ephesians and their great goddess Diana, now telling them that nothing has been done by anyone that would cast aspersions on their worship and their goddess.

He then turns his attention to Gaius and Aristarchus,

proclaiming to the crowd that they had done nothing wrong, proclaiming that they had not blasphemed their goddess.

He then says that if Demetrius and the craftsmen with him have proof of anything, they can settle it in open court. Otherwise, they had best leave well enough alone. He then provides the clincher.

If Roman peace is broken, and we are to blame, we can bring upon ourselves Roman anger, which no one wants to do. He went on to say that the simple reason is, no one can point to any one thing that's been done that would occasion this outburst. He then dismissed the assembly. So, we have to confess that the Lord used a heathen to intervene, which he capably did. As well, Gaius and Aristarchus were released.

MACEDONIA AND GREECE

"And after the uproar was ceased *(the mob had dispersed)*, Paul called unto *him* the Disciples, and embraced *them (speaks of some of the Believers of the Church in Ephesus)*, and departed for to go into Macedonia *(pertained to his care for the Churches in that region)*.

"And when he had gone over those parts *(no doubt included Philippi, Thessalonica, and Berea)*, and had given them much exhortation *(refers to the teaching of the Word of God, as is obvious)*, he came into Greece *(probably refers to a repeat visit to Athens, Corinth, and Cenchrea, as well as other places)*,

"And *there* abode three months *(he probably spent most of this time at Corinth [I Cor. 16:6])*. And when the Jews laid wait for him, as he was about to sail into Syria *(these were most probably Jews from the synagogue at Corinth, who planned to kill him)*, he purposed to return through Macedonia *(basically presents the opposite direction, actually to Philippi, from where he would then turn toward Syria)*.

"And there accompanied him into Asia Sopater

of Berea; and of the Thessalonians, Aristarchus and Secundus; and Gaius of Derbe, and Timothy; and of Asia, Tychicus and Trophimus *(some expositors believe that some of these men were chosen by various Churches to travel with Paul, and take their offerings for the poor in Jerusalem [Acts 19:29; 27:2; Rom. 15:25-28; I Cor. 16:3; II Cor. 8:19-23])*.

"These going before tarried for us at Troas *(by the use of the pronoun 'us,' Luke indicates that he has once again joined Paul and his party)*" **(Acts 20:1-5).**

THE CHURCHES

Paul had spent two years or more in Ephesus, and the teaching and instruction that they received from him made this Church into one of, if not the strongest, that he under the Lord was able to raise up. In fact, he stayed longer in Ephesus and Corinth than he did any other place. It seems that he had very little problem with the people at Ephesus but tremendous problems in Corinth. In fact, for a while it looked like the Church at Corinth would be lost. But the Lord undertook, and the efforts of the Evil One were rolled back, and the Lord prevailed.

Instead of going into a dissertation here as to the situation at Corinth and how Paul handled it, I would advise the reader to get our book, *"THE APOSTLE PAUL AND THE CHURCH AT CORINTH,"* which should be out in the near future.

PAUL AT TROAS

"And we sailed away from Philippi after the days of unleavened bread *(speaks of the Passover Week)*, and came unto them to Troas in five days *(evidently portrays the length of time it took to make the voyage by ship)*; where we abode seven days.

"And upon the first *day* of the week *(Sunday)*, when

the Disciples came together to break bread *(Sunday had become the main day of worship)*, Paul preached unto them, ready to depart on the morrow; and continued his speech until midnight *(proclaims him preaching possibly for several hours)*" **(Acts 20:6-7).**

THE FIRST DAY OF THE WEEK

There is no particular Scripture in the New Testament that pointedly changes the sacred day, one might say, from Saturday, the Jewish Sabbath, to Sunday, the first day of the week, the day of our Lord's Resurrection. However, even as the Seventh Verse states, *"And upon the first day of the week, when the Disciples came together to break bread,"* it proclaims the fact that they were accustomed to doing such on the first day of the week. Undoubtedly, this was done for several reasons, the foremost being that this was the day, as stated, in which Jesus rose from the dead.

In writing to the Church at Corinth, Paul stated, *"Upon the first day of the week let every one of you lay by him in store, as God has prospered him,"* once again refers to a gathering of the Church on the first day of the week **(I Cor. 16:2).**

As well, it was said of John the Beloved when he wrote the Book of Revelation, *"I was in the Spirit on the Lord's Day"* **(Rev. 1:10).** Here, the Holy Spirit through John refers to Sunday, the first day of the week, as *"The Lord's Day."*

Furthermore, as it regards Saturday, the Jewish Sabbath, Paul, after proclaiming to us what Jesus did at the Cross **(Col. 2:13-15),** said, *"Let no man therefore judge you in meat, or in drink, or in respect of an holyday, or of the new moon, or of the Sabbath Days which are a shadow of things to come; but the Body is of Christ"* **(Col. 2:16-17).**

The meaning of the phrase, *"but the Body is of Christ,"* proclaims the fact that Jesus is the New Covenant, and that everything in the Old Testament pointed directly to Him. When He came, this fulfilled the Law, including all Sabbath Days, etc., in totality. In fact, Paul also said:

"**For Christ** *is* **the end of the Law for Righteousness** *(Christ fulfilled the totality of the Law)* **to everyone who believes** *(Faith in Christ guarantees the Righteousness which the Law had, but could not give)*" **(Rom. 10:4).**

WHAT ABOUT THE FOURTH COMMANDMENT, REMEMBER THE SABBATH TO KEEP IT HOLY?

The Scripture says, *"Remember the Sabbath Day, to keep it holy.*

"Six days you shall labour, and do all your work:

"But the seventh day is the Sabbath of the LORD your God: in it you shall not do any work, you, nor your son, nor your daughter, your manservant, nor your maidservant, nor your cattle, nor your stranger that is within your gates:

"For in six days the LORD made Heaven and Earth, the sea, and all that in them is, and rested the seventh day: wherefore the Lord blessed the Sabbath Day, and hallowed it."

The notes on these Passages from THE EXPOSITOR'S STUDY BIBLE give us the following:

"The seventh day was not so much to be a day of worship, as we think of such now, but rather a day of 'rest.' Even the very beasts, pressed into man's service since the Fall, shall rest. All were to observe this day. Everything pertaining to the Law of Moses, in some way, spoke of Christ. The 'Sabbath' was no exception. It was meant to portray the fact that there is 'rest' in Christ and, in fact, that there is rest 'only in Christ' [Mat. 11:28-30]. So, when a person presently accepts Christ, they are in effect keeping the Sabbath, which speaks of the 'rest' that we have in Christ – rest from self-effort to attain unto Righteousness. Even though there was no written command by the Holy Spirit to do so, gradually we find Believers, during the time of the Early Church, as recorded in the Book of Acts, making Sunday, the first day of the week, the day of our Lord's Resurrection, their day of worship, etc., which

is different than the Sabbath of old, because Christ has fulfilled in totality the old Jewish Sabbath."

THE TEST UNDER GRACE

What distinguishes God's people is participation in God's Rest. Christ is God's Rest (Heb. 4). The honor, or dishonor, done to the Sabbath was the test under Law. The honor, or dishonor, done to Christ, the test under Grace. Death was the penalty of dishonoring the Sabbath under the old Law; a similar penalty (spiritual death) attaches to dishonoring Christ.

THE APOSTLE PAUL

Trying to bring the Law into the New Covenant and attach it to Grace constituted Satan's greatest effort in the Early Church. In fact, if a lesser man than Paul would have been at the helm, so to speak, the Evil One may very well have succeeded.

Paul continued to hammer the Truth that Jesus fulfilled the Law of Moses in every respect, which He was ordained to do. In fact, the Law of Moses, given to Israel, was never meant to be permanent but only temporary. Actually, every facet of that Law, and I mean every facet, pointed to Christ in some way, whether in His Atoning, Mediatorial, or Intercessory Work. As we have stated, the great Apostle said, *"For Christ is the end of the Law for Righteousness to everyone who believes"* (Rom. 10:4). He even went so far as to say, *"that if you be circumcised, Christ shall profit you nothing"* (Gal. 5:2).

He then said, if one goes the way of the Law, *"Christ is become of no effect unto you"* (Gal. 5:4).

And then to round it off, so to speak, he said, *"whosoever of you are justified by the Law; you are fallen from Grace"* (Gal. 5:4).

To say the least, these are extremely serious statements. In other words, they leave no wiggle room. The Law must go, which includes the Jewish Sabbath of old, Circumcision, Feast Days, the Sacrificial system and, in fact, the entirety of the

Temple. Because the Jewish Christians were so slow to come to this Truth, in A.D. 70, the Lord used the Roman General Titus to completely destroy the Temple, and in every capacity, making it impossible for the Mosaic Law to be carried forth.

THE MIRACLE

The Scripture says:

"And there were many lights in the upper chamber *(evidently spoke of a third story room, which would seat two or three hundred people)*, where they were gathered together *(this was the meeting place or Church in Troas)*.

"And there sat in a window a certain young man named Eutychus, being fallen into a deep sleep: and as Paul was long preaching, he sunk down with sleep, and fell down from the third loft, and was taken up dead *(the Greek Text declares that he was a lifeless corpse; the fall had killed him)*.

"And Paul went down, and fell on him, and embracing *him* said *(presents the example of Elijah in this, which is probably what Paul intended [I Ki. 17:17-21])*, Trouble not yourselves; for his life is in him *(does not mean, as some claim, that the boy had merely been knocked unconscious, but rather that he had been dead, and that the Lord had infused life back into him; he was raised from the dead!)*.

"When he *(Paul)* therefore was come up again, and had broken bread, and eaten, and talked a long while, even till break of day *(this all night Message was interrupted only by the raising of the boy from the dead; he had much to tell them, and there was much they needed to hear)*, so he departed.

"And they brought the young man alive, and were not a little comforted *(what a night it had been!)*" (Acts 20:8-12).

MUCH TO BE TAUGHT

The Believers in Troas, no doubt, desired that the Apostle teach them the Word of God. What a privilege they had for the man to whom the meaning of the New Covenant was given to answer their questions and deal with subjects which were so necessary to be properly understood. He would use the entire night for this most important task, stopping only when the boy fell from the window and was taken up dead. Then the Lord mightily and wondrously performed a Miracle as Paul prayed for the lad, with him being totally healed. After this occasion, Paul immediately went back to explaining the Scriptures to them, and doing so *"even until break of day."* They had heard the Word of God as few had heard it, and they had seen a display of the Power of God as few had seen it.

In each one of these cities where Churches were founded, the Elder, or Pastor, would be selected from among the people. But as it would be understood, their Knowledge of the Word of God, especially what Paul taught, was very lacking, to say the least. So, when Paul came among them, that was an answer to prayer. So, every available minute must be used in order to teach the Word.

Today, due to technological advancement, which Paul would love to have had, many people can be reached with a single message.

THE MESSAGE THAT GOD
HAS GIVEN THIS MINISTRY

I think I can say presently, without fear of contradiction, that the Gospel of Jesus Christ has come full circle. It was to Paul, as we've stated over and over again, to whom the Lord gave the meaning of the New Covenant. It was *"Justification by Faith"* (Rom., Chpts. 4-5), and *"Sanctification by Faith"* (Gal., Chpts. 1-6). In fact, virtually 90% or more of Paul's writings dealt with *"Sanctification by Faith,"* in other words, how we as Believers are to live for God. Being Saved is not a difficult thing, and neither is it complicated. It is simply one calling on the Lord with a promise that whosoever does such will be Saved (Rom. 10:13). But living for the Lord on a daily basis, how we order our behavior, how we conduct ourselves, and how we grow in Grace and the Knowledge of the Lord, is something else altogether. That's the reason that virtually all of the Bible is given over to this particular subject.

Paul had the totality of the Gospel. He knew the Law of Moses as no other human being in the world of that day, and, as well, it was to him, as stated, that the Lord gave the meaning of the New Covenant, which included every single iota of the Plan of Redemption (Gal. 1:12).

THE REVELATION

In 1997, the Lord gave me a Revelation of the Cross of Christ, which incorporated the method of the Holy Spirit, as to how He works within our hearts and lives. It was nothing new, actually that which had already been given to the Apostle Paul (Rom. 8:1-2). But now, in that we are entrusted with this Message, the Message of the Cross, we must take it to the whole world. As stated, the Gospel has finally come full circle. This Message deals not only with the Cross of Christ as it refers to Salvation, but, as well, the Cross of Christ as it refers to our Sanctification. In other words, how we live for God. The simple Truth is, unless one knows the Truth of the Cross, and we mean the complete Truth of the Cross, while one can be Saved without this information, one without this knowledge simply cannot live a victorious life. In fact, that's what the entirety of the Seventh Chapter of Romans is all about.

After Paul was Saved and then baptized with the Holy Spirit some three days later, and then immediately beginning to preach the Gospel, the Truth is, even though the Apostle had had a tremendous experience with the Lord, he simply at that time did not know how to live for God. That's the reason he said:

"I was alive without the Law once: but when the Command-
ment came, sin revived, and I died" **(Rom. 7:9).**

This means that the Apostle for the first few years of his
life tried to live for God by the means of keeping the Law. He
found he couldn't, and neither can anyone else. It was not
until the Lord gave him the meaning of the New Covenant that
the Apostle then knew how to live for God, which information
was given to us in his fourteen Epistles.

That's the reason that the Lord, I believe, has assigned us
the responsibility of starting THE SONLIFE TELEVISION
NETWORK. This is television programming 24 hours a day, 7
days a week. The entirety of this network is given over to preaching and teaching the Message of the Cross. This Message must
be gotten to the entirety of the Church, and I mean throughout
the entirety of the world. The Church under the Apostle Paul
some 2,000 years ago began with this Message. It will end with
this Message. That's what I mean by coming full circle.

THE JOURNEY

"And we went before to ship *(refers to Luke and the*
men of Verse 4, but not Paul, at least at this time), **and**
sailed unto Assos *(a short distance of about forty miles*
around Cape Electum), **there intending to take in Paul:**
for so had he appointed, minding himself to go afoot
(by land it was about twenty miles; he would walk this
distance alone, no doubt desiring to be alone with the Lord
in prayer).

"And when he met with us at Assos, we took him
in, and came to Mitylene *(presented another approximate*
forty miles by ship).

"And we sailed thence, and came the next *day* over
against Chios *(presents another Island about the size of*
Lesbos; it lay due west of both Smyrna and Ephesus, about
a hundred miles in distance); **and the next *day* we arrived**
at Samos, and tarried at Trogyllium; and the next *day*

we came to Miletus.

"For Paul had determined to sail by Ephesus *(not stop there),* because he would not spend the time in Asia *(tells us, I think, he did not want to tarry, having settled this thing with the Lord respecting this eventful trip):* for he hasted, if it were possible for him, to be at Jerusalem the Day of Pentecost *(the Holy Spirit has warned him of the coming difficulties he will face on this trip, and it is almost as if he must haste, lest he draw back because of these coming difficulties)*" (Acts 20:13-16).

PAUL

If it is to be noticed, Luke continues to use the personal pronoun *"we,"* meaning that he continues to be with Paul.

Paul at this time could have gone to Ephesus, but he feels he must be in Jerusalem on the Day of Pentecost. As we shall see, he will have a meeting with the Ephesian Elders, who will have to come about 30 miles to meet with him at Miletus, which they gladly consented to do. The Apostle evidently felt that if he went to Ephesus, he would be tempted to stay for several weeks, which would keep him from being in Jerusalem on the Day of Pentecost. As we have stated, all of these Churches were very dependent on the Apostle Paul for teaching and instruction. While he had others with him who, no doubt, could do an excellent job at proclaiming the Message, still, as would be obvious, Paul had greater knowledge than any.

THE EPHESIAN ELDERS

"And from Miletus he sent to Ephesus, and called the Elders of the Church *(it was about thirty miles to Ephesus; he wanted the Elders to come meet him at Miletus before he left).*

"And when they were come to him *(probably represents two or three days from the time the Messenger was originally sent),* **he said unto them, You know, from the first day that I came into Asia** *(takes them back to the very beginning of the Church at Ephesus),* **after what manner I have been with you at all seasons** *(indicates him nurturing them with the Gospel of Jesus Christ),*

"Serving the Lord with all humility of mind *(presents that which was the very opposite of the Judaizers and other false teachers, who were attempting to draw a following after themselves),* **and with many tears** *(Paul's emotions ran deep),* **and temptations** *(a provocation to deal with a situation outside the Ways of the Lord),* **which befell me by the lying in wait of the Jews** *(the constant plots against Paul by the Jews were never ceasing):*

"And how I kept back nothing that was profitable unto you *(he did not allow anything to silence his voice respecting the great Doctrine of Jesus Christ and Him Crucified),* **but have showed you** *(explained the Scriptures),* **and have taught you publickly, and from house to house** *(most Churches were then in houses),*

"Testifying both to the Jews, and also to the Greeks *(the Gospel is the same for all),* **repentance toward God, and Faith toward our Lord Jesus Christ** *(presents the Gospel in the proverbial nutshell; Faith in Christ pertains to Faith in what He did at the Cross)"* **(Acts 20:17-21).**

THE MESSAGE OF PAUL TO THE EPHESIANS

Evidently Paul sent a runner, so to speak, from Miletus to Ephesus, a distance, as stated, of about 30 miles, requesting of the Elders in the Church in Ephesus that they would come with all haste to him in Miletus. Knowing that they would probably have to walk the 30 miles, and that it would be a great hardship on them, undoubtedly, the Apostle felt in his spirit that he should do this, meaning that he would never see them again. In fact, there is no record that Paul was able to go to Ephesus again. And yet, these men, hungry to hear what

Paul had to say to them, eagerly made the journey. How many there were, we aren't told. As to exactly how long he was able to spend with them, we aren't told.

The final words he gave to them, Luke records, or at least the gist of what was said.

Paul begins his message by going back to his establishing the Church in Ephesus. Considering that he had spent more time in Ephesus than any other place, well over two years, he was able to teach them again and again the great Truths of the Word of God, which made this Church one of, if not the greatest founded by the Apostle. Ever how many were there that day, they were privileged to hear these words. It is certain that all could not come and for various reasons, but for those who were able to do so, they would cherish this moment for the rest of their lives.

BOUND IN THE SPIRIT

"And now, behold, I go bound in the spirit unto Jerusalem *(speaks of the Holy Spirit, and the desire of the Spirit that Paul take this trip, irrespective of the coming difficulties)*, not knowing the things that shall befall me there *(the Holy Spirit tells him to go to Jerusalem and that there will be great problems, but doesn't tell him exactly what they will be)*:

"Save that the Holy Spirit witnesses in every city *(tells us that such happened, but gave no information about the actual events)*, saying that bonds and afflictions abide me *(the Holy Spirit didn't tell Paul exactly how these things would come about)*.

"But none of these things move me *(proclaims Paul putting himself entirely in the hands of the Lord)*, neither count I my life dear unto myself *(his life belonged to the Lord, and the Lord could do with it as He so desired)*, so that I might finish my course with joy *(and that he ultimately did)*, and the ministry, which I have received of the Lord Jesus, to testify the Gospel of the Grace of God *(proclaims basically what this 'course' actually is; his Message was Jesus Christ and Him Crucified)*" **(Acts 20:22-24).**

THE WITNESS OF THE HOLY SPIRIT

It is remarkable that the Holy Spirit had Luke to include the entirety of the Message here delivered by Paul, or at least the gist of what was said.

The Apostle mentions as to how the Holy Spirit has stated in city after city, and time and time again, as to the trouble that will come his way as it regards the coming trip to Jerusalem.

Why did the Holy Spirit do this?

Many have stated that the Holy Spirit was trying to get him to not go to Jerusalem, but there is no proof of that.

We must also understand that everything that happens to a Child of God is a test of Faith. How will we act? How will we react?

Paul evidently felt in his spirit that he must go to Jerusalem. What his reasons were, we aren't exactly told; however, I personally feel that he was ever mindful at the potential of a split in the Church over the Law/Grace issue. He felt, no doubt, that he could deal with James, and put to rest anything that would occasion such a split. He knew if such happened, it would set the Work of God back for many, many years, if not destroy it totally.

And yet, he would not and, in fact, could not trim his Message to accommodate the Law. And at the same time, he knew that the Church in Jerusalem was still immersed in the Law, which had caused and was causing him tremendous problems in all of the Churches. So, whatever the reason for the demand in his own spirit that he go to Jerusalem, and at whatever cost, no doubt, the problem of the Law/Grace issue loomed ever large in his mind and thinking.

By the Grace of God he was successful in avoiding a split.

In fact, he took up offerings from all the Churches to help alleviate the problem in Jerusalem concerning the many thousands who had been excommunicated from the synagogue, meaning that they now had no visible means of support. He, no doubt, felt this would show the Church in Jerusalem that he wanted nothing but that which the Lord desired.

THE KINGDOM OF GOD

"And now, behold, I know that you all, among whom I have gone preaching the Kingdom of God *(he had faithfully preached the Message to these Ephesians)*, shall see my face no more *(he knew this would be the last time he would see them, and therefore, the reason he had sent for them)*.

"Wherefore I take you to record this day *(the Heavenly record will show)*, that I *am* pure from the blood of all *men* *(means that he had delivered the Gospel to everyone who heard him preach, exactly as it was given to him by the Lord)*.

"For I have not shunned to declare unto you *(refers to the fact that the temptation was always there to trim the Message)* all the Counsel of God *(all the Word of God, holding back nothing)*" (Acts 20:25-27).

ALL THE COUNSEL OF GOD

It is incumbent upon every true Preacher of the Gospel, and I refer to those, of course, who are truly called of God, to preach the whole Counsel of God, holding back nothing, but proclaiming in totality that which the Word declares. This is the weakness of the modern church. Too many preachers are preaching what people want to hear, instead of what people need to hear.

I heard the man interviewed who is the father of the *"Seeker Sensitive Movement."* The term refers to the fact that nothing will be said or done in the church that upsets anyone. He stated, in effect, that sin was never mentioned, Hell is totally ignored, the Wrath of God completely ignored, and the Cross and the Blood are never mentioned as well.

He went on to state that some of the songs about the Cross were beautiful, but they would never sing them in his church because it might offend someone. No person is to be made to feel they are a sinner. In fact, anything that might have a tendency to upset anyone in any capacity is ignored and actually forbidden. Only what makes the people feel good will be preached, so that means that he is preaching a *"feel good Gospel,"* whatever that is.

It must have been about ten years ago that I heard that interview. And then about a year ago, I read an article that either had been written by this particular pastor, or else someone was quoting him. At any rate, the article went on to relate as to how a poll had been taken in their church—a church, incidentally, averaging 25,000 or 30,000 in attendance. The questionnaire was anonymous, so the people could tell the truth.

The pastor, the father of the *"Seeker Sensitive Movement,"* made the statement, *"What we're preaching must not be working, so we're going to have to rethink our presentation."*

He found out when he looked at the questionnaires, thousands of them, that his church was filled with people who admitted to every type of sin that one could think. That's why he said, *"We're going to have to rethink our presentation."*

No, he doesn't have to rethink anything. He just needs to start preaching the Gospel, that is, if he was ever called of God to begin with, which I seriously doubt.

IS EVERYTHING IN THE WORD OF GOD POPULAR?

If the truth be told, there is very little in the Word of God, if anything at all, that is popular with the world. The Bible teaches that man is a sinner. In fact, due to the Fall, man is born in original sin. That's the reason he must be Born-Again, and if not, he will die eternally lost.

Yes, there is a place called Hell, and it is a place where the fires are never quenched, and the smoke of their torment ascends up forever and forever. To be sure, Hell is no joke. It's not merely a figment of someone's imagination. It is a place located in the heart of the Earth, and the sad, horrible thing about it is, most of the human race who has ever lived has gone to this place called Hell. And most that are alive today are going to this place called Hell.

That's the reason that Jesus said, *"Broad is the way, that leads to destruction, and many there be which go in thereat"* (Mat. 7:13).

The Bible teaches that the only way that a person can escape eternal Hell, and it is eternal, is by accepting the Lord Jesus Christ as one's Saviour, believing that what He did for us at the Cross makes Salvation possible. The Bible also teaches that there is no other way of Salvation. It is Jesus Christ alone!

The Bible also teaches that every human being who has ever lived is going to one day face the Lord Jesus Christ. If they are unsaved, they will face Him at the *"Great White Throne Judgment,"* and if a Believer, they will face Him at the *"Judgment Seat of Christ"*; however, face Him we will!

Now, the Bible can be denied or ignored, but what it says is the Word of God. It does not merely contain the Word of God, it is the Word of God. As I've said many times, the Bible is the roadmap for life, and the blueprint for eternity. There is no other! Ignoring what it says does not at all absolve one from eternal responsibility. Please remember that! So, these preachers who have compromised the Word of God, or who ignore it altogether, will one day be judged from the Book that they have maltreated. Of that, one can be certain!

Paul stated, *"Wherefore I take you to record this day, that I am pure from the blood of all men."* How many others can say that? God help us that we follow in the train of the great Apostle.

GRIEVOUS WOLVES

"Take heed therefore unto yourselves, and to all the Flock *(this word is directed to the Pastors who had come from Ephesus to meet him)*, over the which the Holy Spirit has made you overseers *(Elders, Bishops, Overseers, Shepherds, and Presbyters all mean the same thing, 'Pastor')*, to feed the Church of God *(to tend as a Shepherd)*, which He has purchased with His Own Blood *(Christ bought us at a great price)*.

"For I know this, that after my departing shall grievous wolves enter in among you, not sparing the Flock *(presents a perfect description of those who merchandise the Body of Christ, and in whatever way)*.

"Also of your own selves shall men arise *(will not come from the outside, but from the inside)*, speaking perverse things, to draw away Disciples after them *(not to Christ, but to themselves)*.

"Therefore watch *(be spiritually vigilant)*, and remember, that by the space of three years I ceased not to warn every one night and day with tears *(Paul not only preached the Truth of the Word, but warned of and pointed out false doctrine and false apostles as well)*" (Acts 20:28-31).

PERVERSE THINGS

The Apostle now warns the Church at Ephesus of those who would come in, preaching another Gospel. He spoke of two different types of individuals. They are:

• *"Grievous wolves:"* these were individuals that came from without, purporting to have a Word from the Lord, when their idea was to *"rape the Flock."*

• And then he spoke of those who would come up out of their own midst, *"speaking perverse things,"* all in order to *"draw away Disciples after them."*

Concerning both of these types, those who came from outside and those who came from inside, if one got to the very bottom of the situation, one would find that money played a big part in whatever would be done. In other words, they would try to draw away the Flock, and at times, would be successful, all in order to line their pockets. Again, the breed continues unto this hour. So, he tells them to *"watch"* for these individuals, whomever they might be.

THE MESSAGE OF THE CROSS

Paul preached the Cross. That was his Message and all who followed him. If they wanted the Will of God, that would be their Message as well.

THE MODERN SCENE VERSUS THE TIME OF PAUL

Then the Churches founded by Paul knew and understood the Gospel as it should be known and understood. They had had Paul as their teacher, who was the very finest that could be provided then or at any time. To hear the Message of the Cross from the very one to whom the Lord had revealed its meaning provided the finest instruction that could be obtained. So, these individuals in the Church at Ephesus had been brought in right, had been anchored correctly in the Faith, and knew the Gospel as it should be known.

Today, I'm afraid it is different. While most modern Preachers, at least those who claim to believe the Bible, understand the Cross of Christ as it regards Salvation, regrettably, they have no knowledge at all as it respects the Cross pertaining to Sanctification, in other words, how we live for God, and how we grow in Grace and the Knowledge of the Lord. And this is the great Truth which the Lord has given this Ministry (Jimmy Swaggart Ministries). It's not something new, it's that which the Lord first of all gave to Paul. In fact, unless the Believer understands this great Truth, while he or she can be Saved, under such circumstances, they simply cannot live a victorious life.

WHAT IS THE MESSAGE OF THE CROSS?

To address this all-important subject as it should be addressed requires much more space than is available at the time. But perhaps the following can give us a clue:

• We must understand that Jesus Christ is the Source of everything that we receive from God (Jn. 1:1-2; 14:6; Col. 2:10).

• The Cross of Christ is the Means by which these things are given to us (Rom. 6:3-5; I Cor. 1:17, 18; 2:2).

• Understanding this, the Cross of Christ must ever be the Object of our Faith (Gal. 6:14; Col. 2:14-15).

• The Holy Spirit superintends all of this (Rom. 8:1-2; Eph. 2:13-18).

When one looks at the little diagram above, as it regards the first statement, most Preachers, if not all, at least those who claim to believe the Bible, would wholeheartedly agree. However, as it regards the statement, *"the Cross is the Means by which all of this is received,"* meaning it cannot be received any other way, and meaning that the Cross of Christ must ever be the Object of our Faith, now that presents a problem. We are now coming to the offense of the Cross.

WHAT IS THE OFFENSE OF THE CROSS?

Paul said there would be an offense (Gal. 5:11).
Why?
The Cross of Christ proclaims God's Way of Salvation and Sanctification, which completely excludes all of man's ways. This is galling to man, and especially religious man. To find out that the Holy Spirit labels our personal efforts, talent, ability, education, intellectualism, motivation, etc., as mere *"flesh,"* presents a problem to most. And we must remember, it doesn't really matter how much we religionize the flesh, it is still flesh, and that which God cannot accept.

In fact, that which the Lord has done is so very, very simple.

We ought to understand that whatever we need from the Lord, we cannot provide it for ourselves. We must understand that the Lord has already provided everything for us. All we have to do to receive it is simply to understand that Christ is the Source, and the Cross is the Means and, thereby, place our Faith. Then, it is freely given to us. Now, that sounds so simple, and because it is simple; however, it does not sit well with religious man. There is a reason it doesn't!

Religious works appeal to our self-importance. So, we like to be involved. But please understand, involving ourselves in all these religious works stops all Spiritual Growth, gives occasion for the advent of the sin nature to once again dominate us, and terribly weakens our Faith.

I think that one reading the great Epistles written by Paul cannot help but come to the conclusion that Paul preached the Cross (Rom. 6:3-5; 8:2; I Cor. 1:17, 18, 23; 2:2; Gal. 6:14). It's his Epistles that, in effect, tell us how to live for God. So, when something else is preached to us, and I speak of something other than the Cross of Christ, we must understand that while it may be coming from a sincere preacher, if it's not the Cross, it's really not the Gospel. What is being said may be something about the Gospel, but that's greatly different than it being the Gospel.

IT IS MORE BLESSED TO GIVE THAN TO RECEIVE

"And now, Brethren, I commend you to God *(he has planted enough of the Gospel in them that they will not turn from the Lord)*, and to the Word of His Grace *(that 'Word' is the 'Cross')*, which is able to build you up *(the Gospel of Grace alone can build one up)*, and to give you an inheritance among all them which are Sanctified *(the Believer is Sanctified only by making the Cross the Object of his Faith, which gives the Holy Spirit the latitude to carry out this work within our hearts and lives; the*

Believer cannot Sanctify himself).

"**I have coveted no man's silver, or gold, or apparel** *(he was not after their money as were these grievous wolves of Verse 29).*

"**Yes, you yourselves know, that these hands have ministered unto my necessities, and to them who were with me** *(refers to Paul repairing tents to support himself [Acts 18:3]).*

"**I have showed you all things** *(means that this particular aspect of unselfishness is to serve as an example),* **how that so labouring you ought to support the weak** *(everything the Believer does is to set a spiritual example),* **and to remember the Words of the Lord Jesus, how He said, It is more blessed to give than to receive** *(these words are not recorded in the Gospels; however, we know that only a tiny part of what He said and did is recorded; Peter, or one of the other Apostles who were with Jesus, evidently related this to Paul)*" **(Acts 20:32-35).**

THE WORD OF HIS GRACE

Paul knows that he will not see the Ephesians again. Undoubtedly, the Lord had related this to him. That is, as well, most likely the reason that he asked for these Brethren to come the 30 or so miles from Ephesus to Miletus. And despite the hardship, I have no doubt, as well, that these men who came from Ephesus sensed that this was a momentous occasion. Could they know that what they did that particular day or so in walking that distance, that is, if that's the way they came, that their act would become a part of the Word of God, and would be read and discussed untold millions of times, even thousands of years in the future?

Anything that's done for the Lord is of supreme significance. We must never forget that. Consequently, whatever it is we do for Him, we should do it with all diligence, understanding the significance of His glorious Work.

So now, Paul closes out his Message to them. Where they were gathered in the city was not clear, but wherever it was, it was a momentous occasion.

He closes out his Message to them by calling to their remembrance the fact that he had not been a burden to them in any capacity. He had *"coveted no man's silver, or gold, or apparel."* He went on to state how that he had met his own needs by working with his own hands, which had to do with repairing tents, which was no more than menial labor, which garnered what we would refer to as minimum wage.

The truth is, there has really never been one exactly like Paul. When the Lord chose him as the *"masterbuilder"* of the Church, He chose the right one. From those small congregations nearly 2,000 years ago, today the Church, be it spiritual or otherwise, girdles the globe. In other words, the foundation was proper.

THEY WOULD SEE HIS FACE NO MORE

"And when he had thus spoken *(represented the last time they would ever hear him speak to them)*, he kneeled down, and prayed with them all *(as well, concerns the last time he will pray with them, even though he will continue to pray for them)*.

"And they all wept sore *(concerns their great love for the Apostle)*, and fell on Paul's neck, and kissed him *(his Message had brought them from death to life)*,

"Sorrowing most of all for the words which he spoke, that they should see his face no more *(so far as is known, these Ephesians never saw the Apostle again until they saw him in Glory)*. And they accompanied him unto the ship *(this was at the port of Miletus)*" (Acts 20:36-38).

THEIR LOVE FOR PAUL

When Paul came to Ephesus several years earlier, sent there

by the Lord to establish a Church, these Ephesians who met with him that day, those years before had been idol worshippers. They had known nothing of the True God of Heaven. Their lives were miserable, to say the least. But now they have found hope in Christ Jesus. In other words, their entire world changed, and for the good, for the better, and a thousand times over.

These individuals knew in their hearts that everything they now had in the Lord Jesus Christ, they owed it to Paul. That's the reason when it came time to leave, that they *"all wept sore and fell on Paul's neck, and kissed him."* As they accompanied him unto the ship, they knew they would not see him again.

As I dictate these notes in the month of May, 2010, every one of these Ephesians is now in the portals of Glory. They are there because they heard the Gospel from the lips of Paul, and they accepted it wholeheartedly. In essence, Paul was their Father in the Lord (I Cor. 4:15-16).

TYRE

"And it came to pass, that after we *(Luke is with the party)* were gotten from them, and had launched *(left the Elders from Ephesus)*, we came with a straight course unto Coos, and the *day* following unto Rhodes, and from thence unto Patara *(located on the West Coast of Lucia and Pamphylia)*:

"And finding a ship sailing over unto Phenicia, we went aboard, and set forth *(they changed ships at Patara)*.

"Now when we had discovered Cyprus, we left it on the left hand *(means they did not stop at this Island)*, and sailed into Syria, and landed at Tyre: for there the ship was to unlade her burden.

"And finding Disciples *(followers of Christ)*, we tarried there seven days *(during this time, his teaching was invaluable to them)*: who said to Paul through the Spirit, that he should not go up to Jerusalem *(would have been better translated, 'who said to Paul in consequence of the*

Spirit'; the idea is that due to what the Spirit of God was portraying to these Believers concerning the coming problems in Jerusalem, the individuals themselves were voicing their own feelings that he should not go; it was not the Holy Spirit saying, 'don't go'; the Spirit was actually constraining him to go [Acts 20:22])" **(Acts 21:1-4).**

DISCIPLES

Every time the word *"Disciples"* is used in the Book of Acts, as it is used in Verse 4, without exception, as stated, it is speaking of followers of Christ. So, when it spoke of *"certain Disciples"* in Acts 19:1, these were followers of Christ. The reason I mention this is that some have claimed that those particular individuals were not even Saved. The use of the word *"Disciples,"* however, proves otherwise.

As they passed Rhodes, they would undoubtedly have seen the prostate mass of the vast Colossus, of which two legs still stood on their pedestal. In fact, the huge mass of copper had been hurled down sometime before by an earthquake. Later on, it would be broken up and carried away on 900 camels, all purchased by a Jew. This monstrous image—one of the wonders of the world of that day—was a figure of the sun. It now is gone, as all such will ultimately be gone.

Eventually they arrived at Tyre, where the ship was to unload its cargo. The Scripture says, *"and finding Disciples, we tarried there seven days."*

In one or more of their meetings that were conducted, the Holy Spirit through one or more there, in essence, portrayed to Paul what was going to happen shortly in Jerusalem.

The way it is translated in the King James Version of the Bible, it sounds like the Holy Spirit is saying that Paul should not go to Jerusalem. But many scholars claim that the translation is not as it ought to be, and as we stated in the notes, it would have been better translated, *"who said to Paul in consequence of the Spirit."* In other words, the Holy Spirit was warning Paul as to the trouble which would befall him in Jerusalem. It was not that he should not go, but that he should be prepared for what would come, and at the same time, that these Believers in Tyre would hold up Paul in prayer, as no doubt others were doing as well.

THE JOURNEY CONTINUES

"And when we had accomplished those days *(the past seven days)*, we departed and went our way; and they all brought us on our way, with wives and children, till *we were* out of the city *(shows the love and affection Paul continued to gain in these last few days, even from the children)*: and we kneeled down on the shore, and prayed *(I think the strength of Paul's prayer life is now obvious)*.

"And when we had taken our leave one of another, we took ship; and they returned home again *(these Believers at Tyre returned to their homes, but with a full heart and an exercised soul)*.

"And when we had finished *our* course from Tyre, we came to Ptolemais *(about thirty miles from Tyre; proclaims the end of Paul's voyage by ship)*, and saluted the Brethren, and abode with them one day" (Acts 21:5-7).

LOVE FOR PAUL

It is obvious from all of these places that Paul and his party visited on their way to Jerusalem, that he was well known and respected highly. The Believers at Tyre evidenced great affection for him, evidently understanding the great touch of God in his life.

I wonder, did they know and understand in all of this what it all meant? Did they realize that this great *"Faith"* would girdle the globe and see untold millions brought to a Saving knowledge of Jesus Christ?

I don't think they did, and, in fact, I don't think anyone

could have seen that far ahead.

Once again, when Paul and his party are about to leave, they *"kneeled down on the shore, and prayed."* It is obvious that Paul had a strong prayer life. As well should we!

CAESAREA

"And the next *day* we who were of Paul's company departed, and came unto Caesarea *(approximately sixty miles; they evidently walked this distance; the 'company' could have been as many as nine)*: and we entered into the house of Philip the Evangelist *(presents the same Philip of Acts 8:40)*, which was *one* of the seven *(Acts 6:5)*; and abode with him *(his house was evidently quite large)*.

"And the same man had four daughters, virgins *(insinuates they had given themselves over to perpetual virginity; meaning they would not marry, but would give their lives totally in serving the Lord)*, which did Prophesy *(the idea is that they were Evangelists exactly as their father, which strikes down the idea that women cannot preach)*" **(Acts 21:8-9).**

PHILIP THE EVANGELIST

At Caesarea, Paul, accompanied by those with him, stayed several days, which were the last happy days of freedom he would enjoy for a long time. The Lord graciously refreshed his spirit by this brief interval of delightful rest. He was staying with Philip the Evangelist. Paul had much in common with this man. It was Philip who had evangelized the hated Samaritans. It was Philip who was privileged to baptize the Ethiopian eunuch. Despite their strange beginnings, the lots of these two men had been closely intertwined. It was the furious persecution tendered by Paul, then known as Saul the Pharisee, which had scattered the Church of Jerusalem. It was in flight from that persecution that the Ministry of Philip had been changed.

Farrar said, *"As Paul and Philip talked together in those few precious hours, there must have flourished in their minds many a touching reminiscence of the days when the light of Heaven, which had once shone on the face of Stephen upturned to Heaven in the agony of martyrdom, had also flashed in burning apocalypse on the face of a young man whose name was Saul."*[3]

How the wheels of God had turned! No doubt, Stephen and Philip knew each other very well, and perhaps were very close friends, and here was Paul who had participated, strangely enough, in the murder of Stephen, now sitting with Philip, in a union which only God could bring about.

I have every confidence that both Philip and his four daughters questioned Paul all the time he was there about the great Gospel of Grace. They undoubtedly knew the great Revelation which had been given to him. No doubt, they unceasingly plied him with questions and, thereby, saw their own lives greatly strengthened and encouraged. I must believe that the great Apostle spared nothing, relating to them all that the Lord had shown him. I must believe, as well, that they eagerly received all that he imparted to them.

THE PROPHET AGABUS

"And as we tarried *there* many days *(waiting for the Day of Pentecost)*, there came down from Judaea a certain Prophet *(the same Brother mentioned in Acts 11:28)*, named Agabus.

"And when he was come unto us, he took Paul's girdle *(a sash worn around the waist like a belt)*, and bound his own hands and feet *(presents that which the Holy Spirit told him to do as an object lesson)*, and said, Thus saith the Holy Spirit, So shall the Jews at Jerusalem bind the man who owns this girdle, and shall deliver *him* into the hands of the Gentiles *(this was designed by the Holy Spirit to test Paul's resolution to obey the inward voice which bound him to go, even as Elijah tested Elisha).*

"**And when we had heard these things, both we, and they of that place, besought him not to go up to Jerusalem** *(but Paul must listen to the Holy Spirit, not men).*

"**Then Paul answered, What mean you to weep and to break mine heart?** *(They kept trying to persuade him, becoming emotionally distraught with some of them weeping.)* **for I am ready not to be bound only, but also to die at Jerusalem for the Name of the Lord Jesus** *(proclaims the consecration already settled in Paul's heart and mind respecting these coming events).*

"**And when he would not be persuaded, we ceased, saying, The Will of the Lord be done** *(means that all had now come to the place where they realized what Paul was doing and the direction he was going were indeed the Will of God; Paul was a chosen vessel to offer the Kingdom to Israel, as well as to proclaim it among the Gentiles; the final offer he would shortly give to Israel was a Divine necessity; but as we shall see, they rejected that offer and went to their doom)*" **(Acts 21:10-14).**

THE WILL OF THE LORD BE DONE

To this band of Believers came down from Judaea the Prophet Agabus, who, in the early days of Paul's work at Antioch, had warned the Church of the impending famine that was soon to come. Now he gives another Word to Paul. To proclaim what the Lord had given to him, he unties the sash from around Paul's waist, and then ties with it his own feet and hands, and then gives the pronouncement, *"Thus saith the Holy Spirit, so shall the Jews at Jerusalem bind the man who owns this girdle, and shall deliver him into the hands of the Gentiles."*

They had been aware of the peril of the intended visit, but no intimation had been given them so definite as this, nor had they yet foreseen that a Jewish assault would necessarily end in a Roman imprisonment.

Upon hearing this Word from the Lord, they earnestly begged him to stay where he was, insisting that they would go to Jerusalem to carry the Gentile contribution. Since the Spirit of God had given him so many warnings, is he certain that he is in the Will of God as it regards his visit to that city, and thus exposing himself in the very stronghold of his most embittered enemies?

To be sure, Paul was not insensible to their entreaties and arguments. But yet, it was not to be. No voice could turn him aside from obedience to the Call which he felt to be from God. As someone has said, *"he was a captive bound to Christ's triumphant chariot-wheel."* That being the case, what could he do? He could not turn either to the right or to the left. *"What are you doing, weeping and breaking my heart?"* he said. *"I am willing not only to go to Jerusalem to be bound, but even to die, for the Name of the Lord Jesus."*

"He saw a Hand they could not see,
"Which beckoned him away,
"He heard a Voice they could not hear,
"Which would not let him stay."

PAUL

THE APOSTLE

CHAPTER TEN

Jerusalem

JERUSALEM

"And after those days we took up our carriages *(referred to their baggage, whatever that may have been)*, and went up to Jerusalem *(it was approximately sixty miles, and they probably walked)*.

"There went with us also *certain* of the Disciples of Caesarea *(meant that the party is now quite large, possibly numbering fifteen to twenty people, or even more)*, and brought with them one Mnason of Cyprus *(he was originally from Cyprus, but now lived in Jerusalem, or nearby)*, an old Disciple *(does not necessarily mean old in age, but thought by some to be one of the original group baptized with the Holy Spirit on the Day of Pentecost)*, with whom we should lodge *(Mnason had invited Paul and his party to stay at his home while in Jerusalem)*.

"And when we were come to Jerusalem, the Brethren received us gladly *(indicates some of the Saints in Jerusalem, but not necessarily the leaders of the Church at this particular time; that would come the next day)*" (Acts 21:15-17).

THE BRETHREN

This great gathering in Jerusalem was the *"Feast of Pentecost,"* meaning that Jews would be coming from all over the Roman Empire, all in order to keep the Feast. Knowing that accommodations were at a premium, thankfully, it seems the Brethren of Caesarea had taken care to secure for Paul and those with him a shelter while in Jerusalem in the house of Mnason, a Cyprian. It is believed that Paul had a sister living at Jerusalem, but it is not known if she was a Believer or not, and in any case, her house, which, no doubt, was known by many Jews, would not be a safe place for Paul to be, as should be obvious. So, for the fifth time, it is believed, since his Conversion, Paul enters Jerusalem. It must have brought back painful memories.

He would have thought of the school of Gamaliel where he had spent several years, the synagogue of the Libertines, the house where the High Priest had given him his commission to Damascus, and then, the spot where the grass had drunk the blood of Stephen. All of this, and without exception, must have stirred in him painful memories.

He was coming into a city where friends were few, and where the very mention of his name might be enough to cause a knife to be pulled from its scabbard, with every effort to snuff out his life. That was the city of Jerusalem! But yet, surely he had some friends in the mother Church in Jerusalem. No doubt, he was cheered to be in the house of Mnason, but he could not remove the deep sense that he was in the city which was the murderess of the Prophets, and even his Saviour.

Farrar said, *"He knew too well the burning animosity which he kindled, because he remembered too well what had been his own, and that of his party, against those who were followers of Christ. The wrath which he had then felt was now a furnace heated sevenfold against himself."*[1]

THE OFFERING

With Paul was Sopater of Berea, Aristarchus and Secundus from Thessalonica, with Gaius and Timothy, both from Derbe, and, as well, Tychicus and Trophimus who were from Ephesus (Acts 20:4). Luke was also with the party (Acts 20:6).

Paul and all of these men were carrying a large sum of money, in fact, offerings which had been taken up from all the Churches founded by Paul. This money, which must have been considerable, was to be given to James to be used to help the destitute in the Church in Jerusalem.

All Jews in Jerusalem who accepted Christ as their Saviour, were excommunicated from the synagogue. That means that they could no longer attend the synagogue, and, as well, their children would be put out of school, and they would be evicted from their apartments, that is, if they were renting a particular place. They would lose all employment, with their family, at least in many cases, actually conducting a mock funeral for them. In regard to this and the great hardship which all of this caused, Paul had taken up large sums of money to be given to the Church in Jerusalem, which was meant to serve another purpose as well.

Paul, ever fearful of a Church split because of the Law/ Grace issue, was doing everything within his power to stop such a rupture. He wanted James and the Elders in the Church in Jerusalem to know and understand that he was doing everything he could to help. In other words, he was a part of the Church and not an antagonist. And yet, even as we shall see, there was that looming problem of Law and Grace. Little did the great Apostle realize what he was about to step into.

GENTILES

"And the *day* following Paul went in with us unto James *(refers to James, the Lord's Brother, who was the Senior Pastor of the Church in Jerusalem)*; and all the Elders were present *(refers to the many Pastors who served with James concerning the Church in Jerusalem; the Church was quite large, perhaps numbering as many as thirty thousand members or more)*.

"And when he *(Paul)* had saluted them *(greeted them)*, he declared particularly what things God had wrought among the Gentiles by his Ministry *(gave an account of his second and third missionary journeys with the planting of many Churches)*.

"And when they heard it, they glorified the Lord *(praised the Lord for what had been done)*, and said unto him, You see, brother, how many thousands of Jews there are which believe *(probably spoken by James, and referring to the Church in Jerusalem, made up almost exclusively of Jews)*; and they are all zealous of the Law *(meaning their new-found Faith in Christ stirred them up to serve the Lord with a new zeal, which they channeled in the direction of attempting to obey the Law of Moses to an even greater degree than ever)*:

"**And they are informed of you** *(concerned itself with charges against Paul relative to what he was teaching concerning the Law/Grace issue)*, **that you teach all the Jews which are among the Gentiles to forsake Moses** *(was not correct, at least in the manner in which it was being said; in fact, Paul preached almost exclusively from the Old Testament, holding up all that it stated as pointing to Christ)*, **saying that they ought not to Circumcise *their* children, neither to walk after the customs** *(once again, this was not exactly what Paul was saying; he taught that Circumcision did not Save the soul, and that no flesh shall be justified by the deeds of the Law [Rom. 3:24-31; 4:21; Gal. 3:19-25])*.

"**What is it therefore?** *(I think this illustrates that James himself was not settled on the matter, respecting Paul.)* **the multitude must needs come together: for they will hear that you are come** *(we aren't told anything about this particular meeting of which James spoke)*" **(Acts 21:18-22).**

WHAT IS IT THEREFORE?

Paul related to James and the Elders present what the Lord had done in cities such as Corinth, Ephesus, the Churches in Galatia, etc. He told of the many souls Saved, the many lives changed, and the countless Gentiles who had come to Christ. And then, one by one, he called forward those with him that they might, with their own hands, lay at the feet of James the sums of money which the Gentile Churches had contributed, some out of their deep poverty. There lay all this money, a striking proof of the faithfulness with which Paul, at any rate, had done his best to be mindful of the poor, and especially those in Jerusalem.

Without a doubt, this offering was far larger than they would have expected, because Paul would have done no less.

THANK YOU?

And yet, Luke makes no mention whatsoever of these funds given to the Church, which were so desperately needed. We are not told about a word of thanks. Farrar says, *"And we see but too plainly that Paul's hardly disguised misgiving as to the manner in which his gift would be accepted was confirmed"*[2] (Rom. 15:31). If gratitude had been expressed, Luke surely would have recorded such.

Farrar continues, *"Though some at least of the Brethren received Paul gladly, the Elders of the Church had not hurried on the previous evening to greet and welcome him, and subsequent events proved too clearly that his chief reward lay in the sense of having done and taught to his converts what was kind and right,"*[3] irrespective as to what others did.

In fact, the collection for the Saints in Jerusalem occupies many a paragraph in Paul's Epistles, even as it had occupied his thoughts. But there is little or no recorded recognition of his labor of love by the recipients of the bounty which, but for him, could never have been collected.

Abruptly, even, it seems, ignoring the most generous gift, James, or at least one of the Elders present, immediately launched into the charges, one might say, that had been brought against Paul. Those charges consisted of the following:

• They spoke of the thousands of Jews who had accepted Christ.

• They went on to relate that *"they are all zealous of the Law."*

• The charge is then made that Paul was *"teaching all the Jews which were among the Gentiles to forsake Moses."*

• He was accused of telling the Jews, so they said, *"that they ought not to Circumcise their children."*

• It is claimed that he was teaching them to forsake the

customs of the Jews.

As it regards all of this, it is finalized with the question, *"What is it therefore?"*

LUKE

Luke does not in any way record what Paul's answer was to these charges. He totally ignored what Paul said, if anything, and considering that this is the Word of the Lord, we gather from the silence that the Holy Spirit was very displeased at these proceedings.

What followed was Paul going into the Temple with four Jews to partake of the completion of the Nazarite Vow.

What happened has been debated from then until now as to the right or the wrong of Paul's actions. I suppose we will have to wait until the portals of Glory to ascertain the truth beyond the shadow of a doubt.

DO WHAT WE SAY!

"**Do therefore this that we say to you** *(proclaims a plan James, it seems, thought might defuse the situation)*: **We have four men which have a vow on them** *(pertained to the Nazarite Vow [Num. 6:14-20])*;

"**Them take, and purify yourself with them, and be at charges with them, that they may shave *their* heads** *(proclaims the fact that Paul was to pay for all of these sacrifices out of his own pocket, which in 2010 money amounted to several thousands of dollars)*: **and all may know that those things, whereof they were informed concerning you, are nothing** *(the thought here is that if Paul was as opposed to the Law as it was claimed, he certainly would not be in the Temple carrying out a Nazarite Vow, which was a part of the Mosaic Law)*; **but *that* you yourself also walk orderly, and keep the Law** *(no answer from Paul is recorded; we know that Paul didn't keep the Law as it regarded all of its rituals and ceremonies; in* *fact, all of that was fulfilled in Christ; the only answer we can give concerning Paul's action in doing what James said is that he was trying to prevent a split in the Church; it is my opinion that James didn't understand the Message of Grace as he should, and was still trying to hold to the Law; about ten years later, the Lord made it impossible for the Law to be kept anymore, in that the Temple was totally destroyed by the Roman Army).*

"As touching the Gentiles which believe, we have written *and* concluded that they observe no such thing *(releases Gentiles from obligation to the Mosaic Law; it is obvious here, however, that James didn't include the Jews in this freedom, which presented a dichotomy and caused great problems in the Early Church)*, **save only that they keep themselves from *things* offered to idols, and from blood, and from strangled, and from fornication** *(this was right; but as stated, James didn't include the Jews, which made that part wrong)*" **(Acts 21:23-25).**

WHAT WAS A NAZARITE VOW?

The Scripture doesn't plainly say that the vow Paul took upon himself was a Nazarite Vow (Acts 18:18), but due to the fact that he shaved his head in Cenchrea, this is probably what it was. As well, the men, whom James requested that Paul go with into the Temple, had taken the Nazarite Vow. Quite possibly, Paul had mentioned to James the same thing concerning himself.

• Under the Mosaic Law, either a man or a woman could take the vow of a Nazarite. All of this is found in the Sixth Chapter of Numbers.

• This vow pertained to them separating themselves unto the Lord.

• The one undertaking such a vow must separate himself from wine and strong drink, in fact, from grapes of any nature, even grape juice.

• All the days of the vow, and it seems as if though the vow could be of any duration, the individual was not to cut his hair.

• He could by no means touch a dead body, even if it were a close loved one. If the vow were to be broken, on the seventh day of the purification process, he was to shave his head.

• On the eighth day, he was to bring two turtledoves to the Temple, and a Priest would offer one for a Sin Offering and the other for a Burnt Offering.

• He had to offer three lambs and one ram for a Trespass Offering, a Burnt Offering, a Sin Offering, and a Peace Offering, and in that order.

• He was to keep his hair after he had shaved his head and give it to the Priest, who would put it in the fire *"under the Sacrifice of the Peace Offering."*

That above was what the individual was to do on a personal basis as it regarded his Nazarite Vow and coming out from that particular vow; however, the Priests, as the Sixth Chapter of Numbers brings out, had a complete process they must undertake as it regarded this vow being completed. This was the Mosaic Law, that which had been given by the Lord. But, of course, and repeatedly stated, our Lord fulfilled all of this when He came, making it now a moot point. In other words, all of these things are now of no consequence.

THE MONETARY EXPENSE

It seems from the terminology given in Verses 23 and 24 that Paul was expected to pay for all of this. If so, he would have had to pay for twenty lambs, four for each one, which were five counting himself. As well, there were other particulars such as *"unleavened cakes,"* etc., which he would have had to provide as well. The entire procedure in the Temple would last for seven days. At any rate, it was an expensive business.

HOW DO WE JUDGE PAUL'S ACTION?

The very object of proclaiming the finish of the Law under

Christ is done so for the purpose of Justification. Paul had written that the teaching of the Judaizers was quite a different gospel to his, and that anyone who preached this gospel of the Judaizers was accursed (Gal. 1:6-9). He had openly charged Peter with hypocrisy for now living like a Jew after he had lived in Gentile fashion, when the individuals came from James in Jerusalem to Antioch (Gal. 2:11-14). It was Paul who laid it down as his very thesis that *"by works of the Law no flesh shall be justified"* (Gal. 2:16). He had also said that to build again what had been destroyed was to prove one a positive transgressor (Gal. 2:18). He had spoken of the Law as a *"curse"* from which Christ had redeemed us and, as well, declared that the Law could never bring Righteousness (Rom. 3:20; Gal. 2:16). He had even stated that the Law was a slavery to *"weak and beggarly elements"* (Gal. 4:9).

ONE SUMMATION

Some years ago a particular writer said, of whom I have no way to ascertain his identity, and I quote, *"And that to suppose the author of the Epistles to the Romans and Galatians standing seven days, oilcakes in hand, in the Temple vestibule, and submitting himself to all the manipulations with which Rabbinic pettiness had multiplied the Mosaic ceremonials which accompanied the completion of the Nazarite vow – to suppose that, in the midst of unbelieving Priests and Levites, he should have patiently tolerated all the ritual nullities of the Temple service of that period, and so have brought the business to its tedious conclusion in the elaborate manner above described, is just as credible as that Luther in his old age should have performed a pilgrimage to Einsiedeln with peas in his shoes, or that Calvin on his deathbed should have vowed a gold-embroidered gown to the Holy Mother of God."*

Understanding all of this, how do we judge Paul at this time?

WAS PAUL RIGHT OR WRONG IN THIS ACTION?

While the Holy Spirit through Luke faithfully gave us the

proceedings, no verdict was given except to relate the circumstances.

For the following reasons I do not believe that Paul was wrong in his submitting himself to what James asked or even demanded:

• First and foremost, Paul was extremely concerned about the possibility of a split in the Church over this very issue of Law and Grace, which could have set the Church back many years, even decades, or destroyed it altogether. As a result, the Apostle did everything within his power to keep such from happening, and rightly so. In other words, he was walking a tightrope here which separated the new from the old, the present from many hundreds of years of tradition.

• Had he refused to do this which James requested and, as stated, in some way even demanded, this may have been the straw that would break the camel's back, so to speak. I firmly believe that he sought the Lord about the matter. I cannot imagine him not doing so. Even though the Scripture doesn't say, I personally feel he had permission from the Holy Spirit to do what he did.

• He had himself stated previously, *"For in Jesus Christ neither circumcision avails anything, nor uncircumcision; but Faith which works by Love"* (Gal. 5:6). The sin came in one placing one's faith in these rituals, whatever they may have been. Paul did what he did to appease the naysayers, and to be sure, he most definitely was not putting his faith in these things, knowing that they had all been fulfilled in Christ.

• As well, and to be sure, there were no Gentiles present at these proceedings so as to cause them to stumble.

• Was not what Paul did the same thing that Peter did in Antioch, when Peter separated himself from the Gentiles, refusing to eat with them, in order to appease those sent from James?

No! What Peter did was in the presence of both Gentiles and Jews and, in effect, nullified the great Gospel of Grace. What Paul did was with Jews only and, as stated, with no Gentiles present. In other words, what Peter did cast a tremendous reflection on the Gospel, while what Paul did cast no reflection at all. In fact, had the Holy Spirit not desired that Luke include this account in the Sacred Text, this action would have been completely unknown.

• Whatever the situation, we do know that there was no split in the Early Church, which Paul did everything to avoid. In fact, when Titus destroyed Jerusalem and the Temple in A.D. 70, the Christian Jews in Jerusalem tried to keep their way alive, living the Law while accepting Christ, but it soon died out. As is known, James was martyred by the Jewish Sanhedrin not too long after this happening with Paul.

PERSECUTION

"Then Paul took the men *(the four men of Verse 23)*, and the next day purifying himself with them entered into the Temple, to signify the accomplishment of the days of purification *(presents something which Paul had, no doubt, done at times in the past)*, until that an offering should be offered for every one of them *(speaks of the sacrifices to be offered at the conclusion of the seven days)*.

"And when the seven days were almost ended *(seven days of purification)*, the Jews which were of Asia *(Jews came from all over the Roman Empire to keep the various Feasts; Ephesus was in Asia, so these Jews knew Paul and were not happy with him at all)*, when they saw him in the Temple, stirred up all the people, and laid hands on him *(they bodily seized him)*,

"Crying out, Men of Israel, help *(Paul was in the innermost Court with other men)*: This is the man, who teaches all *men* every where against the people, and the Law, and this place *(once again portrays one of Satan's favorite tactics of twisting what has actually been said to make it mean something else entirely)*: and further brought Greeks also into the Temple, and has polluted this Holy Place *(was an entirely false accusation; the four men with Paul were Jews).*

"**(For they had seen before with him in the city Trophimus an Ephesian, whom they supposed that Paul had brought into the Temple.)** *(They jumped to conclusions!)*

"**And all the city was moved** *(the claim that Paul had brought a Gentile into the Innermost Court spread like wildfire)*, **and the people ran together: and they took Paul, and drew him out of the Temple** *(actually means they dragged him out, beating him as they went; he was dragged into the Court of the Gentiles, which was the Outer Court)*: **and forthwith the doors were shut** *(referred to the doors of the Court of the Gentiles, and the Court of Women).*

"**And as they went about to kill him** *(such is religion!)*, **tidings came unto the Chief Captain of the band, that all Jerusalem was in an uproar** *(pertained to the Roman Tribune who commanded a cohort of approximately a thousand soldiers).*

"**Who immediately took soldiers and centurions, and ran down unto them** *(probably represented about two hundred men)*: **and when they saw the Chief Captain and the soldiers, they left beating of Paul** *(which, no doubt, saved Paul's life)*" **(Acts 21:26-32).**

THE LIE!

At some point, when the seven days of purification were almost ended, there were some Jews in the Temple among the hundreds, some from Ephesus and perhaps other cities of Asia. It may even be possible that Alexander the coppersmith was one of them. At any rate, one of them recognized Paul. This individual, whomever he may have been, instantly attracted others toward him as he cried, *"This is the man who teaches all men everywhere against the people, and the Law, and the Temple."* Then this individual, no doubt joined by others, began to cry that Paul had brought Greeks into the Temple and had polluted this holy place. The Scripture says that some of these Jews had seen Paul on the streets of the city previously with Trophimus, who was an Ephesian Gentile, and they were claiming that Paul had brought him into the Temple. All of a sudden, the crowd becomes a mob, and they grab Paul and forcibly drag him out of the Temple with every intention of killing him.

No doubt, the rumors flew from lip to lip that this was Paul, the follower of the one called *"the Hung."* This is the one who taught and wrote that Gentiles were as good as Jews—the man who blasphemed the Torah—the man whom the synagogues had scourged in vain—the man who went from place to place getting them into trouble with the Romans; and now he has been caught taking with him into the Temple a Gentile dog. The punishment for that crime was death.

For Paul to defend himself was impossible. What voice could be heard in the midst of the wild roar of these intent upon murder.

THE CHIEF CAPTAIN

But then the Roman Centurion, stationed with his soldiers on the roof of the enclosure, became aware of the wild commotion that had suddenly sprung up. He could see hundreds of Jews running toward a particular area, actually the Court of the Gentiles. It was quite obvious that in another moment the floor was going to be stained with blood. Without a moment's delay, the Centurion sent a message to the Commandant that the Jews had seized somebody in the Temple and were trying to kill him.

In fact, the Romans were very much accustomed to situations somewhat similar to this, and it was known throughout the Roman Empire that there was no place in that vast Empire quite like Jerusalem and the Jews. They could instantly become a burning, senseless, and incomprehensible savagery.

Lysias, the Chief Captain, and his soldiers forced their way straight through the throng to the place where Paul was being held and rescued him from this enraged mob.

There is no way that Lysias could have even remotely understood that his action that day would go down in Biblical history to be read and studied by untold millions through the centuries. He saved Paul's life, which fell out to being an untold blessing to untold future generations. And yet, I'm afraid that to what he was exposed; he hardly had opportunity to know, which was the Christ whom Paul preached. How many down through history come close but not quite close enough!

ARRESTED

"Then the Chief Captain came near, and took him, and commanded *him* to be bound with two chains *(refers to him being bound to a soldier on each side)*; and demanded who he was, and what he had done *(speaking to the Jews)*.

"And some cried one thing, some another, among the multitude *(generally proclaims the conduct of a mob, for this is what the crowd now was!)*: and when he could not know the certainty for the tumult, he commanded him to be carried into the castle *(he gave instructions for Paul to be taken into the Fortress, or Tower of Antonia)*.

"And when he came upon the stairs, so it was, that he was borne of the soldiers for the violence of the people *(in order to protect him the soldiers were forced to lift him up, possibly even above their heads)*.

"For the multitude of the people *(the Jews)* followed after, crying, Away with him *(presents the cry of those who had also thirsted for the Blood of Jesus Christ [Lk. 23:18])*" (Acts 21:33-36).

WHO IS HE AND WHAT HAS HE DONE?

When Lysias and his soldiers forced their way through the mob to the place where Paul was being held, actually being beaten, they had to forcibly take him from his bloodthirsty enemies. When the soldiers had seized Paul, no doubt, beating back the enraged Jews, he quickly locked two chains onto Paul and chained him to a soldier on each side. He then asked the question, *"Who is this man, and what has he done?"* As they, no doubt, tried to answer him with guttural screams, Lysias quickly learned that he could find out nothing from this enraged mob, so he ordered his soldiers to take Paul into the barracks. But no sooner had he gotten to the stairs which led to the top of the roof and, thereby, into the fortress, than the mob, fearing that they would be deprived of their vengeance, made another rush at Paul, screaming, *"Kill him! Kill him!"* The Apostle was, no doubt, saved from being torn to pieces chiefly by the fact that Lysias kept close to him, with his soldiers beating back the crazed mob.

RELIGION

When one surveys this scene, one is looking at the end result of religion.

Religion is that which is conceived by man, devised by man, and birthed by man. Whatever is conceived makes the claim that this is the way to reach God or to better oneself in one way. If it is conceived by man, then God cannot have anything to do with it.

The world is filled with religion. I speak of Hinduism, Islam, Buddhism, Mormonism, Catholicism, etc. In fact, much of that which goes under the label of Christianity is not in truth that which is Biblical, but is that which is devised by men and, thereby, corrupt. Biblical Christianity is that which was conceived by the Godhead, with the price paid by the Lord Jesus Christ at Calvary's Cross and, thereby, empowered by the Holy Spirit. It is received and lived strictly by Faith (Rom. 5:1-2).

JESUS CHRIST AND HIM CRUCIFIED

True Christianity, meaning that which is totally and

completely Biblical, is all wrapped up in the Lord Jesus Christ and what He did for us at the Cross. At the Cross our Lord satisfied the demands of the broken Law and did so for every human being, at least those who will believe (Jn. 3:16). As well, He atoned for all sin, past, present, and future, again, for those who will believe. In fact, the New Covenant is the Lord Jesus Christ. It is Who He is and What He did.

We must ever understand that our Lord did all of this for you and me. In other words, He did it for sinners. To have all imputed to us, and I mean all for which He paid such a price, the only thing that is required of us is simple, childlike Faith (Rom. 5:1-2; 6:1-14; 8:1-2, 11; I Cor. 1:17, 18, 23; 2:2). Unfortunately, while the world has ever been trying to create another god, the church has ever been trying to create another sacrifice.

While the modern church understands somewhat the Cross of Christ as it regards Salvation, it understands the Cross of Christ not at all as it regards Sanctification, in other words, how we live for God, how we order our behavior, and how we grow in Grace and the Knowledge of the Lord. In fact, the same thing that is required for Salvation is required for Sanctification. It is, as stated, simple Faith in Christ and what He did for us at the Cross. Actually, our Lord said that if we didn't deny ourselves, which means to deny our own strength and ability, and take up the Cross and follow Him, we could not be His Disciple (Lk. 9:23; 14:27).

So, when we observe this scene at the Temple in Jerusalem with this hellish mob trying to kill Paul, we are observing religion in action. In fact, the entire crux of Judaism had been so polluted by man, so perverted by man, and so twisted by man that anymore it resembled not at all that which had originally been given by God to Moses. In fact, Jesus came as the last Preacher of the Law to show the nation of Israel what the Law really was, and how it should be administered; however, as we all know, they did not accept Him at all and, in fact, crucified Him. It must be remembered that it wasn't the thieves or the harlots that crucified Christ, but rather the religious leaders of Israel. Always remember, anything that's not Christ and Him Crucified, always and without exception, leads to self-righteousness. And that is what nailed Christ to the Cross—self-righteousness!

PAUL

"And as Paul was to be led into the castle, he said unto the Chief Captain, May I speak unto you? *(This presents Paul speaking to the Captain in the Greek language, which was actually the major language of the Roman Empire.)* Who said, Can you speak Greek? *(The next Verse explains the reason for this question.)*

"Are not you that Egyptian, which before these days made an uproar, and led out into the wilderness four thousand men who were murderers? *(This question portrays how this Captain was mistaken about Paul's identity.)*

"But Paul said, I am a man *which am* a Jew of Tarsus, *a city* in Cilicia, a citizen of no mean city *(presents an entirely different scenario to this Roman Captain, inasmuch as Tarsus was famous for philosophy and learning)*: and, I beseech you, suffer me to speak unto the people *(Paul was, no doubt, impressed by the Holy Spirit to do this).*

"And when he *(the Roman Captain)* had given him licence *(told him he could address the crowd)*, Paul stood on the stairs, and beckoned with the hand unto the people *(presents the last time the Holy Spirit will appeal to Israel as a Nation, at least as far as is recorded).* And when there was made a great silence, he spoke unto *them* in the Hebrew tongue, saying, *(it is possible that Paul was speaking in the ancient Biblical Hebrew, which was read every week in the synagogues; as stated, it was the last appeal by the Spirit)*" **(Acts 21:37-40).**

A JEW FROM TARSUS

With a startling turn of events, Paul turned to the Chief

Captain and said to him in Greek, *"May I speak a word to you?"*

The Roman Captain was somewhat startled that Paul could speak Greek, thinking that he was an Egyptian. A short time before, an Egyptian Jew, claiming to be the Messiah, had succeeded in raising up 30,000 followers, with the claim that the walls of Jerusalem would fall flat before him. Four thousand of these poor deluded Jews seem to have actually accompanied him to the Mount of Olives. There Felix fell upon them, killing some 400, and taking a multitude of them prisoner, which brought the whole thing to an impotent conclusion. The Egyptian, somehow, made good his escape and, in fact, was never heard of anymore.

All of this proclaims the fact that the flesh attracts flesh. We wonder why Believers, so-called, can be deceived so readily by that which is obviously wrong. The reason is obvious; their faith is not in Christ and the Cross but rather something else. Therefore, they do not have the Holy Spirit leading them, for the Holy Spirit works exclusively within the parameters, so to speak, of the Finished Work of Christ (Rom. 8:1-2, 11; Eph. 2:13-18).

Upon the question of whether he was that Egyptian, Paul quickly answered, *"I am a Jew, a native of Tarsus, in Cilicia, a citizen of no undistinguished city, and, I entreat you, allow me to speak to the people."*

The Roman Captain was, no doubt, taken aback by this turn of events. He probably contemplated the question for a few moments and then told Paul that he could address the crowd. Evidently, he loosed the chain from one of Paul's hands.

Standing on the stairs above the crowd, which may have numbered several hundreds, or even more, he raised his hand and when he did, the mob grew deathly quiet. He then *"spoke unto them in the Hebrew tongue."*

Speaking in the Hebrew tongue portrayed to them that this man was a scholar, extremely knowledgeable in the great Law of Moses. This was the sacred tongue of the synagogue, so to speak.

Little did they realize it but this man who stood before them that day understood the great Law of Moses as no other individual in Israel. But, as we shall see, they cared precious little for that.

PAUL'S DEFENSE

"**Men, Brethren, and Fathers** *(presents the beginning of Paul's final address to Israel, at least which is recorded, which will culminate the next day with the Sanhedrin)*, **hear you my defence** *which I make* **now unto you** *(presents some of the greatest words they will ever hear; Paul was the instrument, but the Holy Spirit was the Speaker).*

"**(And when they heard that he spoke in the Hebrew tongue to them, they kept the more silence: and he said,)**

"**I am verily a man** *which am* **a Jew, born in Tarsus,** *a city* **in Cilicia, yet brought up in this city at the feet of Gamaliel** *(automatically gave Paul credibility),* ***and*** **taught according to the perfect manner of the Law of the Fathers, and was zealous toward God, as you all are this day** *(all of this means Paul was a scholar in the Mosaic Law).*

"**And I persecuted this Way** *(the Way of the Lord Jesus Christ)* **unto the death** *(his persecution of Believers had resulted in the death of some),* **binding and delivering into prisons both men and women** *(proclaims that he showed no mercy).*

"**As also the High Priest does bear me witness, and all the estate of the Elders** *(even though this happened some twenty-five years before, there, no doubt, were some Jewish Leaders present who knew what he was talking about)*: **from whom also I received letters unto the Brethren** *(Acts 9:1-2),* **and went to Damascus, to bring them which were there** *(followers of Christ)* **bound unto Jerusalem, for to be punished"** (Acts 22:1-5).

THIS WAY

As Paul begins to speak to this great crowd, combining the

address he will make the next day to the vaunted Sanhedrin, this will be the last appeal, of which we have record, of the Holy Spirit to Israel. If they had accepted Paul's statement and turned to Christ, the nation would not have been destroyed by Rome, as it was a little over ten years from this time (70 A.D.). In other words, their response to his plea would decide their destiny. And that's exactly what happened!

They rejected what Paul said and did with a finality. In 70 A.D., Titus, the Roman General in charge of the mighty Tenth Legion, laid siege to Judah, culminating in Jerusalem. When the conflict ended, over one million Jews had been slaughtered. In fact, so many crosses had been erected around the city, on which each one hung a Jew, that there was no other place to put crosses, it is said! Hundreds of thousands of others were taken as slaves into the major cities of the Roman Empire. But yet, they hardly realized that their response that day to the Message of this man called *"Paul,"* had such import. But it most definitely did!

As he spoke to them, he first proclaimed that he could entirely sympathize with them in this outburst of zeal because he had once shared their state of mind, and that nothing short of Divine Revelation had altered the course of his life.

He went on to tell them that he had been brought up under the great Gamaliel, and that he was not merely a Jew, but rather a Pharisee who had studied the inmost intricacy of the Law. He stated that he was so like themselves in being a zealot for God that he had persecuted *"this Way"* to the very death, dragging into prison not only men but also even women. He then appealed to the memory of the ex-High Priest Theophilus and many still surviving members of the Sanhedrin who had given him letters to Damascus, where he was to continue his rampage, even breathing out threatenings and slaughter. So, he knew their spirit, he knew their zeal, and he knew their murderous intent!

There were, no doubt, some in that crowd that day, even though these things happened some twenty-five years before, who knew that what he was saying was the truth.

HIS CONVERSION

"And it came to pass, that, as I made my journey, and was come near unto Damascus about noon *(a day Paul would never forget)*, suddenly there shone from Heaven a great light round about me *(would later be described by him as brighter than the noonday Sun [Acts 26:13])*.

"And I fell unto the ground *(knocked down by the Power of God)*, and heard a Voice saying unto me, Saul, Saul, why do you persecute Me? *(When we oppose those who truly belong to the Lord, and I speak of opposing their Righteousness, we are at the same time opposing God.)*

"And I answered, Who are You, Lord? *(Paul knew that it was Deity to Whom he was speaking.)* And He said unto me, I am Jesus of Nazareth, Whom you persecute *(describes the Lord using the very Name so hated by Paul)*.

"And they who were with me saw indeed the light, and were afraid *(tells us that all of Paul's Testimony could be confirmed by witnesses)*; but they heard not the Voice of Him Who spoke to me *(should have been translated, 'they did not hear what the Voice said, they only heard the sound')*.

"And I said, What shall I do, Lord? *(At this moment, Paul accepted Christ as his Lord and Saviour.)* And the Lord said unto me, Arise, and go into Damascus; and there it shall be told you of all things which are appointed for you to do *(proclaims the Plan of God for Paul's life and Ministry)*.

"And when I could not see for the Glory of that Light *(the Light shining from Christ was so bright that it blinded Paul)*, being led by the hand of them who were with me, I came into Damascus *(presents Paul coming into the city in an entirely different posture than he had heretofore reckoned)*" **(Acts 22:6-11).**

The Conversion of Paul on the road to Damascus was, without a doubt, one of the greatest Conversions that the world has ever known. Here was a man who hated Jesus. In fact, he hated that name with a passion. Of course, denying that Jesus had been raised from the dead, and feeling that he must do all within his power to stamp out those who were followers of Christ, he did so *"breathing out threatenings and slaughter."*

Considering all of this, what was it that changed the whole spirit of his life, in fact, so dramatically was he changed that a little later he would change his name from *"Saul"* to *"Paul."*

That which changed him, and did so completely, was nothing less than a Divine Vision of Jesus of Nazareth, Who he had seen in such a light that it blinded him.

In a moment's time, he now knows that Jesus Christ was and is the Son of God, in other words, Deity. As well, he knows that Jesus is the Messiah of Israel. He also knows that this One was crucified by Israel and the One he had been persecuting so terribly for the last year or so.

He had been utterly, completely, totally, and absolutely changed, and in a moment's time, from Saul, the raging persecutor—Saul who had imprisoned and beaten the Believers throughout the synagogues—Saul at whose feet had been laid the clothes of them who slew Stephen—to Saul the Christian, the Believer, the Child of God, the follower of Jesus Christ, and that in totality, and yes, the Preacher of the Gospel of Jesus Christ. Would this not have an effect upon those who were listening to him now?

Also, those with Paul saw the light and heard the sound of the Voice that spoke with Paul but did not know what was said.

He then tells this audience, who just a short time before had been a mob, that he asked the Lord, *"What shall I do?"*

The answer came back immediately that he was to go into Damascus, and *"there it would be told him of all things which are appointed for him to do."* In fact, even though he left

Jerusalem a raging persecutor of those who followed Christ, in a few moments time everything had changed. Let me say something in respect to that:

A VISION OF JESUS

If we Preachers will preach Jesus, preach Him as the Saviour, preach Him as the Healer, preach Him as the Baptizer with the Holy Spirit, preach Him as our Redeemer, preach Him as the One Who died on the Cross for all of mankind, and preach Him as risen from the dead, if that can be done, there will be very favorable results. But our problem is, we are preaching everything but that!

One could have argued with Paul until his hair turned white and would have made no impression upon this bigot; however, when he saw Jesus, everything changed, as everything will change for anyone who is told about Him and accepts Him.

PAUL WAS A CHOSEN VESSEL

"And one Ananias, a devout man according to the Law, having a good report of all the Jews which dwelt *there (he was a follower of Christ, but still was loved and respected by the Jews who were not friendly to Christ)*,

"Came unto me, and stood, and said unto me, Brother Saul *(referred to him in this manner because Paul was already Saved)*, receive your sight *(he was healed immediately, and it seems at that moment baptized with the Holy Spirit, with the evidence of speaking with other Tongues [Acts 9:17])*. And the same hour I looked up upon him *(Acts 9:18 says, 'there fell from his eyes as it had been scales')*.

"And he said, The God of our Fathers has chosen you *(Paul was chosen by the Lord for a particular task)*, that you should know His Will *(what the Lord wanted, not what Paul wanted)*, and see that Just One *(Jesus Christ was to be the focal point of all things)*, and should hear the Voice of His Mouth *(this made Paul a witness to His Resurrection on the same level as those who saw Him alive before His Ascension).*

"For you shall be His witness unto all men of what you have seen and heard *(this speaks of his Great Commission to take the Gospel to the world of that day).*

"And now why do you tarry? *(In essence, this presents Ananias telling Paul that it is time to begin.)* arise, and be baptized, and wash away your sins *(refers to a present action being done because of a past action; he was being baptized in water because his sins had already been washed away by the Blood of Jesus),* calling on the Name of the Lord *(your sins were washed when you called on the Name of the Lord)*" (Acts 22:12-16).

THE MESSAGE DELIVERED BY ANANIAS TO PAUL

The Message that the Lord gave to Ananias, which was to be given to Paul, is as follows:

1. *"The God of our Fathers has chosen you;"*
2. *"That you should know His Will;"*
3. *"That you should see that Just One;"*
4. *"That you should hear the Voice of His Mouth;"* and,
5. *"You shall be His witness unto all men of what you have seen and heard."*

So, Ananias had a fivefold Message to deliver to Paul, which he did. Let's look at each one of these.

THE GOD OF OUR FATHERS HAS CHOSEN YOU

Why didn't the Lord choose Simon Peter, or John the Beloved, or one of the other chosen Disciples of His for this most important task?

That's a good question!

It is somewhat ironical that the Lord chose a man who had breathed out threatenings and slaughter as it regarded

Believers, with some having even died because of the maltreatment as a result of what Paul did. In fact, he held the clothes of those who were throwing the stones at Stephen, in effect, stoning him to death, and was totally in favor of what this pack of animals did! And yet, the Lord chose him to be the one to whom the meaning of the New Covenant would be given, in fact, the greatest Word that the Lord ever gave any human being and would ever give a human being. Also, in with this Call, he would be the *"masterbuilder"* of the Church. That means that the Lord would give him the responsibility of laying the Foundation, which was and is the Message of the Cross. In fact, Paul used the word *"Cross"* so much that it could be said to be a synonym for the entirety of the Gospel Message.

But none of that, even though it tells us what he was to do, tells us why the Lord chose him to do it.

The Lord knew that with the same zeal that Paul had persecuted the Church, he would now build the Church. He also knew that the great Apostle would never turn aside from the Message. He was called to preach the Cross, and that's exactly what he would do. The Lord knew that Paul, even in the face of terrible persecution, would not turn from the Message at all but would keep it in its purity.

Men look on the outward, but God looks on the heart. And God Alone knows what's in the heart. Considering what Paul had to face in coming years, He knew the Apostle would not allow anything to deter him.

THAT YOU SHOULD KNOW HIS WILL

This concerns the meaning of the New Covenant, which, in effect, was and is the meaning of the Cross. That's why Paul told the Church at Corinth, *"For I determined not to know anything among you, save Jesus Christ, and Him Crucified"* (I Cor. 2:2). This was the Will of God, and Paul was not to allow anything to compromise, hinder, or pollute that Will. The Lord knew that Paul would be faithful to carry out that Will in totality. The Lord was not to be disappointed!

TO SEE THAT JUST ONE

Paul was to see that Jesus Christ must be the focal point of all things. It was Christ Who paid the price on Calvary's Cross, and He would be the One Whom the Holy Spirit would glorify. Paul never too much mentioned, if at all, the Life and Ministry of Christ during His earthly Sojourn, but instead, proclaimed the great Victory that Jesus won at the Cross. In fact, the entirety of his teaching centered up on Christ and the Cross.

SHOULD HEAR THE VOICE OF HIS MOUTH

He personally stated that the great Revelation which had been given to him, which was the meaning of the New Covenant, was not given to him by any of the Apostles, but rather by the Lord Jesus Christ Personally (Gal. 1:11-24). It was Who Christ was, the Son of the Living God, and What He did, which is the price paid at Calvary's Cross. In effect, that was the gist of Paul's Message.

YOU SHALL BE HIS WITNESS UNTO ALL MEN
OF WHAT YOU HAVE SEEN AND HEARD

The entirety of his fourteen Epistles is made up of what he had seen and heard. That concerns his initial Salvation experience on the road to Damascus, and then the great Revelation given to him, which was the meaning of the New Covenant, which was and is the meaning of the Cross.

THE GENTILES

"And it came to pass, that, when I was come again to Jerusalem *(pertains to Acts 9:26)*, even while I prayed in the Temple, I was in a trance *(speaks of his high regard for the Temple, and at the same time refutes the accusation by some of the Jews that he would pollute the Temple)*;

"And saw Him *(Jesus)* saying unto me, Make haste, and get thee quickly out of Jerusalem *(presents the Lord once more indicting this city, His City, but now in total rebellion against Him)*: for they will not receive your testimony concerning Me *(they not only have rejected the Message of Christ, but would kill Paul as well, if given the opportunity)*.

"And I said, Lord, they know that I imprisoned and beat in every synagogue them who believed on You:

"And when the blood of Your martyr Stephen was shed *(presents this event which undoubtedly had a lasting effect on Paul)*, I also was standing by, and consenting unto his death, and kept the raiment of them who killed him *(this makes Paul a party to the death of this man)*.

"And He *(Jesus)* said unto me, Depart: for I will send you far hence unto the Gentiles *(this was the particular calling of Paul, even as he had been told by Ananias at the time of his Conversion)*" (Acts 22:17-21).

THE TRANCE

Now Paul mentions to the great crowd listening to him and, no doubt, with rapt attention that some twenty years ago, while worshipping in this very Temple, he had fallen into a trance and again had seen the risen Jesus. While the Sacred Text doesn't say that he used the Name *"Jesus,"* but rather the pronoun *"Him,"* they knew of Whom he spoke. And then the Lord bluntly said, *"for they will not receive your testimony concerning Me."*

Paul answered and implored the Lord in that the Jews knew how he had opposed Christ at every turn, and he even brings up the death of Stephen which, no doubt, haunted him all of his life.

But the Lord ignored what Paul said and bluntly told him,

"Depart: for I will send you far hence unto the Gentiles."

THE RESPONSE OF THE JEWS

"And they gave him audience unto this word *(speaks of the word 'Gentiles')*, and *then* lifted up their voices, and said, Away with such a *fellow* from the Earth: for it is not fit that he should live *(presents these people claiming they are Scriptural in their demand for Paul's life)*.

"And as they cried out, and cast off *their* clothes, and threw dust into the air *(portrayed their anger)*,

"The Chief Captain commanded him to be brought into the castle, and bade that he should be examined by scourging *(a most terrible form of torture)*; that he might know wherefore they cried so against him *(considering that Paul was speaking in Hebrew, the Roman Captain little knew what was taking place)*" (Acts 22:22-24).

SELF-RIGHTEOUSNESS

When any way is accepted other than Jesus Christ and Him Crucified, it always, and without exception, leads to self-righteousness. And to be sure, *"religion,"* which is that devised solely by men, is the greatest cause of self-righteousness. This is why Jesus said when speaking to the religious leaders of Israel, *"that the publicans and the harlots go into the Kingdom of God before you"* (Mat. 21:31).

No, Jesus by no means condoned stealing and harlotry. He was rather saying that the publicans and the harlots knew what they were doing was wrong, and some of them would repent; however, these religious leaders of Israel would not repent.

They had so distorted the Law of Moses that it no longer even remotely resembled what had originally been given. So, in essence, they had made up their own religion which, as stated, always falls out to acute self-righteousness.

In essence, Paul was telling this great crowd of Jews

assembled before him that Jesus had plainly told him that they would not receive his Message, and that he was to rather turn to the *"Gentiles!"*

Farrar said, *"That fatal word, which hitherto he had carefully avoided, but which it was impossible for him to avoid any longer, was enough. Up to this point they had continued listening to him with the deepest attention. Many of them were not wholly unacquainted with the facts to which he appealed. As well, his intense earnestness and mastery over the language which they loved charmed them all the more."*[4] But now, he told them that a vision from heaven had bidden him to preach to *"sinners of the Gentiles,"* which meant that he was giving the hallowed privileges of the Jews to those dogs of the uncircumcised. Farrar continues, *"The word 'Gentiles,' confirmed all their worst suspicions, and fell like a spark on the inflammable mass of their fanaticism. No sooner was it uttered than they raised a scream of 'Away with such a wretch from the earth; he ought never to have lived!'"*[5]

Now we see a mob that is once again totally out of control, beside themselves with impotent rage, howling, yelling, cursing, flinging about their arms, and casting dust into the air by handfuls, and this is their religion! Doesn't it remind one of the religion of Islam?

However, despite all of their rage, Paul was out of the reach of their personal fury. Observing all of this, the Roman Commandant ordered the prisoner to be led into the barracks, where the *"cat"* would be applied to his back, and then the *"Chief Captain"* would know what all of this was about.

A ROMAN CITIZEN

"And as they bound him with thongs *(getting him ready for the beating that would now be inflicted)*, **Paul said unto the Centurion who stood by, Is it lawful for you to scourge a man who is a Roman, and uncondemned?** *(Paul did not shrink from torture when it was directly connected*

with the Name of Jesus, but he quietly and with much dig-
nity avoided it when ordered by official ignorance.)

"When the Centurion heard *that*, he went and told
the Chief Captain, saying, Take heed what you do: for
this man is a Roman *(the rights of Roman citizens were*
guarded as something sacred by Rome).

"Then the Chief Captain came, and said unto him,
Tell me, are you a Roman? He said, Yes *(in fact, the*
Chief Captain had broken the law even by binding Paul).

"And the Chief Captain answered, With a great sum
obtained I this freedom *(proclaims one of the ways*
Roman citizenship could be gained). And Paul said, But
I was *free* born *(Paul was born a Roman citizen, either*
through some service performed for Rome by his family, or
else because of living in the city of Tarsus).

"Then straightway *(immediately)* they departed
from him which should have examined him *(refers to*
those who were going to scourge Paul quickly retiring):
and the Chief Captain also was afraid, after he knew
that he was a Roman, and because he had bound him.

"On the morrow, because he would have known
the certainty wherefore he was accused of the Jews, he
loosed him from *his* bands *(he was no longer restricted,*
but at the same time held in custody that the Captain may
hopefully gain some information), and commanded the
Chief Priests and all their Council to appear *(the Jewish*
Sanhedrin, the highest Jewish Council, and ruling Civil
and Religious body), and brought Paul down, and set
him before them" (Acts 22:25-30).

I WAS FREE BORN

The shirt is ripped from Paul's back, and he is bent forward with bare back, so the whip can do its work. Three times
Paul has suffered such beatings by the Romans. Five times he
has suffered the lash of Jewish thongs. The Jews had a law

that no more than forty stripes could be laid on a person's back; however, the Romans had no such law. They could beat a person as long as they so desired, and, in fact, many died under the Roman whip.

It is believed by some that these beatings had caused Paul great difficulties to where it was even a chore to walk. It was thought that if he had suffered one more beating, it would so have affected his spine that he would have been unable to walk at all.

Just before the whip is laid across his back, he asks a question that he had, no doubt, asked the other times when Romans had inflicted such pain on him, but then, which had been to no avail. It might be useless now, but it was worth trying. He, therefore, asked in a quiet voice, *"Is it lawful for you to scourge a Roman who has not been tried?"*

The question was asked of the Centurion, who was standing nearby to see that the torture was duly administered. To say the least, he was startled by the appeal.

Could it be true that this man was actually a Roman, and yet, he cannot imagine anyone falsely making this claim, for the penalty of such was death. In observing Paul, it was quite obvious that he was not a man given to such stupidity. So he told the soldiers to stop and went to the Chief Captain and relayed the information that Paul had given him.

The Chief Captain must have been very much nonplussed, for he had already broken the law twice by binding Paul's hands and then giving orders to put the whip to him, that is, if he were really a Roman citizen.

So, he quickly comes up before Paul. One can imagine Paul standing there, his back bare, with the Captain saying to him, *"Tell me, are you a Roman?"*

Paul immediately answered, *"Yes!"* The Chief Captain must have wondered how in the world that this poor Jew could have come by the privilege of Roman citizenship?

He went on to say to Paul, but as much to himself as anything else, *"With a great sum obtained I this freedom."* And then Paul quickly answered, *"But I was free born."*

At this stage he really does not know what to do with Paul. So, he summoned the Chief Priests to gather the Sanhedrin the next day for a trial of sorts.

Little did this Roman Captain realize that his informing the Chief Priests that they should call the Sanhedrin together would be the last time that the Holy Spirit would appeal to the nation of Israel. He could not have known that, but that's exactly what happened.

THE SANHEDRIN

"And Paul, earnestly beholding the Council *(evidently speaks of all seventy-one members of the Sanhedrin, with the High Priest Ananias serving as its President)*, said, Men *and* Brethren, I have lived in all good conscience before God until this day *(means that whatever he had been doing, he had thought it right at the time, whether true or not)*.

"And the High Priest Ananias commanded them who stood by him to smite him on the mouth *(this man would have hated Paul; history records he was appointed about nine years before this through political influence; he ruled like a tyrant in Jerusalem, and was a glutton according to the Jewish Talmud; Zealots assassinated him in A.D. 66 for his pro-Roman sympathies)*.

"Then said Paul unto him, God shall smite you, *you* whited wall *(in effect, says, 'you whitewashed wall,' meaning that the whitewash covered a black heart)*: for you sit to judge me after the Law, and command me to be smitten contrary to the Law? *(This presents Paul knowing the Law of Moses to a far greater degree than any of these members of the Sanhedrin.)*

"And they who stood by said, Do you revile God's High Priest? *(Paul did not know this man was the High Priest.)*

"Then said Paul, I did not know, Brethren, that he was the High Priest *(it was very difficult at that time for a visitor to Jerusalem, as Paul was, to know who was High Priest; the Romans made and unmade them at their pleasure, in addition to those made and unmade by the Sanhedrin; in other words, the High Priest was no longer a son of Aaron, as Scripturally they should have been)*: for it is written, You shall not speak evil of the Ruler of your people *(Ex. 22:28)*" (Acts 23:1-5).

YOU WHITED WALL

When Paul said, *"Men and Brethren, I have lived in all good conscience before God until this day,"* something in these words rubbed the High Priest wrong. Despising Paul, he may have disliked the use of the term *"Brethren."* As well, Paul asserting his perfect innocence, no doubt, angered this reprobate Priest, for that's what he was.

Ananias had been appointed to his position by Herod, and history proved him to be one of the worst, if not the very worst, specimen of the Sadducees. The Talmud states that he was a tyrant who, in his gluttony and greed, reduced the other Priests almost to starvation by defrauding them of their rightful duty. He held the High Priesthood for a period which, in these particular times, was unusually long. When fortunes turned against him, as they ultimately did, with individuals wanting to kill him, he was dragged out of his hiding place, which was a sewer, and perished as someone sank a dagger deep into his body.

His conduct toward Paul gives us a picture of his character. Scarcely had Paul begun his defense when this wretch ordered the officers of the court to smite Paul on the mouth. Paul answered the blow by stating, *"God shall smite you, you whited wall!"* And to be sure, that is ultimately and exactly what happened.

When Paul was told that the man who gave instructions for him to be smitten was the High Priest, the great Apostle apologized, stating that he was not aware this man was the High Priest. Had he known, he would not have referred to him as a *"whited wall."* Paul most definitely knew the phrase, *"you shall not speak ill of a Ruler of your people"* (Ex. 22:28).

Some may not understand Paul not knowing that this man was the High Priest; however, it must be understood that at that time, the Romans, and even Herod, were constantly setting up one High Priest and putting down another, and at their own whim. This means that the High Priesthood was for sale to the highest bidder. Also, the office had become more corrupt than one could begin to imagine.

A PHARISEE

"But when Paul perceived that the one part were Sadducees, and the other Pharisees *(we aren't told how he came about this information)*, he cried out in the Council, Men *and* Brethren, I am a Pharisee, the son of a Pharisee *(expresses the party with which Paul had been associated before his Conversion, and his father having been the same)*: of the hope and resurrection of the dead I am called in question *(the whole Christian Faith is built around Christ, His Death on the Cross, and His Bodily Resurrection; without Faith in both, men are lost)*.

"And when he had so said, there arose a dissension between the Pharisees and the Sadducees: and the multitude was divided *(speaks of the Sanhedrin itself, but typifies the majority of the church world presently)*.

"For the Sadducees say that there is no Resurrection, neither Angel, nor spirit *(they were the modernists of that present time)*: but the Pharisees confess both *(they were the fundamentalists of that time, which means to profess belief in all the Bible)*.

"And there arose a great cry: and the Scribes *who were* of the Pharisees' part arose, and strove, saying, We find no evil in this man *(proclaims the situation being*

decided on the basis of Doctrine, and not on Paul person-
ally): **but if a spirit or an Angel has spoken to him, let**
us not fight against God.

"**And when there arose a great dissension, the Chief**
Captain, fearing lest Paul should have been pulled in
pieces of them, commanded the soldiers to go down,
and to take him by force from among them, and to
bring *him* **into the castle** *(portrays the fact that the situa-*
tion had gotten completely out of hand)" **(Acts 23:6-10).**

THE DISSENSION BETWEEN THE PHARISEES AND THE SADDUCEES

In the Sanhedrin, the ruling body of Israel, seeing that it was
made up of both Pharisees and Sadducees, and Paul very well
knowing the animosity between them, cried out in the midst of
the furor, *"Brethren, I am a Pharisee, the son of a Pharisee."*

Some would question Paul taking this course, feeling that
it was beneath him.

In actuality, Paul was totally opposed to the Pharisees in
every fundamental particular of their system. In fact, the
Pharisaical spirit is the very opposite of the Christlike Spirit.
In Paul's Epistles to the Romans and the Galatians, he had
proven their whole theology, as such, to be false in every capacity. It was the Pharisees more than any others who demanded
the Crucifixion of Christ.

I AM A PHARISEE?

When Paul cried out to the crowd, *"I am a Pharisee, the*
son of a Pharisee," considering where he was, he was merely
stating what he had been for so many, many years. At the same
time, the bedrock of doctrine regarding the Pharisees, as it
pertained to the resurrection of the dead, which the Sadducees
denied, Paul, in essence, is stating that this is still his belief. In
fact, there was no one in the world at that time who knew more

about the Resurrection than did Paul. It was to Paul that the meaning of the Resurrection was given, which he gave to us in the Fifteenth Chapter of I Corinthians.

Paul was not subscribing at all to the disposition of the Pharisees but merely stating his belief of Doctrine. In fact, in that setting, he would have been wrong not to have done that.

When he made this great statement that day, all the Pharisees in that crowd shouted out, *"We find no evil in this man."* They went on to state, *"but if a spirit or an Angel has spoken to him, let us not fight against God."*

Seeing that the thing was again about to get out of hand, even as the two parties, the Pharisees and the Sadducees, began to fight each other, Lysias, the Roman Captain, felt that he must move Paul to safer quarters, or else the whole thing was going to turn into a city wide riot. So he led him to the barracks of the Romans.

THE LORD STOOD BY HIM

"And the night following the Lord stood by him, and said *(presents another appearance by Jesus Christ to Paul [Acts 22:8, 14, 18; I Cor. 9:1; 15:8; II Cor. 12:1-4])*, **Be of good cheer, Paul** *(evidently, Paul was greatly discouraged at this time, hence, the needed admonition given by Christ)***: for as you have testified of Me in Jerusalem, so must you bear witness also at Rome** *(this meant that despite the hatred and great efforts of his enemies, the Jews in Jerusalem would not be able to take his life, which they didn't)*" **(Acts 23:11).**

BE OF GOOD CHEER, PAUL

If Paul had displeased the Lord by going into the Temple before other Jews as it regarded the Vow of Purification, and had his reply regarding him being a Pharisee been displeasing to the Lord, to be sure, the Lord would not have appeared to him at this time, and above all, encouraged him as He did.

Without a doubt, Paul would have been extremely discouraged, even to the point of being depressed, at the action of the Jews who he had encountered the last few days. In fact, he could not help but feel as he did. But the very words of the Lord to him were, *"Be of good cheer, Paul."* Our Lord proudly proclaimed the fact that Paul had *"testified of Me in Jerusalem."*

As we have stated, when Paul addressed the mob hours before and had given a ringing declaration of the Lord Jesus Christ, and had done so, as well, in a sense, to the Sanhedrin, every indication is that our Lord was perfectly pleased with the Apostle. And now He tells him, *"so must you bear witness also at Rome."* And so it would be, but the trip to the capital of the world of that day would most definitely not be uneventful.

As it regards Paul's actions, not knowing the circumstances and, in fact, not knowing them at all, it is most easy at this present time, ten thousand miles distance and two thousand years later, to find fault with the Apostle. But I remind all and sundry that immediately after these happenings, our Lord appeared to Paul and gave a ringing declaration of approval as it regarded the conduct of the Apostle and, as well, what he had said. So that should settle the question.

THE JEWS

"And when it was day, certain of the Jews banded together, and bound themselves under a curse *(their 'curse' was a religious curse, which sought to put God in a position where He would have to do their will; their thinking was ridiculous!)*, saying that they would neither eat nor drink till they had killed Paul *(such is religion!)*.

"And they were more than forty which had made this conspiracy.

"And they came to the Chief Priests and Elders, and said, We have bound ourselves under a great curse, that we will eat nothing until we have killed Paul *(they now seek to make their efforts official)*.

"**Now therefore you with the Council signify to the Chief Captain that he bring him down unto you tomorrow, as though you would enquire something more perfectly concerning him: and we, or ever he come near, are ready to kill him** *(proclaims the depth of infamy to which the religion of the carnal heart can sink cultured and religious people)*" **(Acts 23:12-15).**

THE CONSPIRACY

In all of this, we continue to see the darkened heart of Israel of that day, and moreover, of the situation becoming even more evil as they are faced by Paul, one of the most righteous men who ever lived. Their spiritual blindness had deceived them into the state of religious murder. Concerning this, Farrar says, *"How dark a picture does it present to us of the state of Jewish thought at this period that, just as Judas had bargained with the Chief Priests for the blood-money of his Lord, so these forty assassins went, not only without a blush, but with an evident sense of merit or approval, to the hostile section of the Sanhedrin, to suggest to them as to how they could murder Paul."* We find that the Sanhedrin readily gave their approval of the plot. Once again, this is religion in action. It *"steals, kills, and destroys"* (Jn. 10:10).

As we've already stated in this Volume, and will possibly state so again, religion is that which is conceived by man, birthed by man, and carried out by man. This means that God has nothing to do with it. It is a scheme that claims to reach God or to better oneself in some way. It is hateful, deceitful, wicked, ungodly, and reprobate.

If one wants to see the beginning of religion, one need only go to the Fourth Chapter of Genesis. There, Cain and Abel, brothers, offered up their sacrifice to God. The Lord had told the First Family that despite being fallen and driven from the Garden, they could still have forgiveness of sins and communion with Him; however, it would be by virtue of the slain lamb, which would be a substitute for the Redeemer Who ultimately would come. This was God's Way and, in fact, His Only Way. It is still His Way presently.

Cain would not offer a lamb on the Altar, but rather brought vegetables or the fruit of his own hands, whatever that was, and tried to offer that to God, which the Lord would not accept. God accepted the sacrifice offered by Abel because it was in keeping with what the Lord demanded. In effect, the offering of the lamb stipulated that man understood that he was a sinner, and that without the shedding of blood there could be no remission of sins. The lamb served as a substitute as, in fact, untold millions of lambs did from then unto the time of Christ.

Angry because God accepted the sacrifice of Abel, and angry because his was rejected, Cain then murdered his brother, Abel. That is the picture of religion, and it has plagued the Earth from then until now. In fact, if one looks far enough, one will find religion as the cause for most of the blood that has been spilled in this world, in whatever capacity, and we speak of wars and rumors of wars.

THE PLOT DISCOVERED

"And when Paul's sister's son heard of their lying in wait *(presents Paul's nephew and all we know of his family other than references in Rom. 16:7, 11, 21)*, he went and entered into the castle, and told Paul *(we aren't told how he came by this knowledge)*.

"Then Paul called one of the Centurions unto *him*, and said, Bring this young man unto the Chief Captain: for he has a certain thing to tell him.

"So he *(the Centurion)* took him *(Paul's nephew)*, and brought *him* to the Chief Captain, and said, Paul the prisoner called me unto *him*, and prayed me to bring this young man unto you, who has something to say unto you.

"Then the Chief Captain took him by the hand, and went *with him* aside privately, and asked *him*, What is that you have to tell me? *(This portrays an honest effort on the Chief Captain's part to obtain the truth in all these matters.)*

"And he said, The Jews have agreed to desire you that you would bring down Paul tomorrow into the Council, as though they would enquire something of him more perfectly.

"But do not thou yield unto them: for there lie in wait for him of them more than forty men, which have bound themselves with an oath, that they will neither eat nor drink till they have killed him: and now are they ready, looking for a promise from you *(a plot to which the Tribune would probably have innocently agreed had the young man not warned him; in fact, what the Jews were doing was totally against Roman Law)*.

"So the Chief Captain *then* let the young man depart, and charged *him, See you* tell no man that you have showed these things to me *(it is believed, although not stated, that the young man went and related to Paul his ready acceptance by the Tribune, which no doubt encouraged Paul greatly)*" **(Acts 23:16-22).**

PAUL'S RELATIVE

Even though we do not desire at all to read more into the silence of this time than we should, as it regards the Early Church in Jerusalem, still, we hear no prayer for Paul from any one of the Elders of the Early Church or, in fact, any of the leaders of the Church.

It is very well understandable that the situation with Paul was extremely toxic, but still, when Peter had been in prison and in peril of execution, the Believers in Jerusalem stayed in constant prayer to God for him day and night, even without ceasing, in order that he might be delivered. But we must understand that feelings toward Peter, at least at that early period, were very much different from those with which the Christian Jews looked upon Paul, who treated the Mosaic Law and its essential Covenant as a thing of the past for converted Gentiles.

We are not saying that the leaders of the Church in Jerusalem were not praying for Paul. Quite possibly they were; however, the Holy Spirit through Luke makes no mention of such, if it did, in fact, happen.

Paul owed to a relative, and not to the Church in Jerusalem, the fact that he had been rescued from this planned murder. Farrar said, *"Paul had a married sister living in Jerusalem, who, whether she agreed or not with the views of her brother – and the fact that neither she nor her family are elsewhere mentioned, and that Paul never seems to have put up at her house when in the city, makes it at least very doubtful that she agreed with her brother as it regards the Law/Grace issue."[7]* But yet, she seemed to have enough natural affection for her brother to make every effort to defeat this plot for his assassination.

All that we know about this is that the son of Paul's sister, Paul's nephew, apparently a mere boy, on hearing of the intended effort of murder, went at once to the barracks of Fort Antonia and then revealed the plot to Paul.

At any rate, Paul was able to get the boy an audience with Lysias. He immediately revealed all he knew about the situation.

It is obvious that Lysias believed what he was told and then made plans to foil the plot.

"Let the song go round the Earth!
"Jesus Christ is Lord!
"Sound His praises, tell His Worth,
"Be His Name adored;
"Every clime and every tongue,
"Join the grand, the glorious song!"

"Let the song go round the Earth!

"From the eastern sea,
"Where the daylight has its birth,
"Glad, and bright, and free;
"China's millions join the strains,
"Waft them on to India's plains."

"Let the song go round the Earth!
"Lands where Islam's sway,
"Darkly broods over home and hearth,
"Cast their bonds away!
"Let His Praise from Africa's shore,
"Rise and swell her wide lens o'er!"

"Let the song go round the Earth!
"Where the summer smiles;
"Let the notes of holy mirth,
"Break from distant isles:
"Inland forest dark and dim,
"Snowbound coasts give back the hymn."

"Let the song go round the Earth!
"Jesus Christ is King!
"With the story of His Worth,
"Let the whole world ring!
"Him Creation all adore,
"Evermore and evermore!"

PAUL

THE APOSTLE

CHAPTER ELEVEN

The Imprisonment In Caesarea

THE IMPRISONMENT IN CAESAREA

CAESAREA

"And he called unto *him* two Centurions, saying, Make ready two hundred soldiers to go to Caesarea, and horsemen threescore and ten *(seventy)*, and spearmen two hundred, at the third hour of the night *(9 p.m.)*;

"And provide *them* beasts, that they may set Paul on *(probably placed the Apostle next to one of the Centurions in the very midst of the force)*, and bring *him* safe unto Felix the Governor *(not exactly a man of kind disposition to whom Paul must answer)*.

"And he wrote a letter after this manner:

"Claudius Lysias *(the Roman Tribune)* unto the most excellent Governor Felix *sends* greeting.

"This man was taken of the Jews, and should have been killed of them: then came I with an army, and rescued him, having understood that he was a Roman.

"And when I would have known the cause wherefore they accused him, I brought him forth into their Council *(Sanhedrin)*:

"Whom I perceived to be accused of questions of their Law *(Law of Moses)*, but to have nothing laid to his charge worthy of death or of bonds.

"And when it was told me how that the Jews laid wait for the man, I sent straightway *(immediately)* to you, and gave commandment to his accusers also to say before you what *they had* against him. Farewell" (Acts 23:23-30).

THE LETTER FROM CLAUDIUS LYSIAS

In this web of deceit and proposed murder, Lysias, no doubt, had much on his mind. Concerning this, Farrar said, *"So corrupt was the Roman administration in the hands of even the highest officials, that if Paul were murdered Lysias might easily have been charged with having accepted a bribe to induce him to turn Paul over to these murderers."*[1] Trying to protect himself as well as Paul, he now feels that he must send Paul away, and do so swiftly and secretly. Knowing how explosive was the situation, so as not to cause more uprising on the part of the Jews, he assembled 200 soldiers, 70 horsemen, and 200 spearmen, all in order to take Paul to Caesarea. Considering this tremendous body of men, we understand the fear that Lysias had as it regarded the Jews attempting to take Paul by force from his protection.

The conduct of Lysias, although not so commendable to begin with, on the whole, would have to be rendered as kind and honorable. Quite possibly Paul informed him, although the Scripture doesn't say, that he would raise no alarm against him as it regarded the conduct of Lysias at the beginning.

The Roman Commandant wrote a letter to Felix, the Governor of the region, as it regarded Paul, and gave it to one of the Centurions for it to be delivered when they arrived in Caesarea.

One thing is certain, Lysias was not taking any chances as it regarded Paul's safety. It is obvious that he knew the Jews, how explosive they could be, and how that small things could quickly erupt into a conflagration.

THE GOVERNOR

"Then the soldiers, as it was commanded them, took Paul, and brought *him* by night to Antipatris *(about forty miles from Jerusalem, with about twenty miles left to Caesarea; the soldiers must have marched without stopping for about fifteen hours).*

"On the morrow they left the horsemen to go with him *(the infantry of about four hundred soldiers returned to Jerusalem, while the Cavalry, consisting of some seventy horsemen, took Paul the balance of the way to Caesarea),* and returned to the castle:

"Who, when they came to Caesarea, and delivered the epistle to the Governor *(the letter written by the Roman Tribune)*, presented Paul also before him.

"And when the Governor had read *the letter,* he asked of what province he was *(the home of Paul)*. And when he understood that *he was* of Cilicia *(this automatically gave the Governor jurisdiction; the fact that Paul was a Roman citizen from this important Province, meant that Felix could not ignore him)*;

"I will hear you *(he speaks to Paul)*, said he, when your accusers are also come *(pertained to members or representatives of the Sanhedrin)*. And he commanded him to be kept in Herod's Judgment Hall *(a part of the lavish Palace built by Herod the Great; it served as the Capitol Building as well as the official residence of the Roman Governors; it evidently had some prison cells within its confines)*" (Acts 23:31-35).

PAUL'S ARRIVAL IN CAESAREA

Having to walk the horses at a pace equal to the pace walked by the soldiers, they must have marched all night long, even up into the next day, for it was a distance of approximately 40 miles to Antipatris. The soldiers would then march back to Jerusalem, with the 70 horsemen escorting Paul the balance of the way to Caesarea, a distance of approximately 20 miles. To which we have already alluded, to appoint that many soldiers to accompany Paul tells us several things:

• Lysias knew the temperament of the Jews and wasn't taking any chances with Paul.

• Considering that Paul was a Roman citizen, and especially of a Province as important as Cilicia, again, he was taking no chances.

• Because Lysias had already broken Roman Law when he chained the hands of Paul to two Roman soldiers, and especially because he had come close to submitting him to a beating, even now the consequences could be serious. So, he felt that he must protect Paul at all costs.

And now arriving in Caesarea, Paul is presented to the Governor who read the letter written to him by Lysias.

A few days before, Paul, with those with him, had left Caesarea on his way to Jerusalem. He now enters Caesarea again, but not at all as he had left it those days before. That would have been quite a sight to behold, some 70 horsemen coming into the city with Paul in the midst of them. This must have attracted many curious eyes.

Philip and the other Christians of Caesarea would have had no knowledge that Paul was being escorted back to their city, as all of this was done in secret. But, no doubt, they would learn very shortly all of that which had transpired the last few days. That ride, in the midst of his Roman bodyguard, was destined to be the last time, as far as we know, that Paul would experience fresh air, till after some two years of imprisonment his voyage to Rome would begin.

PAUL BEFORE FELIX

"And after five days Ananias the High Priest descended with the Elders *(represented members of the Sanhedrin who were Sadducees)*, and *with* a certain orator *named* Tertullus, who informed the Governor against Paul *(he served as the prosecutor for the Jews)*.

"And when he was called forth, Tertullus began to accuse *him*, saying, Seeing that by you *(Felix)* we enjoy great quietness, and that very worthy deeds are done unto this nation by your providence *(Josephus said that even though Felix did suppress some of the robbers and murderers in Judaea, he was himself 'more hurtful than them all')*,

"We accept *it* always, and in all places, most noble Felix, with all thankfulness.

"Notwithstanding, that I be not further tedious unto you, I pray you that you would hear us of your clemency a few words *(Felix was not a man of clemency)*.

"For we have found this man a pestilent *fellow*, and a mover of sedition among all the Jews throughout the world, and a ringleader of the sect of the Nazarenes *(presents the name for followers of Christ coined by the Jews)*:

"Who also has gone about to profane the Temple *(Paul didn't profane the Temple in any manner)*: whom we took, and would have judged according to our Law *(presents another outright lie; they had no intention of giving him a trial as the word 'judge' implies, but rather were attempting to beat him to death before he was rescued by the Tribune)*.

"But the Chief Captain Lysias came *upon us*, and with great violence took *him* away out of our hands *(is meant to throw the Roman Tribune in a bad light; it was a bad mistake on the part of Tertullus; no doubt, the Holy Spirit had him go in this direction)*,

"Commanding his accusers to come unto you: by examining of whom yourself may take knowledge of all these things, whereof we accuse him *(refers to the fact that the situation is now in the Court of the Governor, even though the Jews do not think it should be here; for all their plotting, they have not helped their cause)*.

"And the Jews also assented, saying that these things were so *(refers to the High Priest and those with him who joined Tertullus with their voices of approval respecting their hired prosecutor's statements; as stated, it was a mistake on their part)*" **(Acts 24:1-9).**

THE ACCUSATION AGAINST PAUL

Roman Law stated that a prisoner sent to a Roman judge had to fix a trail within three days. But, due to bringing the accusers from Jerusalem, it was the fifth day after Paul's arrival at Caesarea that he was brought to trial. Ananias in person accompanied handpicked Jews, all eager for revenge. Paul had called him a *"whited wall,"* which was, in essence, saying that he was a *"plastered tomb."* In the Jewish world of that day, one who walked over a tomb was defiled. So, all of this riff-raff lusted for Paul's blood. They would leave no stone unturned until they had had their vengeance.

TERTULLUS

These Jews, more than likely ignorant of the procedure in Roman courts, hired a man by the name of Tertullus to represent them. He was a Gentile who tried to conduct himself as though he were a Jew.

He began his dialogue, as it regarded the accusation against Paul, before this Roman Governor by complimenting Felix. In essence, he went on to state what a great man that Felix was, with the truth being that Caesarea had probably never been governed by one so corrupt.

Evidently Luke was present and, thereby, faithfully recorded all that took place.

Having finished with the flattery, he brought three charges against Paul. They were:

1. He was a public pest who lived by stirring up trouble among all the Jews all over the world.

2. He was a ringleader of the sect called the *"Nazarenes."*

3. He had attempted to profane the Temple.

As is obvious, even before Paul makes his defense, his accusers had no case against him.

When Tertullus finished his tirade, the Jews present chimed in with their accusations, which, again, had no substance, which was extremely obvious to the Governor. As well, Tertullus did not endear himself to the Governor when he accused the Chief Captain Lysias of using great violence against them to rescue Paul. Sooner or later, the Devil always overplays his hand. He would do no less here.

PAUL'S DEFENSE

"Then Paul, after that the Governor had beckoned unto him to speak, answered *(presents that which the Holy Spirit had said that Paul would do, 'to bear My Name before the Gentiles, and Kings, and the Children of Israel' [Acts 9:15])*, Forasmuch as I know that you have been of many years a judge unto this nation, I do the more cheerfully answer for myself *(there was no one in the world at that time who knew Mosaic Law any better than Paul; as well, being a Roman citizen, he was also quite knowledgeable of Roman Law)*:

"Because that you may understand, that there are yet but twelve days since I went up to Jerusalem for to worship *(in essence, Paul is stating that what they were accusing him of was impossible, considering the short period of time)*.

"And they neither found me in the Temple disputing with any man, neither raising up the people, neither in the synagogues, nor in the city *(refers to the fact that absolutely nothing had been done that could be misconstrued in any way, referring to these charges)*:

"Neither can they prove the things whereof they now accuse me *(they couldn't prove their charge because they never happened)*" **(Acts 24:10-13).**

THE DENIAL

Felix was probably already impatient at this time with the conviction that this was, as Lysias had informed him, some Jewish squabble about Mosaic Law, of which he had little interest. So, he probably nodded to Paul that he could now begin his defense, which he did.

Paul's defense was totally different than the manner chosen by Tertullus.

He opened his statement by stating that he knew that Felix

was very familiar with Jewish affairs, and as that was the case, Felix would know and understand that of which he spoke.

He went on to state that he had not caused any disturbance anywhere, neither had he had a disagreement with anyone, nor had he attracted a crowd in any capacity, either in the Temple or in the synagogues, or in any part of the city. So, the Apostle head-on denies the charges brought against him, which were ridiculous, to say the least. He then challenged the Jews to produce any witnesses who could claim otherwise than what he was stating.

Reading carefully the charges, which are superficial at best, one wonders as to why the High Priest would take up his time, come all the way from Jerusalem to Caesarea, a distance of approximately 60 or more miles, to present before the Governor such flimsy charges. And then again, charges which he could no wise substantiate.

True, there had been a riot, but for that, he was not responsible. It had been stirred up by certain Asiatic Jews, who claimed that he had brought a Greek into the Temple, which, of course, was totally untrue. So, if they were so certain of their case, why did not these Jews come and present their evidence? In fact, their very absence was a proof of the weakness of the case against him.

THE WORSHIP OF THE GOD OF MY FATHERS

"But this I confess unto you, that after the Way which they call heresy *(following Christ)*, so worship I the God of my Fathers *(places Christianity as the fulfillment of the great Promises and Predictions given to the 'Fathers,' i.e., all the Old Testament Worthies)*, believing all things which are written in the Law and in the Prophets *(the entirety of the Old Testament)*:

"And have hope toward God *(in essence, states that the Law and the Prophets were not complete within themselves, only pointing to the One Who was to come)*, which they themselves also allow *(even his enemies among the Jews believed in the coming Messiah, but not that He was Jesus)*, **that there shall be a resurrection of the dead, both of the just and unjust** *(proclaims, as is obvious, two Resurrections)*.

"**And herein do I exercise myself** *(diligence constantly practiced by Paul so that his life and conduct please the Lord in all things)*, **to have always a conscience void of offence toward God, and** *toward* **men** *(Mat. 22:37-40)*" **(Acts 24:14-16).**

A CONSCIENCE VOID OF OFFENSE TOWARD GOD, AND TOWARD MEN

Now Paul says that he will confess to the Governor what he believes, and what he is. He states unequivocally, *"that after the Way which they call heresy, so worship I the God of my Fathers."* While he didn't use the Name of Jesus, he did use the term *"the Way,"* which all the Jews in the room understood perfectly as to refer to the Lord Jesus Christ. He admitted that the worship of Christ was referred to by these individuals as *"heresy."* In fact, he had once sat on that side of the fence, so to speak. He now states unequivocally that he *"believes all things which are written in the Law and in the Prophets."*

In essence, the Apostle is saying that while they may vehemently disagree with him regarding as to Who Jesus Christ is, and What He has done, namely the Cross, still, he has broken no Roman Law by that which he believes. He now states his belief in the *"resurrection of the dead, both of the just and the unjust,"* which, of course, was believed by the Pharisees as well. While the Sadducees, of which party belonged the High Priest, did not believe in a Resurrection, still, the Pharisees did, and for that they could not condemn him. As it regards this part of his defense, he states before all that he has a *"conscience void of offence toward God, and toward men."* He will now go to the heart of their charges against him.

LACK OF EVIDENCE

"Now after many years I came to bring alms to my nation, and offerings *(probably refers to the six or seven years Paul had been away from Jerusalem).*

"Whereupon certain Jews from Asia found me purified in the Temple, neither with multitude, nor with tumult *(refers to the fact that absolutely nothing was going on at that time which could have given any type of credence to these accusations).*

"Who ought to have been here before you, and object, if they had ought against me *(the ones who accused him were not present here; the High Priest and the members of the Sanhedrin who were present had not witnessed any of these so-called infractions).*

"Or else let these same *here* say *(now puts the High Priest and those with him on the spot)*, if they have found any evil doing in me, while I stood before the Council *(shifts the attention away from those not present to those who are),*

"Except it be for this one voice, that I cried standing among them, Touching the resurrection of the dead I am called in question by you this day *(this had to do with Jewish Law, which interested the Romans not at all)*" (Acts 24:17-21).

NOTHING DONE THAT WAS WRONG

As we have stated, for the riot which had ensued, he was not responsible. It had been brought about by certain Jews, more than likely from Ephesus, accusing him of bringing a Gentile into the Temple confines, which he had not done. And furthermore, if they believed what they were saying was true, why were they not here as witnesses against him. In fact, their very absence was a proof of the weakness of the case against him. And then he turned toward the High Priest and those with him, in effect stating, if they had any charge against him specifically, now was the time to bring it out. And, of course, they had no charge other than what they said, which, in reality, was no charge at all. While they tried their best to lay something before the Governor which would stick, the truth is, their case was broken down, simply because they had no case at all.

At this particular time he had no reason at all to try to justify himself for being a follower of Jesus Christ, since, at that time, such had not been declared by Rome to be an illicit religion, so to speak.

Some 25 years before, Paul had been the champion of the Sanhedrin, with that ruling body giving Paul their wholehearted approval for his *"breathing out threatenings and slaughter,"* as it regarded the followers of Christ. In other words, he was slated for big things in Israel, which, in one of his Epistles, he mentioned. He said:

> "For you have heard of my conversation *(way of life)* in time past in the Jews' religion *(the practice of Judaism)*, how that beyond measure I persecuted the Church of God, and wasted it *(Acts 9:1-2)*:
> "And profited in the Jews' religion above many my equals in my own nation *(he outstripped his Jewish contemporaries in Jewish culture, etc.)*, being more exceedingly zealous of the traditions of my fathers *(a zeal from his very boyhood)*" **(Gal. 1:13-14).**

But the Damascus Road experience had changed all of that and had done so in a few moments time. One glimpse of Jesus and there was absolutely no doubt now in Paul's mind as to Who He was.

THE DECISION OF FELIX

> "And when Felix heard these things, having more perfect knowledge of *that* Way *(Felix had greater*

knowledge of Christianity than Tertullus, and the Jews present at that trial were willing to give him credit), **he deferred them, and said** *(means simply that he refused to give a verdict at this time)*, **When Lysias the Chief Captain shall come down, I will know the uttermost of your matter** *(he was trying to delay the matter, hoping it would defuse the situation; moreover, there is no record he ever sent for Lysias)*.

"**And he commanded a Centurion to keep Paul, and to let** *him* **have liberty** *(tells us that Felix considered Paul someone above the ordinary; he was under house arrest, but basically had the run of the place)*, **and that he should forbid none of his acquaintance to minister or come unto him** *(he could have as many visitors as he liked, with no restraint on such activity)*" **(Acts 24:22-23).**

THE KNOWLEDGE OF THAT WAY

In some way, Felix had gained some knowledge of Christ and the questions which surrounded Him. In fact, he knew much more about Christ than the Jews and their advocate supposed. Understanding that, he was not going to hand Paul over to the Sanhedrin, which would be wrong, but at the same time, he did not wish to offend these individuals. So he refused to give any type of decision now, stating the absence of Lysias as the reason, this man who, incidentally, was a material witness. However, there is no record that Lysias was ever summoned by Felix to Caesarea.

Felix knew that Paul was totally innocent of all of these ridiculous charges, that is, if they could be labeled as such, therefore, he gave instructions to the Centurion that Paul was to be given freedom within certain boundaries. He could have as many visitors as he so desired, and as often as he so desired. No doubt, Luke and Aristarchus were with Paul constantly during the two years of his stay in Caesarea, and, doubtless, Phillip the Evangelist and other Christians came to visit him often.

It is quite possible, and undoubtedly a fact, that Paul conducted services in the prison, and often, especially considering the freedom which was accorded him. One cannot imagine Paul not taking every opportunity to present the Gospel. As well, I am certain that the Believers in Caesarea availed themselves of this wonderful opportunity to hear the Apostle again and again. So his time spent there, even though incarcerated unjustly, still, was not wasted at all.

RIGHTEOUSNESS, TEMPERANCE, AND JUDGMENT TO COME

"And after certain days, when Felix came with his wife Drusilla, which was a Jewess *(his wife was the young daughter of Herod Agrippa I, the Herod who killed James [the Brother of John] with a sword [Acts 12:1-2])*, he sent for Paul, and heard him concerning the Faith in Christ *(it seems to imply that his interest was sincere)*.

"And as he *(Paul)* reasoned of Righteousness *(Righteousness can only come through Christ)*, temperance *(the bondages and vices which affect humanity)*, and judgment to come *(all must one day stand before God)*, Felix trembled, and answered *(proclaims tremendous Holy Spirit Conviction)*, Go your way for this time; when I have a convenient season, I will call for you *(presents the sinner's excuse when under Conviction and refusing to surrender)*.

"He hoped also that money should have been given him of Paul, that he might loose him *(the love of money was probably one of the reasons he would not give his heart to the Lord)*: wherefore he sent for him the oftener, and communed with him *(there is no record that he ever came to Christ; so close, but so far off!)*.

"But after two years *(gives us no hint as to what took place during this particular time)* Porcius Festus came into Felix' room *(means that Festus now replaced Felix as Governor)*: **and Felix, willing to show the Jews a pleasure, left Paul bound** *(presents a terrible travesty of Justice)*" **(Acts 24:24-27).**

A MORE CONVENIENT SEASON

Felix summoned Paul into his presence and, with his wife Drusilla, gave ear to what Paul had to say.

A short time before this, Felix used the machinations of Simon Magus, a sorcerer, to induce Drusilla, the younger sister of Agrippa II, to leave her husband and to become his wife. It was a strange thing, and one which must have required all the arts of Simon to effect, that this young and beautiful princess, who was at this time only 20 years old, should have abandoned all her Jewess prejudices, and risk the deadliest abhorrence of her race, by leaving a prince who loved her, and had even been induced to accept circumcision to gratify her national scruples, in order to form an adulterous connection with this cruel and elderly profligate, which describes Felix.

When Paul addressed this man and his wife, he did not launch into a diatribe concerning this adulteress union, even though it is no doubt that he knew of such. Instead, he spoke of Faith in Christ which dealt with Righteousness, temperance, and Judgment to come. To be sure, it was a powerful message.

RIGHTEOUSNESS

He dealt with Righteousness, no doubt, claiming the fact that there was nothing that man could do to attain to such, but that it could be freely given him as Faith is evidenced in Christ and what Christ did for us at the Cross. That and that alone is the Righteousness of God. And Faith in Christ Alone is the only manner in which it can be received.

TEMPERANCE

The Greek word for temperance is *"egkrateia,"* **and means**

"self-control." This is the crowning sin of the unredeemed. As someone has well said, *"Lust ever demands and lust is never satisfied."*

Solomon gave the greatest description of this of anyone, I think, in history, then or now. Here was a man, if we judge by comparisons, who was the richest man who ever lived. As well, he had wisdom that had been given to him by God, which meant that he was more wise than any other human being. In other words, he could indulge himself in the worst forms of vice, because he had the money to purchase such, and his wisdom, sadly, could be turned to artful ways of supposedly enjoying such evil. As such, he gave himself over in totality to try to satisfy the lusts of the flesh. When it was all over he said, *"All is vanity and vexation of spirit"* (Eccl. 1:14).

The only way that one can be temperate, in other words, exercise proper self-control, is for one first of all to know the Lord Jesus Christ as one's Saviour, and then to place one's Faith exclusively in Christ and the Cross and maintain it there, which will then give the individual the help of the Holy Spirit (Rom. 6:1-14; 8:1-2, 11). Otherwise, temperance may be looked at and admired but will prove to be unreachable.

JUDGMENT TO COME

One day man is going to have to answer to Jesus Christ, of that, the unredeemed do not desire to hear. Any individual can face the Lord Jesus Christ now by accepting Him as Saviour and Lord, which means that every sin was answered at Calvary, or else one will stand before Him at the Great White Throne Judgment. But one way or the other, every human being who has ever lived is going to face Jesus Christ. We must not forget that!

The world, and even the church, has become so psychologized that the idea of individuals having to face a Judgment is denied. Psychology teaches that man is not responsible for his actions, but that such responsibility rests in his environment or others. The Bible teaches the very opposite.

There are Books in Heaven (Rev. 20:12), in which is recorded everything that anyone does, good and bad. The bad can be erased in totality, if one will accept Christ as one's Saviour and Lord. Otherwise, it remains, with the individual having to answer in the coming Great White Throne Judgment.

If every person believed that, would we have a different world? Undoubtedly we would, but the truth is, there are very few who believe what the Bible says regarding this coming day.

When Felix heard this given by Paul, the Bible says that Felix *"trembled."* The word *"trembled"* in the Greek is *"emphobos,"* and means, *"to fear, to be alarmed, to be affrighted and that exceedingly."* In other words, Felix came under powerful Holy Spirit Conviction.

His answer to the Lord and to Paul was, *"go your way for this time; when I have a convenient season, I will call for you."* That convenient season never came, as it never comes for most. The Scripture plainly tells us that *"today is the day of Salvation."*

And now we learn that Felix was holding Paul, despite the fact of knowing that he was innocent of all these charges, hoping that someone would pay him a large sum of money for Paul's release. He didn't realize that Paul would never adopt any illicit method to secure his liberty, nor in any case would he burden those who loved him to request of them a ransom to give to this man.

And then the Scripture tells us that *"he sent for Paul the oftener, and communed with him."* As we said in the notes, he came so close, but yet, was so far off. Unless he made his peace with God at a later date, and we pray he did, but barring that, at this moment, he is in Hell, and, no doubt, he has remembered every single word of these conversations, wishing that he had just one more opportunity to get right with God. But remember this:

There are no unbelievers in Hell, and at the same time, there is no Salvation in Hell!

At a later time we find that Porcius Festus became Governor in the place of Felix. To ingratiate himself with the Jews, he *"left Paul bound."*

PAUL BEFORE FESTUS

"Now when Festus was come into the Province *(refers to him taking the position of Governor at Caesarea in the place of Felix)*, after three days he ascended from Caesarea to Jerusalem *(according to topography, he ascended; but according to geography, he descended; Jerusalem is about 2,500 feet above sea level, while Caesarea, situated on the coast, is just a few feet above sea level)*.

"Then the High Priest and the Chief of the Jews informed him against Paul, and besought him *(they began to besiege Festus with repeated accusations against Paul)*,

"And desired favour against him, that he would send for him to Jerusalem, laying wait in the way to kill him *(proclaims the idea, as thought by some, that this was to be done by the same forty men who had originally made the vow to kill Paul [Acts 23:16])*.

"But Festus answered, that Paul should be kept at Caesarea, and that he himself would depart shortly *thither (seems to imply that the Governor had about had his fill of the hatred and hypocrisy of these Jews)*.

"Let them therefore, said he, which among you are able, go down with *me*, and accuse this man, if there be any wickedness in him *(in effect, he is saying Paul is a Roman citizen and must be treated as such)*" (Acts 25:1-5).

ALL RELIGION CAN DO IS KILL

At least one of the reasons that Felix was replaced by Festus is a riot of sorts which occurred in Caesarea. The city being half Jew and half Greek, there was always a perpetual feud between them. The Jewish population was large and wealthy, and since Herod had done so much for Caesarea, they claimed it as their own.

It was quite true that, but for Herod, Caesarea would never have been heard of in history. Its sole utility, at least that which made it what it was, consisted of a harbor, which had been constructed at enormous cost of money and labor, but yet, which was greatly needed. The Greeks maintained that it was their town, seeing that it had been founded by Strato and called *"Strato's Tower,"* until Herod had altered the name to Caesarea, in effect, naming it after Caesar.

At a point in time, the Greeks and the Jews began to quarrel openly in the marketplace until fighting erupted, with Felix then appearing with a cohort of soldiers, and then ordering the Jews to disperse. He was not instantly obeyed, and not having any fondness for the Jews, as well, he sided with the Gentile faction and turned his soldiers loose on the Jews. In fact, they killed many Jews that day. The Jews laid a formal complaint against Felix for his conduct, and he was called to Rome to answer these charges. What happened to him we do not know. At any rate, he was replaced by Festus, who it is believed was a more honorable ruler. He seemed to try to administer a real justice and did not stain his hands with bribes.

JERUSALEM

Almost immediately after arriving in Caesarea, he went directly to Jerusalem. It seems that one of the first questions he had to face was the mode of dealing with Paul. So, when he reached Jerusalem, the High Priest, along with other Jewish leaders, demanded the death of Paul. While there was a new High Priest, Ishmael Ben Phabi, still, he thirsted no less for the blood of the great Apostle. But they were to find that Festus was not a Governor who would bow to the whim of the Jews in order to win popularity. The Jews found that he could not be coerced into any direction he did not desire to take.

They strongly requested, even demanded of Festus, that Paul might be brought to Jerusalem, where he might be tried by the Sanhedrin. Actually, they had no plans at all for Paul to face the Sanhedrin once again, but that they would hire assassins to kill Paul between Caesarea and Jerusalem. It didn't take much for the new Governor to see through these reprobates, so he tells them he will take everything they have stated under advisement. Instead, he told these Jewish leaders, if they so desired, they could come to Caesarea and lay their charge against Paul face-to-face with the Apostle.

THE SAME CHARGES AGAINST PAUL

"And when he had tarried among them more than ten days, he went down unto Caesarea; and the next day sitting on the judgment seat commanded Paul to be brought *(this meant the Governor was calling for a new official trial; Festus could do this because Felix had never officially handed down a decision)*.

"And when he was come, the Jews which came down from Jerusalem stood round about *(evidently some Jews from Jerusalem had immediately come to Caesarea in order to testify against Paul)*, and laid many and grievous complaints against Paul, which they could not prove *(undoubtedly proclaims the same complaints they had registered some two years before; they charged that Paul had indeed violated Roman Law in some manner at which the next Verse hints, but which Luke did not specify)*.

"While he answered for himself, Neither against the Law of the Jews, neither against the Temple, nor yet against Caesar, have I offended any thing at all *(it seems they were claiming that Paul had instigated a new religion, which, if true, would have been against Roman Law)*.

"But Festus, willing to do the Jews a pleasure, answered Paul, and said, *(Festus feared these Jewish leaders, knowing that if they were willing to bring these types of false charges against Paul, they would not hesitate to do the same against him to Rome)*, **Will you go up to Jerusalem, and there be judged of these things before me?** *(This presents the compromise of the Governor)*" **(Acts 25:6-9).**

I HAVE NOT OFFENDED IN ANYTHING AT ALL

Almost immediately after Festus had arrived back at Caesarea, he called the case of Paul the Apostle to order. The Jews had not again hired a practice barrister to help them, so the trial quickly degenerated into a scene of clamor, in which Paul simply met the many accusations against him with calm denials. The Jews claimed that Paul was guilty of heresy, which pertained to being a follower of Christ, and sacrilege, once again claiming that he had defiled the Temple, and treason, claiming that he had broken Rome's laws. But once again, they did not produce a single witness who would testify to these accusations, so Paul had no need to do more than to recount the facts.

It quickly became obvious to Festus that there was not a grain of truth in these Jewish accusations, meaning that Paul was not guilty of anything approaching to a capital crime. Festus, unlike Felix, wished to put an end to this thing for nothing was more odious to the dignity of an educated Roman than the scowling faces of these despised Jews. So Festus, trying to settle the situation, asked Paul whether he was willing to go up to Jerusalem and be tried before the Sanhedrin under his protection.

Paul knew very well that he had far more chance of justice at the hands of the Romans than at the hands of these Jews. In fact, the crimes of these reprobates were now dragging Jerusalem ever closer to her destruction. Every Gentile tribunal before which he had stood, Gallio at Corinth, the city leaders of Ephesus, the Roman Tribune Lysias, and then Felix, all had found him innocent of these charges brought against him

ever by the Jews. To fall into their hands was to invite death. He did not see and, in fact, could not see at all that this was the Will of God. So he decided, no doubt, after praying about the matter very, very much, to change the course completely.

CAESAR

"Then said Paul, I stand at Caesar's judgment seat, where I ought to be judged *(proclaims the Apostle seeing through this ploy, and knowing that if he went to Jerusalem, the Jews would find some way to kill him)*: to the Jews have I done no wrong, as you very well know *(proclaims that which is true, and which Paul hammers home, and rightly so!)*.

"For I be an offender, or have committed any thing worthy of death, I refuse not to die *(in effect, Paul is attempting not so much to save his life, but rather to declare his innocence)*: but if there be none of these things whereof these accuse me, no man may deliver me unto them. I appeal unto Caesar *(means it is the Will of God for him to stand before Caesar, and not the Jews)*.

"Then Festus, when he had conferred with the Council, answered *(refers to the legal advisory Council of the Governor, which evidently advised Festus that he acquiesce to Paul because of Roman Law)*, Have you appealed unto Caesar? unto Caesar shall you go" (Acts 25:10-12).

THE APPEAL

As a Roman citizen Paul had one special privilege—the right to appeal to Caesar, which privilege he seized upon. In effect, he was saying, *"I am standing at Caesar's tribunal, and not before the Sanhedrin. It is before Caesar that I ought to be judged, not others."*

He probably turned to Festus and said, in the words of Farrar, *"Even you, O Festus know full well that I never in any respect wronged the Jews. If I am an offender, and have committed any capital crime, it is not against them, but against the Empire; and if I am found guilty, I do not refuse to die. But if all the accusations which these bring against me are nothing, no one can sacrifice me to them as a favor."[2]*

It seems that the appeal by Paul came as a surprise to Festus. He did not expect to have his jurisdiction superseded by an *"appeal"* to a superior on the very first occasion that he took his seat on the tribunal.

Festus took the matter to his Council, evidently highly placed Romans who served in this capacity, as to whether the appeal was legally admissible or not. Even though any Roman citizen had the right to appeal, still, just any appeal for any cause would not be recognized, as should be obvious. Apparently, it didn't take long for a decision to be reached by the Council, to which Festus, after a moment's thought, acquiesced. He turned to Paul and stated, *"Have you appealed unto Caesar? unto Caesar shall you go."*

AGRIPPA AND FESTUS

"And after certain days king Agrippa *(pertains to the second son of Herod Agrippa who is mentioned in Acts 12:1)* and Bernice *(she was Agrippa's sister)* came unto Caesarea to salute Festus *(to pay their respects to the new Governor)*.

"And when they had been there many days, Festus declared Paul's cause unto the king, saying *(Festus thought Herod had a better understanding of Jewish Law than he did, which was true)*, There is a certain man left in bonds by Felix *(speaks of Paul)*:

"About whom, when I was at Jerusalem, the Chief Priests and the Elders of the Jews informed *me*, desiring *to have* judgment against him *(means that the Jews did not really want another trial for Paul, but rather that Festus accept their accusations at face value and pronounce the death sentence on Paul without any further trial or investigation).*

"**To whom I answered, It is not the manner of the Romans to deliver any man to die, before that he which is accused have the accusers face to face** *(presents this heathen as having a better sense of justice than the religious Jews who, of all people, should have known better)*, **and have licence to answer for himself concerning the crime laid against him** *(portrays the justice of the heathen Government of Rome, with Israel, who was supposed to be God's chosen, having no justice whatsoever).*

"**Therefore, when they were come hither, without any delay on the morrow I sat on the judgment seat** *(proclaims, as is obvious, the recounting of this episode to King Agrippa by Festus)*, **and commanded the man to be brought forth**" **(Acts 25:13-17).**

FESTUS SENSES THAT THERE IS MORE TO PAUL THAN MEETS THE EYE

Only a day or two had elapsed after the appeal by Paul when Agrippa II, the last of the Herods, and his sister Bernice came down to Caesarea to pay their respects to the new Governor. In fact, the power of Agrippa, the King of this area, depended not at all on popular support but simply and solely on the will of the Emperor. In fact, he was merely an instrument to keep order for the Romans, and it was essential for him to remain on good terms with them.

During the visit of this pair, Festus took the opportunity to refer to the perplexing case of Paul.

In the words of Farrar, Festus said, *"He told Agrippa of the fury which seemed to inspire the whole Jewish people at the mention of his name, and of the futile results of the trial just concluded."*[3] So, Festus now recounts the activities of that trial and of the demands of the Jews, and how that Paul had appealed to Caesar.

JESUS

"Against whom when the accusers stood up, they brought none accusation of such things as I supposed *(he really didn't understand their accusations)*:

"But had certain questions against him of their own superstition *(he was actually saying, 'against him of their own religion')*, and of One Jesus *(shows that Paul, in his defense, readily preached Jesus to the Governor and these Jewish leaders; in this account as given by Luke, we only have a capsule sketch)*, which was dead, Whom Paul affirmed to be alive *(proclaims the Resurrection which, in its manner, was the most astounding Miracle the world had ever known; Jesus had been Crucified; the Roman records could show this, and Festus could check if he so desired; as well, Roman soldiers made the Tomb secure; all of this, as stated, was a matter of record)*.

"And because I doubted of such manner of questions *(he was at a loss as to how to decide such questions)*, I asked *him* whether he would go to Jerusalem, and there be judged of these matters.

"But when Paul had appealed to be reserved unto the hearing of Augustus *(Nero)*, I commanded him to be kept till I might send him to Caesar" (Acts 25:18-21).

JESUS IS ALIVE

Festus continues as he claims to Agrippa that ever how much the Jews tried to misrepresent the real questions at issue, it was clear that they turned on Mosaic technicalities, with which he was not familiar and, as well, *"on One Jesus Whom the Jews claim to be dead, but Whom Paul alleged to be alive."* Concerning these matters of Mosaic technicalities, Festus would have had no knowledge of such. And of the One called *"Jesus,"* of this he had no knowledge at all.

Little did this Governor realize as to the significance of all these proceedings. And yet, I think he sensed something about Paul that was different than anything he had ever encountered. However, there is no record that Festus talked with Paul privately as had Felix. And I think, if such had been the case, Luke would have reported it.

Of all the things going on in the world of that day, little did this Governor, in this obscure Province of Judaea, know and understand that what was taking place in his court was the single most important thing on the face of the Earth. Rome was very important in that day, actually, an Empire such as had never been; however, it is mentioned in the Sacred Text only in its relationship to those who knew the Lord, and mostly with Paul.

KING AGRIPPA

"Then Agrippa said unto Festus, I would also hear the man myself. To morrow, said he *(Festus)*, you shall hear him.

"And on the morrow, when Agrippa was come, and Bernice, with great pomp, and was entered into the place of hearing, with the Chief Captains, and principal men of the city *(the King and his sister took this opportunity to let the city of Caesarea see their glory)*, at Festus' commandment Paul was brought forth *(it is suggested that Luke was in attendance this particular day as well, and was a witness of all the proceedings)*.

"And Festus said, King Agrippa, and all men which are here present with us, you see this man, about whom all the multitude of the Jews have dealt with me, both at Jerusalem, and *also* here, crying that he ought not to live any longer.

"But when I found that he had committed nothing worthy of death, and that he himself has appealed to Augustus, I have determined to send him.

"Of whom I have no certain thing to write unto my

lord *(once again refers to Nero; the Governor is com-
plaining that he is going to send a man to Caesar for a
trial, but he has no idea what to tell the Emperor he has
done).* **Wherefore I have brought him forth before you,
and especially before you, O king Agrippa, that, after
examination had, I might have somewhat to write** *(he
hopes the King, being a Jew, might be able to define the
charges a little better).*

   **"For it seems to me unreasonable to send a prisoner,
and not withal to signify the crimes *laid* against him**
*(the Roman world found no fault in Paul, even as Pilate
found no fault in Jesus; but the world of religion did, as the
world of religion always does!)*" **(Acts 25:22-27).**

WHAT HAS HE DONE?

   After Festus relates all of this to Agrippa, the King quickly
states that he would like to hear this person himself. Actually,
this is exactly what Festus wanted, hoping that Agrippa could
define Paul's crimes because, as of yet, the Governor had
not heard anything that resembled a crime. So, the next day
Agrippa and his sister would hear Paul in person.

   Actually, this was not a trial that was conducted because
Agrippa was without judicial authority, and, as well, even the
authority of the Governor had been cut short by the appeal. It
was just to be an audience of curiosity.

   It seems that Festus ordered everything to be prepared for
the occasion and, in fact, invited all the chief officers of the army,
and even the principal inhabitants of the town. The Herods were
always in favor of a good show, and Festus would gratify them
by a grand processional display. In other words, the glitter and
the glamour of Caesarea would be represented, and to be sure,
Festus, along with Agrippa and Bernice, would take advantage
of the occasion to present themselves in all their pomp and glory.

   When Agrippa came into this room, did it come to his
mind of his great-grandfather Herod, who had murdered all

the innocent babies in his efforts to kill baby Jesus? Or, what about his great-uncle Antipas, who had murdered John the Baptist? Or, did he think of his father Agrippa I and the execution of James the Elder?

Also, did he remember that each of them had died soon after their terrible crimes against the Lord or had been disgraced soon after? It is doubtful at that moment that those things entered his mind.

Farrar asked, *"Did he realize how closely, how unwittingly, the faith in that 'One Jesus' had been linked with the destinies of his house? Did the pomp of today remind him of the pomp some sixteen years earlier, when his much more powerful father had stood in the theatre, with the sunlight blazing on the tissued silver of his robe, and the people shouting that he was a god, with him dying very soon thereafter a most miserable death? Did none of the dark memories of the place overshadow him as he entered that former palace of his race? It is very unlikely."*[4]

Self-importance probably absorbed the mind of this King, and then Paul is brought in. He would have looked with curiosity on this poor, worn, and shackled prisoner who was led in at his command.

Festus called the meeting to order by proclaiming how the Jews wanted Paul dead, and how that he personally could not see that he had committed any capital crime. Since he was a Roman citizen and had, in fact, appealed to Caesar, it was necessary that he state the crimes the man had committed. It didn't seem sensible to send someone to Caesar and not spell out that of which he was accused. So, he says to King Agrippa that perhaps after he had heard Paul, he could make clearer to Festus what this man's crime was or, at least throw some light on the subject, giving Festus some intelligence about the matter. He was to be disappointed!

PAUL'S DEFENSE

"Then Agrippa said unto Paul, You are permitted

to speak for yourself. Then Paul stretched forth the hand, and answered for himself:

"I think myself happy, king Agrippa, because I shall answer for myself this day before you touching all the things whereof I am accused of the Jews:

"Especially *because I know* you to be expert in all customs and questions which are among the Jews *(this was not offered as flattery; in fact, Agrippa's father, King Agrippa I, was zealous for the Jewish Law up to almost the end of his life)*: wherefore I beseech you to hear me patiently.

"My manner of life from my youth, which was at the first among mine own nation at Jerusalem, know all the Jews *(concerns Paul being immersed in Jewish Ritual and Law from the time he was old enough to begin his advanced studies, which was probably about twelve years of age)*;

"Which knew me from the beginning *(means simply that what he is saying can be easily proven)*, if they would testify, that after the most straitest sect of our religion I lived a Pharisee *(pertains to this group being the most strict in doctrines and moral practices)*.

"And now I stand and am judged for the hope of the promise made of God unto our Fathers *(this 'hope' was the Messiah, the Lord Jesus Christ Whom the Jews rejected)*:

"Unto which *promise* our Twelve Tribes, instantly serving God day and night, hope to come. For which hope's sake, king Agrippa, I am accused of the Jews *(many of the Jews were looking forward to the fulfillment of the Prophecies regarding the coming Messiah; the great dissension was over Jesus)*" (Acts 26:1-7).

PAUL'S SALUTATION

As Paul stood there that day in front of Festus, Agrippa,

his sister, and many more notables of the city of Caesarea, in a sense, how out of place he must have looked. The Scripture plainly says that Agrippa and his sister have entered the proceedings *"with great pomp."* I'm sure that all there that day had heard of Paul, with his detractors doing all they could to disgrace him, and to be sure, they would have had little opportunity to hear that which was correct. At any rate, whatever it was they had heard aroused their curiosity.

Someone such as Paul, that is, if there could ever be anyone such as Paul, always arouses the curiosity of the world. They know something is different, greatly different, but they have no idea as to what it is.

Paul was in chains that day as he stood before this crowd.

After all the formalities had been dealt with, then Agrippa turned to Paul and told him, *"You are permitted to speak for yourself."*

Evidently told that Agrippa wanted to hear him, Paul addressed his first remarks to the King. Apparently, he knew that Agrippa had at least a working knowledge of Jewish Law, i.e., *"the Law of Moses."* And yet, Paul also knew that Agrippa had absolutely no knowledge whatsoever of the One Who had given the Law. His approach to Agrippa and those who were there that day was different than had been his approach to Festus, because he knew that Festus had little knowledge, if any at all, concerning the Law of Moses. But, as stated, Agrippa did!

Paul began by proclaiming the fact that he had lived as a Pharisee, of which the King would have been greatly familiar, and that he adhered to the Law of Moses in every respect, and in every way, to the best of his ability.

And then he mentioned *"the hope of the promise made of God unto our Fathers,"* which, of course, pertained to the Messiah. And now, that's where the difficulty is.

Paul is claiming, as is obvious, that Jesus Christ, in fact, was and is that Hope and Promise. The Jews as a nation had rejected that and, in fact, had crucified Christ. And because

Paul grandly proclaimed the fact that Jesus Christ is the Messiah of Israel, infuriated the Jews to no end, especially considering that Paul had once been the greatest enemy of *"that Way,"* which pertained to the Lord Jesus Christ, as to Who He was and is, the Son of the Living God, the Messiah of Israel, and What He did to redeem humanity, which pertained to the Cross.

The phrase that he used, *"I am accused of the Jews,"* pertained totally and completely to the dissension regarding Jesus Christ. The nation of Israel was not content to let the followers of Christ go their way. While the religious leadership of Israel went their way, they felt they had to snuff out every voice that was lifted in favor of Christ. But again, that's exactly what Paul had once done. But now the Lord has made Paul the greatest champion of Christ, the one who proclaimed Him as possibly no other.

JESUS OF NAZARETH

"Why should it be thought a thing incredible with you, that God should raise the dead? *(Israel's history was one of Miracles, so the dead being raised, as extraordinary as it is, should not come as a surprise.)*

"I verily thought with myself, that I ought to do many things contrary to the Name of Jesus of Nazareth *(presents Paul taking himself back to his dreadful time of unbelief)*.

"Which thing I also did in Jerusalem: and many of the saints did I shut up in prison, having received authority from the Chief Priests; and when they were put to death, I gave my voice against *them (we know of Stephen; however, there may have been more)*.

"And I punished them oft in every synagogue, and compelled *them* to blaspheme *(should have been translated, 'and attempted to compel them to blaspheme,' because the Greek Text implies that he was not successful in this effort)*; **and being exceedingly mad against them, I persecuted** *them* **even unto strange cities** *(indicates that Damascus was not the only city, other than Jerusalem, where Paul was practicing his deadly wares).*

"**Whereupon as I went to Damascus with authority and commission from the Chief Priests** *(intending to continue his persecution in that city)*" **(Acts 26:8-12).**

THE PAUL THAT ONCE WAS

As Paul speaks, not at all glossing over the terrible crimes he had committed before his Damascus Road experience, it becomes quickly obvious that he is completely at ease. As one reads the Text, one can instantly tell that the Lord anointed him mightily. Even though he was in chains, so to speak, held as a prisoner, still it is overly obvious that Paul is the man. Everyone there, including the Governor and the King, is subservient to him. And yet, we have to understand that in the way that it is meant to be understood. This is not proud ego of which I speak, but rather the place and the position of the lowliest Child of God, which is higher than any other office or position that the world has to offer. God looks at this world in only two ways. In other words, there are two types of people in this world as far as He is concerned, the Redeemed and the unredeemed. He does not look at it regarding nationalities, the color of one's skin, etc., totally and completely rather as to whether the person is Born-Again or not. Those who aren't Born-Again have absolutely nothing to offer this world, but in actuality, constitute a drag upon its impulses. That's the reason that Jesus said of all Believers that we are the *"salt of the earth,"* and the *"light of the world"* (Mat. 5:13-16).

THE BORN-AGAIN EXPERIENCE

The Born-Again experience is not merely a change from one philosophy to another. It constitutes a miraculous change that takes place in the person's heart and life, and is done so instantly. Concerning this, Paul wrote:

"If any man *be* in Christ *(Saved by the Blood)*, *he is* a new creature *(a new creation)*: old things are passed away *(what we were before Salvation)*; behold, all things are become new. *(The old is no longer useable, with everything given to us now by Christ as 'new')*" (II Cor. 5:17).

These people gathered that day to hear Paul realized not at all the opportunity they then had. There is no record that any of them gave their hearts to Christ, even though they had abundant opportunity. Now, as I dictate these notes, nearly 2,000 years have passed. If none of them eventually came to Christ, and there is no record they did, they have been in Hell for these last 2,000 years. They have relived this scene with Paul over and over again, but as we have previously stated, while there are no unbelievers in Hell, at the same time, there is no Salvation in Hell either.

THE TESTIMONY OF HIS CONVERSION

"At midday, O king, I saw in the way a Light from Heaven *(proclaims one of, if not, the most dramatic Conversions the world has ever known)*, above the brightness of the Sun, shining round about me and them which journeyed with me *(this was the Glory of Jesus Christ)*.

"And when we were all fallen to the earth *(the Power of God was so strong that Paul and all his associates with him fell to the ground)*, I heard a Voice speaking unto me, and saying in the Hebrew tongue *(actually speaks of all hearing the Voice, but only Paul knowing what was said [Acts 9:7])*, Saul, Saul *(his Hebrew name)*, why do you persecute Me? *(This proclaims the fact that when we persecute those who belong to the Lord, we, in fact, persecute the Lord.)* *it is* hard for you to kick against the pricks *(proclaims a common idiom of that day and even now; in other words, you will only succeed in hurting yourself; you will not stop the Plan of God).*

"And I said, Who are You, Lord? *(This proclaims the fact that Paul knew he was speaking to Deity.)* **And He said, I am Jesus Whom you persecute** *(proclaims the Lord using the Name Paul hated the most—Jesus)*" **(Acts 26:13-15).**

A LIGHT FROM HEAVEN

When Paul spoke before Felix and the Jewish leaders approximately two years earlier, there is no record that he mentioned his Damascus Road experience, but now he goes into detail. Actually, the account of his Conversion was given some three times (Acts 9:3-9; 22:6-11; 26:13-18).

I wonder what the thoughts and ideas were of these individuals who heard Paul give this account this particular day? As we shall see, we know somewhat as to what Festus was thinking.

In this account, Paul relates several things. Some of them are:

• That he saw a Light from Heaven brighter than the Sun, which was the Glory of the Lord Jesus Christ.

• He felt the Power of this event which, in fact, knocked him, plus all who were with him, to the earth.

• Beyond the shadow of a doubt, the Voice speaking to him identified itself as *"Jesus Whom you persecute."*

One thing is certain, Paul was instantly changed as a result of that Vision and, in fact, would never be the same again.

TO MAKE YOU A MINISTER

"But rise, and stand upon your feet *(very similar to what the Lord had said to Job many years before [Job 38:3])*: **for I have appeared unto you for this purpose**

(specifies that the Lord has a very important work for Paul to do), **to make you a Minister and a witness both of these things which you have seen, and of those things in the which I will appear unto you** *(in fact, it would be to Paul that the Lord would give the meaning of the New Covenant, which, in effect, was the meaning of the Cross [II Cor. 12:1-12])*;

"**Delivering you from the people** *(refers to the Jews)*, **and *from* the Gentiles, unto whom now I send you** *(the Lord would not allow the death of the Apostle until he had finished his Mission; his primary Mission was to take the Gospel to the Gentiles, which he did)*,

"**To open their eyes, *and* to turn *them* from darkness to light, and *from* the power of Satan unto God, that they may receive forgiveness of sins, and inheritance among them which are Sanctified by Faith that is in Me** *(the Apostle pointed out that man is blind, enslaved, impure, immoral, poverty-stricken, and unholy, but he can receive sight, liberty, forgiveness, true wealth and holiness upon the Principle of Faith in Christ and what Christ has done at the Cross)*" **(Acts 26:16-18).**

I SEND YOU UNTO THE GENTILES

Paul now launched into the full impact of the Vision he had had on the Road to Damascus. He does not mince words at all, plainly proclaiming the fact that Jesus had appeared to him, had spoken with him, and had identified Himself by that Name that he had once hated, the Name of Jesus. He goes on to relate what the Lord said to him, how he would minister to the Gentiles, which, of course, was totally and completely out of sorts for a Jew to do such. Of course, most, if not all, to whom he was speaking that day were Gentiles. When he plainly delivers this word, and by the Power of the Holy Spirit, without a doubt the words hit home and powerfully so.

He, in effect, tells them that despite their place and position, and despite their riches and wealth, still, they are dwelling in darkness, actually under the power of Satan. But then he tells them that most definitely they can *"receive forgiveness of sins,"* and, as well, they can become a part of the Family of God, but only by accepting Jesus Christ as their Saviour and their Lord.

THE HEAVENLY VISION

"Whereupon, O king Agrippa, I was not disobedient unto the Heavenly Vision *(Paul had faithfully carried out that which the Lord had called him to do)*:

"But showed first unto them of Damascus *(he preached Christ in Damascus immediately after being Saved)*, and at Jerusalem, and throughout all the coasts of Judaea *(pertains to Paul going to Jerusalem immediately after Damascus, and then later to other areas of Judaea)*, and *then* to the Gentiles *(speaks of the far greater majority of his Ministry, even up to this particular time)*, that they should repent and turn to God, and do works meet for repentance *(turn from the heathen idols to God)*.

"For these causes the Jews caught me in the Temple, and went about to kill *me (Paul is saying that the Jews do not hate him because of their stated reasons, but rather because of his preaching Jesus)*.

"Having therefore obtained help of God, I continue unto this day, witnessing both to small and great *(proclaims the fact that God has sustained him through some very difficult times)*, saying none other things than those which the Prophets and Moses did say should come *(Paul claims total Scripturality for his Message, which it certainly was)*:

"That Christ *(the Messiah)* should suffer *(means that he would die; in other words, that was the reason He came [Isa., Chpt. 53])*, *and* that he should be the first who should rise from the dead *(Jesus is the 'Firstfruits' of the Resurrection and, therefore, the guarantee of the Resurrection of all Believers [I Cor. 15:1-23; Rev. 1:5])*, **and should show light unto the people, and to the Gentiles** *(refers to the Lord Jesus Christ as being the only 'Light,' and for all people)*" **(Acts 26:19-23).**

PAUL PREACHED CHRIST

Paul first of all proclaims an account of the Vision which the Lord had given him on the Road to Damascus. And now he states that *"I was not disobedient unto the Heavenly Vision."* He goes on to say how that immediately he began to preach Christ in the synagogues in Damascus, and after that, Jerusalem, and then in certain areas of Judaea. He then reiterates how that he had taken the Message, even as he had been compelled to do, to the Gentiles. The Message was simple, *"that they should repent and turn to God, and do works meet for repentance."* Now, in essence, he is saying, *"that is my crime,"* of course, which is no crime at all.

He then plainly says that this, preaching Christ and preaching to the Gentiles, is the reason the Jews want to kill him.

He then proclaims to King Agrippa that everything that he is doing is first of all given in the Law of God as given by Moses and continued in the Prophets.

In essence, he is saying that the entirety of the Old Testament points to Christ, Who would give His life on the Cross of Calvary, and that He should rise from the dead, Whose Sacrifice would be both for the Jews and the Gentiles.

WHY WHERE THE JEWS SO THREATENED BY THIS MESSAGE?

The answer is somewhat simple. Men sin, and then they seek to justify their sin.

Jesus fulfilled every Passage in the Old Testament as it

regarded the Messiah. Through Joseph, His foster Father, His Lineage went back to David through David's son, Solomon. Through Mary, His Lineage went back to David through another son, Nathan. So, His Lineage was perfect, even as any Jew could have ascertained by looking at the genealogies in the Temple. Furthermore, He performed untold numbers of Miracles, which could not be questioned. In fact, the Jews, even His most strident enemies, never refuted His Miracles, because it was so obvious that they were real. So they claimed that He was performing these Miracles by the power of Satan. Those who did that blasphemed the Holy Spirit. They were attributing the Works of God to Satan (Mat. 12:24-32). In effect, the religious leaders of Israel that day sealed the fate of their nation when they claimed that Jesus was performing these Miracles by the power of Satan, when He most definitely was performing them by the Power of God.

FESTUS

"And as he thus spoke for himself, Festus said with a loud voice, Paul, you are beside yourself; much learning does make you mad *(as a heathen, Festus could not understand as Agrippa could the great argument that the Atoning Death and Resurrection of the Messiah fulfilled the predictions of the Prophets, and were necessary in order to effect the Salvation of sinful men)*.

"But he said, I am not mad *(insane)*, most noble Festus; but speak forth the Words of Truth and soberness *(presents the only 'Truth' the Governor and others present had ever heard)*.

"For the king *(Agrippa)* knows of these things, before whom also I speak freely: for I am persuaded that none of these things are hidden from him; for this thing was not done in a corner *(King Agrippa most certainly knew of Jesus; it would have been impossible for him not to have known)*" (Acts 26:24-26).

THIS THING WAS NOT DONE IN A CORNER

King Agrippa, no doubt, knew of the things of which Paul spoke, and, as well, this King was the focus point of this meeting. But yet, Festus, the evidence tells us, listened with open-mouthed astonishment as Paul began to relate of the Visions and Revelations, and of the ancient Prophecies, and above all, of Jesus Who had been crucified, and yet, had risen from the dead and, in actuality, was Divine. Paul went on to state how that this One could forgive sins and take away the darkness of the Jews as well as the Gentiles. Festus had never heard anything like this, which meant, if it were true, this One of Whom Paul spoke was greater even than the Caesars. In effect, He was God.

All of a sudden, Festus breaks the stillness of the room, save for Paul's voice, and blurts out, *"Paul, you are beside yourself; much learning does make you mad."*

One can imagine the silence that filled the room upon this outburst, and even though it would have caused Paul to hesitate for a moment, he answers with a calm voice, *"I am not mad, most noble Festus; but speak forth the Word of Truth and soberness."*

He then quickly added, *"For the King knows of these things, before whom also I speak freely: for I am persuaded that none of these things are hidden from him; for this thing was not done in a corner."*

Paul knew that Agrippa had read Moses and the Prophets and had heard from multitudes of witnesses some, at least, of the facts to which Paul referred as it regarded Christ. I think it is safe to say that the King did not believe them in the slightest, but yet, he knew of them.

I keep coming back to the idea of the golden opportunity these individuals had to accept Christ, but at the same time, even as Paul had said elsewhere, *"For you see your calling, Brethren, how that not many wise men after the flesh, not many mighty, not many noble, are Called"* (I Cor. 1:26).

It is hard for the mighty and the noble to come to the place that they understand that they must come the same way to Christ as the uneducated, the poverty stricken, etc.

The Scripture doesn't say that none of this nature is called, but rather, *"not many."* Thank God, there are a few of this character who respond to the clarion Call of the Gospel.

THE ALTAR CALL

"King Agrippa, do you believe the Prophets? *(This presents an Altar Call being given to this King and his sister, which drilled straight to the heart of this profligate Jew.)* I know that you believe *(presents the Apostle answering for the King, which saved him from embarrassment)*.

"Then Agrippa said unto Paul, Almost you persuade me to be a Christian *(the Greek Text does not give any more indication of what the King actually said; it is not known if he was really moved and then said sincerely, 'you almost persuade me to be a Christian!' or 'do you think you can easily make me a Christian?!')*.

"And Paul said, I would to God, that not only you, but also all who hear me this day, were both almost, and altogether such as I am *(the Apostle, through and by the Gospel of Jesus Christ, proclaims the position of the Believer in Christ as being above any other office or position in the world)*, except these bonds *(this must have been a dramatic moment when, coupled with the majesty of his words, Paul lifts up his manacled hands forming a picture of arresting grandeur)*" **(Acts 26:27-29).**

ALMOST PERSUADED!

Paul immediately turned to the King, knowing that he had read at least some of the Prophets in the Old Testament, and then simply asked him, *"King Agrippa, do you believe the Prophets?"*

Paul didn't wait for an answer, quickly adding, *"I know that you believe."*

What did Paul mean by that statement?

He wasn't meaning, as would be overly obvious, that King Agrippa had believed to the Salvation of his soul, but rather that he believed the Prophets were from God, and what they spoke was the Word of God.

There are untold millions of people who believe that the Bible is the Word of God, but they are not Saved. Their believing, as King Agrippa, is only that they give mental assent, in other words, a superficial belief. To believe, as it regards Salvation, means that one believes that the Bible is the Word of God, and most of all, that *"Jesus Christ and Him Crucified"* is the story of the Bible, and that for one to be Saved, one must accept Him as Saviour and Lord. When one does that, he is instantly *"Born-Again"* (Jn. 3:3).

Then Agrippa said unto Paul, *"Almost you persuade me to be a Christian."* Not having any punctuation marks or even sentence endings in the Ancient Hebrew Text, it is not known if Agrippa was making a statement or asking a question. At any rate, I personally believe that the Holy Spirit through Paul's Message touched the heart of the King. Whatever actually was his response, the record is that he did not accept Jesus Christ, the One Paul preached, as his Saviour and Lord. Unless he made things right with God immediately before he died, he has been in Hell now for nearly 2,000 years. He has relived that statement or question, whatever it was, *"almost you persuade me to be a Christian,"* over and over. And, in fact, it is a statement or question that begs to be answered, but one must remember, first, second, third, and fourth chances, etc., are on this side of the grave. After death, there is no such thing as a purgatory, only Judgment.

Then Paul made the following statement not only to Agrippa but, as well, to Festus and to all who were in that room that day, *"I would to God, that not only you, but also all who hear me this day, were both almost, and altogether such as*

I am, except these bonds." And how true that was and is.

If one has the Lord Jesus Christ as one's Saviour, then whatever else it is he doesn't have is of little consequence. And, in fact, if one has everything else, all the riches of the world, all the acclaim, grandeur, and glory, but doesn't have the Lord Jesus Christ as his Saviour, then what has it profited him?

THIS MAN DOES NOTHING WORTHY OF DEATH OR OF BONDS

"And when he had thus spoken, the King rose up, and the Governor, and Bernice, and they who sat with them *(they did not want to hear anymore, so they rose and thus closed the audience, and their opportunity for Eternal Life)*:

"And when they were gone aside, they talked between themselves, saying, This man does nothing worthy of death or of bonds *(they had been brought face-to-face with themselves, and above all, with God; and as such, they would never be the same again, even though they had rejected the appeal and the plea)*.

"Then said Agrippa unto Festus, This man might have been set at liberty, if he had not appealed unto Caesar *(implies that the appeal had already been registered, and now must be carried out; behind it all, the Lord wanted the Apostle to go to Rome)*" (Acts 26:30-32).

THE WILL OF THE LORD

Whatever those in the room that day saw as it regarded Paul, they were most certainly made to realize that this was indeed no common prisoner. One who could speak as he had spoken, and, of course, they had no knowledge whatsoever of the Anointing of the Holy Spirit, still, they knew there was something about this man that was different. How could anyone stand manacled in chains, raise his arm to the clank of that chain, and state with a straight face that he wished everybody in the world was exactly as he was, with the exception of the bonds! And to be sure, when he said that word, it was not merely the clever word of an argument but something altogether different. In other words, even though they all rejected it, or so it seems, they knew beyond the shadow of a doubt that something here was different.

Whatever way they regarded Paul, they had to come to the conclusion that he was in no sense a criminal.

Agrippa, by rising from his seat, gave the signal for breaking up the meeting. The others rose at the same time, and as this assembly dispersed, they were heard remarking on all sides that Paul was undeserving of death or even of imprisonment. Farrar said, *"Agrippa was far too little of a Pharisee, and far too much of a man of the world, not to see that mere freedom of thought could not be, and ought not to be, suppressed by external violence."* He went on to say, *"The proceedings of that day probably saved Paul's life for several years afterwards. Festus since his own opinion, on grounds of Roman justice, was so entirely confirmed from the Jewish point of view by the Protector of the Temple, could hardly fail to send to Nero a ringing declaration which freely exonerated the prisoner from every legal charge; and even if Jewish intrigues were put in play against him, Nero could not condemn to death the man who Felix, and Lysias, and Festus, and Agrippa, and even the Jewish Sanhedrin, in the only trial of the case which they had held, had united in announcing innocent of any capital crime."*[5]

Of course, the Sanhedrin wanted Paul dead, but in the trial before Felix, they were able to bring no charge against him at all that was of criminal intent.

> *"Jesus, Saviour, pilot me,*
> *"Over life's tempestuous sea;*
> *"Unknown waves around me roll,*
> *"Hiding rocks and treacherous shoal;*
> *"Chart and compass come from Thee,*

"Jesus, Saviour, pilot me."

"As a mother stills her child,
"You can hush the ocean wild.
"Boisterous waves obey Your Will,
"When You say to them 'Be still!'
"Wondrous Sovereign of the sea;
"Jesus, Saviour, pilot me."

"When at last I near the shore,
"And the fearful breakers roar,
"Between me and the peaceful rest,
"Then, while leaning on Your Breast,
"May I hear You say to me;
"'Fear not, I will pilot thee.'"

PAUL

THE APOSTLE

CHAPTER TWELVE

Paul Sails For Rome

PAUL SAILS FOR ROME

"And when it was determined that we *(Luke is still with Paul)* should sail into Italy *(the time has now arrived when Paul will now go to Rome)*, they delivered Paul and certain other prisoners unto *one* named Julius, a Centurion of Augustus' band *(this was an elite 'band' directly responsible to the Emperor)*.

"And entering into a ship of Adramyttium, we launched, meaning to sail by the coasts of Asia; *one* Aristarchus, a Macedonian of Thessalonica, being with us *(proclaims another of Paul's converts being with him along with Luke; consequently, Festus allowed Paul two traveling associates [Acts 20:4])*.

"And the next *day* we touched at Sidon *(a port about seventy miles north of Caesarea).* And Julius courteously entreated Paul, and gave *him* liberty to go unto his friends to refresh himself *(Paul and his associates were allowed to stay with these people in Sidon until the ship sailed; this shows how much trust the Centurion placed in Paul)*.

"And when we had launched from thence *(from Sidon)*, we sailed under Cyprus, because the winds were contrary.

"And when we had sailed over the sea of Cilicia and Pamphylia, we came to Myra, *a city* of Lycia.

"And there the Centurion found a ship of Alexandria sailing into Italy; and he put us therein *(they changed ships)*.

"And when we had sailed slowly many days, and scarce were come over against Cnidus, the wind not suffering us, we sailed under Crete, over against Salmone *(the winds were not favorable, so they were not making good time)*;

"And, hardly passing it, came unto a place which is called The Fair Havens; near whereunto was the city *of* **Lasea.** *(There was no town at Fair Havens for them to replenish their stores, with Lasea being about five miles distant)*" **(Acts 27:1-8).**

THE WAYS OF THE LORD

During the winter months, the way the winds blew in that part of the world, travel by sea was all but impossible. In fact, on September 24, which that year was the Great Day of Atonement, the Jewish season for navigation was now over. In other words, they didn't try to sail after that time. However, the Gentiles did not regard the sea as closed until November 11. So, with that thought in mind, somewhere around September 1, Paul, along with Luke and Aristarchus, set sail for Rome under Roman protection. While Rome, considering that he was a prisoner, would pay for Paul's passage, whatever the amount of money may have been, Luke and Aristarchus had to provide their own funds. Quite possibly the Believers at Caesarea had helped with this expense. Also, it is understandable that Festus allowed Luke and Aristarchus to be companions of Paul, which they were during the great part of his Roman imprisonment. They, no doubt, were passengers, not prisoners and, as stated, they had to pay their own expenses.

It is most certain that when it was determined that Paul would be sent to Rome to stand before Caesar, Luke and Aristarchus made plans to be with him. No doubt, the Lord instituted this event and, as would be obvious, they were a great help to Paul. Without them an already difficult journey would have been made worse.

JULIUS

The Scripture tells us that Festus, *"delivered Paul and certain other prisoners unto one named Julius, a Centurion of Augustus' band."* This man would prove to be a great friend to Paul, which again, no doubt, the Lord instituted.

Julius was a Centurion, which means he was in charge of one hundred soldiers. It is doubtful that this entire cohort accompanied him. More than likely he selected eight or ten for the journey.

The *"Augustus band"* was, if the title is true to form, a prestigious group. The one hundred soldiers in this group would have come from the most distinguished Roman regiments in order to serve as the bodyguard for the Caesar. At times, however, they were sent out on very special missions.

It is believed that Julius was sent to Caesarea upon the arrival of Festus as the new Governor. This Province over which Festus was in charge was one of the wealthiest in the entirety of the imperial provinces, but yet, one of the most troublesome.

It is believed that quite possibly this Julius may very well have been Julius Priscus who afterward rose to the splendid position of one of the two Prafects of the Praetorians. As stated, we see enough of him during this voyage to lead us to believe that he was a sensible, honorable, and kindly man. At least, that was the side of his character that he showed to Paul.

It is almost positive that he was in the meeting when Paul addressed Agrippa with all the notables of Caesarea, and could very well have been moved greatly by Paul's Message that day.

ROMAN SOLDIERS

In these types of situations, Roman soldiers were responsible with their own lives for the security of their prisoners. In other words, if a prisoner escaped, the soldier who allowed him to do so, or under whose watch he escaped, would be executed. So, to make certain that such did not happen, or seldom happened, the prisoners, whomever they may have been, were kept safe by chaining them with a long light chain by the right wrist to the left wrist of soldiers, who relieved each other in turn. It's probably unlikely that this was done while they were on-board the ship, but at any other time, it most definitely was carried out.

It should be understood as to how trying it must have been to have no moment and no movement free, and to be fettered in such proximity, more than likely, to a soldier who would, the far greater majority of the time, have been coarse, vulgar, reprobate, etc.

No doubt, Festus was in a hurry for the ship to sail, for every day made the weather more uncertain and the voyage more perilous. So, Festus, more than likely, hurried Julius, to whom this commission was entrusted, to get the journey underway. While they would trade ships several times, the first was a coasting merchantman of the Mysian town of Adramyttium.

The voyage began without incident. The wind seemed to be favorable, and they sailed without incident to Sidon, a journey of approximately 70 miles. And then Julius, whom we have said was entrusted with this mission, allowed Paul, no doubt accompanied by Luke and Aristarchus, to go into Sidon without guards, which was probably for several days. It must be understood that a Roman Tribune, who, as stated, was responsible for these prisoners with his life, seldom allowed a prisoner to be released on his own cognizance. But, it is obvious that Julius so trusted Paul, so trusted the word of the Apostle, that he allowed the Apostle this privilege.

"TO REFRESH HIMSELF"

The heading, *"to refresh himself,"* probably gives some credence to the thought that Paul had not done well physically on the short trip just undertaken. Perhaps there had been seasickness or something of that nature. But, above all, to have this liberty given to him that he could be among Christian friends and not be chained to a Roman soldier, ever how long it was, no more than a few days, if that, had no problem at all proving itself to be a Godsend to the Apostle. Of course, Luke and Aristarchus would have been with him.

When they set sail from Sidon, from that day forward, the entire voyage became a succession of delays and accidents, which, after nearly two months of storm and danger, culminated in a hopeless shipwreck. Farrar said, *"No sooner had they left the harbor of Sidon than they encountered the baffling Etesian winds, which blow steadily from the northwest. This was an unlooked-for hindrance, because the Etesians usually cease to blow towards the end of August, and are succeeded by south winds, on which the captain of the merchantman had doubtless relied to waft him back to his port of Adramyttium."*[1] But it was not to be.

When they docked at Myra, the former capital of Lycia, they found a large Alexandrian wheat-ship, which could easily accommodate Paul and the other prisoners, along with the small cohort of soldiers. They then sailed for Cnidus. However, even though that was their intended destination, the wind would not allow them to put in at Cnidus, or to continue their direct voyage, which would have passed north of Crete. The only alternative left them was to make for Cape Salmone, at the eastern end of the island. But they found they could not make the Cape their destination, and because of adverse winds, they were obliged to put in at Fair Havens, *"near whereunto was the city of Lasea."*

MUCH HURT AND MUCH DAMAGE

"Now when much time was spent *(spoke of several days with still no favorable winds)*, and when sailing was now dangerous *(pertained to any time after September 14th)*, because the fast was now already past, Paul admonished *them (pertained to the Great Day of Atonement, and was actually a one day fast, which Paul and his two associates, no doubt, kept)*,

"And said unto them, Sirs, I perceive that this voyage will be with hurt and much damage, not only of the lading *(cargo)* and ship, but also of our lives *(presents that which the Lord had evidently already related to Paul)*.

"Nevertheless the Centurion believed the master and the owner of the ship, more than those things which were spoken by Paul *(they would find to their chagrin that they had chosen wrong)*.

"And because the Haven *(Fair Havens)* was not commodious to winter in, the more part advised to depart thence also, if by any means they might attain to Phenice, *and there* to winter; *which is* an haven of Crete, and lies toward the southwest and northwest *(pertains to a harbor which, in fact, was commodious, and where some imperial grain ships actually did tie up for the winter; it was about fifty miles west of Fair Havens)*.

"And when the south wind blew softly, supposing that they had attained *their* purpose, loosing *thence*, they sailed close by Crete *(pertains to a wind direction for which they had been waiting)*" (Acts 27:9-13).

THE THINGS WHICH WERE SPOKEN BY PAUL

Considering that Fair Havens was not desirable at all for a ship to be tied up for three or four months in a place so dreary and desolate, the opinion was that they would try to make Phenice, which afforded a very commodious harbor. Actually, the Scripture is somewhat peculiar in describing it as it *"lay toward the southwest and northwest."* This expression is given in this manner because this is the way that sailors saw it. Its two openings at the extremities of its sheltering island looked precisely in the opposite directions, namely, northeast and southeast. In fact, this harbor, which was on the south of Crete and was safe in all weathers, fronted a much larger town, which was a much better place if one had to spend several months there.

Understanding all of this, the Captain of the ship, and

Julius, the Roman Centurion, along with, no doubt, all the soldiers and other passengers, threw in their vote, although it could be dangerous, to make for Phenice.

Paul had, no doubt, been in prayer very much about this voyage, and at a point in time he stated what he believed the Lord had given to him. Some claim that this was only his opinion; however, the way he makes the statement leaves no doubt that the Lord had spoken to him. He said:

"Sirs, I perceive that this voyage will be with hurt and much damage, not only of the lading and ship, but also of our lives."

So, the Centurion had to make a choice.

The Captain of the ship and, as well, its owner had strongly opted for Phenice. Knowing that this man was a professional sailor, the Centurion accepted his advice and gave instructions that the ship was to weigh anchor, which would later prove to be much to his regret.

Almost immediately, a soft south wind sprang up, which was exactly what they needed. So, they set sail.

Considering the favorable wind that is now blowing, it is not known what was said about Paul's advice, if anything; however, at this stage it looked like the great Apostle was dead wrong. It was to prove to be otherwise.

THE STORM

"But not long after there arose against it a tempestuous wind, called **Euroclydon** *(this was a hurricane).*

"And when the ship was caught, and could not bear up into the wind, we let *her* drive *(means that the helmsman simply could not hold the wheel for the force of the wind; so he could do nothing but let the ship drive toward whatever the direction the wind wanted it to go).*

"And running under a certain island which is called **Clauda**, we had much work to come by the boat *(the 'boat' of which Luke speaks was a little skiff they were pulling, which was the custom then and remained so for* *many centuries; due to the storm, they had great difficulty getting this small boat on-board)*:

"**Which when they had taken up, they used helps, undergirding the ship** *(these were large ropes which were pulled under the ship and made sure, helping to hold the vessel together in the storm)*; **and, fearing lest they should fall into the quicksands, strake sail, and so were driven** *(this way they would be driven by the wind, but with few or no sails stretched at all; hopefully the wind would change before they were driven onto the rocks)*.

"**And we being exceedingly tossed with a tempest, the next** *day* **they lightened the ship** *(they had to throw certain things overboard)*;

"**And the third** *day* **we cast out with our own hands the tackling of the ship** *(pertains to the third day after leaving Clauda; they now threw overboard ship equipment, even that which was desperately needed)*.

"**And when neither sun nor stars in many days appeared, and no small tempest lay on** *us,* **all hope that we should be saved was then taken away** *(now all on-board knew that they should have listened to Paul)*" **(Acts 27:14-20).**

THE WORDS OF PAUL COME TRUE

They had not long enjoyed the favorable wind when almost immediately things changed. It was like with a siren song they were being lured to their destruction. They ran smack into the middle of a hurricane. As hurricane force hit them, the condition of the ship quickly became hopeless. It became utterly impossible for her to set any type of course. She could only go where the wind took her.

Farrar said, *"Happily the direction of the wind, and the fact – in which we see the clear Hand of Providence – that the storm had burst on them soon after they had rounded Cape Matala, and not a little later on their course, had saved them from being dashed upon the rocks and reefs, which lie more to the northwest between both Candia and Clauda."²* They were thankful for that, but still, their condition was quite desperate.

With the force of the wind hitting them, they were scared that the ship was going to literally break up. The only recourse for that was to undergird the ship as best they could, which they did by putting ropes under the prow and then pulling them to the middle of the vessel and binding them as tightly as possible. How much help that would give is anyone's guess, but perhaps, it would help a little.

Evidently the vessel had already started to break up and was seriously taking on water, despite the undergirding, the problem only increased. They then resorted to throwing everything overboard that wasn't nailed down, so to speak, in order to lighten the ship. Despite all of that, the situation looked about as bad as it could look, with the crew fearing that they would not escape with their lives. In other words, death was staring them in the face. But then, there came an extremely encouraging word from the man whose advice they should have taken to begin with, but didn't.

THE VISION

"But after long abstinence *(does not refer to a 'fast' as some claim, but rather that they hadn't had a prepared meal for some days)* Paul stood forth in the midst of them, and said, Sirs, you should have hearkened unto me, and not have loosed from Crete, and to have gained this harm and loss *(is not really meant as a reprimand by the Apostle, but rather to give foundation to what he is about to say).*

"And now I exhort you to be of good cheer: for there shall be no loss of *any man's* life among you, but of the ship *(plainly tells us that the ship will be lost with its cargo of wheat, but not a person will lose their life).*

"For there stood by me this night the Angel of God,

Whose I am, and Whom I serve *(the statements 'Whose I am,' 'Whom I serve,' and 'I believe God' [Vs. 25] form a noble confession of Faith)*,

"**Saying, Fear not, Paul** *(said in this manner because there had been fear in Paul's heart, as well as everyone else on-board)*; **you must be brought before Caesar** *(not because of Paul's appeal to Caesar, or because of the charges brought against him by the Jews, but rather because of the Divine Plan)*: **and, lo, God has given you all them who sail with you** *(every Saint had better know as to what Preacher he is 'with')*.

"**Wherefore, sirs, be of good cheer: for I believe God, that it shall be even as it was told me** *(insinuates that possibly some did not believe what Paul was saying)*.

"**Howbeit we must be cast upon a certain island** *(the Angel evidently did not tell Paul what island)*" **(Acts 27:21-26).**

BE OF GOOD CHEER

In the midst of what looked like certain destruction, Paul says to the Captain and the Centurion, and whoever else was standing nearby, a statement to them that was absolutely phenomenal, to say the least.

He began his remarks by stating that they should have listened to him previously when he advised the Captain and the Centurion not to loose from Crete because the voyage would prove to be extremely harmful. He did not make this statement to rub it in on them that their decision had been very costly, but rather to lay a foundation for what he is about to say.

He then went on to state that during the last evening, an Angel of the Lord had appeared to him and had stated, *"Fear not, Paul; you must be brought before Caesar: and, lo, God has given you all them who sail with you."*

As we also said in the notes, the Angel said to him, *"fear not,"* simply because, evidently, there had been some fear on

Paul's part.

Now, many would look at the situation and remind themselves that the Lord had told Paul over two years before that he *"must bear witness also at Rome"* (Acts 23:11). That being the case, there was no way that Paul was going to be killed before he reached Rome.

However, it is always very easy to judge another man's experience. Had we been in the midst of that storm and feeling the ship coming to pieces under our feet, all types of thoughts might have entered into our minds.

Paul may have wondered if he had actually heard from the Lord that some two years previously. And then, the Angel appeared.

THE MINISTRY OF ANGELS

The Scripture says, *"For He shall give His Angels charge over you, to keep you in all your ways"* (Ps. 91:11).

While the greater thrust of this Passage speaks of Angels watching over Christ in His earthly Sojourn, at the same time, it most definitely can apply to Believers. In a sense, Angels have charge over all Believers. To be sure, their business is to carry out the Commands of the Lord, which means that Believers cannot order Angels around, as some teach.

Jesus said, concerning Angels and Believers, *"Take heed that you despise not one of these little ones; for I say unto you, That in Heaven their Angels do always behold the Face of My Father which is in Heaven"* (Mat. 18:10). This tells us that every true Believer, as stated, is assigned an Angel, who reports to the Heavenly Father any and all things pertaining to that Believer.

Paul said, *"Are they not all Ministering spirits, sent forth to Minister for them who shall be heirs of Salvation"* (Heb. 1:14)?

But let us again emphasize, Angels who are assigned to every Believer do only what the Lord tells them to do. They cannot be ordered to do thus and so by Believers, which some erroneously claim. However, I think one can say without much fear of contradiction that the Ministry and Work of Angels was somewhat more pronounced in Old Testament times, which includes the four Gospels, than they are now under the New Covenant. The reason could be that we now have the Holy Spirit, Who is God, abiding in our hearts and lives permanently, and Who constantly helps us. But having said that, every once in awhile, even as we are now studying, an Angel will appear, even as the Angel did with Paul that particular night.

In essence, Paul then stated to the Captain and the Centurion that the ship would be lost, but the lives of all on-board would be spared, and they would be *"cast upon a certain island."*

THE SHIPWRECK

"But when the fourteenth night was come *(pertained to the length of time after leaving Fair Havens; so the storm had lasted now for about two weeks)*, as we were driven up and down in Adria, about midnight the shipmen deemed that they drew near to some country *(they could hear waves breaking on the beach, or rocks, at some distance)*;

"And sounded, and found *it* twenty fathoms *(a depth of about 120 feet)*: and when they had gone a little further, they sounded again, and found *it* fifteen fathoms.

"Then fearing lest we should have fallen upon rocks, they cast four anchors out of the stern, and wished for the day *(were anxious for the night to be over, so they could see where they were)*.

"And as the shipmen were about to flee out of the ship, when they had let down the boat into the sea *(portrays some, if not all, of the ship's crew about to take the only small boat they had and attempt to escape to shore, in effect, deserting the ship)*, under cover as though they would have cast anchors out of the foreship *(presents their deception, but Paul was watching)*" (Acts 27:27-30).

PAUL WAS WATCHING

The storm had now lasted for some 14 days, and one can well imagine the physical condition of the men on-board. Then, some of the sailors claimed that they could hear waves dashing on the rocks ahead, meaning they were close to land. This being the case, evidently the sailors on-board had determined to take the only small boat that they had with them and make for the shore, leaving the prisoners and soldiers to a certain death. In fact, they had just let down the small rowboat into the sea and were about to get on-board when Paul called such to the attention of the Centurion.

THE GREAT PROMISE OF GOD

"Paul said to the Centurion and to the soldiers, Except these abide in the ship, you cannot be saved *(to obtain God's Promises, we must abide by His Conditions).*

"Then the soldiers cut off the ropes of the boat, and let her fall off *(the Centurion now believes Paul).*

"And while the day was coming on, Paul besought *them* all to take meat, saying, This day is the fourteenth day that you have tarried and continued fasting, having taken nothing *('nothing!' the Greek word used here means they had eaten no regular meal).*

"Wherefore I pray you to take *some* meat: for this is for your health *(they should attempt to force at least some food down, irrespective of their seasickness, which, no doubt, some of them still had)*: for there shall not an hair fall from the head of any of you *(that is, if you will do what I say).*

"And when he had thus spoken, he took bread, and gave thanks to God in presence of them all *(which every Believer should to do at every meal, as well)*: and when he had broken *it*, he began to eat.

"Then were they all of good cheer, and they also

took *some* meat *(some food)*.

"And we were in all in the ship two hundred three-score and sixteen souls *(276 people on-board, which meant the ship was quite large)*.

"And when they had eaten enough, they lightened the ship, and cast out the wheat into the sea. *(What was left of the cargo still on-board)*" **(Acts 27:31-38)**.

PAUL TAKES CHARGE!

It is obvious at this stage that Paul has taken charge of the ship, and most definitely with the well wishes of the Captain and the Centurion. No doubt, the thought was readily in their minds that if they had listened to him to begin with, they more than likely would not have lost the ship.

When he spoke to the Captain and the Centurion a couple of weeks before, he said to them that this voyage would be with great hurt and much damage, with the ship being lost as well as its cargo, with even their lives in danger. It does not say that he told them that the Lord gave him this information, and, at any rate, even if he did relay such to them, the Centurion was not willing to take his advice, as it regarded the weather, over and above that of the Captain. But now they know, and beyond the shadow of a doubt, that they must heed what he says, and which they do so willingly.

Paul bluntly tells the Centurion and his soldiers that whosoever at this stage tries to escape the ship will be drowned. Immediately, the Centurion gave instructions to his soldiers to cut the ropes to the small boat below in which the crewmen had proposed to escape the ship. In other words, by now, they believed Paul explicitly. Considering that there were 276 people on this ship, this means it was quite large.

They had not had a solid meal since the storm began some two weeks earlier, but the Text doesn't mean that they had eaten nothing for fourteen days, but only that they had not had a meal as they should have had. Some have thought that the entire ship went on a two-week fast. However, and to be sure, of the 276 souls on-board, only Paul, Luke and Aristarchus, knew the Lord. The others would not have gone on a two-week fast, thinking it would help them to survive. In fact, they needed all the strength that they could muster. While it was a *"fast,"* it was not by choice, and now Paul encourages them to eat whatever it is they can find that they may have some physical strength for what lay ahead. He then assured them, *"there shall not an hair fall from the head of any of you."* He thanked the Lord for the food in the presence of them all, and all of them began to try to eat something, which they did. As is obvious, the food cheered them up with them gaining strength.

In all of this, we see the tremendous value of the Child of God in the midst of this sinful world. As we've already stated in this Volume, this is the reason that Jesus said Believers are *"the salt of the Earth"* and *"the Light of the world"* (Mat. 5:13-14). In other words, the only thing in this world keeping it on a halfway even keel is the Children of God. This is one of the reasons that the world is going to sink into such a deplorable condition in the Great Tribulation, which is yet to come. Every Child of God will be taken out in the Rapture. This will leave the world with no restraining influence. While there will be hundreds of thousands, if not millions, who will give their hearts to Christ during this terrible time, still, there is a vast difference in a new convert and a seasoned veteran in the Lord. Had it not been for Paul, all of these men would have drowned.

THEY ESCAPED ALL SAFE TO LAND

"And when it was day, they knew not the land *(they did not know where they were)*: but they discovered a certain creek with a shore, into the which they were minded, if it were possible, to thrust in the ship *(they wanted to take the ship as close to the shore as possible)*.

"And when they had taken up the anchors, they committed *themselves* unto the sea, and loosed the rudder bands, and hoisted up the mainsail to the wind, and made toward shore *(once again, trying to get as close as possible!)*.

"And falling into a place where two seas met, they ran the ship aground; and the forepart stuck fast, and remained unmoveable, but the hinder part was broken with the violence of the waves *(they had not gotten in as close as they desired)*.

"And the soldiers' counsel was to kill the prisoners, lest any of them should swim out, and escape *(the reason for this is that Roman Law condemned guards to death if prisoners escaped under their watch)*.

"But the Centurion, willing to save Paul, kept them from *their* purpose *(presents this man now knowing Paul was not just another prisoner)*; and commanded that they which could swim should cast *themselves* first *into the sea*, and get to land:

"And the rest, some on boards, and some on *broken pieces* of the ship. And so it came to pass, that they escaped all safe to land *(fulfilled exactly that which the Angel had conveyed to Paul)*" (**Acts 27:39-44**).

THE SHIP DESTROYED

Exactly as Paul had said some two weeks earlier, the ship with all of its cargo was lost, and had it not been for the Angel of the Lord which appeared to Paul, their lives would have been lost as well.

As daylight finally came, driving back that black night, none of the shoreline was recognizable. At any rate, they would now try to push the ship as close to the shore as was possible. They were not to be too very successful. A ways from shore, the ship stuck in mud, and with the water still very tempestuous, a leftover from the hurricane, the hinder part of the ship began to be battered to pieces.

Roman Law stated that if soldiers who were given the watch

over prisoners allowed them to escape, the soldiers themselves would be executed. Knowing that, and fearing that the prisoners on-board, including Paul, might escape, the soldiers proposed to kill all the prisoners. No doubt, at this time, and needing every hand they could get to try to save the ship, they had taken the chains off all the prisoners, so they might be useful. The Centurion, overhearing what was being proposed, and knowing that Paul could not be killed, the Scripture says, *"kept them from their purpose."* In fact, everyone was commanded to throw themselves into the water, taking refuge on broken pieces of the ship, and anything they could find, to get them all safe to land, and that's exactly what happened.

They all somehow swam to shore and finally stood shivering on the bank on that stormy November morning. At the moment, they did not know that they were on the island of Malta.

The Scripture doesn't say, but undoubtedly, Paul, along with Luke and Aristarchus, and quite possible others, as well, standing on that shore, began to thank the Lord for saving them. In fact, their escaping this storm with their lives could be construed as none other than a Miracle.

MELITA

"And when they were escaped, then they knew that the island was called Melita *(it is now called Malta, and is about fifty miles south of Sicily in the Mediterranean)*.

"And the barbarous people showed us no little kindness *(is not meant by Luke to be an insult; it just referred to people who were not influenced by Greek culture)*: for they kindled a fire, and received us every one, because of the present rain, and because of the cold" (Acts 28:1-2).

THE GREAT KINDNESS

Even though Luke gives us no information, still, according to what little was said, it seems to be obvious that very soon the people of the island spotted the group. It was raining and cold, and Luke says that they *"showed us no little kindness."*

He refers to them as *"barbarous people,"* which was not meant as an insult. It just meant, as we said in the notes, that they were not influenced by Greek culture.

It seems the first thing they did was to help get a fire started for all of these people who were shivering cold. And, as well, the *"kindness"* mentioned could very well have included food also and, no doubt, did.

Once again, we see the Hand of God in all of this. The ship could have wrecked on a shore of an island occupied by people who were the very opposite of these at Melita, but the Lord had them to beach among some of the kindest people in that part of the world.

THE MIRACLE

"And when Paul had gathered a bundle of sticks, and laid *them* on the fire, there came a viper out of the heat, and fastened on his hand *(presents Satan, having been unsuccessful in killing Paul with a storm, now trying another tactic)*.

"And when the barbarians saw the *venomous* beast hang on his hand, they said among themselves, No doubt this man is a murderer, whom, though he has escaped the sea, yet vengeance suffers not to live *(they knew that the poison of this particular type of viper would kill any man)*.

"And he shook off the beast into the fire, and felt no harm *(doesn't mean that he did not feel the pain of the bite, but rather did not begin to swell, as instantly was the case normally!)*.

"Howbeit they looked when he should have swollen, or fallen down dead suddenly *(they had personally seen the snake bite Paul, even hanging on his hand; so they knew the reptile had bitten full force)*: but after they had looked a great while, and saw no harm come to him, they changed their minds, and said that he was a god *(probably referred to Hercules; he was one of the gods of the Phoenicians and was worshiped on Malta under the title of 'dispeller of evil').*

"In the same quarters were possessions of the Chief man of the island, whose name was Publius *(this man had a Roman name, so it probably means he was the Roman official on this island)*; who received us, and lodged us three days courteously" (Acts 28:3-7).

A SECOND EFFORT BY SATAN FOILED

Some have argued that there are no venomous snakes on the island of Malta. While that may be true presently, it most definitely was not true 2,000 years ago.

Paul, along with all the others, was trying to scrape up wood so they could keep the fire going. They desperately needed the heat because of the rain and the cold.

I think it obvious that Paul was not too very much akin to many modern preachers, who think they are too good to do anything of this nature. Here we find Paul, whom I believe to be the greatest man of God on Earth of that time, out gathering sticks with the others, and even in the rain and the cold, at that. In other words, he was not too good to do such.

As the Apostle gathered a group of sticks together, the Scripture says, *"there came a viper out of the heat, and fastened on his hand."* In other words, he suffered a severe bite. Quite a few of the natives saw what had happened and knowing the snake was poisonous, they automatically assumed that Paul was a murderer or something of that nature. They watched him as *"he shook off the beast into the fire, and felt no harm."*

They evidently kept staring at him, expecting the hand that had been bitten to begin to swell, which it normally would have, and then when a little time passed, expecting at any moment for him surely to fall down dead, but they found that such was not to be.

They observed him for a period of time and saw no harm come to him, and then as superstition does, they changed their minds from thinking that he was a murderer to thinking that he was a god. He was neither! Yet, in the coming three months, all of those who were with these islanders were to see many things accomplished that only God could do, and do so by using His Servant Paul.

With a newfound respect for Paul, they took him to the *"Chief man of the island, whose name was Publius."* He was probably the Roman Governor, of sorts, of the island, inasmuch as he had a Roman name.

When Luke said, *"Who received us, and lodged us three days courteously,"* he doesn't exactly state what the pronoun *"us"* meant. More than likely, it pertained only to Paul, Luke, and Aristarchus. For his courteous treatment of Paul and others, we will find that the Lord would repay him many times over, even as the Lord always does. What a mighty God we serve!

HEALING

"And it came to pass, that the father of Publius lay sick of a fever and of a bloody flux *(presents a medical term which Luke would have used, being a Physician; the man had a reoccurring fever and dysentery)*: to whom Paul entered in, and prayed, and laid his hands on him, and healed him *(the Lord is still the Healer)*.

"So when this was done, others also, which had diseases in the island, came, and were healed:

"Who also honoured us with many honours *(evidently indicates material things such as clothing, food, and even gifts of money, etc.)*; and when we departed, they laded *us* with such things as were necessary *(no doubt, refers to the entirety of the 276 people who had been shipwrecked)*" **(Acts 28:8-10).**

THE LAYING ON OF HANDS

Paul believed that the Lord healed the sick and conducted himself accordingly. Unfortunately, much unbelief fills the modern church world, with little faith evidenced in the Power of God.

"The father of Publius," the Scripture says, *"lay sick of a fever and of a bloody flux."* Whether Publius asked Paul to pray for his father or not, we aren't told. At any rate, Paul went to the man's dwelling, no doubt accompanied by Luke and Aristarchus, *"and prayed, and laid his hands on him, and healed him."*

Evidently, the news spread all over the island, and everyone came who had diseases or sicknesses of any kind, and the Scripture says they *"were healed."*

What a beautiful thing the Lord did on this island. There is no record that Paul established a Church here, but one can be certain that he most definitely did preach to them the Gospel of Jesus Christ. Even though Luke is silent about the matter, a Church could very well have been established and, in fact, many could have come to Christ, and no doubt did.

These people were so happy with Paul and his party, respecting the three months they stayed with them, that they loaded them down with goods when they left. It could have been money, clothing, etc., because they had lost nearly everything in the shipwreck. The record is that all were blessed, the crew of the ship, the soldiers, etc.

The Lord has set in the Church, *"Apostles, Prophets, Evangelists, Pastors and Teachers,"* all *"for the perfecting of the Saints, for the work of the Ministry, for the edifying of the Body of Christ: till we all come in the unity of the Faith, and of the knowledge of the Son of God, unto a perfect man, unto the measure of the stature of the fulness of Christ."*

Paul went on to say, *"That we henceforth be no more children, tossed to and fro, and carried about with every wind of doctrine, by the sleight of men, and cunning craftiness, whereby they lie in wait to deceive; but speaking the Truth in love, may grow up into Him in all things, Who is the Head, even Christ"* (Eph. 4:11-15).

The point being, if it had not been for Paul, the entire crew of this ship would have drowned, and because of Paul, and above all the Love of God in him, they were treated very kindly on this island, and given many things to meet their needs. The point is this:

Every Believer must find a Preacher of the Gospel on whom the Lord has laid His Hand, and who is preaching the pure Gospel of Jesus Christ, and attach themselves to that Preacher, and then be blessed. Unfortunately, all too often, men choose that which appeals to the flesh, and, as such, there is no profit but rather a great loss.

BRETHREN

"And after three months we departed in a ship of Alexandria, which had wintered in the isle, whose sign was Castor and Pollux *(evidently portrayed another grain ship from the same city where the wrecked ship had been based [Acts 27:6]; the two signs mentioned here were the favorite divinities of Mediterranean seamen at that time; it was the custom to have their images, whatever they were, on the head and stern of their ships)*.

"And landing at Syracuse, we tarried *there* three days *(Syracuse was the capitol of Sicily, about eighty miles north of Malta)*.

"And from thence we fetched a compass *(took a heading)*, and came to Rhegium: and after one day the south wind blew, and we came the next day to Puteoli *(Puteoli was the chief port on the Bay of Naples)*:

"Where we found Brethren *(those who were followers of Christ)*, and were desired to tarry with them seven days *(the Centurion allowed Paul to remain with these Brethren and, no doubt, preach the Gospel to them for this length of time)*: and so we went toward Rome *(finds them finishing this perilous journey on foot).*

"And from thence, when the Brethren *(from Rome)* heard of us, they came to meet us as far as Appii forum, and The Three Taverns *(a runner evidently went to the Capitol informing the Brethren that Paul was coming; consequently, it seems a group went to meet Paul)*: whom when Paul saw, he thanked God, and took courage *(refers to the fellowship the Apostle and those with him greatly enjoyed)*" (Acts 28:11-15).

THANKFULNESS TO THE LORD

When it was time to leave the island of Malta, Julius found another Alexandrian corn ship which was going their way, so the entire group of some 276 persons boarded this ship. They traveled to the lovely Bay of Puteoli and there docked. Their journey by ship, although it had been extremely eventful, was now over.

There they found some followers of Christ, but as to exactly how this came about, we aren't told. At any rate, these Believers pressed upon Paul to stay with them for seven days. It seems that Julius allowed Paul, who, no doubt, was accompanied by Luke and Aristarchus, to spend an entire week with them.

When the week was ended, Julius, along with his cortege of soldiers, escorted Paul toward Rome. They would finish this perilous journey on foot. From Puteoli to Rome was a distance of about 140 miles.

When they had traversed approximately 100 miles, at a place called *"Appii Forum,"* they were met by a group of Believers who had come from Rome to meet them, a distance of about 40 miles. Evidently, a runner had gone into Rome and had informed Believers there that Paul was on the way. So, they would come to meet him.

Even though Paul had never been in Rome, still, it is obvious that there were a group of people there who knew him well, believed in him, and would readily show that affection.

No doubt, this encouraged the great Apostle greatly. It says, *"He thanked God, and took courage."*

ROME

"And when we came to Rome, the Centurion delivered the prisoners to the Captain of the Guard *(pertained to the Commander of Nero's Praetorian Guard)*:
but Paul was suffered to dwell by himself with a soldier
who kept him *(obviously means Paul was treated differently from the other prisoners; he was evidently granted
special favors)*.

"And it came to pass, that after three days Paul
called the Chief of the Jews together *(not only refers to
the main Jewish leader in Rome, but the other leaders as
well)*: and when they were come together, he said unto
them, Men *and* Brethren *(the following account seems
to indicate that the Brethren of Verse 15 had no connection with these Jewish leaders)*, though I have committed
nothing against the people, or customs of our Fathers,
yet was I delivered prisoner from Jerusalem into the
hands of the Romans *(proclaims the Apostle relating the
situation exactly as it had happened)*.

"Who, when they had examined me, would have let
me go, because there was no cause of death in me *(pertained
to the Romans, not the Jews, as the next Verse explains)*.

"But when the Jews spoke against *it*, I was constrained to appeal unto Caesar *(proclaims the Apostle
having done this in order to save his life)*; not that I had
ought to accuse my nation of *(he was in no way in Rome
to bring charges against the Jews or to cause them problems in any manner)*.

"For this cause therefore have I called for you, to
see *you*, and to speak with *you*: because that for the
hope of Israel I am bound with this chain *(in effect, he
is saying that all of this is because of his proclamation*

of Christ as the Messiah of Israel, and the Saviour of the world)" (Acts 28:16-20).

FOR THE HOPE OF ISRAEL

What were the thoughts of Paul when he came into the outskirts of Rome, the capital of the world of that day? While he had been in many great cities, to be frank, there were none like Rome. This was the center of worldly power, the city that would rule the world of that day for nearly 1,000 years. And, of the untold thousands who would crowd its roads and its streets coming into the city and leaving the city, in that polyglot of humanity, none could even begin to realize that one was coming into the city whose Message, the Message of Jesus Christ and Him Crucified, would literally change the world.

Farrar said, *"How many a look of contemptuous curiosity would be darted at the chained prisoner and his Jewish friends as they passed along with their escort of soldiers!"*[3]

As they passed ever-lengthening rows of suburban villas and ever-thickening throngs of people, they would reach the actual precincts of the city, catch sight of the Capitol and the Imperial Palace, pass the Circus Maximus on their left, and were finally brought to the barracks of the Praetorian cohorts which kept guard over the person of the Emperor. And, thus in March, and it was believed to be in A.D. 61, in the seventh year of the reign of Nero, under the consulship of Caesennius Paetus and Petronius Terpilianus, Paul entered Rome.

JULIUS

After a very eventful journey, exactly as Paul had said that it would be, here the charge of the Centurion Julius ended, and one must wonder at the thoughts he had regarding the experiences of the past few months. He owed his own life, and also the lives of the other prisoners entrusted to him, to Paul. Officially, when he handed Paul and the other prisoners over to the charge of the Praefect of the Praetorian guards, his commission was finished.

No doubt, when Julius officially turned Paul over to the authorities, he did so with every kind word. And besides that, the letter that had been written by Festus actually contained no charge against Paul. As that Governor had stated, how could he send a prisoner to Rome without even stating what his crime is supposed to have been? But that's the way the situation played out. As a result of all of this, Paul was treated much differently than the other prisoners. For instance, he was allowed to rent his own house, whatever type of dwelling that would have been, but at his own expense. As well, even though given this freedom, he was still chained to a Roman soldier. While he could have as many visitors as he so desired, and for as long as they desired, he was still always chained to a Roman soldier. This was the Law under the Roman system.

That this was extremely irritating may be seen from his several allusions to his *"bonds,"* or the *"chain,"* which he mentioned in basically every Epistle of his captivity (Eph. 6:20; Phil. 1:7, 13-14, 16; Col. 4:3; 4:18).

Where he came by the money for this hired house, we aren't told, but it is obvious that the Lord made a way.

THE CHIEF OF THE JEWS

After Paul had been there some three days, he called the leader of the Jewish community in Rome, along with other Jewish notables, to come meet with him, which they did.

He addressed them as *"Brethren,"* and assured them that he had done nothing to the Jews in Jerusalem or anywhere else. Despite this, they had thirsted for his life and caused him to be seized at Jerusalem and handed over to the Roman power. Yet, he went on to relate as to how the Romans, after thoroughly examining him, found no fault in him, and would have set him free were it not for the opposition of the Jews, which compelled him to appeal to Caesar.

He lets these Jewish leaders know that he is not going in

any way to make any accusations against the Jewish leaders in Jerusalem, or anywhere else, for that matter. He closes out his statement to them by stating, *"For this cause therefore have I called for you, to see you, and to speak with you: because that for the hope of Israel I am bound with this chain."*

PAUL

"And they said unto him, We neither received let-ters out of Judaea concerning you, neither any of the Brethren who came showed or spoke any harm of you *(probably pertained to the fact that Roman Law punished unsuccessful prosecutors of Roman citizens; it is difficult to comprehend that these Jewish leaders in Rome had never heard of Paul, but it seems somewhat that this was the case, or else their knowledge of him was scant).*

"But we desire to hear of you what you think *(pro-claims a great opportunity now presented to Paul)*: for as concerning this sect *(Christianity)*, we know that every-where it is spoken against *(true Bible Christianity contin-ues to be 'everywhere spoken against').*

"And when they had appointed him a day, there came many to him into *his* lodging *(it is believed that he was allowed to rent a house, and there abide during his stay in Rome)*; to whom he expounded and testified the Kingdom of God, persuading them concerning Jesus, both out of the Law of Moses, and *out of* the Prophets, from morning till evening *(they heard the 'Word' as they had never heard the 'Word' before; above all, they heard about Jesus, to Whom the Word pointed).*

"And some believed the things which were spoken, and some believed not *(some embraced Christ as Lord, Messiah, and Saviour, and some did not)*" (Acts 28:21-24).

THE KINGDOM OF GOD

When Paul was imprisoned in Rome, it is said there were

seven synagogues in Rome at that time. So, those who came to hear Paul were probably leaders of each of these synagogues. Actually, his small dwelling, whatever it was, and wherever it was in Rome, could not have accommodated very many, as would be obvious.

The first meeting with the Chief Jews, as called by Paul, seemed to be for the purpose of seeing exactly what these men had been told about him, if anything at all. He spoke some things to them concerning his trial before the Governor in Caesarea, but never went into any detail whatsoever regarding his Ministry.

They answered him, basically stating that they had not received letters out of Judaea concerning him. And, as well, they said the Jews who came by the synagogues, Jews from Judaea, did not show or speak any harm of him.

That seems a little far-fetched, considering the hatred that the High Priest and the Jewish leaders had of him, even going to all lengths to try to kill him. But, at any rate, this is the information we have which Luke gave to us. Whether these Jewish leaders were lying to Paul that day, only the Lord knows. However, they said, *"We desire to hear of you what you think: for as concerning this sect, we know that everywhere it is spoken against."*

So, Paul set a specific day to where they could come. As stated, these were, no doubt, the leaders of the respective synagogues in Rome. The Scripture says that to these individuals, whomever they may have been, *"he expounded and testified the Kingdom of God, persuading them concerning Jesus, both out of the Law of Moses, and out of the Prophets, from morning till evening."*

Luke then adds, *"And some believed the things which were spoken, and some believed not."*

THE CHURCH IN ROME

When the Jewish leaders proclaimed the fact that they knew little about *"this sect,"* speaking of Christianity, that was probably correct. It must be remembered that Rome at that time was a city of more than two million inhabitants. As well, we know there was a Church in Rome at that time because some of its members, as we have previously noted, came to meet Paul at a place called *"Appii Forum."* In addition, some time before, Paul had sent his great Epistle to the Romans to these very people.

But having said that, we must conclude that the Church in Rome could not have been very large, so it is quite possible that the Jews, who were noted for keeping to themselves, had little knowledge, if any at all, concerning the Christian Church in Rome.

THE JEWS

"And when they agreed not among themselves, they departed, after that Paul had spoken one word, Well spoke the Holy Spirit by Isaiah the Prophet unto our Fathers *(proclaims the instrument as Isaiah, but the Speaker as the Holy Spirit),*

"Saying, Go unto this people, and say, Hearing you shall hear, and shall not understand; and seeing you shall see, and not perceive *(Isa. 6:9-10; presents the sixth of seven times this is recorded by the Holy Spirit [Isa. 6:9; Mat. 13:14; Mk. 4:12; Lk. 8:10; Jn. 12:40; Acts 28:26; Rom. 11:8]):*

"For the heart of this people is waxed gross, and their ears are dull of hearing, and their eyes have they closed; lest they should see with *their* eyes, and hear with *their* ears, and understand with *their* heart, and should be converted, and I should heal them *(this is a willful rejection of Truth, which brings about a willful judgment of the hardening of the heart).*

"Be it known therefore unto you, that the Salvation of God is sent unto the Gentiles, and *that* they will hear it *(presents Paul's last statement to the Jewish leadership of Rome that day; in effect, he says that the 'Salvation of God' is found only in Jesus).*

"**And when he had said these words, the Jews departed, and had great reasoning among themselves** *(discussing greatly what he had said)*" **(Acts 28:25-29).**

THE SALVATION OF GOD

Even though some believed what Paul said, more than likely, the majority did not. As well, from the way that Paul closed out this session, there is a good possibility that those who believed not, in other words, they refused to believe what the Bible said about the Lord Jesus Christ, their disapproval must have been very vocal and very strident. He closes by quoting to them the great words of Isaiah the Prophet, *"Hearing you shall hear, and shall not understand; and seeing you shall see, and not perceive."* In other words, from the way that Paul closed this session, the idea is that despite the overwhelming evidence in the Word of God as it regarded the Lord Jesus Christ, Who He is, and what He did, still, they would not believe. It was, as stated in the notes, a willful rejection of Truth. That being the case, such rejection always brings about a willful judgment of the hardening of the heart. He then proclaimed to them, *"that the Salvation of God is sent unto the Gentiles, and that they will hear it."*

Little did they realize that this Gospel being portrayed to them by this man called Paul would ultimately bring down, or rather change, the mighty Roman Empire and, as well, would touch the entirety of the world.

ROME

"**And Paul dwelt two whole years in his own hired house** *(rented house)*, **and received all who came in unto him** *(no doubt, strengthened the Church mightily in Rome).*

"**Preaching the Kingdom of God** *(refers to the Rule of God in the human heart and life)*, **and teaching those things which concern the Lord Jesus Christ, with all confidence, no man forbidding him** *(it is said that even some from Caesar's household were converted [Phil. 4:22])*" **(Acts 28:30-31).**

PREACHING THE KINGDOM OF GOD

So Luke concludes the great Book of Acts by saying several things. Some of them are:

• Paul was incarcerated some two years in Rome.

• Although chained to a Roman soldier, he had the privilege of renting his own house and being kept there for the two year period instead of being kept in a jail cell.

• He was at liberty to have as many visitors as he liked and for as long as he liked, who, in fact, came to him constantly to hear the Word of the Lord.

• During these two years, he *"preached the Kingdom of God, and taught those things which concerned the Lord Jesus Christ."*

• Thus was fulfilled the Word of the Lord given to him some four years earlier when the Lord appeared to him and said, *"Be of good cheer, Paul: for as you have testified of Me in Jerusalem, so must you bear witness also at Rome"* (Acts 23:11).

For other information concerning his two years in Rome, we have to derive that from his Epistles.

From what little information we do have, it is believed that Luke remained with him that entire time and, as well, that Aristarchus attended him so closely as to earn the designation of *"fellow-prisoner"* (Col. 4:10). As well, from Colossians 4:10, we learn that Mark was with Paul in Rome for a considerable period of time. This means, of course, that whatever problem there had been in the past with Mark was no longer in the present. We know, as well, that Tychicus brought him news from Ephesus (Eph. 6:21). Also, Epaphroditus came from Philippi, bringing Paul a very generous offering, which was, no doubt, very much needed (Phil. 2:25; 4:18). As well, Epaphras came to consult him about the heresies that were beginning to creep into the Churches at Laodicea, Hierapolis, and Colosse (Col. 1:7; 4:12).

PAUL'S RELEASE FROM PRISON

It is believed that Paul was released from house arrest in Rome in A.D. 63. There is no record that he had a trial at that time before Nero, or anyone else, for that matter, simply because there were actually no charges against him. It is believed that he visited Spain after his release, but of that there is no concrete evidence. It is thought that he may have been arrested again in A.D. 66 or 67, and there gave his life.

> *"I am the Lord's! O joy beyond expression,*
> *"O sweet response to Voice of Love Divine;*
> *"Faith's joyous 'Yes' to the assuring Whisper,*
> *"'Fear not! I have redeemed you;*
> *"'You are Mine'."*
>
> *"I am the Lord's! It is the glad confession,*
> *"Wherewith the Bride recalls the happy day,*
> *"When love's 'I will' accepted Him forever,*
> *"'The Lord's,' to love, to honor and obey."*
>
> *"I am the Lord's! Yet teach me all it means,*
> *"All it involves of love and loyalty,*
> *"Of holy service, absolute surrender,*
> *"And unreserved obedience unto Thee."*
>
> *"I am the Lord's! Yes; body, soul, and spirit,*
> *"O seal them irrecoverably Thine;*
> *"As You, Beloved, in Your Grace and Fullness,*
> *"Forever and forevermore are mine."*

PAUL

THE APOSTLE

CHAPTER THIRTEEN

The Last Words Of Paul

THE LAST WORDS OF PAUL

The last words of Paul are found in his last Epistle, written from the Mamertine Prison in Rome. Last words are very significant, especially when the individuals know that their time is drawing to an end, and most of all, someone of the caliber of Paul.

A PERSONAL EXPERIENCE

In our last visit to Rome, which was in 1995, that is, if I remember correctly, the highlight of that trip was our visit to the Mamertine Prison.

Actually, this prison is very small, containing only a few cells. The part where Paul was incarcerated is below ground, actually carved out of solid rock. There are stairs that lead down into this part presently, but then, the only way for entrance was through a trapdoor that was in the ceiling, which opened to a room above. So, when Paul was incarcerated there awaiting his trial before Nero, the guards would have tied a rope around his waist and then lowered him through this trapdoor into the cell below. What little food he got would have come through that trapdoor as well.

It is said that this cell in which Paul was incarcerated began its existence as a granary. In other words, it was carved out of solid rock to serve as a storage place for grain. Later on, not so long before Paul was incarcerated there, cells were built on top of the ground, with it then being called the Mamertine Prison. Little did Rome know nearly 2,000 years ago, when the Apostle Paul was placed in this dungeon, there to await his death, that millions of people down through the centuries would desire to visit this place, because of their respect for the man Paul, who faithfully gave to us that which the Lord had given to him, as it regards the meaning of the New Covenant. Rome is no more, as far as the Empire is concerned, having long since faded into oblivion, but in the hearts and minds of untold millions, there is eternal gratitude to the man who faithfully held up the image of Christ.

MY VISIT THERE

The day that we visited the Mamertine Prison, once again, if I remember correctly, as we walked down the steps into this room where II Timothy was written, our party was the only ones there. Taking only a few moments to look at the bleak surroundings, wondering where the table sat, in fact, if there were a table, on which Paul had penned his last Epistle, which is the Word of God, all of us stood transfixed in our own thoughts.

After making a few remarks, I opened my New Testament to II Timothy 4:6, and began to read.

"For I am now ready to be offered, and the time of my departure is at hand. I have fought a good fight, I have finished my course, I have kept the Faith."

I was unable to continue any further, the tears started to flow, and the Spirit of God settled over that room like a hovering blanket, as all of us felt, for at least a few moments, the significance of what had transpired here.

I think I can say without fear of exaggeration that Paul may very well have been the greatest example for Christianity ever produced by Christ. Not meaning at all to take away from the innumerable men and women of Faith that helped bring to us what we have today, but yet, Paul, the man to whom the Lord Jesus Christ gave the meaning of the New Covenant, which the Apostle faithfully delivered to us, this man, in my opinion, stands alone with no one being his equal.

How that Paul got the Epistle of II Timothy delivered, in fact, to Timothy, we aren't told. But it is overly obvious that it was safely delivered to his son in Christ.

PAUL'S ARREST

As we have stated, the Acts of the Apostles ends with the

statement that Paul remained a period of two whole years in his own hired lodging, and received all who came in to visit him, *"preaching the Kingdom of God and teaching the things concerning the Lord Jesus Christ, and doing so with all confidence."*

The question as to why Luke discontinued his account of Paul and his Ministry at this point, of that we have no clue. We will have to surmise that it was the Will of God for the account to be discontinued at this point. All types of suggestions have been offered, but they are only suggestions, with no validity in fact.

It has been generally believed that at about the beginning of the year A.D. 64, Paul was tried, acquitted, and liberated, or else set free without a trial. And then, approximately two years later, he was once more arrested, and was, after this second imprisonment, put to death at Rome.

In July, A.D. 64, the great persecution against the Christians in Rome and elsewhere broke out. It is obvious that Paul had been released from prison by this time, perhaps only a few weeks earlier, and had that not been the case, he, no doubt, would have been arrested then. So, we have every reason to believe that he was released at the beginning of the year A.D. 64.

SPAIN

Paul had stated in his Epistle to the Romans that he intended to go to Spain (Rom. 15:24, 28). That he may very well have done; however, there is no record of Paul having gone to Spain, as well, there is no record of any Church established by him in the country of Spain. If he went at all, which he probably didn't, it would have to have been immediately after his release from prison. What little information is derived after the Book of Acts leads us to believe that he rather went about establishing the Churches, and to be sure, the need for such would have been very great. He had been away for some four years, incarcerated some two years in Caesarea and some two years in Rome. He probably felt that task more important at the time than anything else. To use his energies to protect these Churches from the subtle leaven of spreading heresies was, no doubt, heavy on his mind.

Farrar says, and in regard to this, *"At Jerusalem and at Antioch he had vindicated forever the freedom of the Gentile from the yoke of the Levitic Law. In his letters to the Romans and Galatians he had proclaimed alike to Jew and Gentile that we are not under the Law, but under Grace. He had rescued Christianity from the peril of dying away into a Jewish sect, only distinguishable from Judaism by the accepted fulfillment of Messianic hopes. Laboring as no other Apostle had labored, he had preached the Gospel in the chief cities of the world of that day, from Jerusalem to Rome, and maybe he even went as far as Spain."*[1] His desire would be, not to attempt the foundation of new churches, as important as that may have been, but to forewarn and to strengthen the beloved Churches which he had already founded.

PAUL ARRESTED

We do know that at Troas Paul stayed in the house of a brother in the Lord named Carpus. Here it was, it seems, that the final crisis of his fate seems to have overtaken him. It is at least a fair conjecture that he would not have left at the house of Carpus his books and the cloak, which was so necessary to him, unless his departure had been hasty and perhaps involuntary.

Since Nero began his persecution of the Christians, to be sure, many Romans or Jews, eager to please the Emperor, could have turned Paul in, so to speak. Some have stated that it was Alexander the coppersmith who was the one who had him arrested. At any rate, Paul did state in his last Letter to Timothy, *"Alexander the coppersmith did me much evil: the Lord reward him according to his works: of whom you beware also; for he has greatly withstood our words"* (II Tim. 4:14-15).

He could have been arrested at Troas and sent under guard to Ephesus to be judged by the Proconsul. While awaiting his trial there, he would have been put in prison; and the fact that his place of imprisonment, it is stated, is pointed out among the ruins of Ephesus, although no imprisonment at Ephesus is directly mentioned in Scripture, still, there is a possibility that this is the way it happened.

Farrar said, *"From the trial at Ephesus, where his cause might have suffered from local prejudices, he may once more have found it necessary to appeal to Caesar."*[2]

Once more the Apostle would make the trip to Rome, but there would be no glad hand extended to him this time. No Disciples from Rome met him at the Appii Forum or the Three Taverns, neither could anything have well occurred to make Paul take courage. In fact, the horrible persecution by Nero had depressed, scattered, and perhaps decimated the little Christian community.

Regarding Paul's first imprisonment, he was allowed to rent his own house and have visitors as long as it was desired. But Christianity was now suspected of political designs and was reduced to the place of an enemy of the State. This time he had no Lysias to say a good word for him, no friendly testimonies of Festus or an Agrippa to produce in his favor. Farrar says, *"The government of Nero, bad almost from the first, had deteriorated year by year with alarming rapidity, and at this moment it presented a spectacle of awful cruelty and abysmal degradation such as has been rarely witnessed by the civilized world."*[3] Now Paul was consigned to the Mamertine Prison.

SECOND TIMOTHY

As previously stated, II Timothy was written in the Mamertine Prison, the last Epistle written by Paul. How he got it out and to Timothy, we have no way of knowing. He said this to his young protégé.

"Do your diligence to come shortly unto me *(Timothy was in Ephesus, about 1,000 miles from Rome; consequently, it was a journey which at best would take several weeks; whether the young Apostle made it there in time or made it at all, is not known)*:

"**For Demas has forsaken me, having loved this present world, and is departed unto Thessalonica** *(presents a sad commentary regarding one who had been blessed with such a golden opportunity)*; **Crescens to Galatia** *(mentioned here only; tradition says he founded the Church in France)*, **Titus unto Dalmatia** *(modern Yugoslavia)*.

"**Only Luke is with me** *(presents the one who wrote the Gospel that bears his name, as well as the Book of Acts)*. **Take Mark, and bring him with you** *(John Mark, who wrote the Gospel of Mark, the nephew of Barnabas)*: **for he is profitable to me for the Ministry.** *(This presents a tremendous commendation by the Apostle concerning Mark.)*

"**And Tychicus have I sent to Ephesus.** *(It is believed Tychicus may have conveyed this very Epistle, the last one written by Paul, to Timothy and was perhaps instructed to replace Timothy at Ephesus, while the young Apostle came to Rome.)*

"**The cloak that I left at Troas with Carpus, when you come, bring *with you*** *(quite possibly it was summer when Paul wrote this Epistle, and if he survived till winter, he would need this cloak)*, **and the Books, *but* especially the Parchments** *(refers to the Old Testament Books)*" **(II Tim. 4:9-13).**

ONESIPHORUS

Paul singles out one particular brother who seemingly did not care what others thought, or in how much danger he placed himself by helping Paul in these last days. His name was Onesiphorus. Concerning him, the Apostle said:

"**The Lord give Mercy unto the house of Onesiphorus**

(from the terminology, it seems this man had died a short time before); **for he oft refreshed me, and was not ashamed of my chain** *(once again, it seems many Believers were, in fact, ashamed of Paul and his situation, but not Onesiphorus)*:

"**But, when he was in Rome, he sought me out very diligently, and found** *me.* *(This man, so kind to the great Apostle, will be among those at the final Judgment to whom the Saviour will say, 'I was in prison, and you came unto Me' [Mat. 25:36]).*

"**The Lord grant unto him that he may find Mercy of the Lord in that day** *(speaks of the 'Judgment Seat of Christ,' which will commence after the Rapture of the Church; only Believers will be there; as well, it will not involve sin, for that was handled at Calvary, but rather our motives, etc.)*: **and in how many things he ministered unto me at Ephesus, you know very well.** *(It seems this man had ever been a help to Paul. Therefore, his name will be proclaimed favorably and forever on the pages of Sacred Writ)*" **(II Tim. 1:16-18).**

NERO

It is believed that Paul had a trial before Nero; however, there is no proof of such. As well, it is not impossible that he may have pleaded his cause before Nero himself. If the trial took place in the spring of A.D. 66, Nero had not yet started for Greece, and would have been almost certain to give personal attention to the case of one who had done more than any living man to spread the Name of Christ.

Nero had personally caused the fire to be set, which engulfed much of Rome, and he strongly desired the blame to be placed on the Christians. Actually, their crime was in the words of Nero, *"haters of humanity."* Nero had been intensely anxious to fix on the innocent Christians the stigma of this conflagration of fire. And now, the greatest of the Christians, the very

leader of the hated sect, stood chained before him.

PAUL BEFORE NERO

If indeed this did happen, what a contrast between these two men—one, the godliest of the godly and the other, the vilest of the vile.

One was the leader of Paganism, the other the Ambassador of Christ. The Emperor's diadem was now confronted for the first time by the Cross of the Lord Jesus Christ, before which, some three centuries later, would pull down the Roman Empire.

Nero, as he sat that day on his gilded throne, was not yet 30 years of age, but was stained through and through with every possible crime and steeped in every nameless degradation.

Farrar said, *"Of all the black and damning iniquities against which, as Paul had often to remind his heathen converts, the Wrath of God forever burns, there was scarcely one of which Nero had not been guilty. A wholesale robber, a pitiless despot, an intriguer, a poisoner, a murderer, a matricide, a liar, a coward, a drunkard, a glutton, incestuous, unutterably depraved, his evil and debased nature, of which even Pagans had spoken as 'a mixture of blood and mud' – had sought abnormal outlets to weary, if it could not sate, its insatiable proclivity to crime."* Farrar went on to say:

"He was that last worst specimen of human wickedness – a man who, not content with every existing form of vice and sin in which the taint of human nature had found a vent, had become 'an inventor of evil things.' He had usurped his throne; he had poisoned, under guise of affection, the noble boy who was its legitimate heir; he had married the sister of that boy, only to break her heart by his brutality, and finally to order her assassination; he had first planned the murder, then ordered the execution, of his own mother, who, however deep her guilt, had yet committed her many crimes for love of him; he had treacherously sacrificed the one great general whose victories gave any lustre to his reign; among other murders, too numerous to count,

he had ordered the deaths of the brave soldier and the brilliant philosopher who had striven to guide his wayward and intolerable heart; he had disgraced imperial authority with every form of sickening and monstrous folly; he had dragged the charm of youth and the natural dignity of manhood through the very lowest mire; he had killed by a kick the worthless but beautiful woman whom he had torn from her own husband to be his second wife; he had reduced his own capital to ashes, and buffooned, and fiddled, and sung with his cracked voice in public theatres, regardless of the misery and starvation of thousands of its ruined citizens; he had charged the fire upon the innocent Christians, and tortured them to death by hundreds in hideous martyrdoms; he had done his best to render infamous his rank, his country, his ancestors, the name of Roman – nay, even the very name of man."[4]

To the contrary, Paul had spent his entire life learning the Word of God, and above all, learning the Lord Himself. He had suffered every hardship to take the Gospel of hope to a dying world. Then, as now, the only hope that man had was in Jesus Christ, and Paul, with tireless effort, brought that hope to untold thousands, and in the final alternative, to untold millions. His life was a life of heroic sacrifice. In fact, I think it might be said that no man toiled like this man, and we might well say that *"Paul was the greatest example for Christianity that Christ ever produced."*

So, here these two stand facing each other; one, the slave of Christ, and the other, the incarnation of the Antichrist.

When Nero died, he had gone on a frivolous expedition to Greece, and when he returned, he found that a revolt in Rome was in the making, and he was the target. He fled the palace at night, attempting to disguise himself, and had to quench his thirst with water from a ditch. Realizing he was cornered, he finally let his trembling hand be helped by a slave to force a dagger into his throat, as he committed suicide. Today he is in Hell, and will be there forever and forever. And to be sure, if, in fact, Paul did stand before him in Rome, he remembers

every word, every moment of that meeting, and will do so forever and forever.

THE LAST CHARGE OF THE GREAT APOSTLE

"I charge *you* therefore *(has the weight of a legal affir-
mation)* before God, and the Lord Jesus Christ *(should
have been translated, 'Our God, even Christ Jesus')*, Who
shall judge the quick *(living)* and the dead *(refers to the
fact that all Believers will stand at the Judgment Seat of
Christ)* at His Appearing and His Kingdom *(refers here
to the Second Advent)*;

"Preach the Word *(refers to the whole body of
revealed Truth, which means the entirety of the Word of
God)*; be instant in season, out of season *(presents the
idea of the Preacher holding himself in constant readiness
to proclaim the Word)*; reprove *(the Preacher is to deal
with sin, both in the lives of his unsaved hearers and in
those of the Saints to whom he ministers, and he is to do so
in no uncertain tones and terms)*, rebuke *(a suggestion in
some cases of impending penalty)*, exhort with all longsuffering and Doctrine. *(This tells us that the 'reproving'
and the 'rebuking' must be done with gentleness. As well,
the 'longsuffering' refers to a gentleness that continues
even when the Message is met with rejection. However, the
'Doctrine' is not to change, even though it is rejected.)*

SOUND DOCTRINE

"For the time will come when they will not endure
sound Doctrine *('sound Doctrine' pertains to over-
riding principles: the Salvation of the sinner, and the
Sanctification of the Saint; the Cross is the answer for both,
and is the only answer for both)*; but after their own lusts
shall they heap to themselves teachers, having itching
ears *(refers to the people who have ears that 'itch' for the*

smooth and comfortable word, and are willing to reward handsomely the man who is sufficiently compromising to speak it; hearers of this type have rejected the Truth and prefer to hear the lie);

"And they shall turn away *their* ears from the Truth *(those who follow false teachers not only turn away their ears from the Truth, but see to it that the ears are always in a position such that they will never come in contact with the Truth)*, **and shall be turned unto fables.** *(If it's not the 'Message of the Cross,' then it is 'fables' [I Cor. 1:18].)*

AFFLICTIONS

"But watch thou in all things *(carries the idea of watching one's own life, Ministry, and the Doctrine which we are proclaiming)*, **endure afflictions** *(carries the idea of not allowing hardships, difficulties, or troubles to hinder one's carrying forth of one's Ministry; it is a sharp command given with military snap and curtness; Wuest says, 'How we in the Ministry of the Word need that injunction today. What a 'softy' we sometimes are, afraid to come out clearly in our proclamation of the Truth and our stand as to false doctrine, fearing the ostracism of our fellows, the Ecclesiastical displeasure of religious leaders so-called, or even the cutting off of our immediate financial income.' ['I would rather walk a lonely road with Jesus than be in a crowd without His fellowship'])*, **do the work of an Evangelist** *(keep trying to get people Saved)*, **make full proof of your Ministry** *(does it match up with the Word of God?)*.

I HAVE KEPT THE FAITH

"For I am now ready to be offered *(the word 'ready' signifies that the Holy Spirit had already told the Apostle that the time had now come; the word 'offered' speaks of* *the Drink-Offering poured out upon the sacrifice about to be offered, which, in effect, was the lesser part poured out upon the most important part; only one who considered himself less than the least of all Saints could write in such deep humility)*, **and the time of my departure is at hand.** *(This presents the fact that the servant of the Lord is immortal until his work is done.)*

"I have fought a good fight *(should have been translated, 'I have fought the good fight'; Paul fought his fight with sin to a finish, and was resting in a complete victory)*, **I have finished** *my* **course** *(he had been faithful in carrying out that which had been assigned to him)*, **I have kept the Faith** *(refers here to the deposit of Truth regarding the meaning of the Cross and the Resurrection of Christ, with which the Lord had entrusted Paul)*:

"Henceforth there is laid up for me a Crown of Righteousness *(the Victor's Crown)*, **which the Lord, the Righteous Judge, shall give me at that day** *(at the Judgment Seat of Christ)*: **and not to me only, but unto all them also who love His Appearing.** *(This Victor's Crown will go to all who consider His Appearing precious)*" **(II Tim. 4:1-8).**

"I heard the Voice of Jesus say,
"'Come unto Me and rest;
"Lay down, you weary one, lay down,
"Your head upon My Breast.'
"I came to Jesus as I was,
"Weary, and worn, and sad;
"I found in Him a resting place,
"And He has made me glad."

"I heard the Voice of Jesus say,
"'Behold, I freely give,
"The Living Water; thirsty one,
"Stoop down, and drink, and live.'

"I came to Jesus, and I drank,
"Of that Life-giving Stream;
"My thirst was quenched, my soul revived,
"And now I live in Him."

"I heard the Voice of Jesus say,
"'I am this dark world's Light;
"Look unto Me, your morn shall rise,
"And all your day be bright.'
"I looked to Jesus, and I found,
"In Him my Star, my Sun;
"And in that Light of life I'll walk,
"Till traveling days are done."

BIBLIOGRAPHY

CHAPTER 1
F.W. Farrar, *The Life and Work of St. Paul: Vol. 1*, Minnesota, Klock & Klock Christian Publishers, Inc., 1981, pg. 58.

H.T. Sell, *Bible Studies in the Life of Paul*, Fleming H. Revell Company, London & Edinburgh, 1904, pg. 15.

F.W. Farrar, *The Life and Work of St. Paul: Vol. 1*, Minnesota, Klock & Klock Christian Publishers, Inc., 1981, pg. 44.

Ibid., pg. 137.

Ibid., pg. 138.

Ibid., pg. 142.

Ibid., pgs. 147-150.

Ibid., pgs. 162-163.

Ibid., pgs. 167-168.

CHAPTER 2
F.W. Farrar, *The Life and Work of St. Paul: Vol. 1*, Minnesota, Klock & Klock Christian Publishers, Inc., 1981, pg. 178.

Ibid., pgs. 181-182.

CHAPTER 4
Kenneth S. Wuest, *Wuest's Word Studies from the Greek New Testament: Volume 1*, Grand Rapids, Michigan, Wm. B. Eerdman's Publishing Company, 1973, pg. 77.

Ibid.

George Williams, *The Student's Commentary on the Holy Scriptures*, Grand Rapids, Kregel Publications, 1949, pg. 856.

Kenneth S. Wuest, *Wuest's Word Studies from the Greek New Testament: Volume 1*, Grand Rapids, Michigan, Wm. B. Eerdman's Publishing Company, 1973, pgs. 82-83.

Ibid., pg. 86.

Ibid., pg. 87.

Ibid., pgs. 87-88.

CHAPTER 6
F.W. Farrar, *The Life and Work of St. Paul: Vol. 1*, Minnesota, Klock & Klock Christian Publishers, Inc., 1981, pg. 289.
Ibid., pg. 339.
Ibid., pg. 344.

CHAPTER 7
F.W. Farrar, *The Life and Work of St. Paul: Vol. 1*, Minnesota, Klock & Klock Christian Publishers, Inc., 1981, pgs. 402-403.
Ibid., pg. 404.

CHAPTER 8
F.W. Farrar, *The Life and Work of St. Paul: Vol. 1*, Minnesota, Klock & Klock Christian Publishers, Inc., 1981, pg. 455.
Ibid., pg. 498.
Ibid., pgs. 501-502.
Ibid., pg. 512.
Ibid., pg. 516.
Ibid., pg. 519.
Ibid., pg. 522.
Ibid., pg. 526.
Ibid., pg. 530.
Ibid., pg. 550.
Ibid., pg. 553.
Ibid., pgs. 567-568.
F.W. Farrar, *The Life and Work of St. Paul: Vol. 2*, Minnesota, Klock & Klock Christian Publishers, Inc., 1981, pgs. 4-5.

CHAPTER 9
F.W. Farrar, *The Life and Work of St. Paul: Vol. 2*, Minnesota, Klock & Klock Christian Publishers, Inc., 1981, pgs. 11-12.
Ibid., pg. 36.
Ibid., pg. 288.

CHAPTER 10

F.W. Farrar, *The Life and Work of St. Paul: Vol. 2*, Minnesota, Klock & Klock Christian Publishers, Inc., 1981, pgs. 291-292.

Ibid., pg. 293.

Ibid., pg. 294.

Ibid., pgs. 315-316.

Ibid., pg. 316.

Ibid., pg. 330.

Ibid., pg. 331.

CHAPTER 11

F.W. Farrar, *The Life and Work of St. Paul: Vol. 2*, Minnesota, Klock & Klock Christian Publishers, Inc., 1981, pg. 333.

Ibid., pg. 350.

Ibid., pg. 352.

Ibid., pg. 354.

Ibid., pgs. 360-361.

CHAPTER 12

F.W. Farrar, *The Life and Work of St. Paul: Vol. 2*, Minnesota, Klock & Klock Christian Publishers, Inc., 1981, pg. 366.

Ibid., pg. 372.

Ibid., pg. 389.

CHAPTER 13

F.W. Farrar, *The Life and Work of St. Paul: Vol. 2*, Minnesota, Klock & Klock Christian Publishers, Inc., 1981, pg. 541.

Ibid., pg. 543.

Ibid., pg. 546.

Ibid., pgs. 554-555.